History of Christianity in the Middle Ages

History of Christianity in the Middle Ages

From the Fall of Rome
to the Fall of Constantinople

William Ragsdale Cannon

BAKER BOOK HOUSE

Grand Rapids, Michigan 49506

To

Mack B. Stokes

Ὁ φίλος ἐστὶν ἄλλος αὐτός.
—Ἀριστοτέλης ὁ φιλόσοφος

And

The Faculty and Students of the Candler School of Theology
of
EMORY UNIVERSITY

Igitur clericus, qui Christi servit ecclesiae, interpretetur primum vocabulum suum et nominis definitione praelata nitatur esse, quod dicitur.

—Sancti Eusebii Hieronymi Epistulae, LII, 5

Preface

CHRISTIANITY IN THE MIDDLE AGES HAS BEEN A CONCERN OF TOO FEW AMONG English-speaking Protestant church historians. Those who have written in this field have, on the whole, produced monographs, that is, scholarly treatises on particular persons and movements; they have not attempted a synthetic history of Christianity in all phases of its development in those centuries between the collapse of the Roman empire in the West and the capture of Constantinople by the Turks and the beginning of the Renaissance.

Even among Roman Catholics the most numerous contributions have been made by German and French scholars, and these, too, largely in the field of biography and analytical history. Mann is the outstanding Britisher, whose *Lives of the Popes in the Middle Ages* puts all medieval scholars in his debt. The best synthetic history is French, written almost a generation ago by the late F. Mourret. It is largely institutional, however, and takes little account of the Byzantine church save where its developments impinge on Western ecclesiastical affairs. There is now in progress another general ecclesiastical history by a group of French scholars several volumes of which deal with the Middle Ages.

Consequently this book is offered to meet a definite and long felt need. It is a synthetic history depicting the development of Christianity from A.D. 476 to A.D. 1453 in all its aspects, doctrinal as well as institutional, the Greek church as well as the Latin.

In the writing of this history I have employed as best I could primary sources, citations to which appear in the footnotes. Likewise, I have tried to consider major monographs and other secondary materials. When I have knowingly utilized them, I have given a reference in the footnotes. Yet it is never possible for the author of a history as broad in its scope as this one, fully to acknowledge his debt to the research of others. Naturally he reads as much as he can, and over a period of years the findings and judgments of

7

others become unconsciously his own. "We are like dwarfs," said Bernard of Chartres, "seated on the shoulders of giants." For the labor of all those the fruits of which have entered into the making of this history, I am grateful.

Especially grateful am I to my former professors of Yale University who taught me the methods of historical research and inspired me by their own labors to this accomplishment: Luther A. Weigle for catholicity of learning; Halford E. Luccock for clarity of expression and interesting style of writing; Kenneth Scott Latourette for painstaking exactness and prodigious industry in research and publication; H. Richard Niebuhr for profundity of insight and originality of judgment; Robert L. Calhoun for undeviating loyalty to original sources and fascinating skill in their interpretation; Roland H. Bainton for making the past live again in both the splendor of its achievements and the shame of its failures and its sin; and, above all else, the late Douglas Clyde Macintosh for the strength of ideas and intellectual integrity which is the foundation of genuine scholarship.

I am grateful, too, to a number of my colleagues: J. Carlton Nunan and Francis Benjamin of the English and History Departments of Emory University for reading and correcting the page proofs; Egon Gerdes of the University of Kiel, Germany, and a research scholar at Emory University, for checking the footnotes; James W. May and John Lawson of the Department of Church History of the Candler School of Theology of Emory University for invaluable criticisms of the manuscript when it was first written; and Miss Sarah Flake, my efficient and gracious secretary, for typing the manuscript from my almost illegible handwriting.

William R. Cannon

Contents

Abbreviations Used Frequently in Footnotes

AS   Acta Sanctorum Bollandiana. 67 vols. Antwerp and Brussels, 1643-1931.

CMH   Cambridge Medieval History. 8 vols., 1936.

CSHB   Corpus Scriptorum Historiae Byzantinae. Bonn, 1828-97.

CSEL   Corpus Scriptorum Ecclesiasticorum Latinorum. Vienna, 1866—in progress.

J. Regesta   Regesta pontificum Romanorum ab Condita ecclesia ad annum post Christum natum 1198. Phillip Jaffé, ed., 1851; 2nd ed., Wattenbach, Loewenfeld, Kaltenbrunner, and Ewald, Leipzig, 1885-1888. 2 vols. 2nd ed. employed throughout.

LP   Liber Pontificalis. 3 vols. Rome, 1886-92. L. Duchesne, ed.

Mansi   J. D. Mansi, Sacrorum Conciliorum Nova et Amplissima Collectio. 31 vols. Florence and Venice, 1759-98.

MGH   Monumenta Germaniae historica. In progress.

MPG   J. P. Migne, Patrologiae Cursus Completus; Series Graeca. 161 vols. in 166. Paris, 1857-66.

MPL   J. P. Migne, Patrologiae Cursus Completus; Series Latina. 221 vols. Paris, 1844-64.

Chapter One

Christendom After the Fall of Rome
(476-590)

LESS THAN ONE HUNDRED YEARS HAD ELAPSED BETWEEN THE DEATH OF THEO-
dosius the Great (395) and the deposition of Romulus Augustulus (476).
Yet in that brief span of time Roman imperial unity had been forever
shattered. The Western half of the empire had been wrecked by the barbarian
invasions; while the Eastern half, though geographically intact and politically
the same as before, had nonetheless been put on the defensive, so that it
was busy preserving what it had rather than expanding into what otherwise it
might have become.

What had taken place in the empire at large was not dissimilar to what
had happened within Christianity itself. The church had not proved sufficiently a unifying and cohesive power to counteract the disruptive and divisive
forces within the secular order. The Arian Controversy over the relationship
of the Son to the Father and the status of Jesus Christ in the Godhead had
been superseded by the Nestorian Controversy over the person of the
historical Jesus and the relationship of the divine and human natures within
his earthly life. Though the official position of the church had been stated,
first at Ephesus in 431 and later at Chalcedon in 451, the results had not
been immediately satisfying. Two patriarchs, Nestorius of Constantinople
and Dioscorus of Alexandria, had been deposed. Separate churches had
emerged in the East along both Nestorian and Monophysite doctrinal lines.
The Roman bishop had been set at odds with the patriarch of Constantinople
because the Council of Chalcedon had decreed that Constantinople was
second only to Rome as an ecclesiastical see, and had given as its reason not
sacred sanction that it had been founded by an apostle, but rather secular
authority that it was the capital of the empire. In North Africa a dispute,
which was still unsettled, had arisen between Augustine of Hippo and
Pelagius over original sin and the degree of man's dependence on divine
grace in salvation. Even vanquished Arianism had revived in the conquering

barbarians, the majority of whom had been won to that heresy by the missionary labors of Ulfilas among the Visigoths in the fourth century.

Consequently, when on August 23, 476, the beardless boy, Romulus Augustulus, had the imperial crown taken from his head and placed on the head of the hairy barbarian, Odovacar, the world of both Roman and Christian antiquity was dead; and a new world for the church as well as for the empire was in the process of being born. In the West, for example, theological concerns gave way to those of missions and evangelism; monasticism ceased to be a byway on which devout but eccentric souls detoured life's major issues and became the highway of civilization itself. The bishop of Rome transformed his prestige as elder statesman into the power of a pope. The church adapted its strategy to the needs of the various and sundry peoples who had broken the established unity of the empire, and politics became a major ecclesiastical enterprise. In the East, though political and social unity made possible the prolongation of the program of the ancient church and though theology and mysticism remained as the chief characteristic of Byzantine piety, heresies led increasingly to schisms. The concerns of church and state coalesced to such a degree that the one was almost indistinguishable from the other. Vast territories of Christendom fell prey to the conquests of Islam. Dogma was made subservient to popular as well as imperial tastes, and Eastern Catholicism was different from what it had been if for no other reason than that it had to adjust itself to a separate and different Catholicism in the West.

I. Christianity Among the Invaders

The map of Europe bore the configuration of the barbarian invasions. With the exception of the Huns, these peoples were immigrants as well as soldiers: they settled in the territories they conquered.

Likewise, the soul of Europe bore the imprint of their spirit. Their religious beliefs came into close contact with the religious beliefs of the inhabitants of the territories over which they ruled. Frequently this led to ideological conflicts, for convictions yield less readily to conquests than bodies and land.

The Vandals, whose North African kingdom was the first to be both established and destroyed, were rapacious Arians who inflicted upon their Catholic subjects intermittent persecutions. Though the lame Gaiseric (428-77),[1] founder and military genius of the kingdom, practiced a suspicious toleration, his successor, Huneric (477-84), was sadistic and persistently cruel. He made it a crime to profess any faith other than Arianism and confiscated the property of Catholic churches as well as of the members who composed them. Arianism itself was established in the kingdom under a

---

[1] Procopius, De Bello Vandalico, I, 1-7.

patriarch whose see was Carthage. Though it made mild gains among the less courageous of the Catholics in times of persecution, it was always a minority movement. It fell into persecuted disrepute with the fall of the kingdom to the invading armies of the Eastern emperor under Belisarius in 534.[2] The entire history of the Vandals was made almost within the space of one century, and was so meager and inconsequential that it was soon lost to memory, like a ruined monument under trackless wastes of desert sand.

The Visigoths in Spain, in contrast to the Vandals, deserved and got a better fate. They too were Arians; but in the course of the sixth century, eager for the consolidation and preservation of their state, they amalgamated with their Latin neighbors and accepted the Catholicism of their subjects as their own. Perhaps they had learned a lesson from their immediate past. Despite the genius for statecraft of Euric (466-84), the founder of their kingdom and one whose hatred of both the Roman empire and Catholicism amounted almost to an insane passion, they had been driven out of Gaul by the Catholic Franks; and their king, Alaric II (484-507), had been slain at Vouglé in Poitou at Clovis' own hands. They learned by bitter experience that they could not long survive among a people the majority of whom was of a faith different from their own.

After they settled in Spain they persevered in Arianism for more than four decades, during which time they formulated in Gothic a liturgy after that creed and set up an episcopacy dependent upon the crown. An abortive attempt at religious revolution (579-85) was staged by Hermenegild under the tutelage of his Frankish wife and the Catholic archbishop, Leander of Seville. Leovigild (ca. 568-86), Hermenegild's father, was a devout Arian and had his son imprisoned and then killed for refusing to give up the Catholic faith. However when Leovigild died one year later, the death knell of Arianism was sounded; his second son, Recared I (586-601), completed the revolution which his first son had begun.

In the month of May, 589, the Third Council of Toledo declared for Catholicism. Recared I has the distinction of being the first king to adapt the anointing ceremony of the Old Testament to Christian usage, having had the sacred oil poured on his head by a bishop, symbolizing thereby for himself and for his medieval successors in all lands their divine right to rule.

The Burgundians, whose territory had increased from their original settlement in Savoy to include the regions from the Rhone and Saône rivers to the Alps and Sarine River and from the north corner of the Jura Mountains to the Durance River, have a short but precious history. They were the first of the barbarians to give up Arianism for Catholicism and to substitute a vulgarized Latin for their rough Germanic dialect. They provided the pagan

[2] Victor Vitensis, *Historia persecutionis Africanae provinciae*, in CSEL, Vol. VII.

Clovis with his Christian queen. When they were defeated by the Franks in 534,[3] they had already codified in Latin their humane laws which exemplified their mild manners, tolerant disposition, and an appreciation of Catholicism acquired by friendly intercourse with Latin bishops and priests whose superior culture they admired. Likewise, under King Sigismund (516-24) they had formally accepted Catholicism,[4] too late, however, to achieve a political unity strong enough to resist the sons of Clovis.

The Franks in Gaul were the most powerful and successful of the barbarian invaders. On the continent their kingdom alone seems to have been able to defy the ravages of time and to secure for itself a permanent place among the nations. Some have attributed its longevity to its early alliance with Catholic Christianity. Be this as it may, the Franks were as ferocious, immoral, and cruel after their conversion as before. Clovis (481-511), their king, on account of either the persuasion or the nagging of Clotilda, his Burgundian wife, promised that if her Savior would grant him victory over the powerful Alemanni he would embrace her faith. The prayer was granted, or at least the victory achieved; and as a result he, together with three thousand of his soldiers, was baptized by Archbishop Remi at Rheims on Christmas Day, 496.[5] Rheims to this day has remained, if not in name at least in fact, the primatial see of France.

Clovis and his people are the first instance among the barbarians of the conversion of a ruler and his subjects from paganism to Catholic Christianity. This intrepid chieftain established Paris as his capital in 508. By inciting a son to murder his father and then by taking vengeance on the parricide, he united the Ripuarian and Salian Franks. Just before his death in 511 he called together a council of bishops at Orleans, established a code of law, and dedicated all his bloody work to the glory of God.

Clovis' pattern of behavior was followed, with some variation in detail, by most of his successors. Chilperic (561-584), for example, who stands on an evil eminence even in an evil age, inflicted blindness as the standard punishment for any disobedience to his commands. It was he who declared against the dogma of the Trinity and who tried to replace doctrinal formularies by the pure Word of God. Is it any wonder that Gregory of Tours styled him both the Herod and the Nero of Frankish history?

Yet despite the general degeneracy of the people and especially of their rulers, who at best were lustful ogres and at worst blood-thirsty tyrants, the Catholic church became the most powerful Frankish institution. Society on

---

[3] Fredegarius, Chronicarum, in MGH, Scriptores rerum Merovingicarum (1888), Vol. II. Isidore of Seville, Historia Gothorum Wandalorum et Sueborum, in MGH, Chronica minora (1892-98), Vol. II. Jordanes, De Getarum sive Gothorum origine et rebus gentis, in MGH (1882).
[4] Apollinaris Sidonius, Epistolae, VI, 12, in MPL, LVIII, 560.
[5] MGH, Epistolae, III, 122.

all its levels seemed to take pride in it. The king had to give his permission before a person could become a clergyman, while the process of selection was rigorous. Bishops were elected in theory by the clergy of their diocese, though in practice the king said first who were eligible. They had heavy responsibility since in addition to their sacerdotal functions they administered the property of the church and in many places superseded civil magistrates in dispensing justice under law. All clergymen were answerable only to ecclesiastical agencies and immune to civil jurisprudence. The church grew wealthy through ample donations from kings and nobles anxious to compensate for their sins. In addition to these donations and the customary gratuities and fees, it collected a tithe on all income in the kingdom. The highest form of both piety and learning was in the monasteries. Out of this rough people came the vision and strength to forge an empire under the religious tutelage of the Catholic church.[6]

Italy was ruled over by the **Arian Ostrogoths**, who maintained their capital at Ravenna, leaving as the most important and powerful person in the city of Rome its Catholic bishop. Since the Ostrogoths had originally entered the empire on the invitation of the government, they were looked upon as colonists; and their domain, at least nominally, was a part of the Eastern empire. This made relationships between them and their Latin subjects easier and more cordial. Odovacar (476-493), the Scirian, had been displaced by Theodoric (471-526), the Ostrogoth, who, when he could not defeat Odovacar in war, made an alliance with him, invited him to a banquet, and then murdered him while he sat at his table as a guest. Theodoric's excuse was that the Eastern emperor had commissioned him to rid the land of Odovacar and to reign in his stead. Though high tempered and illiterate, Theodoric nonetheless ruled with the patience and foresight of an enlightened monarch, practicing tolerance and benevolence for twenty-five out of his reign of thirty-three years. A conscientious and zealous Arian, he watched the affairs of Catholicism from 493 to 518 with benign indifference. He did not interfere in the contest of Symmachus and Laurentius for the Roman episcopacy until years of synods and ecclesiastical debate had made the decision for him that Symmachus was the rightful bishop. He lent protection to the Jews, and riots against them were severely punished. His public works included churches for Arians and Catholics alike. If he looked toward an ultimate assimilation of Goths and Romans, it was on the basis of religious toleration, not uniformity. "To pretend to a dominion over the conscience." Theodoric wrote Justin, the Eastern emperor, "is to usurp the prerogative of God."

[6] Gregorius Turonensis. *Historia Francorum*, II, 40-43; IV, 28; V, 44; VI, 46; VIII, 36; IX, 27, 34; X, 8.

Then in 518 Theodoric's policy changed, and this most understanding and tolerant of sovereigns became an intolerant and ruthless persecutor of those whose religious opinions were contrary to his own. To be sure, the breakdown in his former policy had been caused by a reversal of religious policy in the East. On the accession of Justin (518-527), Arianism became a crime to be severely punished throughout the empire. In the West, especially in Italy where Theodoric reigned, Catholics rallied to the position of the Eastern emperor. Consequently Theodoric began to suspect even his most trusted counsellors who were not Arians. The statesman Albinus was accused of high treason; and when Boethius, the philosopher and friend of Theodoric, rushed to Albinus' defense, he too was arrested, thrown into prison, and later killed with excruciating torture. Theodoric had a cord twisted tightly around Boethius' forehead and then his skull beaten in with a club. While languishing in prison before he died, Boethius wrote his classic, *The Consolations of Philosophy*, which earned him the title, "the last of the Romans." Strange he found comfort in Athens—not Jerusalem; turned to Socrates and Plato—not to Jesus Christ! The Roman bishop, John I (523-526), whom Theodoric sent unwillingly in the spring of 525 on a mission of conciliation to Justin, was imprisoned and killed on his return home. Theodoric survived John less than four months, dying of dysentery in August, 526. The Arian kingdom capitulated after several wars to the armies of Justinian in 553.[7]

Theodoric's work outlasted him only twenty-seven years, having been built on the insubstantial foundation of confidence in the success of religious toleration and belief that political and social unity could be forged out of peoples of different faiths. In the sixth century, religion and politics were one. It was not possible to build a state out of opposing and contradictory religious ideologies.

However, as a secular prince Theodoric deserves a place in ecclesiastical history as the artificer of the instrument of papal elections which prevailed until the establishment of the College of Cardinals in the eleventh century. One month before his death he decreed that the bishop of Rome should be elected by the free suffrages of the clergy and people of Rome and confirmed by the secular sovereign. This decree was prompted by the protest of the populace against Theodoric's attempt to appoint the bishop of Rome without their consent. Its result was the consecration of Felix IV, July 12, 526.

The ability of barbarian states to survive depended in the main on the acceptance and successful use by their leaders of the beliefs and forms of Catholic Christianity. These invaders had the military might and brute force

[7] Ennodius of Pavia, *Opera*, MGH, *Auctores Antiquissimi*, Vol. VII.

to subdue the Western Roman empire; they had not the education or experience properly to govern it. In every principality where they ruled they were a minority of the population, the majority of which was Roman and Catholic. The conquerors needed the superior culture of the conquered to be able to endure. Only the kingdoms of the Franks in Gaul and the Visigoths in Spain survived among those of the invaders at the close of the sixth century. Both were vigorously Catholic.[8]

II. Western Literature and Theology

The light of learning during this period of the establishment of the barbarian states in the West, though it was not entirely extinguished, gave only a flickering and sporadic glow. The court of Theodoric the Ostrogoth in Italy was bright and beaming, while the rest of Europe west of Greece was almost entirely in darkness with an occasional burst of light in Gaul and Spain.

Classical antiquity in Christian guise was transmitted to the Middle Ages by **Boethius**[9] (480-524) and **Cassiodorus**[10] (478-573). Both were Romans, courtiers of Theodoric, and devotees of the past rather than spokesmen of the present or prophets of the future. Boethius established the quadrivium as the basis of western education. Arithmetic, music, geometry, and astronomy were therefore added to grammar, rhetoric, and logic (the trivium) as the fundamental discipline in all the schools. He likewise translated Aristotle's *Categories*, together with Porphyry's introduction, which precipitated the realist and nominalist debates of the eleventh and twelfth centuries. Cassiodorus adapted classical knowledge to the needs of the religious life. After having served Theodoric in a position of state for fifty years, during which time he wrote his *History of the Goths* and composed his famous letters, he retired to a Benedictine monastery. There he wrote a treatise on the soul and prepared a syllabus for the education of monks. In the syllabus he advised the monks to learn the seven arts of antiquity, history, and geography as well as the Scriptures and the writings of the Fathers. This versatile old man was the editor of a compilation of Latin orthography as well as a commentary on the Psalms.

Gregory of Tours[11] (538-594), in contrast to these two classicists, wrote the history of his own people (the Franks) in crude and barbaric style. He likewise prepared the earliest of the medieval liturgical manuals, in which the various nocturnal offices are determined by the position of the stars. He wrote twenty biographical sketches of ecclesiastics living in Gaul and seven

---

[8] Full bibliographies in CMH, I, 658-659, 675; II, 728-738.
[9] MPL, Vols. LXIII, LXIV.
[10] MPL, Vols. LXIX, LXX.
[11] MGH, *Scriptores rerum Merovingicarum*, Vol. I.

books on miracles. With the single exception of **Venantius Fortunatus** [12] (530-610), whose Vexilla regis has become a part of Roman Catholic liturgy, the literature of Gaul became worthless after the death of Gregory of Tours.

The only event of general theological significance to occur in the West during the first half of the sixth century was the **pronouncement made on sin and grace** by a small synod, entirely local in character, held at **Orange** in Gaul, during July of 529. The occasion of the meeting was nothing more than the dedication of the town basilica by the leading ecclesiastic of the area, Caesarius,[13] archbishop of Arles (470-543).

Caesarius came from the Isle of Lerins. The quality of religion on this Isle decidedly influenced the Christianity of Gaul. The monks of Lerins could not accept the predestinarian implications of Augustinian anthropology, but at the same time they did not subscribe to the self-sufficiency of man in working out his own salvation as proclaimed by the Pelagians. In his doctrine of the absolute dependence of man on divine grace Augustine had affirmed the doctrine of total depravity. Every man is born in sin and is helpless to save himself. He taught that God predestines some few to eternal life. He abandons the rest to eternal damnation. Divine election works irresistibly through grace in the lives of the chosen. Pelagius by contrast had taught that man himself decides for or against God, that he merits salvation through his own good deeds, that grace but aids and strengthens him to do what otherwise he could have done through his own natural power, and that if he is damned he has no one to blame but himself.

This controversy had raged in the church for the better part of a century. The Pelagians never had much of a following because their teaching made the work of Christ in redemption incidental to the living of a good life and put the moral man on a parity with the Christian. If man could save himself, why did Christ come into the world at all? But at the same time few people were willing to subscribe to the extreme tenets of Augustinianism. Consequently the Semi-Pelagians, so called, emerged. They were willing to give God sole credit for man's salvation, yet they were not willing to blame him for man's damnation. They were Augustinians without being predestinarians. Caesarius belonged to the Semi-Pelagian school, and to him belongs the honor of concluding the controversy by formulating a position satisfactory to the majority of the church at large.

Caesarius was diplomatic in his procedure of operation. He submitted to the bishop of Rome, Felix IV (526-530), a thesis on the subject.[14] Felix criticized and corrected it; then Caesarius edited it again and submitted it on

[12] Opera, MGH, Auctores Antiquissimi, Vol. IV.
[13] MPL, LXVII, 1001-1166.
[14] Mansi, VIII, 722-724.

July 3, 529, to his episcopal colleagues at Orange; they ratified and signed it.[15] Boniface II (530-532), Felix's successor in office, approved it and commended it to the whole church, and gradually without special conciliar action the church accepted it as Christian dogma on sin and grace.

Thus the canons of this synod declare that man's free will is incapable of moral goodness without the aid of divine grace and that God's help is needed for the first movements of man in salvation. However, the canons do not affirm the doctrine of predestination, nor do they consign unbaptized infants to hell. The Synod of Orange salvaged Augustinianism for the church by making it human. According to its teaching man is free to damn himself by his sinfulness. He is not free to save himself by his goodness but is dependent altogether upon the gracious mercy of God.

III. Irish and Benedictine Monasticism

The most salutary social institution to emerge in the West during this period between the fall of Rome and the pontificate of Gregory the Great was Benedictine monasticism. This institution became the primary, if not the sole, preserver among the barbarians of the classical writings of antiquity. Rome employed it as its chief agency of evangelism and instruction in the Christian faith.

Monasticism itself was the product of Eastern Christianity during the early stages of its history, witnessing to the fact that the Greek mind and spirit, rather than the Latin, pioneered in practical or applied Christianity as well as theology. Anchoritic, or solitary, monasticism had grown up in the arid climate of Egypt in the third century and had flowered into a popular movement, due to the inspiration of Antony, in the first half of the fourth century. Pachomius before 350 had inaugurated coenobitic, or communal, monasticism; and Basil of Caesarea in the middle of the same century had established the laws which were to govern Eastern monasticism throughout its long future.

The monasticism of the East had been transported to the West almost without modification. Even in coenobitic establishments, such as those which had been set up in the fourth century in Gaul by Martin of Tours after the Pachomian pattern, the ideal of the anchorite had prevailed; and the Marmoutiers had become little more than hermit villages. The same had been true of the establishments in Ireland and Britain. Each monastery had tended to set its own pattern of life, oscillating at times between impossible extremes of asceticism and the relaxations of an easy life.

To be sure Irish monasticism was a powerful and effective instrument of evangelism in this period, and the Ionian establishment deserves more than passing notice. Both Ireland and Celtic Scotland and Wales, lying as they

[15] *Ibid.*, Cols. 711 ff.

did outside the pale of the Roman empire, had developed ecclesiastically along divergent and irregular lines. Neither Ninian (d. 432) nor Patrick (389-461), trained as they both had been in Gaul, had reproduced the Roman pattern on the mission field. The British (Celts) and the Irish (Scots) differed from Rome in their date for the celebration of Easter and in the form of the tonsure (they shaved the front of the head from ear to ear, while the Roman Catholics shaved the top of the head, around which hair was allowed to grow like a crown). Unlike the Romans they named their churches after persons still alive. In the rite of baptism they immersed only once, while the Romans did it three times. There were differences in the prayers of the mass and in the rite of episcopal consecration (they did not require three bishops to consecrate). In addition Irish Christianity was monastic in organization and discipline, disregarding the diocesan pattern almost entirely. An Irish monastery, for example, had many smaller establishments including village and to n churches. It was governed by an abbot who was succeeded after his death   members of his own family. Bishops, priests, and monks resided together in the monastery, all under the absolute control of the abbot. Indeed, bishops were employed by the abbot to carry out under his direction episcopal functions such as the ordination of priests, the dedication of churches, and the founding of new missions.

The most famous, effective, and enduring of these Irish monasteries was that of **Iona**, off the coast of Scotland, founded by Columba in 563. It contained 150 monks, was constructed of wood, with the refectory and the church in common. There was a private wattle hut for each of the monks. Life was ordered by the ideals of chastity and humility, and no monk was allowed to own anything of his own. No distinct rule however was formulated.

Columba (521-597), reared in Ireland, had gone to Scotland with twelve companions, like Jesus and the twelve apostles, to preach to his fellow countrymen beyond the sea. Columba's ministry at Iona lasted for thirty-four years. So gentle and sweet was he that even the animals loved him. His last act outside his cell and church was to permit a horse to lick his breast. He died before the altar of the church in the presence of his monks, having gone there with them at midnight for matins.[16]

The Irish evangelistic mission was extended to the continent by **Columban** (ca. 543-615). He was trained at Bangor, a famous establishment in County Down well known for its scholarly pursuits and the classical learning of its monks. In the year 585, Columban and twelve companions left Ireland on their mission. This intrepid missionary and evangelist worked in the countries of Vosges, France, Burgundy, Switzerland, and finally Italy itself. He died

[16] Adamnan, *Vita S. Columbae* (Dublin, 1896).

24

at his own establishment, Bobbio, in the Apennines. Yet neither Columba nor Columban[17] was able to provide everything that was required. Both were great but not great enough. The West needed, if monasticism was to be an effective institution, what the East had already found in Basil of Caesarea: some strong and practical statesman to design a pattern of communal behavior and then to inspire men with the desire to live by it. Such a person was **Benedict of Nursia.**

We do not know too much about the life of Benedict. Though his disciple, Pope Gregory I, wrote his biography, that work contains so many legends and its evaluations are so distorted by extravagant praise that it serves better the purposes of a eulogy than of an honest account of the career of a man. Benedict was born (ca. 480) of an affluent Roman family in the village of Nursia which is situated in the beautiful region of Umbria. By the time he was twenty years old the dissolute society about him had so afflicted his sensitive nature that he fled from it and set up for himself the life of a hermit in a cave near Subiaco. He was evidently a very hairy man; and clad as he was in the skins of animals and with his own body half exposed, a band of shepherds who happened on him mistook him for a wild beast and started to kill him. This encounter with Benedict led to the shepherds' conversion, and they became the first emissaries of his name and fame. Crowds came to his solitary quarters seeking guidance and instruction, and the anchoritic phase of his life ended when some neighboring monks invited him to be their abbot. They soon groaned under his discipline, having been accustomed to an easy and unregulated way of life. Since they did not want to embarrass Benedict by expelling him from his newly acquired position, they decided to poison him instead. He discovered their perfidy and murderous resolve and fled south to the region between Rome and Naples. On the high hill of Monte Cassino, a belated pagan shrine, Benedict expelled the gods of antiquity and set in their place monasticism's altar to the one true God. In the year 529 he established the Abbey of Monte Cassino which became the parent house of the Benedictines, or Black Monks. There he experimented with his brethren and formed and perfected his famous *Rule.* He died after at least fourteen more strenuous years (ca. 543).[18]

Though we know all too little about Benedict's life, we know everything about his thought and work, for he gave these to posterity through his **Rule.** The rule is not a list either of moral prohibitions or of spiritual maxims. Rather it is a legal code, very practical in nature, covering every phase of a monk's life. It is the translation of the Roman conception of civil law into the service of the highest form of the Christian life—that of self-abnegation and unselfish devotion to God and the needs of others.

[17] MPL, LXXX, 209-326.
[18] MPL, LXXVII, 149-430.

The daily activity of the monk is divided into three portions: first, the services of formal worship, the *Opus Dei*, chanted in choir, which consume four and a half hours; secondly, manual work in cloister and field, which occupies the monk for six to seven hours, and finally reading and study, especially of the Scriptures and the church Fathers, which demand three to five hours. The hour for rising and retiring, which varies with the season, is specified. Each person is expected to take eight hours' sleep; to eat what is needed to do his work; and to wear the simple prescribed garb of a peasant—a black garment, conspicuous by its sameness. The type work done is determined by the living conditions and the needs of the establishment. There is of course flexibility in service: a good teacher should spend more time instructing pupils than in household chores; a cook should be in the kitchen, while the copyist should be in the library. Still every monk does what he is told to do by his superior; and the vows of poverty, chastity, and obedience have full sway over all. The command to engage in self-inflicted punishment is conspicuous by its absence, and one will look in vain in the *Rule of Benedict* for such penitential exercises as the use of hair shirts, spiked belts, and scourging. Even fasts are regulated by the physical constitution of the devotee. The vow of stability is enforced: a monk cannot transfer from one establishment to another; he spends all his days in the house where he took his vows. The abbot is elected by the monks for life; he chooses his own officials; he consults with the older brethren, but once he has made a decision his will is law.[19]

Benedictine monasticism was disseminated over Europe when the Lombards sacked Monte Cassino from 580-590. It was already popular in Rome, on account of its adoption by Cassiodorus, before Benedict's death. With Gregory I it ascended the papal throne.

IV. Eastern Christianity Prior to Justinian

Monasticism in the East, hoary with age and universally accepted as the highest expression of piety and devotion, had become the effective weapon of the church, or at least of a zealous faction within the church, for enforcing its will upon the empire. Indeed, in less than a year after Romulus Augustulus had been robbed of the imperial crown in the West, the Eastern empire witnessed the expulsion of the usurper, **Basiliscus** (475-476), by the hermit **Daniel,** because Basiliscus had openly declared himself a supporter of Monophysitism. Immediately after the imperial encyclical was issued branding the doctrinal proceedings of the Council of Chalcedon as heretical, Daniel (d. 493), the spiritual successor to Simeon Stylites (ca. 390-459), descended from his pillar on the Black Sea. Through defiance of the inhospitable elements of nature Daniel had become the oracle of God to the people of

---

[19] *Regula Magistri* (ed. H. Vanderhoven and F. Masai, Brussels, 1953).

Constantinople. He entered the capital and preached with such power and success that he produced the unbelievable spectacle of a proud emperor fleeing for his very life before the fury of a half-naked monk.[20] The Emperor Zeno was restored (476). Acacius (471-489), the patriarch, who had draped his cathedral and clergy in black as a sign of mourning over the heresy of Basiliscus, welcomed the restoration of orthodoxy as a miracle of the Lord.

Unfortunately for the securing of religious peace and harmony, the doctrinal temper of monasticism was not the same throughout the East. The monks of Egypt, for example, still looked upon the findings of Chalcedon as a concession to Nestorianism. The see of Antioch had been held intermittently for a decade or more by an avowed Monophysite, Peter the Fuller (476-477; 485-489). Even Jerusalem, the parent see of Christendom, was not in sympathy with the two-nature doctrine. Alexandria had witnessed the murder of one bishop (Proterius, 457) in the baptistry of his cathedral during Holy Week by the supporters of his rival, and twenty ensuing years of doctrinal warfare between the two claimants of his see—Timothy the Cat (457-477) and Timothy Solofaciolus (460-482).

Zeno (474-491) was determined at any price to give religious peace to his entire empire. In this determination he was supported by the patriarch of Constantinople, Acacius. The doctrinal positions with which these men were faced were: (1) the Eutychean, or Monophysite, teaching adopted by the Robber Synod of Ephesus (449) and repudiated by the Council of Chalcedon (451), that though Christ was of two natures—the divine and the human—before the Incarnation, he possessed only one nature—the divine—after his birth; and (2) the Chalcedonian teaching that through the Incarnation Christ was one person with two separate and distinct natures, each with its own peculiar characteristics, the divine and the human. The third school of thought, Nestorianism, which went so far as to separate the persons of the divine and human in Christ by saying that Jesus of Nazareth was a complete human being in whom dwelt the Second Person of the Trinity as a man dwells in a house, was no longer a live issue. Most of the people of this persuasion had formed another church in North Syria.

Zeno, under his own seal, issued in the year 482 what he styled the *Henotikon*, or *Edict of Union*. He hoped to bring together in one communion both the Monophysites and the adherents of the two-nature doctrine, and to do this he skillfully avoided the declaration of any principle which might divide them. He tried for unity by means of ambiguity and vagueness. For example, he affirmed Christ to be one person, born of the Holy Ghost and Mary, one with the Father according to his divinity and one with us according to his humanity, but then he avoided any mention of Chalcedon as a

---

[20] Evagrius, *Historia ecclesiastica*, III, 7.

legitimate conclave of the church and referred rather to Nicaea (325) and Constantinople (381) as having been fully authorized to define Christology.[21]

At first the Henotikon brought into union the major sees of the East, Constantinople, Alexandria, Antioch, and Jerusalem and, with their aid, lulled into quiescence the theological fury of the empire. But it had a contrary effect on the West. Felix III's (483-492) first act as bishop of Rome was to anathematize all the bishops who had subscribed to this edict. Despite its theological acceptability, it offended Rome at two points. First, it ignored the work of Leo I at Chalcedon. Secondly, it presumed to settle an issue of faith by the diplomacy of state. The Roman church preferred ecclesiastics who for conscience' sake would defy potentates as Leo I did Attila the Hun; it despised a bishop like Acacius who cringed before the throne of a lewd, semibarbarous sensualist like Zeno. Acacius reciprocated in kind and, in a formal ceremony on August 1, 484, excommunicated Felix. A schism was thus precipitated between the Western and Eastern churches which lasted for thirty-six years.

Even within the borders of the Eastern empire the Henotikon soon failed. Anastasius, who succeeded Zeno on the imperial throne in 491, tried desperately throughout his twenty-seven-year reign to preserve the compromise. Evidently he had the reputation of being a sweet-spirited man, for he was acclaimed on the day of his coronation by the cry of the populace: "Reign as you have lived!" But in a time of partisan strife a man who tries to be impartial is the most hated of all. The claims of justice pushed Anastasius more and more into sympathy with the Monophysites. He could not abide the fanatical fury of the Chalcedonian monks about Constantinople. He deposed and exiled two patriarchs of Constantinople, Euphemius (490-496) and Macedonius (496-511), because of their Chalcedonian bias and supported Severus, the Monophysite (512-518). Severus had driven Flavianus (498-512) from his see in Antioch, slaughtered the monks and clergy of orthodox persuasion, and fed their dead bodies to birds and beasts. Anastasius resisted the demands of Hormisdas of Rome (514-523) with the firm reply "We can bear insults and contempt, but we cannot allow ourselves to be commanded." He even overcame the violence of the mob by appearing without purple or diadem in the Hippodrome and offering to abdicate to restore peace. The sight of their feeble, eighty-one-year-old emperor evoked pity from the people, and they continued him in office until he died in his eighty-seventh year (518).

The crude, ignorant soldier **Justin I** (518-527), whose only qualification as a ruler was that he was orthodox, ended the schism by recognizing Chalcedonian Christology as dogma and by forcing the two-nature doctrine upon the Eastern church. Only in Egypt, loyal to the memory of Dioscorus, did Monophysitism maintain its strength, though it had occasional flourishes

[21] *Ibid.*, III, 14.

28

throughout the next reign elsewhere, even in Constantinople. On March 30, 525, with pomp and ceremony Justin received the bishop of Rome at Constantinople as his guest, kissed him, and requested his blessing.

V. The Church Under Justinian

The imperial title and crown were transferred on the death of Justin to his nephew Justinian (527-565), though the power and responsibility of government had been his from the outset, since Justin had had neither the sense nor the education to rule. Justinian had been only thirty-six years old at the time his uncle had won the purple and yet had taken his assignment of running the empire with the self-confidence of a veteran. Nine years of experience had given him no qualms when he became emperor himself at the age of forty-five. He reigned for thirty-eight years, surrendering his office reluctantly to death at the age of eighty-three.

Justinian's chief advisor for twenty-one out of his thirty-eight years was his beautiful and charming wife, Theodora. Before she met her husband and won his love she had been an actress and show girl and, if we can believe Procopius, who was the contemporary historian, a prostitute as well.[22] Certainly her background was not the best, since her father was only an animal trainer in the Hippodrome, and since Justinian had to seek a royal dispensation to marry her. But once this woman confined her amorous skills to one man her power was unlimited: Justinian ruled the empire, but in many matters Theodora ruled Justinian.

Indeed, the works of the emperor were more than commensurate with his character. During his reign, North Africa, Sicily, Italy, and the territories of Illyricum and Dalmatia were reclaimed for the empire. Unity was given to the church in the principal sees of the West as well as the East, though at the cost of ecclesiastical independence, since Justinian had to control everything with which he had any dealings. Taxes were successfully collected, art flourished, imperial and Christian law was codified, and the world appeared civilized once again. Yet the emperor personally was effeminate and cowardly, vain as a peacock, egotistical and selfish, mercenary and extravagant, despotic and cruel, and entirely missed greatness himself.[23] Like a frightened rabbit, he prepared to flee when a riot broke out between the Greens and Blues in the Hippodrome; but Theodora, who was not of a mind to forego without a struggle the social recognition she had striven all her life to win, screwed his courage to the sticking point.[24]

Husband and wife did not always see eye to eye, especially in theological matters; and their differences of opinion, at least in their effects upon others,

---

[22] Procopius, Anecdota, xi.
[23] Ibid., viii, 24.
[24] Procopius, History of the Wars, I, 24.

were registered in the history of Christianity. For example, Theodora leaned toward Monophysitism, while Justinian tried to be orthodox. When the Roman bishop, the aged Agapetus (535-536), came on a mission from the Goths to Constantinople, she tried to persuade him to commune with the Monophysite bishop, Anthimus of Trebizond, whom she had in mind to place on the episcopal throne of Constantinople. But when Agapetus refused Justinian heard him out, accepted the validity of his arguments, selected Menas (536-552) in Anthimus' place, and invited Agapetus to consecrate Menas in the cathedral of the city.[25]

Both the emperor and his queen however were one in deeming Nestorian tendencies in theology more dangerous than Monophysite. Consequently Justinian advanced what is known as the "**Three Chapters,**" an anathematizing supplement to Chalcedon, which condemned the faith and writing of Theodore of Mopsuestia, the teacher of Nestorius; Theodoret, the opponent of Cyril of Alexandria; and Ibas of Edessa, a friend of Nestorius.[26] These men, it is true, if one examines the niceties of their doctrine, were not in line with the position of the councils of Ephesus and Chalcedon, and Theodore was far more Nestorian than Nestorius. But they were all dead; the Fathers at Chalcedon had not disturbed them; and the West objected to the emperor's tampering with the decisions of an ecumenical conclave. Unfortunately however the most influential Western prelate, Vigilius (538-555), who was bishop of Rome at the time, was both a sycophant and a coward. Since he owed his position to Justinian and Theodora, he secretly pledged himself to the "Three Chapters," while openly he did not contest the teachings of the West. His vacillation and weakness were unmasked however when Justinian imported him to Constantinople to convene an ecumenical council for the sole purpose of adding the "Three Chapters" to the dogma of the church. At first Vigilius tried to reason with the emperor and to persuade him not to take any action at all. When he failed against Justinian's stubborn determination, he fled for safety to the altar of a church. The emperor's soldiers tried to drag him out for punishment. But Vigilius was a huge man. He held so tenaciously to the base of the altar that he pulled it down. The congregation, moved by compassion, constrained the emperor to spare him.

Justinian nonetheless convened the conclave. There were 160 Eastern bishops, including all the patriarchs, who participated. Five bishops came from North Africa and supported their Eastern peers. Though Vigilius of Rome and his Western bishops took no part in the council, the poor man was terrified into ratifying the pronouncements. Consequently the three

[25] Procopius, Anecdota, xvii, 5.
[26] Mansi, IX, 375 D., 376 A.

heretics were officially condemned; this conclave (553) became the fifth of the General Councils of the church; and Justinian as usual had his way.[27]

The antipathy of the emperor to what he took to be heresy within Catholicism was intensified into **intolerance** and hatred of any religion or any system of ideas other than Christianity. This was in keeping of course with his world view: God ruled over everything, and the divine economy of creation ought to be imitated in the structure and operation of the empire. Church and state were one, and the *imperator* was *pontifex maximus* as well. Justinian was the personification of Caesaropapism, and he acted in all religious matters with a confidence in his own infallibility comparable to that of any pope. Consequently, by royal fiat, he closed the pagan academies of philosophy in Athens, destroyed the few remaining temples of Egypt, and persecuted the Samaritans in Palestine. This was 529—the same year of the Synod of Orange and the establishment of Monte Cassino in the West.

He was more tolerant of the Jews, since he did not proscribe their religion or deprive them of their civil rights. He enjoined them to read their Scriptures in Greek or Latin instead of Hebrew and selected for them the Septuagint as the authorized version of the Old Testament. Nevertheless he segregated them by excluding them from the state service, and he despised them personally, referring to them as "abominable men who sit in darkness."

Justinian's two major contributions to Christianity and to civilization were in jurisprudence and the arts.

The work in jurisprudence consumed the first decade of his reign, the first edition of the *Codex Justinianus* (now lost) having been issued in 529 and the revised famous second edition (still extant) in 534. With this was issued the *Digest* or *Pandects*, prepared by a legal commission over a period of three years (530-533) by which the laws were systematized and indexed and pertinent excerpts were given. The *Code of Justinian*, though a marvelous compilation and harmonization of the laws of the Roman empire, was a Christian document as well. It was a conscious effort to do through the law of the realm what the emperor had attempted in every other phase of his administration—to make his empire conform at least in theory to the ideals of a Christian commonwealth. Whereas heretofore the Christian religion had been grafted on to a culture already in existence, with the *Code of Justinian* the law of God became the parent plant, the branches of which were adaptations of basic principles to historic conditions.

Consequently the Code opens with an affirmation of faith and anathemas against the heretics. Its subsequent chapters deal with enactments governing persons, property, and crime. In the legislation regarding slaves, for example, the rights of every man as created in the image of God are clearly recognized;

[27] *Ibid.*, Cols. 414-419, 457-488; MPL, LXIX, 122-128, 143-178.

though slavery as an institution is not proscribed, still the slave is accepted as a person, precious in the sight of God, and cannot be dealt with carelessly like a piece of real estate. He is put under full protection of the law, and his punishment is restricted by legal enactment. This *Code of Justinian*, with its 432 subjects, became immortal, the foundation of Christian jurisprudence for the Middle Ages and modern times.[28]

Justinian was a **builder in stone** as well as legislation. Early in his reign the Nika Revolt (532) had wrecked the city of Constantinople and destroyed its principal public buildings. This gave the emperor an opportunity to rebuild his capital on a scale more lavish and magnificent than that of Augustus or Nero. Palaces, the Senate, churches, monasteries, public baths, theaters, the aqueduct, and even fortifications were designed as works of art. Each was an object of beauty in itself and all together blended with the natural terrain into a design which made Constantinople the supreme wonder of the world.

Saint Sophia, or the Church of the Holy Wisdom, was Justinian's masterpiece. It took him more than five years to build and cost him in money the sum of all his wars to regain the Western empire. On its completion the emperor exclaimed, "I have vanquished thee, O Solomon!" This church is the parent of Byzantine architecture. Prior to its construction churches in East and West had been modeled after the Roman basilica, or court house, not after the temple. This was because the basilica had a large assembly room and the temple had not. Justinian's architects borrowed from the Oriental as well as the Greek and Roman and thereby created a new pattern by which they were able to express in a unique way the genius of the Christian religion. Saint Sophia is a rectangular structure, the ground plan of which is a Greek cross. Its outstanding feature is that four small domes rise above the four ends of the cross and cluster around a large central dome which rests not on central pillars, but on arches in the ceiling. This gives it the appearance of being suspended, as Procopius testifies, "by a chain of gold from the height of the sky." When one enters, he feels that he is in a building not made by human power. His soul is lifted to the sky and he realizes God is close by and takes delight in his earthly temple.[29]

In addition to Saint Sophia, Justinian tore down and rebuilt the Church of the Holy Apostles, where the emperors were buried from the time of Constantine the Great to the eleventh century. This church, scarcely less magnificent than Saint Sophia, was perhaps more significant in ecclesiastical affairs, for it was the seat of the patriarch and the place of worship for the imperial family. Likewise, he constructed the majestic monastery of Saint Catherine on the lonely slope of Mount Sinai and scattered in prodigality

---

[28] *Codex Justinianus,* ed. Krüger (Berlin, 1906).
[29] Procopius, *Buildings,* I, 1-10.

mosaics of incomparable beauty from the Sinaitic peninsula to Ravenna in Italy.

The literary arts also flourished under Justinian. Poetry was not of the highest quality. Dioscorus, the last Greek poet of Egypt, was an ungrammatical amateur. Crippus, also a North African who lived in Constantinople and wrote eulogies on a Byzantine general and Justinian, was little better. However, the poetical description of Saint Sophia by Paul the Silentiary and the hymns of Romanus the Melode were genuine art. Cyril of Scythopolis, a Palestinian monk, made an interesting collection of monastic lives. John Climacus, who lived on Mount Sinai, wrote the *Spiritual Ladder*, a description of spiritual ascension by means of asceticism to moral perfection. Leontius of Byzantium, one of the first ecclesiastics to prefer Aristotle to Plato, championed the cause of orthodoxy against Nestorianism and Monophysitism; while the great John of Ephesus wrote in Syriac his treatises in defense of Monophysitism, the *Lives of the Eastern Saints*, and his *Ecclesiastical History*. Two or three excellent works on geography, political science, and a statistical survey of the empire were written. Evagrius' *Ecclesiastical History* gave the account of events from the Council of Ephesus to 593. Peter the Patrician wrote a history of Rome from Augustus to Julian the Apostate and in another work described the ceremonies of the spiritual court of Justinian. The greatest writer of the period however was the historian Procopius. He wrote two works, *History* and *On Buildings*, which lend exaggerated praise to the name and fame of Justinian. However, he wrote a third book *Anecdota*, which is a vicious attack on Justinian, Theodora, the general Belisarius, and practically everyone else of importance whom Procopius knew.

Ironically enough Justinian, who had spent all of his mature life defending orthodoxy and promoting Christianity, fell a victim in old age to aphthartodocetism—Monophysitism in its most extreme form—which affirmed that the body of Jesus Christ was different from ours and had been incapable of injury and corruption, even on the cross. Consequently he who caused the church to anathematize others was himself anathematized by the church and his soul consigned to perdition forever. Fortunately his great work has outlived his personal fate.[30] The epoch of Justinian is known as the Golden Age of Byzantine art and literature.

VI. Organization and Worship

The organization and worship of the church during the sixth century were a consummation of the achievements of antiquity and a projection, partial in the West, almost entire in the East, of the long future of the Middle Ages.

Christendom was divided among five great patriarchates—Rome, Con-

---

[30] Evagrius, op. cit., IV, 39, 40.

stantinople, Alexandria, Antioch, and Jerusalem. The patriarchs of these sees were the spiritual fathers and governors of the church universal, though in the size of their areas and the force of their influence the first two were elevated above their brethren, while the fifth, save for the fact that he presided over the parent see of Christendom, was scarcely a patriarch at all. The patriarch of Constantinople, even in the eyes of the Eastern emperor himself, was slightly less in ecclesiastical stature than the patriarch of Rome, though this latter was in no sense absolute monarch of Christendom and shared his title of pope with his Alexandrine brother.

Each patriarchate was in turn divided into **provinces.** Over every province was a metropolitan, sometimes called archbishop, whose cathedral was usually situated in the chief city of the province, the metropolis. Under the metropolitan were his bishops, who ruled over **dioceses** which were generally coterminous with the chief cities of the province and their outlying areas. There were a few dioceses which were autonomous—that is, their bishops were independent of the metropolitan and answerable directly to the patriarch himself. Such dioceses were styled "extra-provincial" or "autocephalous." Sometimes their bishops as well as the metropolitans were called archbishops. The patriarch of Constantinople, for example, ruled in the year 535 over thirty metropolitans and 150 bishops.

The **non-episcopal orders** were composed of priests, deacons, subdeacons, readers, and cantors. To become a priest a man had to be at least thirty-five years of age; a deacon or subdeacon, twenty-five; a reader or cantor, eighteen. Marriage was allowed but not encouraged. A priest could maintain his wife and children if he had married before he became a subdeacon. If his wife died, he was to remain unmarried.

The **duties of the clergy,** then as now, were manifold: pastoral, sacerdotal, administrative, sometimes even political, varying in degree with the importance of the position held. A metropolitan was judge of all clergy, including bishops, under his charge; while a priest acted as chief shepherd to his people, assigning to his staff of deacons, subdeacons, readers, and cantors the business and administrative chores of the parish. Women lent assistance as deaconesses, though they were excluded from the ranks of the clergy. There were special diocesan officials such as archdeacons, protopresbyters (rural deans), deans, and syncelli or chaplains as well as minor functionaries such as stewards, almoners, church wardens, sacristans, archivists, who executed the orders of their bishops.

Clerical privileges were innumerable: exemption from taxes and civil responsibilities and exclusion from the rigors of the law. Clerics were accorded their own juries and their own jails. A bishop was the chief local magistrate in his city and had the statutory powers of an official of the empire.

In the East the church was completely subservient to the emperor; in the West, though the imperial power was asserted by Justinian, it was at least resented and at times even resisted, as if to indicate it was considered illegitimate and therefore transitory. Ecclesiastical organization in the East and West at this time was substantially the same.

In regard to worship—the rites, forms, and ceremonies of the church—the pattern in the East was fixed through the liturgical enactments of Justinian's Code. The West, though greatly influenced by Eastern practices and at this time under the same liturgical mandates where the rule of Justinian prevailed, still maintained a certain flexibility which left to the future the establishment of those patterns it would ultimately adopt. After all, its vehicle of expression was Latin, in contrast to the Greek of Eastern Catholicism and the various and sundry languages of the schismatic and heretical bodies.

The central act of worship in all of Christendom was the Eucharist. It began, according to the Byzantine Rite, with the service of the catechumens. It was introduced with music and the burning of incense in censers as the deacons carried in the Gospels. Before the reading of Scripture the deacon's litany was said. Then lessons were read and heard: from the Old Testament, the Epistles, and the Gospels; the people standing throughout. A sermon or homily was delivered, after which the unbaptized were dismissed. Then began for the faithful behind closed doors the great act of consecration and worship. The elements were prepared in the prothesis, prior to the public service, at the time when the clergy vested. The people listened to the prayer for the faithful. The diptychs of the dead and living were recited by the deacon. The offering of the host was performed by the priest and, after the expressions of praise and thanksgiving in litany and song, each communicant received in his own hands the elements of bread and wine from the priest. The elements which were left over were consumed, not by the priests, but by little children of the congregation. The Eucharist constituted what came to be called "The Service," the rites and ceremonies of which composed "The Liturgy." It could be celebrated only on Sundays and Holy Days.

Other rites and ceremonies supplemented "The Service." The canonical hours came to be observed by priests as well as monks. Though Justinian's Code stipulated only three, in the West and gradually in the East also, seven were observed. Processions, in which the clergy carried crosses, lights, incense, and the Gospels, were popular and took place every Friday evening during a regular season as well as on special occasions when the people sought grace and favor. Masses were said for the dead; holy water was sprinkled on the sick; relics were offered as miracles and cures.

The sixth century witnessed the establishment of saints' days throughout Christendom as well as the observance of great feast days celebrating the cardinal events of Christ's life and work. Likewise, the administration of the

Eucharist was regularized. Baptism, performed by triune immersion, was performed in a baptistry designed for the purpose and situated just outside of the church. It was administered, except in cases of emergency, only at Christmas, Epiphany, Ascension Day, Feast of the Assumption of Mary, and Easter—more especially Easter. Confirmation, at least in the East, was inseparable from baptism and was given to infants as well as adults at baptism. Public penance had ceased, and private confession to a priest was beginning to take its place. Ordination was performed by the laying on of hands. Marriage was a civil act, legal without the blessing of the church; and extreme unction was unknown.[31]

The morals of the people, in the East and in the West, were no better than they had been in preceding centuries. Commitment to the Christian faith was not necessarily an act of personal will. It frequently reflected politics —an act of civic obligation, a requirement of society. In the barbarian states a man was unpatriotic if he did not embrace the religion of his chief. In the empire of Justinian one might risk the penalties of theft, extortion, gambling, cruelty, adultery, sodomy, castration, even murder itself; he dared not run the risk of failing to call himself a Christian.[32]

[31] *Justiniani Novellae* (Leipzig, 1881), 2 vols. F. E. Brightman, *Liturgies*, I, 533 ff.
[32] B. J. Kidd, *The Churches of Eastern Christendom* (London, 1927), pp. 62-75.

Chapter Two

The Papacy and the Evangelization
of the West
(590-756)

THE DEATH OF JUSTINIAN LIFTED THE HEAVY HAND OF IMPERIAL AUTOCRACY
from the neck of the church in the West. No longer did the bishops of Rome
respond to every beck and call of the Eastern emperors and make their way
obsequiously to the court at Constantinople to receive orders from their
royal masters. Justinian had bequeathed to his successor an almost bankrupt
empire. There was scarcely enough wealth or military power to maintain
stability in the East, much less to consolidate and control Western conquests.
Consequently, if the church was to be useful at all in furthering the imperial
interests, it had to be treated as an ally and equal. It could no longer be
commanded as a slave.

In any case the greater part of Western Europe was beyond the reach of
Eastern imperial policy and power. The Roman empire even at its zenith
had never included the lands that are now Ireland, Scotland, Denmark,
Sweden, Norway, and Finland; while only segments of what we know as
Holland, Germany, Austria, Hungary, and Russia were ever within its bounds.
In what had been its ancient and long held territories, there were now
established, as we saw in the last chapter, autonomous and aggressive
barbarian kingdoms. Even Italy had fallen prey to the ferocious and rapacious
Lombards (568),[1] the last and most tyrannical of her invaders.[2] The Eastern
exarch, more often than not, was a self-appointed exile in his marsh-protected
capital of Ravenna and preferred the cowardice of security to the heroism of
battle which could issue as readily in defeat as victory.

Even in its decadence the largest and most influential city in the West was
Rome. The first citizen of Rome was its bishop. More and more the peoples
of the West looked to him for leadership. The seventh century witnessed

[1] Velleius Paterculus, II, 96.
[2] *Leges Langobardorum*, MGH, Leges, IV.

37

the transformation of the Roman episcopate into the papacy. This and the succeeding century marked an extensive expansion of Christianity in Western Europe. The chief agents in this expansion were missionaries of the Roman and Celtic churches.

I. Gregory I

The head of the Roman church at the end of the sixth century was a man of consummate ability. He, more than any of his predecessors, seemed to divine the universal scope of his office. He both laid the foundation of the medieval papacy and mapped the strategy of a successful missionary enterprise which enabled Rome to direct ecclesiastical affairs for almost a thousand years in the Western world.

Gregory was born in Rome of a noble house, probably in the year 540, and boasted among his ancestors two bishops of Rome, Agapetus I (535-536) and Felix IV (526-530), who was his great-grandfather. If his was the famous Anicius family, there then flowed in his veins the blood of Roman generals and statesmen whose deeds of glory harkened back to the Gallic wars of the second century. It was also reported that Benedict of Nursia was his kinsman. His father was a senator.

When Gregory was no older than six years, the savage Totila, purposing to erase from history the very knowledge of where Rome stood, depopulated the city and left it for a time as the habitation of jackals and other beasts of the field. Gregory saw in his early teens the last Goth subjugated and the power of Justinian set up in Italy. Between the death of Justinian and his own elevation, three men preceded him in the office of Roman bishop: John III (561-574), Benedict I (575-579), and Pelagius II (579-590). Gregory served as minister to the imperial court at Constantinople under Pelagius II. Before going to Constantinople however he had been prefect of Rome which was the city's highest secular official. His duties involved caring for Rome's public buildings and food supply—and that at the age of thirty-three. Out of the patrimony of his father he had established and endowed six monasteries in Sicily and one in Rome, the latter being his ancestral home on the Coelian Hill. By this time he himself had taken the monastic vows.

Gregory's six years (579-585) in Constantinople were only moderately well spent in the service of his bishop. He apprised the Emperor Maurice of the deplorable conditions of Italy under the Lombards and won his sympathy, if not his military support. He saved the Patriarch Eutychius from the heresy of believing our bodies will be impalpable after the general resurrection and therefore unidentifiable with our present bodies. He championed the claims of Naples and won for that city its civil rights. Above all else he learned how to control men by persuading them to forsake their opinions for his.

His next four years (585-590) were of the same piece. He was back in Rome as state secretary to the bishop and abbot over his own monastic establishment. During this time he tried to win (without success) the schismatic bishops of Istria back into communion with the church by convincing them of the wisdom of the Fifth Ecumenical Council regarding the Three Chapters, and governed his monks with a discipline far more severe than any Benedict ever recommended or practiced. It seems now as if all his years from 540 to 590 were preparation for the last thirteen and a half which were to follow them. Every one of Gregory's enduring accomplishments came after he became bishop of Rome.

This major event in the history of the church, which Gregory tried almost frantically to prevent, took place in the midst of the bubonic plague. Pelagius II, one of the first victims of the plague, died on February 7, 590. Immediately, presumably on the same day, the whole **people chose Gregory to be pope.** The humble man wrote a letter to the Emperor Maurice in Constantinople asking him to veto the action of the Roman people. To escape enthronement he hid among the merchandise of tradesmen and was transported out of the city. Fortunately his letter never reached the emperor. After three days he was discovered, so legend has it, by a heavenly shaft of light which pointed out to the people the cave where he was hiding. They seized him and carried him by force to Saint Peter's, where he was consecrated September 3, 590, seven months less four days after his election. Legend also narrates that during the time between the election and consecration of Gregory, as the population engaged with its bishop in the penitential procession asking divine deliverance from the pestilence, the people of Rome saw the Angel of Death astride Hadrian's Mausoleum sheathing his sword; and they knew the plague was ended. From that day until now the Mausoleum has been called the Castle of Sant' Angelo.

"Gregory," so writes Bossuet, "gave the world a perfect model of **ecclesiastical government.**" [3] He became the artificer of the medieval papacy by demonstrating through the conduct of his episcopacy the proper form that institution should take. At the same time he had a clear notion of the goals he wanted to accomplish. Through service he brought his age into conformity with his own stupendous ends.

The Eastern empire was too poor and too weak to provide what the times required. The Roman church, through Gregory, stepped into the political and social breach which the state was unable to fill. Destitute fugitives, made homeless by the Lombards, were given shelter and food and the means of making for themselves new homes. On every feast day and on the first day of each month Gregory himself presided at the distribution of meat,

---

[3] Bosset, Jacques B., *L'Histoire universelle*, eleventh period.

wheat, vegetables, wine, fish, and clothing. He organized his charities to a minute degree, ascertaining the exact needs of recipients and avoiding waste and graft. Likewise, for the protection of his people, he exercised political, even military, prerogatives when required. He dispatched soldiers against the Lombards (592). Later, to lift the siege of Rome, he negotiated a truce with them without the consent of the Eastern exarch (594). As the church served the people in social and political ways, they were led gradually to look upon it as their state.

Gregory's political concerns did not in the least diminish his zeal in prosecuting the purely ecclesiastical interests of his see. Its physical properties, the so-called patrimonies of the apostle Peter, received the same businesslike care from this watchful pontiff as they would have from one whose only job in life had been that of a large landowner. At the head of each patrimony (estate) was a steward who had responsibility for its material prosperity and for the proper distribution of its revenues among the poor. The lands themselves were parceled out among farmers, the terms and conditions of whose leases depended almost entirely upon the quality of their work and the quantity of their yield. They worked the tenant help, assigned to the soil, through their superintendents who directed labor in the field. The pope himself kept an eye on the officials of every patrimony through itinerating magistrates who reported directly to him. Though Gregory bought and sold slaves and used them for profitable ends as did any layman in his diocese, still he treated them as if they had souls and made provision for their emancipation when he considered them socially fit to sustain themselves as free men.

Likewise Gregory was keen about the proper execution of sacerdotal functions. His orderly mind insisted on an orderly liturgy. Consequently he amended the Sacramentary by deleting from it many of the long and irregular prayers of the preceding centuries, bringing back old usages, and making it conform in most places to the Greek. What he thus arranged became the groundwork of the Roman Missal as we know it today: brief, direct, and within the compass of a single book. He inspired, if he did not actually originate, the chant called by his name and created the *schola cantorum*, which still sings in the Roman church according to ancient melodic principles. He emphasized preaching, for he knew "The living word moves the heart more than a reading, which requires an intermediary." Most important of all he devised his *Pastoral Rule*, delineating the nature and characteristics of the priesthood, describing the life of the pastor, giving the rules for apostolic preaching, and showing that the source of all is the interior, spiritual life. His diocese was as well organized for religious success as his patrimonies for material gain.

Gregory did not confine his labor to Rome or its metropolitan environs.

In deeds as well as name he was patriarch of the West. He ordered the African bishops to oppose the Donatists and the civil authorities to suppress them by force. He severely punished those of his own lands who had fallen into Manichaeism, for he believed "that torture of the body should serve at least the good health of the soul." He thereby set the precedent for the inquisitions of subsequent ages. He nursed Spain from Arianism into orthodoxy, set up and directed the missionary campaign in Britain, encouraged or rebuked the important prelates of the West as circumstances required, chided the Emperor Maurice on his restrictions concerning the admission of soldiers to sacred orders, and did whatever else he deemed needed to be done to govern the entire church.

This led him into open conflict with the patriarch of Constantinople, John the Faster. John styled himself "Ecumenical Patriarch," which Gregory looked upon as a dangerous attempt to lift his see in prestige and power above the other patriarchates of the church and a flagrant violation of the primacy of Rome. He called upon John to surrender that vain and arrogant title and to give an account to the papal nuncio in Constantinople of his maltreatment of one of his priests. In one of his letters to John, after making reference to his reputation for extreme asceticism and personal piety, Gregory sarcastically remarked that it would be better for more food to go into his mouth and less lies to come out of it. "I know not what bishop," asserted Gregory, "is not subject to the Apostolic See."

In addition to his heavy administrative and pastoral duties, Gregory found time for study, reflection, and writing. Though his style is crude and many of his ideas are superficial and borrowed with little creative interpretation from the Fathers, especially Augustine, still his works are such that they appealed to the masses of his day, and through them he was able to set the theological pattern of the Middle Ages. He popularized and made convincing the old ransom theory of the atonement. His *Morals on the Book of Job,* written while he was still nuncio in Constantinople, was a leading text on ethics until the Renaissance. His *Dialogues* were the model for later hagiographers. His *Pastoral Rule* on church administration is his masterpiece. Gregory, even in the history of thought, is one of the four Doctors of the Latin church.[4]

Gregory, more than any of his predecessors, deserves the title of pope. The power of his influence made him head of the universal church during his lifetime, and his behavior formed the pattern of government which transformed the Roman episcopate into the papacy. He died, age sixty-four,

---

[4] Johannes Diaconus, *Vita,* in MPL, LXXV, 59-242. Paulus Diaconus, *Vita,* in MPL, LXXV, 41-60. LP, I, 312-314. Gregorius Magnus, *Opera,* in MPL, LXXV-LXXVIII. F. H. Dudden, *Gregory the Great* (London, 1905), 2 vols.

March 12, 604. His life was the personification of his title: "Servant of the Servants of God."

II. Conversion of Britain

Both **British and German Christianity** find their main roots in the program of evangelization which Gregory inaugurated and which his and successive missioners carried out. To be sure, this work of the Roman church was complemented by similar labors on the part of Irish and Celtic monks, so that it would be unfair to the historical record to say that these northern peoples were won solely by the efforts of Rome and the emissaries of the popes. Italy herself received a visitation from afar in the person of the Celt Columban, and his monastery of Bobbio succeeded among the Lombards who had burned Benedict's Monte Cassino to the ground. However, in the end the Celtic missions were either superseded or absorbed by the Roman, and Western Europe as it was constituted into a Christian hegemony bore the papal imprint.

While still a young man, Gregory had volunteered his own personal services as a missionary to the Anglo-Saxons. He had observed some Angle boys being auctioned as slaves in the marts of Rome; and so fair had been their countenance that he had called them angels. He wanted to free them from the eternal wrath of God, and expressed the hope that through his personal efforts alleluias might be sung in the domains of their king. Though Gregory's immediate resolve was thwarted by circumstance, he eventually achieved his purpose. After he became pope he commissioned Augustine, a Benedictine monk who was trained in Gregory's monastic establishment in Rome, to go with twelve companions and accomplish this mission for him. The year 596—midway in his pontificate—witnessed the sending of Augustine via Frankish Gaul on this ambitious undertaking.

The Roman Mission in England progressed largely along the geographical lines of the Heptarchy, which was in the sixth and seventh centuries the political expression of what is now England. Augustine landed at the northeast corner of Kent on the Isle of Thanet. He addressed his message to Ethelbert, who was ruler of the Jutes, and brought Ethelbert and ten thousand of his subjects to baptism on Christmas Day, 597. Augustine established himself as primate over a new province of the church with his see at Canterbury. When he died in the early part of 605, not many months after his master, Gregory the Great, his mission was still small and inconsequential. His efforts among the East Saxons scarcely survived him; for Mellitus (d. 624), the first bishop of London, was expelled from his see within little more than a decade of his consecration. Paulinus (d. 644), who had been sent by Gregory I from Rome (601) to the aid of Augustine, won Edwin of Northumbria to the faith, baptized him and the leaders of his nation

42

on Easter, 627, and was himself established as the first occupant of the episcopal see of York. This mission also proved abortive. With the defeat and death of Edwin, martyr prince, on the field of battle, October 12, 633, the Northumbrian kingdom itself was decimated—Christianity destroyed by Christians—and the gains of Rome almost entirely liquidated. Indeed, after thirty tireless years of almost superhuman exertion, the mission of Pope Gregory the Great had succeeded in establishing nothing save in the tiny kingdom of Kent.

Failure however was not to be the final verdict. Though the particular expression of Christianity which Paulinus had brought to Northumbria went temporarily into eclipse, **the faith itself in Celtic usage was renewed by Aidan** (d. 651) in 633 and was vigorous enough to withstand two more onslaughts of invasion by that merciless pagan, Penda, king of Mercia. Wessex capitulated to the preaching of Birinus (d. 649), commissioned by Pope Honorius of Rome, in 634 and 635. The East Angles embraced the faith the same year. Mercia, the principality of that recalcitrant pagan, Penda, who in the course of twenty-two years killed five kings, all of whom were Christians, witnessed the penetration of Christianity into its territory in 653. Peada, son of Penda, embraced the faith at the instigation of King Oswy of Northumbria. Sixteen years later (669) its king applied to Canterbury for the establishment of a bishopric. Essex, which had lapsed back into paganism in 619, was won again through the conversion of its king, Sigebert the Good, in 653; and finally Sussex, which had been isolated from the Roman mission by forest and marsh, embraced the gospel preached by Wilfrid in 681. Thus the Anglo-Saxon Heptarchy entered upon the eighth century as a part of Christendom.

Roman Christianity from the very beginning met keen competition from Celtic Christianity in Britain. The monks of Bangor in Wales for example had been repulsed by the arrogance and authoritarianism of Augustine. Perhaps this was no more than an excuse for their indifference, since they did little or nothing on their own toward the conversion of their pagan conquerors. However, quite a different spirit was manifested by the spiritual sons of Columba, who emerged from their retreat on the Isle of Iona to vie with the heirs of Gregory the Great for the mastery of Northumbria and the whole of Britain. It was Aidan the Celt, not Paulinus the Roman, who converted and nurtured the peoples of Northumbria; and his ministry of twenty years with its center at Lindesfarne laid the real foundation for Christian Britain.

Indeed, a Celt trained in this very establishment yet self-convinced of the superiority of Roman customs—Wilfrid (634-709) by name—persuaded the Northumbrian king, Oswy, and his thanes to declare themselves for the Latin expression of the faith. **The Synod of Whitby** (664) is famous. There

Wilfrid debated with the Celtic spokesman, Colman (d. 676), over the observance of Easter, contending in favor of the Roman practice against those who observed the custom claimed to have been established in the East by John. Oswy and his thanes declared themselves in favor of Rome on the pragmatic assumption that, since Roman Christianity derived from Peter and since our Lord had entrusted to Peter the keys to the kingdom of heaven, it would pay them in the end to entrust their salvation to the followers of him who could open and shut the gates of paradise.

It was Theodore, a Greek monk from Tarsus, the city of Paul's birth, who occupied the see of Canterbury from 668 until his death in 690, rather than the controversial Wilfrid, who succeeded in uniting Anglo-Saxon Britain in Roman practices. This he did by appointing worthy Celts to important ecclesiastical sees and by traveling among all the people instructing his clergy in Greek, Latin, theology, liturgics, music, and even the sciences. Literally, the people sang themselves into harmony with the customs of the Roman church. Gradually, outside Anglo-Saxondom, the churches of Celtic persuasion gravitated toward Rome, so that Iona itself accepted the Roman Easter in 716. Much of Ireland had been won to the new usage earlier, in the last decade of the seventh century by Adamnan (c. 624-704), a Roman Celt, though its total ecclesiastical structure was not brought into conformity until the eleventh century.[5]

III. The Expansion of Christianity on the Continent

What had taken place in Britain was re-enacted on the continent. This time however the members of the cast in the missionary drama were supplied by the monastic establishments of Ireland and England. The Frankish church was so secular and spiritually depleted that it could scarcely maintain itself, much less supply aid to its pagan neighbors, while Rome was too busy with politics to do more than give direction and counsel to the evangelists who came from other parts. In the beginning the British Celts shared with their compatriots of the Roman persuasion in the adventures and successes of the gospel. Later their missionary enterprises either coalesced with those of the larger body or else became isolated and ineffective.

The first area outside the bounds of the old Roman empire to be reached by Christian evangelists was the **Low Countries**—that is, what is now Belgium, Holland, and the German shores of the North Sea. This area was inhabited by the Frisians—a people stubborn in their paganism and therefore at first recalcitrant to the Christian appeal. The earliest Irish and British missions to them were unsuccessful. Their resistance to Christianity

---

[5] Baeda, *Historia Ecclesiastica* (ed. C. Plummer, Oxford, 1896); Montalembert, *Monks of the West* (tr. Gasquet, London, 1896), Books X, XV.

began to weaken before the labors of Willibrord, whom history has labeled "Apostle to the Netherlands."

Willibrord, who was born probably on November 6, 658, in Saxon Northumbria, was the offspring of a godly couple who had married it seems for no other purpose than to bring into the world a child who would benefit many peoples. It was said that on the very night of her son's conception, the mother of Willibrord had a dream in which she beheld the thin new moon expand immediately into the full moon, drop from its place in the heavens, and enter into her own mouth so that her bosom was suffused with light. This dream she interpreted as a portent of her son's mission. Willibrord was therefore placed quite early in the establishment of Wilfrid at Ripon, where he remained until his patron's banishment from the see of York in 678. He then spent twelve years in the monastic schools of Ireland, where he acquired the missionary zeal. Not until his thirty-third year, however, after he had zealously striven to prepare his own soul for salvation, did he attempt to bring the light of the gospel to those who lived in the darkness of paganism and sin. He and eleven companions, imitating as best they could the twelve disciples of our Lord, left Ireland in the year 690 for Frisia. Unfortunately, both the method of operation and most of the major events in Willibrord's long Frisian mission of approximately fifty years are lost to history. All we really know is that when Willibrord died at the age of more than four score years, he had won the support of the powerful Franks for his Frisian enterprise, had been established in Rome in the archiepiscopal see of Utrecht, and had by his personal labors brought about the conversion of most of the people in the southern part of the Low Countries.[6]

Winfrid, Willibrord's younger contemporary and for three years (719-722) his co-laborer and assistant, was the chief figure in the evangelization of Germany, the artificer of institutional Christianity among the German people, their first archbishop, and, judged by the extent and significance of his work, perhaps the greatest missionary since the apostle Paul. He is deservedly known in history by his nickname, **Boniface**, doer of good.

We do not know the exact place or date of Boniface's birth, probably near Exeter in Devon in the Anglo-Saxon Kingdom of Wessex between 672 and 680. It seems that he was predestined for his mission; for at the age of four or five years, against the punitive opposition of his father, he determined upon the monastic life. Consequently he was transported from the parental care of his own home to the disciplined upbringing of the Monastery of Examchester, where he modeled his behavior on the lives of the early saints. By assiduous study into the meaning of scripture and ceaseless vigilance in meditation he sublimated the normal passions of youth. When the brothers

[6] AS, Nov. III (1910), pp. 435-457.

of Examchester had taught him all they knew, he was transferred to the Monastery of Nursling between Southampton and Winchester. Here he became proficient in grammar and rhetoric, acquired the taste for writing verse, and developed his skill in the exposition of scripture. So adept a student was soon entrusted with tutorial responsibilities. He was incomparable in the classroom because he did not refuse to learn from his pupils. This attitude of tolerance was to stand him in good all his life. Later, as a missionary, by being willing to learn from the heathen, he was able at the same time to teach them the saving knowledge of Jesus Christ.

After work at home for both his king and the archbishop of Canterbury, he went as a missionary to the Frisians, whom he failed to win to Christianity. Radbod, their king, when he was told his pagan ancestors were in hell, asserted that he preferred their companionship wherever they were to the delights of heaven. Disillusioned, Boniface went to Rome, where he was delegated by the pope to travel as his agent among the savage peoples of Germany. So successful was he in this enterprise that Pope Gregory II ordained him a missionary bishop to Germany (December 1, 722).

Generations before Boniface's time Christianity had been replanted in what is now Switzerland, Southern Germany, and Western Austria; but its growth had not been uniform, and each unit of its expression was more or less a law unto itself without hierarchical organization or an institutional link with the main body of Christendom. Consequently one of Boniface's greatest achievements was the consolidation of existing churches into one ecclesiastical body. For example, he constituted the state of Bavaria into four dioceses, each with its own bishop, and made himself metropolitan, or archbishop, over all. As a result, the pope awarded him the pallium, recognizing in name the exalted position he had already earned in fact. Boniface kept up a regular correspondence with the papacy, not only reporting, but also asking pertinent questions and abiding by the answers he received. In that way he guaranteed to his younger churches communion with Rome.

Boniface's mission did reach out to the recalcitrant pagans; and like the apostle Paul, he was willing to employ every means to effect their conversion. The most dramatic instance of this was the hewing down of the giant Oak of Jupiter at Geismar. He did this to convince the Hessians, many of whom wanted to combine Christianity with the nature worship they were asked to give up, that there was no spiritual potency in trees and springs, and that they could not divine the future by inspecting the entrails of animals or control the elements by legerdemain and incantations. Consequently he took his life in his hands, for a great crowd of pagans stood by cursing him in their hearts as he swung the axe and cut the first notch on the trunk of the tree. That was all that it was necessary for him to do. It is said that a mighty wind blew through the branches of the tree causing it to fall of its own weight to the ground and split into four parts of equal length. The pagans were convinced and helped Boniface build an oratory to Peter out of the wood of the tree. Before he was sixty years of age Boniface brought within the communion of the Roman church practically the whole of Thuringia (much of which had been irregularly Christian before his time) and also Hesse, and won and baptized large numbers of people to the very borders of Saxony in the east. His sphere of operation was that part of Germany which lay east of the Rhine and north of the Danube.

The correspondence of Boniface gives us the most vivid picture which we could ever hope to find of the real conditions of this period in which Christian missionaries were called to labor and to die. These letters also afford us a glimpse of the personality of their author. He seems intent upon his mission, yet he found the time and the tenderness to comfort nuns, to instruct students, and to care for serfs. He showed the disposition and found the leisure to continue his studies, the courage and strength to admonish a king, and even the obliging willingness to find two falcons to send to a friend. It is little wonder that such a person was able to enlist as his assistants some of the best talent of the age. Such were Gregory, a Frankish nobleman who at the age of fourteen deserted home and heritage to follow this man of God; Willibald, his own relative of the royal line of Kent who had been educated at Monte Cassino and became bishop of Eichstätt in Bavaria; and his own pupil, Lul, who worked by his side in Germany, succeeded him in the archiepiscopal office, and commissioned another Willibald to write his life.

Though Boniface's missionary tactics seem not to have been different from those of the other missionaries who had gone before him, he was an innovator to the extent that he used women to evangelize as well as men. He and his companions addressed their message first to the king or ruler of a region, knowing that if they could win him they could win his people too. They itinerated, lived off the land, worked with their hands, and at key points constructed abbeys and monasteries. The most famous of these monasteries was Fulda, where Boniface expected to retire and to die.

But this relentless protagonist of the faith could never retire. He kept an active hand in the affairs of the church in Bavaria, sought aid and laborers for his work from among the British pilgrims in Rome, and addressed himself to the reorganization of the Frankish church and the improvement of the Frankish nation. To this end, with the consent of Rome, he crowned Pepin the Short as king, bringing to an end in the year 751 the Merovingian dynasty of do-nothing kings.

Boniface was of such a disposition that he could not accept success in one sphere of activity as compensation for failure in another. Consequently he returned to Frisia to take up where he had left off some thirty years before. Thus he ended his apostolate at the site of its beginning. The Frisians rewarded his missionary concern for them with martyrdom. On a day in June, 754, beside the River Bordne in Dutch Friesland he and his helpers had gathered to baptize a company of converts; he was waylaid by robbers turned assassins who slaughtered many of his companions and sealed his ministry with his own blood. The robbers had expected to find gold in the chests he carried. Instead they found only manuscripts and relics.

King Pepin decreed that Boniface's remains should be interred at Utrecht, though the martyr had wanted to rest at Fulda. However when the emissaries from Lul came to claim his body, the decree of Pepin gave way to that of a Higher Summoner. The bells of the church miraculously pealed forth his release from Frisia to the Germany he had loved and served. The tomb of Boniface is at Fulda.[7]

The missionary accomplishments of this period between the landing of Augustine in Kent in 597 and the death of Boniface in 754 were most impressive. Not all however was expansion and gain. Spain, for example, which had honorably transmitted the conciliar habits of antiquity to the emerging Middle Ages through her successive councils of Toledo and whose scholarship had glowed in a shaft of light through the encyclopedic learning of Isidore of Seville, now gave way completely to the invading armies of Islam. Her nobility dissipated its strength in warring factions. Her clergy capitulated to corruption and license, countenancing mixed monasteries of men and women. Her people sustained a divided allegiance to Arianism and Catholic Christianity. Even her church persecuted the Jews. Consequently when in the year 711 one of her own noblemen, Count Julian, aided and abetted by a traitorous bishop, Oppas by name, invited the Saracens into Spain, the nation capitulated to Islam with scarcely even a fight. The valiant Pelayo alone formed an underground movement of opposition which was to last for centuries.[8]

What happened to Christianity in Spain might have happened throughout Western Europe had it not been for Charles Martel (ca. 690-741). He was mayor of the Palace under the Merovingian king of the Franks. The Moslems had crossed the Pyrenees and spilled into what is now southern and central France. Charles Martel stayed their expansion at Tours (732) and forced them back over the mountains into Spain. Tours was one of the decisive battles of history. Had its issue been different the civilization of Western Europe might have been Islamic rather than Christian; the Koran, not the Bible, might have shaped its laws and determined its morals; and the muezzin on the pinnacle of his mosque might have called its people to the service of

---

[7] Willibald, Vita Sancti Bonifaeii and other early lives of Boniface, in MGH, Scriptores rerum Germanicarum in usum scholarum (1905). Opera, MPL, LXXXIX, 597-892. Epistolae, MGH, Epistolae, Vol. III (1892). M. Tangle, Epistulae Selectae, I (1916).

[8] Continuationes Isidorianae, MGH, Chronica Minora, IV-VII. CMH, II, 180-93.

Allah rather than the priest at the altar to the service of the God of Jesus Christ.

The gains to the church in the West, territorially and numerically, were greater by far than the losses, so that the addition of Britain, the Low Countries, and the heart of Germany softened the blow of the demise of Christian Spain.

IV. *Christian Mythology and the Emerging Culture*

The means of converting these Germanic peoples became at the same time the agencies of their civilization and, conversely, also the catalysts for the transformation of Christianity into something other than what it was in the East and what it had been in the West prior to the seventh century. This was true certainly in the social expression of Christianity and to a degree at least in its spirit, if not in its doctrinal core. Not only did Christianity influence directly its environment, but its **environment indirectly influenced it**, so that the reaction of the one upon the other produced almost an entirely new culture and civilization.

Latin missionaries, having obtained their grand strategy from Rome and having been left to work out their tactics in keeping with local needs, did not destroy pagan shrines or entirely disabuse the people who worshiped in them of pagan notions. The buildings were consecrated and changed to Christian usage. Likewise the services of Woden, Thor, and the other Norse gods and goddesses were not abrogated but rather transferred to angels like Michael and Gabriel who, though of lesser rank in the new hierarchy than their pagan antecedents had been in the old, were nevertheless more accommodating and efficient. The sprites which had haunted woods and mountains and had either inconvenienced or injured men, depending upon whether they were mischievous or evil, did not disappear with the emergence of Christianity; they just changed their allegiance and became imps or devils of the army of Satan. Indeed the general tendency to apotheosize heroes gradually particularized itself into the adoration of the Virgin. This religious cult, though developed and popularized in subsequent times, existed at least embryonically in this period in the monasteries and oratories where the ordinary providence of God gave place to a perpetual interposition of saints, angels, and especially the Mother of Jesus. Even the sorcery of paganism, though proscribed by law, was thereby recognized as a reality; and a demonic spell cast by a witch could scarcely be broken by anything less than the prayers of a saint or the sacerdotal incantations of a priest.

It is not surprising therefore that **relics, the graves of martyrs and saints, church property, the rites and ceremonies of Christianity, and even the clergy themselves came to have in the minds of these untutored peoples a veneration and sanctity comparable almost to the worship of the Deity**

whom they represented. Pope Gregory I, for example, was content to send the Eastern empress no more than a little filing dust from the alleged chains of the apostle Paul, since in his mind the miraculous power of the relic was compensation enough for the smallness of its bulk.[9] It was related that a Lombard thief who tried to prize loose a link from the gold chain of Peter with a knife had the knife to dart from his hand and cut his own sacrilegious throat.[10] The tombs of Peter and Paul in Rome and even of Martin of Tours in the distant land of the Franks did not fail to yield, almost daily, supposedly miraculous benefits to those who came to them in faith. Good people found rest for their souls in the sanctified precincts of church and monastery, while the sacred soil reputedly refused the corpses of the wicked, and the ghosts of martyrs were said to expel from their chapels the corrupt bodies of evildoers.

The people were impressed by the pageantry of religion, and the bread from the altar representing the body of their Savior could, so they believed, do almost anything, and they came both to love and to fear it. Pope Gregory related that two women who in life had been excommunicated from the church for scandal and yet who in death had been buried within its walls were observed to flee from their graves every time holy mass was celebrated. Because of their God-ordained functions the clergy were sacrosanct. The story was told that an entertainer with a monkey and bells was struck dead for having interrupted the prayers of a priest. Heaven and hell were made familiar to many, since the Angel of Death apparently sometimes made mistakes and summoned the wrong victim to the judgment. When the mistake was discovered, the victim was allowed to return to earth, always with vivid descriptions of what he had seen: angels struggling with demons to rescue a soul, inviting meadows of exquisite flowers peopled by saints in white garments, and sulphurous flames of unquenchable fire emitting the stench of burning bodies.[11]

It is not unfair to style these developments Christian mythology, though in the minds of the people of this age they were often as real as the events of their daily lives and frequently more regulative than the Bible itself because they were better understood.

Public worship, with the doctrinally undefined **sacrifice of the mass** as its central act, tended in the popular mind to be a matter of the material and sensible. This service was conducted entirely in Latin, which, a dead language to the converted barbarians, became in the West the exclusive language of the Christian church. Missionary preaching, the marriage ceremony, and confession were the only rites of Christianity performed in the language of the people. The liturgy was not uniform. There were three major forms: the

---

[9] Gregorius Magnus, *Epistolae*, III, 30.
[10] *Dialogorum Libri* (Venice, 1744), VI, 23.
[11] *Ibid.*, I, 9, 10; II, 22, 23; IV, 50; VI, 23.

Ambrosian in Milan, the Mozarabic in Spain, and the Gregorian in Rome. Still the Roman liturgy obtained the ascendency through Boniface in France and Germany and also in Britain where the Gregorian Latin chants were sung. Even participation in congregational singing except for the Kyrie eleison was denied the people, for Latin hymns had to be sung by a trained choir. The first organ came to the West from Greece during the time of Pepin the Short. The order of the mass itself took definite form, each item of the service with its peculiar subject and contribution being rigidly defined. However, the literary expression of it was allowed to vary with different liturgies for different days and in different churches. The Roman Canon of the Mass, which comes to us from the hands of Pope Gregory I, is terse, crude, in places even ungrammatical, but it possesses massive strength. It, more than any other, is the parent of the English rite written in the Book of Common Prayer.[12]

So significant was the mass that it was looked to for securing all sorts of benefits and gratuities. One bishop, for example, ordered masses to be said to obtain good weather. However, they were employed most for the relief of the dead, for whom low masses (celebrated by a priest only with the aid of an assistant) were said. Leagues for the dead—corporations to provide for their members indefinite masses after their death—were organized; and in Spain this practice became so lugubrious that a law had to be enacted forbidding people to celebrate masses in prayerful expectation of their own speedy death.[13]

The **religious duties of the people** consisted in taking the sacrament at mass (preferably three times a year, certainly once on Thursday of Passion Week), visiting shrines and the graves of saints, attending church services regularly once a week, and making offerings and gifts which were guaranteed to obtain merit. Penance as deeds of satisfaction became a fixed institution so that an individual who was discovered in a fault not only had to ask forgiveness for his wrong, but was assigned a specific work of satisfaction to perform. We know that as early as Archbishop Theodore's time in the Anglo-Saxon church, public confession had been entirely replaced by private confession to a priest who held the sinner's fault in confidence and allowed him to do penance in secret. Indeed these Anglo-Saxon peoples, to whom a man's business was his personal concern alone, seem to have occasioned in the church the transformation of public into private confession. Christianity permeated legal enactments, if it did not actually decree them; and marriage, which had been in antiquity a civil institution, was now regulated entirely by the church. In theory the church upheld the indissolubility of the nuptial bond, though in practice it often had to compromise with the Germanic right of a man

---

[12] L. Duchesne, *Origine du culte chrétien. Etude sur la liturgie latine avant Charlemagne* (Paris, 1889).
[13] *Concilium Toled.*, Mansi, XVII, 5.

to dismiss his wife and take another at will. It recognized as grounds for the annulment of marriage adultery, desertion and neglect, banishment from the nation, leprosy, and the inability to perform the sexual functions. Preaching, which was in the popular vernacular, was often little more than the proclamation of the current Christian mythology and an enforcement of Christian morals through threats and promises.

Scholarship in the form of literary productions did exist in isolated places and among a few rare individuals during this period. Isidore of Seville (ca. 560-636), who had imbibed the spirit of the famous councils of Toledo which combined ecclesiastical and civil legislation to a remarkable degree, knew more perhaps than any other man of his times and bequeathed to the Middle Ages an encyclopedia of ancient thought and learning. He was little more than a compiler, yet he won by his learning the title "the last of the Church Fathers" and set the style of subsequent medieval textbooks.[14] Bede (ca. 672-735) in Britain composed the history of the world from creation and put all of us in his debt by writing the ecclesiastical history of his own people. Famous monasteries in Ireland and Britain became depositories of the knowledge of antiquity as they fostered communities of scholars where the individual submerged his own talents in the accomplishments of the group.

Theology unfortunately was but the systematization and the attempt to rationalize the mythology which possessed the thought and feelings of the people. Pope Gregory I was its sole exponent. The doctrine of purgatory, for example, which was implied in the writings of Augustine, was for the first time searchingly and penetratingly treated by Gregory, who saw in it the prolongation beyond death of the domain of temporality and who consequently put it under the control of the church. The majesty of Christ's person was clouded in Gregory's teaching because Christ's work was made effective through the sacerdotal agencies. God, for Gregory, was an omnipotent being who left no sins unpunished yet who was gracious enough to devise methods and means whereby man might requite him for his guilt and divine justice might ultimately be satisfied. The devil ruled this world as a tyrant, but God baited his own Son on the fishhook of his wisdom, so that the devil took him in fair exchange for us only to be caught and cheated by his own folly. Gregory's religion rested on the motives of fear and hope rather than the Pauline motives of faith and love, and God's free grace in Christ was exchanged for a mechanical system of merits issuing finally in rewards and punishments. Hence he magnified the mass as the sacrifice of Christ repeated for man, its appeasing wafer shortening the time in purgatory.[15] Augustine may have been Gregory's theological master, but the

[14] MPL, LXXXI-LXXXIV.
[15] Gregorius Magnus, Mor., XXXIII, 7, 14 ff.; Dial., IV, 39, 55, 58.

Augustinianism which Gregory bequeathed to the Middle Ages was debased to such a degree that it is hardly recognizable.

The interest of the seventh and eighth centuries therefore was single. Cassiodorus in his day might have been both a monk and a statesman after the Roman imperial pattern and Boethius a pagan philosopher in Christian garb. But now all that had passed away. Christianity was everything in the West. Literature, even the very language of its expression, had become altogether ecclesiastical. It was not that society hated or even envied the accomplishments of Roman antiquity. It was just indifferent to them.

V. The Papal States

In such an atmosphere, where the chief concern of mankind was religion, the Roman church acquired political dominion over the peoples and territories contiguous to its bishopric. As a result the pope became a political as well as spiritual potentate, and the states of the church emerged as a **new phenomenon in history.**

It appears in retrospect as if all this took place by accident. No master mind conceived the deed and carefully planned in advance the innumerable actions necessary to its achievement. The result of all that happened came as either a pleasant surprise or an unbelievable disappointment to the various participants. The pope left Italy a fugitive appealing for mercy to the Franks. He came home again to be made a king and eventually the father of kings and princes. The Lombards sought to expand their territory by conquering Ravenna and Rome. They thought they were fighting a local war. Before they were through however the war had become international and the territory of the Lombards contracted rather than expanded. The Eastern empire watched a little barbarian state expand into its Western rival. And the half-civilized Franks became the benefactors of the church and the creators of its political principality.

Certain fundamental factors underlay this development. (1) The Eastern empire was unable to maintain itself in the West; and (2) the Lombard rule, which had replaced it, was altogether unacceptable to the vast majority of the population of Italy. Then too (3) Rome had developed a civic pride and a patriotic self-confidence which are the heralds of political independence on the part of any progressive people. It felt it belonged outright to the apostle Peter and that it had in its church and bishop all it needed to be constituted a state. Public opinion, therefore, was prepared in advance to welcome the creation of the papal states.

The Franks lent the military aid which gave political reality to the states of the church. If the pope was to rule Rome and its adjacent territories, then the land had first to be freed of its present overlords. The Lombard kings and the Roman bishop could not be sovereign at the same place at the same time.

The ruling house in Frankland was already in debt to the papacy. Pepin the Short (741-768), its founder, had displaced the Merovingian dynasty with the knowledge and approval of the church. When he drove the effeminate and incompetent Childeric III from his throne (751) and incarcerated him in a monastery, Pope Zacharias (741-752) gave moral and spiritual sanction to his action. Archbishop Boniface, the famous missioner, in the name of Rome stood sponsor to his kingly accession. It was not difficult therefore for Zacharias' successor, Pope Stephen III (752-757), to solicit his and his people's aid in the creation of the states of the church.

The precipitating event of this famous accomplishment was a **threatened attack on Rome by the Lombards** and the probable enslavement of its people. Aistulf, the Lombard king who had come to power in 751, vigorously prosecuted his will to create a powerful kingdom by immediately invading the provinces of the Eastern emperor, whose exarch, Eutychius, fled before him, so that he was able to take Ravenna itself (751). He then lifted his eyes toward Rome.

The Romans hated the Lombards with a fierce passion. Their untrimmed beards and savage attire, the peculiar odor of their bodies, and their rough manners frightened the people of the Eternal City. Rumors spread abroad that their "atrocious king, shaking like a lion, kept uttering the most terrible threats against the Romans; he spoke of cutting off the heads of all the inhabitants of Rome." When Pope Stephen sent two men of high ecclesiastical rank to negotiate and attempt to appease Aistulf, he beat them and ordered them to return to their charges without so much as a report to the pope. Even Stephen, who bravely risked his own safety by going in person to the Lombard king at Pavia, was treated as a subject who must receive commands, not as an equal come to parley and negotiate. Consequently, the pontiff slipped away from Pavia like an escaped captive, for that precisely was what he was. He made the perilous journey across the Alps into the land of the Franks, and threw himself in behalf of his people on Pepin the Short as a suppliant. He gave spiritual sanction to Pepin's usurpation of the throne of the Franks by crowning him with his own hands at Soissons, July 28, 754, thus renewing in a grand spectacle what his predecessor, Pope Zacharias, had permitted in 751. In return Pepin and his army invaded Italy, brought Aistulf to terms, and forced him to swear to leave the church unmolested.

Scarcely had Pepin returned home than Aistulf was harassing Rome again. He besieged it in mid-winter, 756, the worst time imaginable for the Franks to cross the Alps and stage an invasion. The Romans sent an urgent call for help in the form of three epistles: one in the name of the pope to King

Pepin; another in the name of the Roman populace to the Frankish people; and a third to king and people alike from the apostle Peter himself, who promised them if they would aid his city now, he would give them succour in the hereafter. The Franks poured into Italy through the Alpine passes, devastated the provinces of the Lombards, and relieved Rome by taking Pavia. Their victory was complete. When the Eastern emperor asked Pepin to restore to him his exarchate, Pepin firmly replied that what he had done he had done solely for Peter; he was under no obligation whatever to the Eastern empire. **Pepin gave outright to the Roman church** and its bishop all the cities won by him from the Lombards including the exarchate of Ravenna in its entirety—that is, the country situated between the Apennines and the sea, the Po and Ancona. Aistulf died as a result of his defeat; the Pope and Pepin decided on his successor, who in gratitude ceded more territory to Rome by giving back what had been captured by Liutprand, Aistulf's predecessor.[16]

What Pepin did he did for the glory of God, the honor of the apostle Peter, and the salvation of his own soul. As a result of his action an entirely new commonwealth was added to the map of Europe, a commonwealth which was to continue in existence from 756 until the unification of Italy in 1870.[17]

This new commonwealth radically changed the office of the papacy. Because of it, the pope became something more than a spiritual pastor of souls. He was a temporal prince as well. Unfortunately, more often than not his temporal responsibilities took precedence over his spiritual duties. The bishops of Rome frequently lost all interest in theology. They left intellectual problems to the East. They were kept too busy being politicians.[18]

[16] *Annales* in MGH, *Scriptores*, I-IV, XIII, XX. *Clausula de Pippini consecratione*, in MGH, *Scriptores*, XV, 1.

[17] CMH, II, 575-94; F. Mourret, *Histoire générale de l'église.* (Paris, 1919-21), III, 283-302.

[18] An excellent treatment of this entire period is L. Bréhier, *Grégoire le Grand, les Etats barbares et la conquête arabe, 590-757* (1947), in *Histoire de l'église depuis les originés jusqu'à nos jours* (ed. A. Fliche et V. Martin, Paris, in progress), Vol. V.

Chapter Three

Doctrinal Divisions and the
Dismemberment of the East
(565-717)

WHAT TOOK PLACE IN THE EAST DURING MUCH THIS SAME PERIOD OF TIME WAS quite different from events in the West.

The monks of Constantinople, Alexandria, and Antioch consumed their energy by either a fanatical defense of Chalcedonian orthodoxy or else a stubborn insistence that such so-called orthodoxy was itself heretical and needed the corrective of a pre-Chalcedonian interpretation. This was their nearest approach to matching the missionary zeal of their Anglo-Saxon and Italian rivals. Indeed, missions were undertaken to spread sectarian differences, and the evangelization of non-Christian peoples was in the name of some doctrinal party or theological faction rather than in the name of the church universal.

The political and social situation was likewise quite different. Whereas the church in the West was confronted already by separate and independent barbarian states, the East, a political hegemony of church and state, was waging a defensive warfare to maintain itself; and as time went on, one important piece of territory after another was lost to the foreign invader. The Western barbarians, religiously and culturally speaking, were at least teachable. The Arab devotees of Islam, to a far greater degree than the Persians who had engaged the power of the Eastern empire before them, were as determined to win a religious and cultural victory as they were to come away conquerors from the fields of military combat. They were disciples of a new faith as well as soldiers in the army of a new nation.

The East continued however to maintain a lively and to a certain degree even creative interest in theology. Its patriarchs and bishops were conversant with speculative religion and knew enough theology to appraise the influence of a doctrine upon the corpus of belief. They spent sufficient time in private study to argue and debate effectively in public on subtle and elusive issues. Controversies of a purely doctrinal sort continued to hold public attention, and the leaders of Eastern Christendom were more than administrators, politicians, and effective evangelists and missionaries. They were theologians as well.

I. Imperial Intolerance and the Monophysite Sects

With the death of Justinian, who in his later years had devoted practically all his time to theological speculation at the expense of statecraft, the affairs of the Church in all phases passed from the emperor into the hands of the patriarch of Constantinople, where they more properly belonged. Whereas the aged Justinian confessed that he had become "cold to the things of this world and aflame only for love of the life to come," [1] his successor once removed, Tiberius II (578-582), impatiently exclaimed to the head of the Constantinopolitan diocese, who sought his advice and importuned his aid: "Trouble me about such things no more. I have as much as I can do with the wars I am engaged in. You must act in church-matters according to what you think right and at your own risk. Look to it yourself. I am free from guilt in this matter." [2]

The patriarchs of Constantinople were not averse to taking responsibility and acting according to the dictates of their judgment and conscience. John III (566-577), better known as John Scholasticus, because of the rigidity of his mind and exactness of his ecclesiastical administration, no sooner placed the imperial crown upon the head of Justinian's nephew and successor, Justin II (565-578), than there appeared an edict in the name of the new emperor in which the sovereign professed his own orthodoxy but deprecated quarrels about persons and syllables. John himself, a lawyer by education, turned his energies to the supplement and refinement of his *Digest of Canon Law*, which he had first composed while still in Antioch before his elevation to the Constantinopolitan patriarchate.

But within less than six years, ecclesiastical tolerance was superseded by an intolerance which issued in persecution, banishments, and even death. John of Ephesus (505-585), the Monophysite historian of this era, explains it by saying that the health of Justin failed, and thereafter John was free to do what he pleased. We do know that Justin was subject to fits of lunacy; after 574 the government was carried on by his wife, Sophia, who associated with herself Tiberius II, who later became Justin's successor. However, the persecution of the Monophysites began on March 20, 571, with an open attack on the convents which Theodora had set aside as a refuge for the persecuted nuns of Asia Minor. It is amazing that the first objects of the patriarch's terrible passion for orthodoxy should have been women. They had excited his ire by refusing to commune with the partisans of the Synod of

[1] MGH, *Auctores Antiquissimi*, III, ii, 133.
[2] John of Ephesus, *Hist. Ecc.*, III, 21.

Chalcedon "which divided Christ our God into two natures after the union and teaches a quaternity instead of a Trinity." [3] In other words these nuns thought Chalcedon had lifted the status of the Jesus of history into the Godhead and had ascribed what Christ became in time to what the Second Person of the Trinity had been with the Father and the Holy Spirit prior to his incarnation. John extended the persecution from nuns to priests and from priests to bishops. Many prelates were deprived of clerical orders; some were jailed.

The eleven-year patriarchate of John III (566-577) gave way to a resumption of the patriarchate of his predecessor, Eutychius, whom Justinian had expelled from Constantinople only about nine months before his death. This second term in office lasted five years (577-582). It was he whom Gregory as papal ambassador in Constantinople chided for his unorthodox opinions on the impalpability of the body in the resurrection and whose works the Emperor Tiberius II (578-582) ordered to be burned. However his own heresy did not stay his heavy hand against the heresy of the Monophysites, whom he began to persecute because he attributed to them the failure of his own theological writings. Only the death of Eutychius and Tiberius II within the same year allayed the persecution. John IV (582-595), called the Faster, was too fastidiously concerned with promoting the acceptance of his title "Ecumenical Patriarch" to bother about the Monophysites; and Maurice, the emperor (582-602), was tolerant and kindly disposed toward everyone. But the damage had already been done. It could not successfully be recalled. Monophysitism, which ceased to be an effective minority voice within the Eastern section of the Catholic church and which was unwilling to exist as an underground ecclesiastical movement, found its fullest life in independent churches. [4]

There was, for example, the **Church of Armenia,** which owed its origin not alone to Monophysitism but also to geographical and political particularity. The land in which it was situated was separated from the Eastern empire by high mountains, marshy lakes, and the forbidding waters of the Black Sea. Politically its members were subjects of the king of Persia. It was but natural for the Armenian Christians to capitalize on their isolation and to emphasize their patriotism by doctrinal divergence from the Eastern church. The Third Synod of Dvin (596) repudiated the legitimacy and therefore the teaching of the Council of Chalcedon. The Arab conquest of their land (654) sealed them in their ecclesiastical separatism and independence.

Consequently their rites and ceremonies developed in isolation. Baptism, marriage, and burial were classified as family festivals. The parents and godparents of an infant carried him to the church. The priest met them at the

---

[3] *Ibid.,* I, 5.
[4] *Ibid.,* Book I; Evagrius, *Hist. Ecc.,* Book V.

entrance, recited prayers over the baby, and led the family group into the church. There the naked baby with his face upright toward heaven and feet pointing east was completely immersed three times. Afterward he was anointed with holy oil, touched by the cross, and clothed in white linen.

Betrothal began before children were three years old. The mothers of the boy and girl decided for them and confirmed their decision by a priest and the gift of a ring to the baby girl. Every year from then until the marriage day the boy had to give the girl a new dress at Easter. Often the two children never saw each other until their wedding. The service itself consisted in the young man's going to the house of his betrothed, leading her from home to church, and together receiving from the priest a crown symbolizing the fact that the union of man and woman in wedlock for the purpose of procreation is the crowning act of creation.

Burial was preceded by a lugubrious act in which relatives and friends came to the home of the deceased carrying lamps which they placed around the coffin. There they sat and sang songs until the next day, when the funeral was held. For a week thereafter the priest visited each day the relatives of the deceased. At the end of the week the mourning ceased. The bereaved family gave a big dinner for all the kinsfolk and acquaintances. The remains of the meal were served to the poor.

Five great festivals marked the calendar of public worship: (1) Christmas, (2) Easter, (3) Transfiguration, (4) Assumption, (5) Exaltation of the Cross. Each festival opened with a day devoted to the church and closed with a day set aside to memorialize the dead. Pagan practices were intermingled with Christian rites. On the eve of the day marking the circumcision of Jesus, for example, bonfires were lit in the yards of the churches and people danced around them and even jumped over them. Consequently this day was called Candlemass.

The highest office in the Armenian Church was the catholicus. The catholicus alone could consecrate the bishops, who had to come from the ranks of the celibate clergy. When a married man was ordained he spent fifty days away from his wife alone in the church. During that time his wife sat on a stool with her mouth, eyes, and ears shut indicating her willingness to be excluded from the duties of her husband.[5]

What had taken place very rapidly in Armenia was duplicated in Syria on a retarded scale. At first the **Syrian Church** tried to remain within the unity of Catholicism. Consequently for one hundred years or more after the Council of Chalcedon the Monophysites had vied with the orthodox for control of the patriarchate of Antioch, many of whose bishops had been heretics.

[5] F. C. Conybeare, A. J. Maclean, *Rituale Armenorum* (1905). M. Jugie, *Theologia Dogmatica Christianorum Orientalium ab Ecclesia Catholica Dissidentium* (Paris, 1935), V, 478-489. S. Weber, *Die katholische Kirche in Armenien* (1903).

Severus for example who held this see from 512-518 was the famous exponent of the Phthartolatrae Party, which contended that the body of Jesus after the Resurrection had been incorruptible and had not been subject to decay. The opponents of the Phthartolatrae Party were the Aphthartodocetae, whose exponent, Julian, contended that even before the Resurrection the body of Jesus had been incorruptible. Severus was the leader of the Monophysites until his death (539) in Egypt, where he had been exiled.

The Syrian Monophysites ceased to struggle within the body Catholic and became a separate body during the reign of Justin II. Jacob Zanzalus, or Baradaeus, a monk from a monastery near Edessa, began to preach Monophysitism openly in the streets of Constantinople in 540. Fifteen years later, 555, he accepted ordination from the imprisoned Monophysite bishops of the capital and went back to Syria to organize his sect. Before his death in 578 he is reputed to have ordained two patriarchs, eighty-nine bishops, and a large number of clergymen, including both Sergius and his successor Paul the Black of Antioch. It was from his given name, Jacob or Jacobus, that his followers got the nickname **Jacobites.** They are called Jacobites to this day, though they trace their sect back to the apostle James, to whom they attribute their chief liturgy.

They employ the leavened bread in the Eucharist, give the sacrament to the sick at home but only on the same day as the consecration of the elements in church, give communion to baptized children, and observe strict fasts in Advent and Lent on both Wednesday and Friday.[6]

The last expression of Monophysitism to emerge during this period was the **Coptic Church of Egypt,** which later was to penetrate also into Numidia and Abyssinia.

The Alexandrian patriarchate, like that of Antioch in Syria, had oscillated between the supporters and opponents of Chalcedon down to the time of Justinian, whose queen, Theodora, always mitigated the severity of her husband's orthodox decrees. Then from 551 to 619 five orthodox patriarchs followed one another in unbroken succession, so that Pope Gregory I of Rome congratulated Eulogius (580-607) of Alexandria on winning over the heretics as readily as his own missionaries were winning over Britain.[7] Yet his praise was premature. The indigenous people of Egypt had never admired the Eastern empire either in government or in religion. They called the Greeks who lived among them Melkites, meaning Imperialists. They were themselves Copts and only too eager to embrace the tenets of Cyril and Dioscorus, former patriarchs whose opinions had been condemned. Consequently with the subjugation of the land, first to the Persians (590-628) and finally to the

---

[6] J. S. Assemani, *Bibliotheca Orientalis* (Rome, 1719-1728) Vol. II. R. Duval, *La literature syriac* (1899).

[7] Gregorius Magnus, *Epistolae,* VIII.

Moslems (642), the Coptic Christians abandoned even the semblance of communion with Constantinople, followed their own elected patriarch, and adopted rites and ceremonies consistent with their native tastes.

The organization of the Coptic church was not radically different from the Greek. A patriarch, who was elected from the Monks of St. Anthony, together with his suffragan bishops, directed its affairs. In doctrine the divinity of Jesus was emphasized, while his humanity was neglected. The priest hailed the elevated host in the Eucharist as "the body and blood of Immanuel our God . . . the quickening flesh which thine only begotten Son our Lord and our God and our Saviour took of the lady of us all, the Holy Theotokos of St. Mary; he made it one with godhead without confusion and without mixture and without alteration." [8] The bread, which alone was given to the laity, was served in little wooden spoons, and confession was required of all who would receive the Eucharist. Women were not allowed beyond the narthex of the church. Boys were baptized when they were forty days old and girls when they were eighty. There were five great fasts: Nineveh (three days and nights before Lent), Lent (fifty-five days), Nativity (twenty-eight days before Christmas), Apostles (just after Ascension Tide), Virgin (fifteen days prior to the Assumption). The festivals in turn were seven: Nativity (Christmas), Baptism of Jesus, Annunciation, Palm Sunday, Easter (the Great Festival), Ascension, Whitsunday.[9]

II. The Nestorian Church

The increase of Monophysitism and the assertion of its ecclesiastical independence were counterbalanced doctrinally by the growth and consolidation of Nestorianism, though this only added to the distress of Eastern Catholicism, since Nestorianism too was heretical.

Whereas Monophysitism had emerged as the aftermath of Chalcedon (451), which had outlawed it, and had struggled for many years to find an outlet of expression, Nestorianism had found already in existence an independent ecclesiastical body willing to accept its tenets and adhere to its faith. To secure the protection of the Persian government, the **Christian church in Persia** had declared its independence of Roman Christianity (Eastern and Western) at the Synod of Markabta in 424, even before the excommunication of him who later had given his name to its theology. Nestorius at that time had been in his patriarchal see at Constantinople. Some years later he had been banished to Egypt, where he had been forced to spend his last agonizing years in the territory of his rival.

[8] F. E. Brightman, *Liturgies*, I, 185.
[9] M. LeQuien, *Oriens Christianus* (Paris, 1740), Vols. I, II. E. Renaudot, *Historia patriarcharum Alexandrinorum Jacobitarum A. D. Marco usque ad finem saec. XIII.* (Paris, 1713) and *Liturgiarum orientalium collectio* (Paris, 1716), Vols. I, II.

Consequently by the middle of the sixth century the Nestorian church was a separate though as yet small body of more than a hundred years duration with an organization as intricate and perhaps as effective as that of the Eastern church. Since from the very outset it had been legally a crime to be a Nestorian, the Christians of this persuasion inside the Eastern empire had had to migrate to the domain of the king of Persia, to those lands which today are Iran, Iraq, and the extreme eastern portion of Syria, and to join the church of Persia.

The bishop of Seleucia-Ctesiphon called, like his Armenian counterpart, the "catholicus" to indicate his independence of all foreign control, was the primate of the church. There were under him a patriarch, five metropolitans, and as many bishops as there were administrative and judicial districts in the Persian empire (for the diocese corresponded with these political units). The catholicus was chosen for life by an electoral college, presided over by the patriarch; and he exercised absolute authority over the affairs of the church. This polity was strengthened by synodical government and the episcopal ownership of all ecclesiastical property within a diocese. The episcopate directed the monastic orders, which were coenobitic. Thus the hierarchy of this church looked on itself as independent entirely of the Western Fathers; considered its catholicus on a parity with the patriarchs of Rome, Alexandria, and Antioch; and appraised its theology as consistent with the gospel and therefore orthodox.

Its famous school, where most of its patriarchs, bishops, and scholars were educated, was at Edessa, later **at Nisibis.** Here **Narsai** (d. 502) had established his fame as a theologian of Nestorianism, as a poet of rare beauty of expression and depth of sentiment, and as a commentator and critic whose work on the liturgy was of great significance in the formation of Eastern rites. In the interpretation of the Eucharist, for example, his writing shows that as early as the fifth century the Nicene Creed was used in the service; a silent prayer was recited; ceremonies employing vestments, incense, fans, and lamps were in use; and the customs of bowing and kneeling were in vogue. At the same time it shows that the screen or veil to shut out from the sight of the people the act of consecration was a later innovation; singing was confined to creed, sanctus, and communion. Narsai belongs therefore to the history of worship in its ecumenical inclusiveness, not just to the particularity of its Nestorian developments.[10]

There were from time to time efforts to secure communion between the Nestorian church of Persia and the church of the Eastern empire. The conciliatory work of the catholicus, Mar Abha the Great (540-552), is the best example. He even admitted the validity of Chalcedon at a synod in 540,

---

[10] R. H. Connolly, *The Liturgical Homilies of Narsai,* in *Texts and Studies* (Cambridge, 1909), VIII, i, 4, 5 ff., 13-118.

but he gave to the symbol his own interpretation.[11] It was he more than anyone else who gave the church of Persia its polity and government, an organization strong enough to endure the misunderstanding and persecution of non-Christian governments and peoples. However when the Fifth Ecumenical Council (553) posthumously condemned Theodore of Mopsuestia, the great teacher of the East, the breach between Nestorian Christianity and the Christianity of the empire was complete.[12] The Arab conquest of Persia (636-640) but emphasized this fact.

This church from the beginning was missionary and evangelistic. The church of Malabar in India—self-styled the Christians of St. Thomas—probably owes its origin to these Persian Nestorians. There were in Malabar as early as 520 bishops who spoke Greek and who had been ordained in Seleucia-Ctesiphon by the catholicus.[13] As late as the ninth century those Indian Christians recognized the authority of the catholicus. In 549 Mar Abha the Great sent a missionary bishop to the Turks on either side of the Oxus River. This act was prophetic of subsequent missionary labors in which the Nestorians from the seventh to the fourteenth century were to carry the gospel across Asia to Peking itself.

The doctrine of the Nestorian church was a belief in the Trinity as set forth in the Nicene Creed, together with a denial of Mary as the Mother of God. The Council neither of Ephesus nor of Chalcedon was recognized. Nestorian Christology lent itself most readily to adoptionism, since its doctrine was that the personality of the human (historical) Jesus was the vehicle for the expression of the personality of the Second Person of the Divine Trinity. Theodore of Mopsuestia, not Nestorius, was held in reverence as its greatest theologian and teacher.

The pattern of public worship was not radically different from that of Eastern Catholicism, since one of its three chief liturgies antedated the Nestorian controversy. Baptism had to take place in a church, and immersion was complete. The priest made the sign of the cross on the child in holy oil with his thumb. The Eucharist was observed with the congregation standing and with mothers feeding their children the consecrated leavened bread, which the priest already had softened with wine. Grown people took both elements separately, but no reservation for the sick was allowed. All services were sung without the aid of instruments. Vestments of a distinctive pattern were used.

The churches were generally small, many built above the ground in the cleft of the rocks with a ladder ascending to the entrance, which was narrow and low and marked only by the sign of the cross. The worshipers stood in

[11] *Synodicon Orientale* (ed. Chabot, Paris, 1902), 556.
[12] *Ibid.*, 398 ff.
[13] MPG, LXXXVIII, 169.

the nave, which was separated from the sanctuary by a stone wall. The men occupied the front of the room, the women the rear. In the wall between nave and sanctuary were shelves of relics, and the altar was oblong in contrast to the square altar of the Greeks. There were no steeples, spires, or domes to the churches. The clergy were generally married; and though no law required this there was scarcely a church anywhere served by an unmarried priest. The most distinctive service was that of the burial of the dead. After the funeral was over the friends and relatives filed by the corpse and took leave of their loved one by kissing his hand before the body was lowered into the ground.[14]

These Nestorian Christians styled themselves The Church of the East.

III. Monotheletism

Monotheletism, which followed directly the separatist movements we have just described, was itself a further stage of the development of Monophysitism. Indeed it was an attempt on the level of theology to achieve the unity which was desperately needed, politically and socially, if the Eastern empire was to hurl back the expanding Persian empire and to resist the fanatically aggressive armies of Islam.

Monotheletism emerged within Eastern Catholicism during the period of the Persian wars (606-629). It was a live issue throughout the uncertain struggle of the Heraclian dynasty against Islam (633-678). The controversy was not actually settled until a year after the famous peace of 679 between the Eastern emperor and the Moslem caliph, when each agreed to recognize the territorial situation that then prevailed, to desist from further military engagements, and as far as possible to let each other alone.

Monotheletism was not confined to Eastern Catholicism however. From the very start it involved the West. At the time of its ascendency in the East it cast the ugly shadow of persecution upon the Roman church and cost one pontiff his life. The issue was not settled without the aid of the papacy and the consent of the Western church. The progress of this dispute illustrates the fact that at this time Roman and Eastern Catholicism was doctrinally speaking one, and that no matter what the situation was politically and socially, Latins and Greeks alike thought of themselves as belonging to the same church.

This doctrine is the ethical corollary of Monophysite Christology. Though the church branded the teaching that Christ had but one divine nature as heretical, there were those theologians who were prepared to affirm a singularity of moral purpose behind the actions and deeds of the Savior. Regardless of the constitution of Jesus' psychological nature, the juxtaposition

---

[14] Assemani, op. cit., Vol. III.

in equal proportion of the human and the divine that underlay his personality, he possessed only one power, or force, of expression. The quality of his deeds was perfect; therefore that energy of his which caused them was single; he was entirely animated by a theandric force. The principle of motivation for his every act on earth was divine. In this early stage of the development of the doctrine, when energy or force was used to describe the activity of Jesus, the proper word to designate the theological position is **Monothelitism.** Its theological synonym would be monergism, the entire control over all phases of personal life by divine grace.

The doctrine emerged as a public issue when it was employed by the Eastern Emperor Heraclius (610-641) for political purposes. He saw in it the basis of a reunion of the Monophysites of Egypt with the orthodox church. He believed that the Monophysites could be persuaded to affirm that Jesus Christ had two natures, human and divine, if the orthodox would affirm that the motivation of his action was single and that such motivation was divine. Consequently on his own initiative he approached Cyrus (630-643), whom he had recently appointed patriarch of Alexandria, to effect the union by giving theological expression to the teaching. In 633 Cyrus issued a document of reunion which stated, "There was but one and the same Christ, working both the divine and human actions by one theandric operation." [15] This statement was officially sanctioned by Sergius (610-638), patriarch of Constantinople.

Immediately this position was opposed. In Egypt itself **Maximus the Confessor** (580-662) lifted a strong voice against it. He was supported by a Palestinian monk named **Sophronius.** Sophronius was elected to the patriarchate of Jerusalem (634-638) and made this issue the theme of his letter of enthronement which he circulated throughout Christendom. Sophronius' argument was simple: a nature is incomplete without a means of expression; since Christ had both a human and a divine nature, each nature had its own power of expression. The power of expression of the human nature caused all his human deeds. The power of expression of the divine nature caused all his divine deeds.[16]

The matter was referred to Rome. **Pope Honorius** (625-638) took it under advisement. He said quite frankly that he did not like the words employed by Cyrus and sanctioned by Sergius because they were not Biblical but he accepted the basic idea they were meant to convey. Consequently he changed energy, force, or power to will. He said, though Christ had two natures in one person, he did not have two wills. Will belongs to person, not nature; therefore all his actions, human and divine, were the expressions of a single divine

[15] Mansi, XI, 561 E., 563-568.
[16] Ibid., Cols. 532 D., 533 A., 536 D. MPG, LXXXVII (3), 3147-3200.

will. Thus Monothelitism became Monotheletism when will superseded force or energy as the descriptive label of the doctrine. Heraclius, under the tutelage of Sergius, issued his *Ecthesis* (638) which, following Honorius, forbids the use of either "one operation" or "two operations" but says instead to confess "one will of our Lord Jesus Christ." [17]

The successors of Honorius quickly withdrew the approval he had given to this teaching and in its place set a condemnation so sweeping that it included Honorius himself. The Byzantine government tried in vain to beat down opposition to its politically contrived Monotheletism. Local synods were held throughout Christendom. Everywhere the position of Sophronius received theological approval and ecclesiastical support. Will must be a function of basic nature. Jesus' actions to be human had to spring from a human will. Likewise his actions to be divine had to spring from a divine will. To deny his human will makes his humanity unreal. In contrast to Jesus of Nazareth as he lived in the flesh, we believe that God has only one will. This must belong to his nature; otherwise there would be three wills in the Trinity, for God exists in three persons.

The Emperor Constans II (641-668), grandson and successor of Heraclius, strove by military as well as political force to maintain Monotheletism. He made Pope Martin I (649-655) pay, first with his freedom, then with his life for the promulgation of the Synod at the Lateran Palace (649) that "just as we believe in Christ's two natures united without confusion, so we also believe in two natural wills, the divine will and the human." [18]

In religious matters Constans' son, Constantine IV (668-685), had better judgment than either his father or his great-grandfather. He turned the Monothelete problem over to the church for a solution. Consequently the **Sixth Ecumenical Council** of the church was held at Constantinople, November 7, 680, through September 16, 681. The Roman pontiff was represented by three bishops, whom he sent, not from any great confidence in their learning, but merely to please the emperor. Pope Agatho (678-681) armed them with a doctrinal tome, telling the council precisely what it should believe. There were one hundred and seventy-four prelates present, including besides the papal legates, George, patriarch of Constantinople (678-683), Macarius, patriarch of Antioch (d. 681), and a presbyter, Peter, who represented Alexandria, the orthodox see of which had been vacant since 652. The conclaves were held in the domed hall of the imperial palace where Constantine IV himself presided at the first and last sessions.

The result of the council was the condemnation of the Monothelete doctrine and the anathematization of its adherents. The pronouncement ran: "Believing that our Lord Jesus Christ, one of the Trinity also after the

[17] *Ibid.*, Cols. 537-544, 579-582, 994 E., 996 C.
[18] *Ibid.*, X, 1150 D.

Incarnation, is our true God, we say that His two natures shown forth in His one person, in which were both the miracles and the suffering throughout the whole incarnate life, not in appearance merely but in reality, the difference as to nature being recognized in one and the same person; for, although joined together, each nature wills and operates the things proper to it. For this reason we glorify two natural wills and operations concurring most fitly in Him for the salvation of the human race." [19]

There was little objection to the pronouncement. Monotheletism, like Monophysitism, had found its strength in North Africa and along the coast of Asia Minor, and these lands were after all in the hands of Moslems.

IV. The Losses to Islam

The Monothelete issue did not arise, grow strong, weaken, and then expire in an ecclesiastical vacuum. Large as this issue loomed in the life of the church during this period, it was but a small piece of the total historical pattern of the times, which were harassed by strife, shaken by wars, and torn asunder by a titanic struggle between two opposing ideologies—the outcome of which was to decide the destiny of empire and civilization. Scarcely had New Rome thrown back the Persian invasion than she was assailed by ferocious warriors from the desert of Arabia. These warriors were fired by a fanatical faith.

In the same year that Heraclius launched the empire upon the Persian wars (622) the Hegira took place in Arabia. The Hegira was the flight of Mohammed and his followers from Mecca to Medina, and it inaugurated the Mohammedan Era. In vain did Heraclius shatter the power of Persia by his five campaigns against that empire. Little profit to him and his people that he carried his armies inside the bounds of the enemy, took the capital, Seleucia-Ctesiphon, and even entered the gates of ancient Nineveh itself. The reputed Holy Cross on which the Savior had been crucified was rescued from the Persians and restored to its proper place in the city of Jerusalem (629) only to be hurried away within less than a decade to Constantinople for safe keeping. Heraclius the Conqueror realized before his day was done that his own conquests were but the prelude to larger conquests to be made in the future by his enemies and that the thousands slain by Rome would not compare with the tens of thousands to be slain by the sword of the prophet. Standing on the deck of his ship in the year 635, he took his leave of the Holy Land: "Farewell Syria. Farewell forever."

The religion of Islam was a product of the mind and spirit of a single individual, Mohammed, its prophet (ca. 570-632).[20] When he was forty

---

[19] *Ibid.*, XI, 640 A. Kidd, *op. cit.*, 106-09; 115-22.
[20] W. Muir, *The Life of Mahomet* (London, 1858-1861), 4 vols.; *Annals of the Early Caliphate from Original Sources* (London, 1883).

years of age this son of the desert became inspired by an uncompromising monotheistic faith which made rigid moral and spiritual demands on himself and his people. The public proclamation of this new faith led, first, to the fanatical devotion of the few and the antagonism of the masses and, finally, to the conversion of the masses and the welding of independent, nomadic tribes into the unity of a nation. Hitherto isolated, relatively unknown, and with no significant place in the history of the East, Arabia emerged in the seventh century into a world power, with the hardihood to carve by the sword for itself an empire. The expansion of Islam was more rapid and extensive than had been the expansion of any other religion. So fanatical was the zeal of its adherents and so strong its armies that it threatened the very existence of both the Christian church and Christian civilization in the East.

Islam subsists under five major doctrines: First, there is no God but Allah, and Mohammed is his prophet. Secondly, God's work to a certain degree is carried on among men by angels, mediating spirits. The greatest and most distinguished among these are four: Gabriel, the angel of revelation, who writes down the divine decrees; Michael, the leader of the heavenly hosts, who fights the battles of the faithful; Azrael, the angel of death; and Izrafil, who sounds the trumpet on the last day. Every mortal has two angels who keep watch over him day and night. One sits on his right shoulder, the other on his left. At the close of each day they fly up to heaven with a written report. Every good action a man does is recorded ten times by the angel on the right. When the man commits a sin that same good spirit pleads with the angel on the left not to write down for seven hours what he has done in the hope that he might repent and pray for forgiveness. Thirdly, the will of Allah is written down in the pages of the Koran, which contains all a Moslem needs to know to obtain salvation. Fourthly, Islam reveres the great figures of Judaism and Christianity but surpasses them, according to its own teachings, in the figure of Mohammed. It distinguishes six prophets: Adam, Noah, Abraham, Moses, Jesus, and Mohammed, the greatest of them all. Finally, there will be a resurrection for every individual and a final judgment for all. Between death and resurrection, there is an interval during which the body rests in the grave, but the soul has a foretaste, in dreams and visions, of its future fate. On the final day of judgment the angel Gabriel will poise a mighty balance, in the scales of which the actions of men will be weighed. The multitudes will follow Mohammed across the bridge, Al Serat, as fine as the edge of a sword, which crosses over Jehennah; and the infidels and sinful Moslems will fall over into the abyss. The good will enjoy Al Jannat, or the Gardens of Paradise. The water of these gardens will be as sweet as honey, as cold as snow, and as clear as crystal; and he who once tastes of it will never thirst again.

In addition to these five major doctrines **there are four binding practices:**

68

First, the devout Moslem is expected to pray five times every day. Always the devotee prays with his face toward Mecca and exercises his body in the manner described in the Koran. Secondly, every person must indulge in religious charity, both of the prescribed type similar to the Jewish tithe, and voluntarily as he is moved to do through compassion for less fortunate persons. Thirdly, for thirty days every year the true believer must abstain rigorously, from the rising to the setting of the sun, from meat and drink, baths, perfumes, sexual intercourse, and all other gratifications of the senses. Fourthly, the last requirement is that the devout Moslem make a pilgrimage to Mecca in the course of his lifetime, either personally or else by proxy.

Underlying both belief and practice is an austere fatalism. Allah, by divine decree, has determined everything that will happen. The deeds of the individuals are but the expressions of Allah's own authoritative, self-determining, inscrutable divine will.[21]

Though the first **military conquests of Christianity by Islam** took place during the lifetime of the Prophet (629), it was only after his death that Islam began to spread like a devouring flame over the East. The first calamitous blow came before the death of Heraclius when Damascus fell in 635. After a long siege under the heroic leadership of its patriarch, Sophronius, Jerusalem was constrained to open its gates (637) to Omar and his desert hosts. The next year (638) saw the fall of Antioch, Tripolis, Tyre, Caesarea, and fifteen other cities along the Mediterranean coast. Indeed by the end of the following year (639), nothing was left in Syria to the Eastern empire. That same year Mesopotamia surrendered to the Moslems and the conquest of Egypt itself began. In less than ten years all North Africa had been shorn from the empire so that the successors of Mohammed ruled from the Oxus in the East to Carthage in the West.

Immediately thereafter Islam began the attack on the North. Its purpose now was to destroy the Eastern empire by capturing Constantinople. In order to do this, a new method of war was employed. The Taurus Mountains appeared insuperable to an army of foot soldiers. Therefore the Moslems organized a navy which surprised Cyprus (648), destroyed Aradus (649), and ravaged Cos and Rhodes (654). All Southern Asia (651) and much of Armenia (652-654) were under the military control of the Arabs. What the Moslems hoped might be a decisive battle was fought by their navy and the navy of the Eastern empire at Phoenix (655), where the Emperor Constans II (641-668) suffered defeat. However this proved to be only a tactical defeat which led later to a strategic victory of the Eastern imperial forces. The Moslems were stretched too far. For five years (673-678) they gambled all they had in a supreme military effort to take Constantinople by land and

[21] The Koran (Palmer translation, 1880).

sea. The Eastern empire was saved by the newly invented "Greek Fire" which the defenders hurled at their assailants, driving them from the walls of their city and setting fire to their navy. Fortunately for the Eastern empire the Moslem fleet was caught in a storm off the coast of Pamphylia, and the elements of nature did what the forces of men could not have done. Finally at Syllaeum (678) Constantine IV (668-685) inflicted a crushing defeat on what remained of the forces of the enemy. This led to cessation of hostilities (679) and the recognition of the territorial situation which then prevailed as the domain of each of the contesting parties.

Thus within a period of forty-five years (633-678), the Eastern empire had lost some of its richest and most populous provinces, had been put constantly on the defensive, and was soon only the shadow of its former self. The peace of 679 was no more than a respite. During the period of the First Anarchy (695-717) when six usurpers contested with one another for control of the empire, the Moslems renewed their conquests so that Cilicia, Galatia, and much of the territory around the cities of the Seven Churches of Asia Minor as far north as Pergamum was in their hands. Social disorder was the natural accompaniment of these wars and by 717 the continued existence of the Eastern empire was problematical.[22]

V. The Consolidation of the Church

The contraction of the empire meant also the **depletion of the Church**. Three of the five patriarchates were now in Moslem territory; and, while Rome struggled successfully for political autonomy and Constantinople enjoyed the luxury of imperial patronage, Alexandria, Antioch, and Jerusalem groveled in the dust under the heel of the victorious infidels. Conditions were so bad in Egypt and Syria that the patriarchs of Alexandria and Antioch lived abroad in voluntary exile, while only the stubborn perseverance of Sophronius permitted him to remain at home in the see of Jerusalem among his conquerors. Multitudes of the people easily exchanged Christianity for Islam so that within the space of almost a single generation the majority of the population of North Africa, Egypt, Syria, Mesopotamia, and even Palestine became Mohammedan. What formerly had been tax-exempt ecclesiastical properties now yielded abundant revenue to the new government, and the enrichment of the state was the impoverishment of the church. The extraordinary gains of Christianity in the West were counterbalanced by excessive losses in the East.

What appeared as well nigh disastrous was in reality, at least to the church within the bounds of the empire, salutary and even beneficial. As a contracted empire had of necessity to become unified in order to survive, so a depleted church had to consolidate its resources in order effectively to discharge its mission. So the patriarch of Constantinople, who heretofore had been one among four equals, became by default the supreme head of Eastern Catholicism. Theoretically at least he presumably still recognized the priority of Rome and on occasions even subscribed to it if it accomplished his ends. Nevertheless he likewise took every opportunity he could to humiliate the papacy. Therefore, together with the emperor, he supported the archbishop of Ravenna, Maurus (648-671), when the latter went to the extreme of excommunicating Pope Vitalian (657-672). The Emperor Constans II, on the suggestion no doubt of his patriarch, excused the see of Ravenna from dependence upon any ecclesiastical superior in the West. Throughout most of the seventh century the popes were omitted from the diptychs of Constantinople. There were 424 dioceses in communion with the see of Constantinople scattered throughout the Balkan peninsula and Asia Minor proper. They were composed of 1 patriarchate, 33 metropolitan sees, 356 suffragan bishoprics, and 34 autocephalous sees called archbishoprics.

The picture of the clergy of this period is a strange contrast of restrictions and requirements. Though they no doubt had privileges in abundance, they are curiously concealed beneath legislation which emphasizes the severity of their calling and the strenuousness of their duties. They were forbidden to frequent inns, horse races, theaters, gambling dens, and brothels or to have any social contacts with women whatever. Even their pastoral responsibilities were so regulated that they were not to be alone with women in their houses at all. They were required at all times to wear clerical dress, to perform their sacramental functions without fees, and to be so diligent in their duties that they would have no time for commercial enterprises of any type. Each cleric was expected to spend his entire ministry in the diocese in which he had been ordained. A deacon was to be humble and not to expect to succeed automatically to the office of bishop after his bishop's death. Though married men were not forbidden to join the clergy, no man above the order of reader or cantor was allowed to marry after his ordination. A married clergyman was expected to refrain from sexual intercourse for several hours preceding his duties at the altar. The only bars to ordination were marriage to a concubine, a widow, or a divorced woman. To enter into marriage contract with a prostitute, a slave, or an actress was a disgrace so terrible that it could not be relieved. Clergymen could not expect to inherit orders or sacerdotal status from their parents. The age for orders was fixed at thirty for the priesthood, twenty-five for the diaconate, and twenty for the subdiaconate.

The regulations governing monasticism in the East were less severe, so it seems, than those governing the secular clergy. Anybody could become a monk, no matter what his previous life had been. Since the monastic religious life was regarded as a state of penitence, the monastery must of necessity open its doors to anyone. A boy as young as ten could volunteer to become a monk. He was expected to live in keeping with his vows of poverty, obedience, and chastity. There was a danger that monasteries might become hostels for failures. The monks were referred to as "the old boys." Consequently the monasteries in the East were not noted for spirituality.

Society in general during this period was, externally at least, intensely religious. There appears to have been an almost abnormal desire on the part of everybody to see, handle, and kiss relics and icons. Every day at all hours recitations of kyries on strings of beads took place. Attendance at church was large and regular even though the service lasted for at least three hours. Despite the outward pomp and circumstance and show of custom, there seems to have been little missionary zeal and evangelistic passion. This is not to say of course that no work of this type took place at all. Heraclius, for example, asked the Roman pontiff to send missionaries to the Croats and Serbs, and we know that many of the Slavs who entered the imperial army very soon became Christians. The army chaplains instructed them and sent them back to their own people to disseminate the faith. The patriarch of Constantinople organized a missionary society to send preachers to the heathen, and so important did this agency become that two patriarchs, Peter (652-664) and Constantine I (674-676), were elected from the position of inspector of missions to the Constantinopolitan see. However, compared with what was going on in the West during this same period, these efforts were small.

The morals of the people in general, so far as we are able to ascertain, were neither exceptionally good nor notoriously bad during this period. There are evidences that cruelty still existed and that men indulged in blinding, slitting the nose, and cutting out the tongues of their enemies. Legislation was passed forbidding men to impersonate women and women to impersonate men. Pagan customs were sufficiently in vogue to necessitate their prohibition by law. Unnatural crimes were possibly few and far between since we find no prohibitory legislation regarding them. The imperial family set a fine example of purity, uprightness, and devotion to duty. The moral precepts of Christianity set the social norm for the laws and customs of the people, by which the majority tried to live.

On account of the terrific strain on the empire imposed by the wars with Persia and Islam there were not sufficient resources to do much in the way of public works. Art in general and religious art in particular suffered as a consequence. Church buildings were mean compared to the magnificent edifices of Justinian. However, the sanctity of the churches was emphasized by forbidding their use as dining rooms, sleeping quarters, or commercial establishments. It was a crime for cattle to be sheltered inside their walls. Apparently for the first time laymen were now forbidden to go inside the sanctuary, which was reserved entirely for the priests. Earlier, no further back than the fourth century, the emperor had sat inside in close proximity to the altar.

Though there was a general impoverishment of decorative arts, **the art of worship itself was exquisitely beautiful.** This is seen especially in **the liturgy.** We have an excellent outline of the service in the *Mystagogia* of Maximus the Confessor, in which he explains the rites in which the congregation actively participates. In the *Missa Catechumenorum*, the service begins with the Introit, which means "Little Entrance," during which the bishop enters the sanctuary and takes his place on the episcopal throne. While this is taking place, the Trisagion is being sung, an anthem addressed formerly at Antioch to the Son, but now addressed throughout the Eastern church to the Trinity. Consequently the Antiochian clause, "who was crucified for us" is deleted. After the Trisagion comes the reading of the three lessons (prophecy, epistle, and gospel), interspersed with chants, the Antiphon, the Alleluia, and the homily (short sermon, generally read from one of the Fathers). At this point there is a decided change in the service. In olden days it was at this juncture that the catechumens were dismissed. Now this act has become more theoretical than practical since the whole of society is nominally Christian. The bishop leaves his episcopal throne and goes directly to the altar for the *Missa Fidelium.* This service opens with the Prayers of the Faithful which take the form of a litany for the church, the clergy, the emperor, and the people. After this follow the oblations of the people which are presented no longer in kind as raw meat, bunches of grapes, produce from the farm, or goods from the store, but rather in currency just as today. Then follows the Great Entrance, when the chalice itself is held before the people. The service continues in the following order: Diptychs, Kiss of Peace, Creed, Anaphora with Salutation, Sursum Corda, Preface, Sanctus, Thanksgiving or Consecration, Elevation, and Communion. The elements are placed in the hands of the people by the officiating clergyman. Gold and silver vessels brought by the communicant in which to receive the elements and convey them to his own mouth are not yet in use. While the people are communicating, the *Communio* is being sung. The service is concluded with the *Troperium*, a hymn written by Sergius, patriarch of Constantinople (610-638). Such then is the picture of the liturgy in the seventh century.

The Eastern liturgy at this time, in contrast to the Western, was polished, finished, and linguistically and artistically perfect. It had centuries of development behind it, while the West was almost for the first time constructing its orders of worship from materials near at hand. The two methods of ordering the Eucharistic ritual were entirely different. In the Western church the propers (parts which change with the season) of the service were variable, while the central prayers were fixed, having been selected from the many dif-

73

ferent ones in use at the time. In the Eastern church the order of the service was itself invariable; nevertheless different Anaphoras, consecration prayers, litanies of Prayers of the Faithful could be used by inserting them at their proper place in the common order. The beautiful and inspiring conceit in the Prayer of Incense—"We offer incense before thy holy glory, O God: receive it upon thy holy and heavenly and spiritual altar, and send down upon us in its stead the grace of thy Holy Spirit"—was an enigma too difficult for acceptance by the literal-minded Latins of the West. The grandiloquent Greeks used it as a matter of course, for its flight of fancy was entirely in keeping with their own mystical piety.

Sacramental worship, not preaching, was central in Eastern Catholicism. Kneeling in church however was looked upon as a dangerous innovation which was forbidden by law as a denial of the Resurrection. The worshiper was expected to stand erect before God as a testimony that his Savior is alive and has freed him from sin and death. The cross was held in such high honor that it could not be placed where it might accidentally be trodden under foot. No longer was Christ represented symbolically as a lamb but actually as hanging on the cross.

Baptism was conferred now upon infants, indicating the belief in its necessity for salvation. This service was not permitted outside a church, and confirmation was an integral part of it. When pagan peoples were converted, catechetical instruction preceded baptism: the catechumen had to recite the creed every Thursday to his priest. Penance was not obligatory at this time, but it was encouraged and was evidently very much used by the people, since special courses of instruction were given for confessors. Marriage was regulated and controlled. Fasting before communion was required, and the worshiper received communion in both kinds through intinction.[23]

The **theological writings** of this period were neither numerous nor great. Sophronius,[24] who ably stated the position of Diotheletism (orthodoxy) against the imperial Monothelete heresy, did not display the same talent for hagiography; nor did his contemporary, Leontius of Neapolis,[25] do any better. Nevertheless the works of both men provide invaluable information on the religious, economic, and political conditions of the time. Much superior however were the writings of Maximus the Confessor.[26] He revived the style and influence of the three great Cappadocians of the fourth century (Basil of Caesarea, Gregory of Nyssa, and Gregory Nazianzen). At the same time he was a mystic, influencing the West as well as the East by

[23] Mansi, XI, 929-1006. Kidd., op. cit., pp. 123-34. L. Bréhier, op. cit., pp. 193-96, 475-76.

[24] MPG, LXXXVII (3), 3147-4014.

[25] MPG, LXXXVI, 1185-2016.

[26] MPG, IV, 15-432; 527-576; XIX, 1217-1280; XC and XCI.

his principles of ascetical contemplation. John Scotus Eriugena borrowed from him. More than any other person Maximus the Confessor was the creator of Byzantine mysticism. Andrew of Crete, a gifted hymnwriter, was the author of the Great Canon which to this day is read in the Greek church twice during Lent. It reviews the chief events of the Old Testament, the deeds and words of our Lord. John of Antioch wrote a universal chronicle from Adam to the beginning of the seventh century, while the author of the anonymous *Easter Chronicle* gave no more than a list of the chief historical events with scattered comments throughout. The most gifted writer of the period was a deacon of Sophia, George of Pisidia. He wrote the history of the times, largely military, in beautiful verse much like the epics of Homer and Virgil.[27] Likewise he composed the *Hexaemeron*, a didactic poem on the creation of the universe with pertinent references to contemporary happenings. George was an ecclesiastic and has been regarded, not because of the *Hexaemeron* but rather because of his epics, as the greatest secular poet of Byzantine history. He shines however like a star apart, for this period was from the viewpoint of literature, art, and general culture the bleakest in the entire history of the Eastern empire.

---

[27] K. Krumbacher, *Geschichte der byzantinischen Litteratur von Justinian bis zum Ende des oströmischen Reiches, 527-1453* (Munich, 1897), 709.

Chapter Four

The Carolingian Renaissance
(756-882)
and the Revival in Britain
(871-899)

THE 126 YEARS IN THE WEST BETWEEN THE DONATION OF PEPIN THE SHORT (756) and the death of Pope John VIII (882)—though a strange medley politically and socially of unity and disunity, order and anarchy, empire and feudalism—form ecclesiastically a single pattern of events and, judged by ideas and doctrines developed therein, constitute one unit in the history of civilization. The schools of Charlemagne, for example, begun under the guiding hand of Alcuin of York in 781, did not bear their ripest fruit in scholarship and intellectual creativity until the days of Eriugena (d. 877) at the court of Charles the Bald in the next century. Likewise the creation of the Holy Roman Empire at the coronation of Charlemagne by Pope Leo III (800) did not find its strongest papal exponent or reach ecclesiastically the zenith of its expression until the pontificate of Pope Nicholas I (858-867). This period therefore, both institutionally and doctrinally, represents a vigorous and progressive phase in the life of the Western church.

The political and social background is that of sharp contrast. Charlemagne created an empire so far reaching and effective that it seemed as if he had reconstituted the domain of the Caesars in the West. Yet from the beginning this empire was more German than Roman. The seeds of its destruction were sown at its birth: (1) It had no standing army but depended entirely on volunteers. (2) There was no stabilizing system of taxation, and voluntary contributions could not sustain an empire. (3) Idle courtiers depleted the royal treasury. (4) The division of the imperial domain among heirs, like the division of private property among wife and children on the demise of a father, was adopted instead of a wise plan of succession which is essential to the continuity of any kingdom.[1] Consequently what Charlemagne gained,

[1] MGH, Leges, I, 15. Mourret, op. cit., III, 368.

his sons lost. The internecine struggles and wars between Louis the Pious and two of his sons (817-840) introduced disaffection into a hitherto unified and harmonious realm. The subsequent tripartite division of the empire at Louis' death (840) brought about the dissolution of the political hegemony of Charlemagne and was the end in nightmare of the first medieval imperial dream.

The picture of society in the West during Charlemagne's reign (768-814) is in the main the picture of one world. Communication had not broken down among the various provinces and regions. Royal commissioners, called missi dominici, traveled in pairs throughout the empire. They kept the emperor apprised of all that went on and applied his laws and regulations to his subjects. Charlemagne promulgated through public assemblies what were known as capitularies—that is, regulations, counsels, maxims. Though these appear now like an odd mixture of diversity and irregularity, showing surprising variety of instruction for different times and places, the import of them all was to give peace and justice to the empire and to remind all peoples that they belonged to one another by being subjects of one king and worshipers of one God.

The immediate aftermath of Charlemagne's time is a scene of particularity with no pattern of social unity outside the church. Feudalism had succeeded to the place of empire. The poor traded freedom for security, sold themselves, together with their labor, to a rich and powerful lord for protection. Consequently castles were built; serfs tilled the land about the castle for its lord; they fled inside when attacked by an enemy. Commerce on any wide scale ceased; industry beyond small crafts for local needs was nonexistent; and men's interests contracted to the scope of what they could see, hear, handle, and feed upon.

Only the church retained some unity. At least for three or four decades after Charlemagne she continued to operate on the momentum he had given her. It took that long also for the light he had caused to be lit in his schools to flicker and then go out, if indeed it ever entirely went out. Consequently there was in the West a brief period of political, social, intellectual, perhaps even to a degree at least, moral and spiritual vitality. It can best be called the Carolingian Renaissance, since Charlemagne more than anyone else initiated it, though its own protagonists were responsible for its success. What Charlemagne did on the continent, Alfred the Great did in Britain, and his reign (871-899) belongs to this same historical situation.

I. The Holy Roman Empire

The political continuum for the events of this period was the Holy Roman Empire. It came into existence itself in the first year of the ninth century and survived until Napoleon Bonaparte discontinued it a thousand years later. It is interesting to observe that the Papal states preceded it in origin by almost twenty-five years, and they outlasted it by more than three decades. Since the Franks honored Rome by giving her people status as a nation, so Rome, as the patrimony of Peter, responded in kind by conferring upon the Frankish king the title of emperor and elevating thereby an aggregation of tribes into the dignity of an empire. The establishment of the Holy Roman Empire by the pope gave to the subsequent years of the Middle Ages their basic structure of political order and, despite the compromises of feudalism and the disruptive claims which Teutonic individualism perennially made, served successfully enough as the secular complement to that ecclesiastical organization which looked on itself as a universal church.

The sudden transformation of an ecclesiastical bishopric into a state was bound to occasion a great upheaval. The pope was not equipped to govern the people, nor were the people willing to be governed by him. Consequently there ensued within the bounds of the new principality a race for power between clerics, many of whom became drunk with the new wine of political responsibility which they tasted now for the first time, and the lay nobility, who hitherto had neglected the church as politically of no consequence yet who realized now that they must either control it or be enslaved by it. The papacy was more than an ecclesiastical honor. It was the political pearl of great price.

The following **ecclesiastical offices** came into immediate prominence: (1) *vidame*, governor of the papal palace; (2) *vestiarius*, treasurer; (3) *sacellarius*, paymaster; (4) *primicerius*, chief notary. These were entirely administrative positions and existed alongside those of the seven papal deacons, who were executives as well and governed the business affairs of the seven ecclesiastical regions, over each of which one of them respectively presided. The pope's spiritual advisers were his twenty-five cardinal priests, each of whom was attached to a presbyterial church and together formed with the pontiff the great official council of the Roman church. There were an archpriest over the priests and an archdeacon over the deacons, and these two officers together with the *primicerius* were the triumvirate which governed the church during the period between a pope's death and the election of his successor. The official clergy below the rank of bishop, admonished to observe celibacy, consisted of priests, deacons, and subdeacons; but there were at the same time unordained clerics—married and ambitious—who composed the administrative ranks and now more than ever clamored for recognition and power in the new ecclesiastical state.

The laymen were not quiescent. Now that the pope was a prince he had to have a standing army, a police force, and the other agencies of political dominion. He was the commander in chief of the army and the commissioner of the police force, but he could not be general and chief gendarme as well, for he was not trained either to fight a war or to apprehend a criminal. The laity gave him his soldiers and constables, and their aristocracy provided him with secular leaders. This meant inevitably the emergence of factions and rival groups.

Laymen contested among themselves for position; clergymen vied with one another for honor; laymen and clergymen struggled alike for power; the papacy itself was victimized and impaired. Some outside, disinterested agency was needed, if for no other reason than to act as umpire, to guarantee a fair fight, and to insure order after it was over.

Pope Stephen III, who had negotiated with Pepin the Short, was succeeded by his mild, charitable, but politically incompetent brother, **Paul I** (757-767). Paul gave up lay government and put the control of his state into the hands of the clergy, who were dominated by the selfish, scheming, ruthless *primicerius*, Christopher, himself unordained. Paul's ten years were wrecked by dissension; and when he died the Roman aristocracy under Duke Theodore actually raised a layman like themselves to the papal rank. Constantine, the soldier-brother of Duke Theodore, was on successive days tonsured; ordained subdeacon, deacon, priest; and lastly, consecrated pope (July 5, 767). The price Constantine paid for his few weeks in office was terrible indeed. The Lombard king, Desiderius (756-774) fought and killed Duke Theodore, defeated his followers, and dragged the cowering Constantine, who had taken refuge under the altar of the chapel, into the streets, where he was degraded and punished by having his eyes gouged out. Desiderius had his own candidate Philip, abbot of St. Guy, proclaimed pope; but he was soon kidnapped by Christopher, the *primicerius*, and exiled to his monastery.[2] **Stephen IV** (768-772) was properly elected in his place.

Stephen, though scholarly and talented, was too timid to govern men successfully. Consequently he was persuaded by Christopher to further humiliate the dethroned pope, Constantine, by subjecting him to a trial. The judges were thirteen Frankish and forty Italian prelates. When Constantine was challenged by his judges to give a reason for accepting so exalted an office as the papacy when he was only a layman, he answered by questioning them: "Sergius of Ravenna, were you not a layman, too, when you accepted archiepiscopal orders; and you, Stephen of Naples, weren't you raised to the episcopacy from lay ranks?" At this his judges became assailants, attacked the accused with their fists, and beat the poor blind man to the ground.[3] Under pressure Stephen turned his favorite Christopher over to the wrath of Desiderius, who blinded him in so cruel a manner that he soon died.[4] However it was during Stephen IV's pontificate, indeed at the same council which

---

[2] LP, I, 463-471.
[3] *Ibid.*, pp. 475-476.
[4] J. Regesta, I, 2388.

condemned Constantine (769), that a law was passed forbidding anyone who had not attained the rank of either cardinal-deacon or cardinal-priest to be elected pope. This council decreed that the Roman clergy and bishops should elect the pope. No layman should be allowed to be present. The election would then be ratified by the Roman populace.[5]

Charlemagne actively projected himself and his army into Italian affairs during the pontificate of Stephen's successor, **Adrian I** (772-795). He did this to offset the grandiose schemes of the Lombard king, Desiderius, whose ambition had tempted him also to dream of empire. Desiderius had given one of his daughters to Charlemagne as wife, but another he had given to Charlemagne's rival and enemy, Duke Tasilon of Bavaria. On the death of Charlemagne's brother and coruler, Carloman, he had accepted Carloman's widow and children at his court and had encouraged treacherous schemes against the Frankish throne. Under pretext of visiting Rome as a pilgrim he had planned to establish himself as its secular ruler and take over the custody of the papacy.

Adrian had resisted his move by calling out the militia and preparing the city against siege. He had threatened Desiderius with anathema if he entered Roman territory. This threat by the pope is the first instance of the use of this spiritual penalty against a temporal ruler.[6] Heretofore it had been reserved entirely for heretics and schismatics. Consequently Charlemagne was only too glad to use all this as a pretext to lay siege to Pavia, dethrone Desiderius, and become the king of the Lombards as well as king of the Franks (774).[7] He then went to Rome, was received in love and joy by the pontiff, and entered into sacred compact with the papal government. He ratified the donation of his father Pepin, made an alliance with the pope, extended considerably the territories of the states of the church, and promised his protection always. He did not claim for himself any right whatever in papal elections. However he did insist that he must hold the privilege of receiving from any official or any Roman nobleman an appeal, even though that appeal might be against the pope himself. These negotiations took place shortly after Easter, in April, 774.[8]

The climax of the whole affair came, however, during the next pontificate. **Leo III** (795-816), Adrian's successor, who had been elected without any interference whatever from Charlemagne, was kidnapped by ruffians in the employment of his own *primicerius* and *sacellarius*, disappointed no doubt that he had been elected pope instead of someone of their choosing. They imprisoned him in the monastery of St. Erasmus, where they attempted

[5] Mansi, XII, 710.
[6] J. Regesta, I, 2401-2402.
[7] *Historiens des Gaules* (1738-1904), V, 131 ff.
[8] LP, I, 496-498.

unsuccessfully to put out his sight and to tear out his tongue. He escaped with the aid of a chamberlain and fled to Charlemagne at Paderborn. Later his enemies too took advantage of the imperial privilege of appeal and made their case against him to the king. Charlemagne ordered an investigation.

The astute Leo stole a long march on his enemies. When a council in Rome, set up in the presence of Charlemagne to investigate the case for and against him, declared that "the Apostolic See has the right to judge everyone but can itself be judged by no one," the pope voluntarily stood up before the conclave of dignitaries in St. Peter's, placed his hands upon the gospels, and swore that he was innocent of every crime with which he had been charged. The congregation broke forth in a litany of praise to God, the Virgin Mary, the Prince of the Apostles, and all the saints in paradise. That was just two days before Christmas.

On **Christmas Day in the year 800,** while Charlemagne was kneeling at the altar in St. Peter's, surrounded by the nobility of his nation and the prelates of Rome, Pope Leo III, evidently with no warning whatever to the king of the Franks, placed an imperial crown on his head. The crowd assembled, having been instructed in advance what to do, cried aloud with one voice: "To Charles Augustus, crowned by God, great and peaceful emperor of the Romans, long life and victory." [9]

That coronation inaugurated the Holy Roman Empire. It signalized that Charlemagne was more than a Frankish prince, the ally and protector of the states of the church, which his father before him had been. He was the supreme ruler of the Western world. At the same time it announced his dependence for this right upon the pope who had voluntarily conferred it upon him.

The new emperor did not altogether like what had happened. He swore that, had he known what was about to take place, he would never have entered the church. He was pleased with what he got but not with the manner in which he had received it. Later he required his son Louis, when he made him emperor co-regent (813), to take the imperial crown from the altar of the church at Aachen. Nevertheless what Leo had done neither Charlemagne nor any of his successors could undo. Leo convinced the people of the Middle Ages that the imperial crown was the gift of the church.

II. Christendom Under Charlemagne

Charlemagne's reputation rests on the fact that he was a creator and disseminator of culture, using Christianity for the improvement of life and of civilization. Perhaps he took himself too seriously. With a naïve view of his own power and his right to use it, he allowed his purview to include every-

[9] LP, II, 4-7.

thing, and he sought to bring all that was into conformity to his sovereign will. The pope might theoretically have been God's vicegerent on earth, but practically the emperor was the divine executive, and pope as well as people bent in obedience to his imperial sway. Fortunately Charlemagne had good advice and knew how properly to appraise and effectively to use it. Consequently the arts of civilization advanced under his patronage.

The picture of Western Christendom under Charlemagne displays itself through five distinct aspects.

First, there is the matter of **church management and discipline.** The church owned extensive land and property, certainly more than any other agency or person in Western Europe, though this ownership was diversified among individual churches, abbeys, monasteries, and other establishments. In other words, there was no central agency that had at its disposal all the accumulated wealth of the Body Catholic. However, this ownership of property threw the church actively into business. She let leases to small farmers who tilled her soil; public markets were held on the premises of abbeys and monasteries; fairs were made to coincide with pilgrimages and feast days; ecclesiastical establishments had their custom houses, toll bridges, sometimes even mints; taxes too were levied and collected. What little industry there was had its ecclesiastical as well as lay participants. Corbie for example under Adalhard's abbatial management prospered through diversified trades: shoes, saddles for horses, wares made by goldsmiths, parchments, and the products of masons, carpenters, fullers, and the like.

The workmen, whether employed by the church or not, soon grouped themselves into guilds, or mutual aid societies, which were for the purpose of supporting one another when an individual's work or property was impaired by fire, shipwreck, or some disaster of nature. These guilds reflected a concern for religion in the carrying out of their functions, showing that as the church engaged in business she likewise left the stamp of her mission upon all that she did. At the same time the world left its mark on her too in greed, avarice, cheating, and other ugly characteristics which the pursuit of gain so frequently occasions if it does not necessarily produce.

In addition to the revenues it received from its properties the church was the recipient of the freewill offering of the people. There was the traditional tithe which, since its inception as the offspring of Judaism, Christianity had taught its adherents belonged to God and should be given by all his children to his church. In addition to this the clergy had come to expect fees for funerals, weddings, and other special services such as masses for the dead. Tremendous properties had been accumulated through wills and bequests. Certain royal lands were put at the disposal of the church, the clerical occupants of which were appointed to their living by the crown. Such ecclesiastical livings were called benefices.

Consequently as a result of such practices abuses arose which required correction. Charlemagne set as his task their correction: (1) People were forbidden by law to give so much of their wealth to the church that they impoverished their own families. (2) Ecclesiastical revenues had to be equally divided among the bishop, the priests, and the poor of the diocese. (3) Fees could not be levied by the clergy for special services such as ordinations, funerals, and special masses, though the people were permitted to make voluntary offerings on those occasions. (4) The church was constrained by law to use properties it had inherited according to the stipulation of the donor. (5) The tithe was not only encouraged, but exacted. (6) The church was continually reminded that its properties were the patrimony of the poor; each monastery was required to establish beside it a hospital for the sick and needy and the stranger within the gates. "He who does not nourish the poor," states one of the capitularies, "is their murderer." [10]

Likewise, Charlemagne took cognizance of ecclesiastical discipline and its enforcement. Gone now in the church were the loose and easy days of the do-nothing Merovingian kings. He required thirty-three different councils to devote their attention to issues of clerical discipline. Priests were admonished to carry out their duties by teaching the people in a clear and simple manner, by hearing confession of penitents as a father would hear his child, by visiting the sick and bereaved, and by supervising the people in their acts of penance. The emperor even offered to lend them the assistance of his government in this last regard. Preaching too required imperial regulation. Homilies were prepared by scholars at the order of the emperor; and the clerics were required to memorize them and deliver them to the people in their own tongue[11] from a low pulpit, raised just a few feet above floor-level, where the preacher would not lose contact with his audience.

The clergy as a general rule lived together in communities, either with their bishop or, when there needed to be many such communities in a diocese, in a house under the supervision of an older priest. Charlemagne decreed that bishops were to be elected by the clergy and people of the diocese in which they were to serve.[12] Yet the election took place always in the presence of his *missus*, and he frequently made a nomination which generally was tantamount to election. Most bishops enjoyed their benefice from him, and he encouraged all high clergymen to come directly to him to settle their disputes.[13] Consequently Henry IV, some two and a half centuries later, had good precedent for his imperial behavior toward the church, despite the complaint and the punitive action against him by Pope Gregory VII.

[10] E. Baluze, *Capitularia regum francorum ab anno 742 ad annum 922*, I, 503.
[11] AS, I, 416.
[12] Baluze, op. cit., I, 779.
[13] *Ibid.*, p. 497.

Secondly, there is the **reformation and revival of monasticism.** Here Charlemagne's personal influence was less direct. He exerted himself to correct the evils that existed in the orders; however the pattern of reform he wisely left to the monks themselves. The resurgence of new life came as a result of the spiritual power within monasticism.

On his succession to the throne Charlemagne found the monasteries in a deplorable condition. Many in Bavaria for example had been distributed as booty to the Frankish warring nobles for their aid in conquest. These had been vacated by sincere persons and were occupied by men seeking to escape military service, misfits in society, and persons of scandalous life. Throughout the realm the abodes of coenobites had become either schools of heresy or resorts of self-indulgence.

Charlemagne tried to enforce the Rule of Chrodegang, who had been minister of state under his grandfather, Charles Martel, and Frankish ambassador to the Lombards under his father, Pepin the Short. Chrodegang had organized the clergy of the episcopal city of Metz, where he had been bishop, into a religious community about the cathedral. The main provisions of Chrodegang's rule, set out in thirty-four chapters, were: (1) a special enclosure for the residence of the clergy; (2) a common dormitory for sleeping; (3) recitation of the divine office in common; (4) study and teaching in addition to the regular sacerdotal performances; (5) a life of utter humility. The practitioners of this rule were known as Canons. This then was the origin of the Canons Regular of the Cathedrals, and Chrodegang's Rule was adopted by many bishops for their clergy.[14]

But Charlemagne could not impose reform on the monasteries from without. It had to come from within. This reform was supplied by Benedict of Aniane (750-821) and the host of monks who came out of his establishment. He had been cupbearer to the emperor. His life was changed from that of courtier to monk by a frightening personal experience. In trying to rescue his brother from drowning, he was himself caught up in the swift current and swept rapidly down stream. His deliverance from disaster was at the same time his conversion. Escape from the river meant for him release from the service of a king of earth to that of the king of heaven. In 779 he founded on his own property in Languedoc a monastery which became the center of monastic reformation and revival in France. He systematized the Benedictine Rule and made a collection of all known monastic regulations.[15] The high quality of life which prevailed at his house of Aniane was imitated by the inhabitants of other monasteries. Likewise, others followed his example in founding monasteries. The most famous of these was Charlemagne's own relative, William of Aquitaine, who established at Gellone the monastery of

[14] *Ibid.*, p. 296. MPL, LXXXIX, 1057-1096.
[15] MPL, CIII, 393-1440.

St. William of the Desert. William had been one of Charlemagne's greatest generals and had successfully repulsed the Saracens.

Thirdly, there are ecclesiastical buildings and customs, the conduct of worship, and the rites and ceremonies appertaining thereto.

Though the distinctive Gothic architecture had not yet emerged, still the Byzantine basilica had been abandoned in the West, and what is known as Romanesque architecture had taken its place. The churches were not polygonal but rather rectangular in the shape of a cross. On the outside, bells, open windows with stone latticework, and sharp arches gave them their common features; while inside their main altar was set in the middle of the choir. Practically every church had a relic of some sort in it. Indeed, before it could be consecrated it was felt that it should have some sacred token of a martyr, an apostle, or of our Lord.[16]

The clergy were now set apart in their dress from ordinary society. They wore their hair short in contrast to the long hair and beards of the Frankish nobility. Their dress consisted of four chief articles: (1) the cassock, a long black garment reaching to the feet and worn at all times; (2) the alb, a white linen vestment with tight fitting sleeves, worn over the cassock at the Eucharist; (3) the chasuble, an ornate outer vestment worn by the celebrant of the mass; (4) and the camail with the pointed capuche, a neck guard which could be drawn over the head as a cowl. These pieces of clothing were reminiscent of the tunic and toga of Roman times and entirely different from the fur jerkin, leather breeches, shirt with short tight sleeves, and the short cloak held on by a metal clasp of the Franks. Perhaps this clerical costume designed after the fashion of the past reminded the people of Christianity's age and history, that the church both was before they came and would be long after they had gone.

Charlemagne was especially attracted to the Gregorian chant, and he brought chanters from Italy to Germany along with their music. He had a beautiful organ constructed for the cathedral at Aachen. Both he and his son, Louis the Pious, continued the liturgical reforms of Pepin the Short so that the Gallican rites competed with the Gregorian rites of Rome in the liturgies of the church and formed a sizeable contribution to the missal.

It was during this period in Western Europe that the baptistry began to give way to the font, and baptism by immersion was displaced by baptism by pouring. Public penance had practically entirely disappeared. Private masses (mostly for the dead) were becoming more and more popular, to the horror of many conservatives who felt that the congregation must participate in order for the Eucharist really to be effective. Unleavened bread, despite vigorous protests from the East, was being more widely used in the service.

[16] L. Duchesne, Christian Worship: Its Origin and Evolution (tr. M. L. McClure, 1919), p. 403.

The elements were still being administered to the people in both kinds, though the communicants were generally given the communion wine through a straw.[17]

Fourthly, there is the area of **Christian doctrine**. The theological issues which arose in the West during the reign of Charlemagne were few and relatively of no great significance.

(1) Ancient Sabellianism arose in Spain (782) through the teaching of Migetius, who claimed that God, though one, had been successively revealed to man under three distinct personal categories: as Father by David, as Son by Jesus Christ, and as Holy Spirit by the apostle Paul.[18]

(2) In refuting this error two Spanish clergy, both bishops, fell into Nestorian Adoptionism. Elipandus of Toledo, for example, said that only the Word was consubstantial with God, but the man to whom the Word attached himself had to be adopted by the Father as his Son. His colleague, Felix of Urgel, attempted to supply the scriptural proof texts for his argument. The natural Son did not know where the body of Lazarus had been laid, what the disciples on the Emmaus Road had been talking about before he joined them, or when the end of the world would come about.[19] Both disregarded Cyril's contribution to Ephesus and Leo's acceptance of it at Chalcedon that, no matter what the limitations of the human nature Christ assumed were, he was still one person whom we adore as God in the flesh. Both errors, Sabellianism and Adoptionism, were condemned at the Council of Frankfurt (794).[20]

(3) The one abiding contribution which the West made to theology during this period was the addition of the filioque to the Nicene-Constantinopolitan creed. The word filioque means "from the Son." It was put in the creed as an affirmation that the Holy Spirit proceeds equally from the Father and the Son. Really it had come out of the Arian disputes in Spain before the land had succumbed to the Moslems. The Council of Toledo (589) had coined the word. It had general acceptance in the West, but great offense was caused in the East when it was chanted by some Western monks in a service in a monastery on the Mount of Olives outside Jerusalem. Charlemagne decided in its favor at a council held at Aachen in 809. Leo III supported this position doctrinally but counseled that, since the word was not in the original Nicene Creed, it would be unwise to insist on its use in the East. He did not forbid the Franks to use it when they repeated the creeds (January, 810).[21] It received general adoption in the West. The East refused it as an un-

---

[17] CMH, III, 556-567.
[18] MPL, XCVI, 859.
[19] MPL, CIV, 37.
[20] Mansi, XIII, 873, 883, 899 ff.
[21] Mansi, XIV, 19 ff.

warranted tampering with tradition. Its churches preferred to say the Holy Spirit proceeds from the Father by the Son.

The final feature of this picture of Western Christendom under Charlemagne is the schools.

Every parish was required by law to provide a school, open to all the children, whether those of freemen or of serfs (decree of 789). It took time of course to implement so sweeping a regulation; unfortunately Charlemagne's reign was not long enough to see it enforced everywhere; after his reign it was neglected. As a result, some dioceses had many and very fine parish schools, while others had only a few poor ones or scarcely any at all. The subject matter of such schools was that of elementary education in that day: simple arithmetic and grammar, the psalter, and the Gregorian chant.[22]

More successful was Charlemagne in his venture in higher education. The Council of Aachen (802) determined the form and scope this education should take. It was entrusted to the two great institutions, both ecclesiastical, which were best suited to carrying it out: the cathedral and the monastery. Qualified lay students were admitted along with clerical, though in the monastic establishments as such the regular were given their own instruction in segregation from the secular and lay pupils. The curriculum consisted of grammar, rhetoric, and mathematics; and the method of procedure was to read aloud the ancient manuscripts in possession of the school, analyzing their style as well as their contents, copying them, and committing large portions of them to memory. Of course there was no substitution for the lecture of the teacher. Schools therefore developed their reputations from both those who taught in them and the number and quality of the manuscripts in their possession. Dissemination of works among many schools became increasingly easier to accomplish through the development of the fine art of copying practiced by all the schools.

The greatest educator of Charlemagne's time was Alcuin of York (b. 735).[23] He was educated in Britain by Egbert, who in turn had been educated by the Venerable Bede. Charlemagne made his acquaintance at Parma (781) and was so favorably impressed by him that he attached him to his person for the rest of his life, made him his chief counselor in all educational matters, and enabled him to become the artificer of those schools which lend an immortal luster to his name. It was Alcuin, who, together with the learned Agobard, archbishop of Lyons, exposed so thoroughly the heresy of Felix of Urgel and Elipandus of Toledo, wrote seven books against it, and prepared the condemnatory findings of the Council of Frankfort. However, Alcuin did not possess a creative or daringly original mind. His scholarship, though vast compared with that of his contemporaries in the West, was neither penetrating

[22] Baluze, op. cit., I, 237.
[23] MPL, Vols. C, CI.

nor expansive relative to the knowledge and ideas of the thinkers of the East. It is dubious whether he even knew Greek. His understanding of Aristotle was confined to those passages which Boethius had preserved. He was neither a philosopher nor a historian. Yet he was an incomparable teacher who knew how to adjust himself to the ignorance of his students and to carry them from the state in which he found them to where he wanted them to go. He led them to an intense study of Augustine and Gregory the Great. He presented them with an abundant supply both of facts and of ideas and enabled them to reach their own conclusions in keeping of course with the orthodoxy of the church. Alcuin, like Charlemagne, sincerely believed that the school is but the vestibule of the church, the learning of man preliminary to the revelation of God in Jesus Christ.[24]

III. The Missions to Saxony and Scandinavia

Charlemagne took his duties as a Christian prince seriously. From the first day he became associated in the government of the kingdom of the Franks with his brother Carloman until he laid down the imperial scepter in death, he gave his stupendous energy to the furtherance of the faith and the territorial expansion of Christianity. His methods were not always wise, and to the degree of his folly the missionary enterprise was impaired. In his impatience and restlessness and indignation at the perfidy of those he had tried to help, he forsook the peaceful manners of Boniface and the earlier missioners and tried to convert the heathen with the sword. Here for the first time in the West people were given the option of Christian baptism or death.

The conversion of the Saxons, for example, was so entwined with **imperialism** in its normal course of expansion and the preservation of peace at home against predatory marauders that it is difficult at this late date to disentangle the two interests. In the mind of Charlemagne, they no doubt were one. It was to the advantage of his kingdom to incorporate Saxony in it and thus to relieve it of military pressure from an outside enemy; Christianity was not optional—it was the religion of everybody in the kingdom. At the same time it was to the advantage of the people of Saxony to become Christians, no matter what their personal desire was, for what does it profit a man to have his own way and lose his soul. To convert a man, even if he had to be frightened into conversion, was nonetheless to save him. If he persistently refused conversion, then he was the enemy of God and a dangerous threat to his fellow men. He was destined for hell anyway. It was of little consequence whether he reached his destination soon or late, so Charlemagne dispensed with the recalcitrant pagans of Saxony with the sword.

[24] CMH, III, 515-518.

It is not fair, however, to this era in history to imply that Charlemagne's action in this regard represented the enlightened Christian conscience of the time. Alcuin of York, the emperor's own counselor and pedagogue, protested strongly against it: "Faith is an act of the will and is not a forced act. Conscience may be appealed to, it must not be constrained by violence. Preachers, not brigands, should be sent to the Saxons." [25]

Yet preachers had been sent to the Saxons already. Their gains were negligible as an influence on Saxon policy in favor of the Frankish state. The Saxons continued to raid and ravage the lands of the Franks. Finally Charlemagne decided on bolder measures. In May, 772, at Worms he won the consent of his high officials and the prayers of his clergy to essay a military expedition against the Saxons and to conquer their lands for Christ. Only a show of power was at first necessary to win them. He overthrew their idols in Westphalia and accepted hostages from them in pledge of their good faith to hear his missioners in peace. Though their raids continued to the extent that the Fritzlard monastery, founded by Boniface, was pillaged and turned into a stable, Charlemagne employed peaceful means. Five years after Worms, at Paderborn in Westphalia, he parleyed with the Saxons, and pled with them through the eloquent tongue of the monk, Sturmio, so that most of their chieftains accepted Christian baptism (May, 777). One significant Saxon leader was missing—**Widukind**, who bided his time in Denmark.[26]

Widukind's hour came in the autumn of 778. Believing Charlemagne had been killed at Roncesvalles beneath the Pyrenees near the border of Spain, Widukind's Saxon soldiers raided Hesse and Thuringia, penetrating as far inland as the left bank of the Rhine. Even Fulda itself was in jeopardy. The monks disinterred the remains of Boniface and carried his coffin a distance of two days' journey from the tomb in which it had lain in honor for twenty-four years.[27] Charlemagne returned in fury, fought hard against the Saxons, and forced Widukind once again into exile in Denmark (779). He then solicited the aid of Willehad, who for two or three years preached and built churches among the Saxons. Like Boniface he was an Anglo-Saxon. His work however was short-lived, for Widukind returned in 782 and swept all that Willehad had done before him like leaves before a whirlwind. Willehad fled to Rome to await more propitious times.[28] Then it was that Charlemagne lost all restraint. That same year he promulgated the capitulary of Saxony which made it a crime punishable by death not to accept Christian baptism or to show disrespect to Christianity by not fasting during sacred seasons. There were 4,500 Saxons beheaded in one day at Verden on the Aller as

[25] MPL, C, 205.
[26] *Historiens des Gaules*, V, 203 ff. *Vita Sturmii*, chapters 3-5, 24, in MPL, Vol. CV, 422 f., 442 f.
[27] MGH, *Scriptores*, II, 36.
[28] MPL, XCIX, 692 ff.

traitors, murderers, and incendiaries. The sanguinary conflict between him and Widukind continued with increased fury for three more years until, both armies exhausted, Charlemagne offered Widukind terms of peace which he accepted. The recalcitrant Saxon warrior asked for and received Christian baptism.[29]

Then the good side of Charlemagne's nature immediately revealed itself. The Act of Speyer (788) gave freedom to the Saxons, stating that Charlemagne wished them to be subjects of God alone. The death penalty for paganism was abolished; Saxons were left to be judged by Saxon law (797).[30]

Thus **Ludger**, the last great apostle to Saxony, was facilitated in his evangelistic mission. He was a native of Frisia, had been selected and trained for his task by a disciple of Boniface, had studied in Britain under Alcuin of York, was ordained priest in 778 at the age of thirty, and after zealous labors among the Saxons for whom he founded the monastery of Werden he died as the venerated bishop of Münster in 809.[31] The monasteries were the centers of Christian instruction in this newly won territory. The most famous of these was *Corbia nova*, an offspring of the celebrated Corbia monastery near Amiens, presided over by Adalhard, who, like Charlemagne, was a grandson of Charles Martel. His own brother Wala and another monk, also named Adalhard, founded *Corbia nova* at the mouth of the Weser River one year (815) after Charlemagne's death. New Corbie (*Corbia nova*) was to Saxony what Fulda had been to northern Germany. Likewise, it became the home base of missionaries to Scandanavia. It leapt into prominence through the effectiveness of its work when Louis the Pious gave it a handsome endowment in 823.[32]

Christianity reached Scandinavia through diplomatic channels and as a result of negotiations between heads of state. Harold of Denmark sent envoys to Louis the Pious of France asking aid of the Frankish emperor. Louis suggested that the aid might be more readily given if the envoys were Christians. They took the hint and very obligingly accepted baptism, carrying back the same suggestion to their king. King Harold, his wife, his son, and four hundred of his warriors were baptized by Bishop Ebbo of Rheims at the royal palace of Ingelheim (May, 826). After Harold got what he wanted from Louis, he lapsed back into paganism.[33]

The real mission to Scandinavia was launched by and prosecuted under the wise surveillance of a former schoolmaster of Corbia nova called **Ansgar**. He witnessed the disgraceful failure both of Ebbo's mission and of his own

---

[29] *Historiens des Gaules*, V, 568-569.
[30] Baluze, op. cit., I, 249-250, 275, 280, 405 ff.
[31] W. Diekamp, *Die Geschichtsquellen des Bisthums Münster* (1881), IV, 3-53.
[32] *Acta Sanctorum ordinis S. Benedicti* (ed. Mabillon, 1733), 710.
[33] *Historiens des Gaules*, V, 130 ff.

personal life. He took up where Ebbo left off. It seems that Ansgar was afflicted by a passionate desire amounting almost to an obsession for martyrdom. This was never granted him. However he did live an austere life of self-denial, wandering back and forth between Denmark and Sweden, witnessing the constant swing of the pendulum between glorious success and abysmal failure. He was just beginning to build a new library, open schools, and construct churches in this heathen territory when pirates raided his chief city, left his constructions in ashes, and dispersed the whole community of newly won Christians in Sweden. Finally the pope appointed him archbishop of Bremen, from which see he successfully directed the operation of effective missions in Scandinavia. At the time of his death at the age of sixty-four (February, 865) these northern peoples were experiencing the humanizing influence of the Christian gospel. Ansgar has been given the title of "Apostle to the Northern Peoples," and he seems to have won them, so ferocious in nature and terrible in battle, by his own extraordinary gentleness.[34]

Nevertheless at the end of the ninth century only a small minority of the original Norsemen—the inhabitants of what is now Denmark, Sweden, and Norway—was Christian.

IV. The Papacy Under Nicholas I

The demise of Charlemagne was at the same time the demise of his empire. The struggles of Louis the Pious against Lothaire and Louis the German were not for the preservation of political unity but for a tripartite rather than a bipartite division of his domain, thereby furthering instead of arresting the dismemberment of the empire. The title Holy Roman Empire continued as did the appellative emperor to designate its sovereign, but both were empty and meaningless. In either case they were the gift of the papacy to confer, and they passed from one geographical area to the next depending upon the territory over which the sovereign ruled who was chosen Holy Roman Emperor.

The weakening of the empire meant the strengthening of the papacy. The seven pontiffs who occupied Peter's throne for the forty-two years between the death of Leo III (816) and the accession of Nicholas I (858), though in no sense uniform in their talents, were nonetheless single in their accomplishment—they prepared the way for a mighty resurgence of spiritual over temporal authority in the person of Nicholas. Pope Paschal I (817-824) won from Louis the Pious a constitution (817) establishing in perpetuity for the Roman church the personal gifts of Pepin (756) and Charlemagne (800). It stipulated that the emperor's interference in Roman affairs should be restricted to putting down disturbances.[35] These provisions were expanded

---

[34] Rimbert, *Vita Anskarii*, in MGH, *Scriptores rerum Germanicarum* (1884).
[35] Baluze, op. cit., I, 791 ff.

in favor of the ecclesiastical establishment under Pope Eugenius II (824-827) by the constitution of 824 (with Lothaire) which permitted Romans to be judged by Roman law and inflicted the penalty of exile on anyone who disturbed a papal election. Likewise, appeals for justice in the area of papal dominion would go first to the pope and later to the emperor only as a last resort. The church imposed its own condition by forbidding simoniacal elections, restricting the absence of bishops from their dioceses to three weeks, requiring concurrence of clergy and people of dioceses in episcopal elections, suspending ignorant priests, and insisting on clergymen wearing at all times their peculiar garb (826).[36] Pope Gregory IV (827-844) acted as an arbitrator in Frankish affairs, setting the precedent of the church's interference in behalf of peace in the government of states. Pope Leo IV (847-855) provided leadership in all phases of government to the extent even of military generalship, showing that the Roman pontiff was quite capable of fulfilling all the duties of a temporal sovereign. He fought the Saracens; he overcame the connivance, the threats, even the violence of the imperial government; he maintained discipline in the ecclesiastical order.[37]

To be sure, there were on occasions during the forty-two years violent outbursts of passion, ambition, and greed, which were portents of the anarchy of feudalism which was to follow: the efforts of the Roman populace to disavow the election of the aged Sergius II (844-847) and to establish the deacon John in his place (844); the appeal to the Saracen infidels by two Italian nobles to win for themselves at the expense of Christendom the duchy of Benevento (Radelgisus and Siconulfus, 835); and the abortive attempt of Arsenius to raise his own son, Anastasius, to the papal throne (855).[38] The positive however outweighed the negative; weakness in the papacy always was repaired by a superior strength.

Nicholas took these gains and consolidated them. He addressed himself to ascertaining the causes of the church's weakness and sought to remedy them. Like Gregory I before him, he was not an innovator; his cannot be styled an original or creative mind; always he operated on old, well-established, traditional lines; he was content to manage the church in keeping with the principles of his predecessors. The point of his greatness was that he did manage it. What others in his position had tried but either had failed to do or else had accomplished only in part, he both essayed and achieved in its entirety. Perhaps more than any other pontiff, he saw the mission of the church in its totality. Whereas Gregory the Great had made the church supreme in Italy, Nicholas I made it supreme in Western Europe. "If," he wrote in regard to the missionary labors among the Scandinavians and Slavs,

[36] Mansi, XIV, 999 ff.
[37] LP, II, 34.
[38] LP, II, 86-90.

"according to the sacred ordinances a new basilica cannot be built without the sanction of the pope, how can a church, i.e., a confederation of Catholics, be established without the approval of the Apostolic See?" [39] "By the power of God," he wrote to Michael the Drunkard, "we have been born the sons and heirs of the apostles Peter and Paul; and, though in merit far inferior to them, we have been made princes over all the earth. . . ." [40]

This remarkable man was sought for the papal office. Nicholas did not seek that position for himself. Indeed, on the news that he had been unanimously chosen after the Cardinal of Saint Mark's had refused election, he tried to emulate his example by fleeing to Saint Peter's. There he was approached and taken by force to the Lateran Palace and placed on the pontifical throne. On Sunday, April 24, 858, in the presence of the Holy Roman Emperor, Louis II, Nicholas was consecrated pope while standing before the altar of the apostle Peter in that martyr's own church. This was the beginning of nine strenuous and stormy years, fraught with physical pain occasioned by chronic illness for the Pope, yet characterized by accomplishment and prestige for the church over which he ruled. His temperament was such that he was always decisive. He knew how to reach a decision quickly, and he had the tenacity of character to stand by what he had decided unwaveringly to the end. Though his letters are long, tedious, and circumlocutious, the actions they take are clear and thorough. With Nicholas there was never any half-way station; compromise was not a possibility; to temporize with an opponent was tantamount to surrendering the cause to him. Nicholas played in the gamble of ecclesiastical and world affairs for big stakes; but, big or small, his intention was constant: he was determined always to win.

Consequently the royal status of Lothaire II (855-869), king of Lotharingia, obtained no special favor from the pope in his divorce proceedings against his wife Teutberga. Though he won approval from his own bishops and by their consent legitimatized into wedlock his adulterous affair with Waldrade, the pontifical judgment of Rome invalidated what their provincial synod had countenanced, so that Nicholas did not hesitate to command the arms of Louis II and Charles the Bald to enforce morality and decency upon their wayward nephew. Likewise, John of Ravenna, archbishop and metropolitan though he was, was constrained, despite the aid and encouragement he had received from the emperor, to defend himself against charges of greed, theft, and maladministration at a trial in Rome, and finally was actually deposed because of the enormities of his crimes. Even Hincmar of Rheims, chief prelate of France and the first person to be accounted with Gallicanism in history, was compelled by force of the papal command to

[39] Ep. 135, in MPL, CXIX, 753-1212 and in MGH, Epistolae, VI, 257-690.
[40] Epistola 86, MPL, CXIX, 926 ff.

restore Bishop Rothade, whom he had deposed, to his see in Soissons. The appeals made to Nicholas for judgment are too numerous, too various, too monotonous to command our attention. However in each minor instance the same deliberation and fairness were given as in the case of major issues, lifting the office of Supreme pontiff in the affections and respect of all the people by convincing them that papal justice reached to the least as well as to the mightiest.

The most notable of all Nicholas' opponents and the one whose contest with the Holy See was in the end to prove the most far reaching in its effects upon the Body Catholic was Photius of Constantinople. The character and career of the man and the details of this affair, which began as an usurpation of patriarchal power by a layman in the diocese of Constantinople, can better be treated in the next chapter where we deal again with the East. Both Photius and Ignatius, whom he displaced, appealed their cases to Rome, and were constrained in order to utilize papal help to recognize papal primacy as well. Though Photius had the backing of the Eastern imperial government, which had placed him in power, and Ignatius had nothing except his own indomitable will, the deposed patriarch won the support of the Roman pontiff. Nicholas was stubbornly steadfast in his negotiations in behalf of Ignatius. He did not live to see the triumph of his position. He died just thirteen days before the news of the final outcome of this issue reached Rome. Yet Ignatius was restored to his see in Constantinople, while Photius was imprisoned in a monastery.

The outstretched hand of Nicholas, who seemed always restless to find new fields of influence and power, reached the hitherto untouched territory of the Slavs of Central Europe. The peoples of this region had already received the emissaries of Christianity, but they had come from Constantinople, not Rome, and their teaching, though the faith of an undivided church, bore a Greek rather than a Latin interpretation. The occasion for Latin intervention was a resolution taken by **King Boris** (852-888) **of Bulgaria** to place his new church in the hands of the pope (866). The pope responded immediately by sending, together with two Latin bishops, detailed instructions for proper ecclesiastical government and a specimen, or type, of a whole new civil constitution for a nation passing from barbarism to Christianity. The principles were derived by Nicholas from the instructions of his predecessor Gregory the Great to Augustine of Canterbury. Christianity is faith and good works. Baptism, properly conducted, makes a man a Christian, but he is sustained in faith by an orderly, moral, well-regulated life. Torture, unnecessary cruelty to enemies, even those not of the faith, is proscribed. Bulgarian soldiers must prepare for battle by prayer, and the standard of the cross must be substituted for that of the horse's tail. Superstition, polygamy, coercion by force of arms are all forbidden. Wicked, unworthy priests must be relieved of their sacerdotal assignments. Such were the essentials of Nicholas' advice to Boris.

Boris asked that Formosus, one of Nicholas' episcopal emissaries, be made archbishop, or patriarch, of his church. This request was not granted. It seems that the motive for Boris' appeal to Rome for guidance was not uncompromised. Perhaps he was afraid that ecclesiastical subservience to Constantinople would lead to the sacrifice of his political independence to the Eastern empire. Or it could be that he was aggrieved at Photius for not granting his new church patriarchal autonomy. No doubt he had hoped to wheedle this favor from Rome. Nicholas' assurance that the Christianity Rome had given him was without spot or wrinkle satisfied him only for the duration of Nicholas' pontificate. Despite the papal assertion, "In this matter we are sufficient ourselves, our sufficiency is from God; and Blessed Peter, who lives and presides in his see, gives the true faith to them who seek it," [41] Boris turned about face and put his church back again under the care of Constantinople, where, owing to the nature of its origin, its proximity to the East, and its cultural background, it more properly belonged.

Nicholas asserted the right of the papacy to censor writings on faith and doctrine and established without equivocation the claim that the Roman church confirms councils by its authority and that the decrees of councils are null and void if they do not have validation by the popes.[42]

It was during his pontificate that the so-called **Forged, or False, Decretals** (so named because of their spurious claim of authorship and date) came into use. They were a collection of ecclesiastical regulations purporting to be the official papal and conciliar decrees of the first seven centuries of Christian history. Their collector and editor was said to have been Isidore of Seville. Hence they are also known as the *Pseudo-Isidorian Decretals*. Their place of origin was unquestionably in the kingdom of the Franks, since Frankish expressions and idiomatic Latin appear in them. They are not vastly different from the *False Capitularies*—their counterpart in civil legislation. Their author cannot now be identified—"a mighty man [who] lived unknown and in seclusion . . . perhaps the most learned of his contemporaries, a man of penetrating mind, sagacious, and in a rare degree initiated in the spirit and needs of his time."

The specific contents of the collection are: (1) preface, in which the author says he has been constrained by the bishops to make this collection of all the ecclesiastical canons; (2) a letter to Pope Damasus (366-384) asking for the papal decrees until his time; (3) Damasus' reply; (4) sixty forged decretals from Clement (end of first century) to Miltiades (310-314); (5) spurious Donation of Constantine (in which the emperor gives Rome and its

---

[41] *Responsa*, 106, in MPL, CXIX, 978-1017.
[42] Ep. 115.

territory to Pope Sylvester and his successors); (6) canons of councils from Nicaea (325) to Seville (619); (7) decrees of the popes from Sylvester to Gregory II, forty of which are forgeries.

The fourfold purpose of these decretals was (1) to unify the church by centering authority in Rome, (2) to free bishops from the tyranny of metropolitans, who would destroy the unity of the church by making themselves supreme in their own areas, (3) to remove ecclesiastical cases from secular tribunals, and (4) to insure the independence of bishops from the temporal powers. Nicholas discovered these decretals in 864, used expressions from them in his own pronouncements, indicating thereby his acceptance of them as genuine, and set the precedent for his successors to employ them in supporting their claims. They were not widely used by the popes until the pontificate of Leo IX (1049-1054), who was himself a native of the region wherein they originated. The *False Decretals* did not supply the cause or even the reason for the assertion of the grandiose claims of the papacy to manage the whole church; these forgeries were useful tools—godsends from foreign quarters which facilitated and hastened the papacy in doing what on its own it had either done from the days of Gregory I or else intended to do.[43]

Nicholas died November 13, 867;[44] yet the momentum of his pontificate extended beyond him for another fifteen years (867-882), during which time his policies were carried out, though without his remarkable vigor and success, by two successive popes. Adrian II (867-872), for example, accepted the penitent Lothaire II and gave him communion at Monte Cassino not long before that prince died; carried out the decisions of Nicholas in regard to Photius;[45] sustained with dignity the anxiety and grief occasioned him by the kidnapping and subsequent murder of his wife and daughter by Eleutherius, the second son of the treacherous and unscrupulous Arsenius; and protested with vigor the Eastern plan for the annexation of Bulgaria to the diocese of Constantinople.[46] John VIII (872-882), a tired old man, mustered all his strength to preserve the prestige of his pontificate. He crowned Charles the Bald Holy Roman emperor as his strongest aid against the Saracens; he made the promise—not to meddle in Bulgarian affairs—the condition of his recognition of Photius, who after the death of Ignatius had been legitimately elected patriarch of Constantinople; he accepted Swatopluk of Moravia and his people under his ecclesiastical governance as Nicholas had accepted Boris and the Bulgarians; and he gave the imperial crown grudgingly

[43] *Decretales Pseudo-Isidorianae et Capitula Angilramni* (ed. Hinschius, Leipzig, 1863). J. Haller, *Nikolaus I und Pseudo-Isidor* (1936).
[44] LP, II, 151-172.
[45] *Sacrosancta Concilia* (ed. Labbé and Cossart, Paris, 1671), VIII, 1224-1228.
[46] Mansi, XVI, ii.

and of necessity to the incompetent Charles the Fat as an act of diplomatic desperation. Yet with it all he kept Italy and the church from political peril during his lifetime.[47] Only after his death did the papacy sink into the abyss of feudal anarchy which already had engulfed most of Western Europe.

History has rightly ascribed to Nicholas I the accolade "Great." Both Adrian's and John's pontificates were a continuation of his, the reaping of the fruits from seed he had already wisely sown. When his harvest had been gathered, there was nothing to grow in its place. All the papal trees were barren, cumbersome burdens on ecclesiastical soil, itself already depleted by spiritual erosion and moral waste.

V. Theology and Philosophy

The debacle which plunged Western society into the Dark Ages was preceded by productive years of scholarship and doctrinal development. These, begun as we have seen during the reign of Charlemagne, continued throughout the reigns of his son and grandsons. They were, chronologically speaking, simultaneous with the institutional history we have just described, though their geographical locale was not Rome and its ecclesiastical principality in Italy as one might expect, but the domain of the Franks in the northwest at the court of kings, in the cathedral schools of metropolitans, and in the secluded fastnesses of monasteries.

The inner circle of brilliant minds which made the ninth century in Western Europe a renaissance of learning and creative thought were the scholars of Corbie Abbey (Corbia near Amiens), presided over by Adalhard and Wala. They included such intellectual worthies as Paschasius Radbertus (ca. 785-ca. 860), the daring and adventurous thinker, Ratramnus (d. 868), and lesser lights like Warin, Hildemann, and Odo of Beauvais. There were also Rabanus Maurus (776 or 784-856) from Boniface's Fulda Monastery and later of the archiepiscopal see of Mainz; the luckless and persecuted Gotteschalk (ca. 805-ca. 868), who began his career at Fulda, who continued it at Orbais in the diocese of Soissons, and who ended it in the dark and damp cells of Hincmar's prison; Hincmar (ca. 806-882) himself, first a monk of St. Denis, then archbishop of Rheims, who for nearly half a century was the theological as well as the ecclesiastical arbiter of the church in France; also the anonymous author of the *Pseudo-Isidorian*, or *False*, *Decretals*; and John Scotus Eriugena (ca. 810-ca. 877), a queer genius who hailed from Ireland or some part of Britain but who displayed his philosophical talent at the court of Charles the Bald in France. The biographical data of these men are of minor consideration. They live in history not for their deeds but for their ideas. What they thought and that to which they gave literary expression

[47] CMH, III, 453-454.

produced some of the chief doctrines and major ecclesiastical practices of the Middle Ages.

The *False*, or *Pseudo-Isidorian*, *Decretals*, for example, were not merely documents on ecclesiastical polity and administration. Like the writings of Cyprian in the third century or Augustine's *City of God* in the fifth, they set forth an ecclesiology in terms of theology. The practices advocated were likewise justified by reasons of faith. The priestly caste, so these documents contend, is exalted above the laity, for Christ is head of the church, and his sovereign powers on earth have been deputed to priests who act in his stead. Consequently priests cannot be judged by civil courts, for it is the prerogative of the Savior alone to pass judgment upon his chosen ones. Now priests are joined to their bishops as the church as a whole is joined to Christ; and the bishops in turn are joined to the pope, who is Christ's chief agent on earth. Thus through him bishops open and shut the gates of heaven; they are to be obeyed by the people of their diocese even if they are in error. However, they are themselves subject to the final judgment of the pope, for God wills that all churches shall adhere to a single belief and shall observe the same practices. They are ordered to be ruled by the Roman church.

The **Virgin Mary**, whom the popular mind had long venerated, adored, and even worshiped, became increasingly among the Carolingian theologians the object of doctrinal reflection. Ratramnus said that Christ had entered the world through the process of birth, yet his birth, like his conception, was miraculous, for Mary's virginity was preserved before, in the process of, and after the birth of Jesus.[48] Paschasius Radbertus went a step further. In reply to a question put to him by some nuns, he said that Mary herself had been spared the curse of original sin, that she had remained pure and without fault in her mother's womb, and that we dare not assume Christ was born according to the common laws of nature.[49] This **doctrine of the parturition of the Virgin Mary** was the theological opinion of Paschasius Radbertus. It was not translated at this time by the church into dogma.

The issue of **predestination** (in the dual sense of foreordination to damnation as well as to salvation) was renewed in the name of Augustine by the unhappy Gotteschalk, a monk not by choice but by parental coercion. To while away the weary hours of monastic seclusion he studied the works of the Bishop of Hippo so assiduously and publicized his findings so enthusiastically that the church regretted the fact that she had ever given him vows and repudiated his theological interpretation by consigning him to prison. The point of Gotteschalk's contention was not aridly scholastic. It was in reality deeply religious, as surely rooted in the soil of faith as Augustine's had been before him and Luther's and Calvin's was to be later. The point at issue to

[48] MPL, CXXI, 11-346.
[49] *De partu virginis*, in MPL, CXX, 1365-1386.

him was God's unchangeableness. The creator of the ends of the earth by his own free will elects men to be saved or rejects them, which is tantamount to their damnation. This predestination cannot be based on foreknowledge, which is merely its accompaniment, for to base it on the foreknowledge of man's behavior would make God himself mutable and governed by temporal affairs.[50]

Gotteschalk at first had some supporters, including Ratramnus of Corbie; but they really did not understand him any better than his assailants. They indeed spoke of a double predestination, but they based God's predetermination of some men to damnation solely on his foreknowledge of their evil deeds which would deserve punishment.[51] Gotteschalk's assailants, on the other hand, including Hincmar of Rheims, thought of predestination only in the positive sense of election to life. God wishes all men to be saved, they claimed, since Christ died on the cross for all men; the fact that some men perish is entirely the result of their own evil deeds.[52] At the two synods of Quierzy (849) and Valence (855) the theological position of Gotteschalk's opponents was ratified as the position of the church.[53] This was the only thing that could have been done if the sacramental system was to be maintained and good works were to have real value in the minds of the people.

More enduring and therefore more significant than the predestination issue was the doctrinal debate over the **nature of the Eucharist.** Paschasius Radbertus wrote in 831 and released thirteen years later (844) a treatise On the Body and Blood of the Lord, in which he contended that the bread and wine of the Eucharist are in reality the body and blood of Jesus Christ—in fact, the very same flesh that was born of the Virgin Mary, that was hanged on the cross, and that arose the third day from the dead; and, likewise, the very same blood that dripped from the nail prints in his hands and gushed from the wound in his side. Admittedly this flesh and this blood lack visible appearance, but they enter the communicant's own body through his mouth and digestive organs, so that he actually feeds upon and is nourished by his Savior.[54] Thus the doctrine of transubstantiation was clearly implied in, though not explained by, Radbertus' teaching.

Ratramnus, in opposition, taught that the bread and wine of the Eucharist are not changed materially in the least; they remain precisely what they were before consecration—bread and wine. It is this material that we eat and digest. Yet to the faithful the act of eating it has a higher, heavenly meaning, so that what is done outwardly has an inward spiritual significance. In the

---

[50] MPL, CXXI, 345 ff.

[51] MPL, CXII, 1554-1562.

[52] Rabanus Maurus' letters to Noting, Eberard, and Hincmar, in MPL, CXII, 1507-1576. Hincmar's De praedestinatione Dei et libero arbitrio, in MPL, CXXV, 65-474.

[53] K. Hefele, Conciliengeschichte (1873-90), IV, 195.

[54] Liber de corpore et sanguine domini, in MPL, CXX, 1267-1350.

soul of the true believer bread and wine become body and blood, and he feeds on Christ by faith in his heart with thanksgiving.[55]

Rabanus Maurus tried to mediate between the two extremes. He contended that, though it is obviously impossible to identify the sacramental elements with the historical Jesus, still the true and real body of Christ is created anew for the communicants by the power of God and fed to them from the altar by the priests. Thus, as the communicant eats, his own flesh is restored to immortality and incorruption by that of his Savior.[56]

Both Rabanus Maurus and Ratramnus were too ethereal for this sensuous age. Hincmar gave vent to the real feelings of the people and expressed the temper of the times: "If what we see is not what we believe, then what we see is only a model, a mere memorial of the body and blood of Christ." [57] The future development of the doctrine of the Eucharist, at least during the Middle Ages, was entirely along the materialistic lines so clearly delineated by Paschasius Radbertus.

Philosophy, in contrast to theology, was during this period almost entirely divorced from the temper of the times. It might be thought of as an anachronism, either as the prolongation from antiquity of Plotinus or else the anticipation of Spinoza in modern times.

What speculation there was had originated in the monasteries of Britain and Ireland and had been transplanted to the continent by Charlemagne with the aid of Alcuin of York. Alcuin's successor in the monastery of Saint Martin of Tours, Fredegisus (d. 834), contended on grammatical grounds that since every noun must have its reference in reality, that nothingness and darkness are actually things themselves and not merely the absence of things. Thus the world was created out of something (unformed matter); and souls, already in existence, were given bodies to inhabit.[58]

But the chief champion of this revival of Neoplatonism and the only philosopher of this period whose work has survived was **John Scotus Eriugena.** He bypassed the predestinarianism of Gotteschalk by contending that evil is unreal to God and therefore God could not have predetermined it; while he gave his support to the spiritual interpretation of the Eucharist in opposition to the materialism of Paschasius Radbertus. These issues were incidental to his main concern, and such problems as they posed would solve themselves once his basic thesis was established.

This thesis was that religion is in reality philosophy and philosophy likewise is religion. Consequently to theorize is to philosophize, and there can be no true philosophy apart from the data of revelation. Reason must use

[55] *De corpore et sanguine domini*, MPL, CXXI, 103-170.
[56] MPL, CXII, 1510 ff.
[57] Hincmar, *De praedestinatione*, ch. 13, in MPL, CXXV, 122-25.
[58] MPL, CIV, 159-174.

these data by incorporating them into the acts of daily living. The method reason employs in handling the data of revelation is dialectics, which operates always in two fundamental ways. One is that of analysis: it starts with individuals, and by proper classification into groups and groups into more inclusive groups it moves up the scale to the basic unity which includes all. The second is that of division: it starts with the basic unity and moves down from genera to species to individuals within species. This method of dialectics Eriugena interprets to be the operation of nature itself—namely, the movement from unity to diversity, and then the ingathering of the diverse elements into their basic unity again.

He is careful to distinguish between being and nature. Being is anything that is precisely as it is—not what it might become. Nature is all that is; it includes potentiality as well as actuality; it is nonbeing as well as being. Nonbeing can be delineated in five different ways: (1) the perfection which escapes our senses and our understanding; (2) what a particular being is not in terms of what, in the scale of being, is either superior or inferior to it; (3) potential being which has not yet been actualized; (4) corruptible things in relation to their incorruptible types; (5) man as the image of God in comparison to man as he is corrupted by sin.

Consequently nature as the totality of being and nonbeing exemplifies four basic divisions: (1) that which creates, yet is not created (God); (2) that which is created yet itself creates (divine ideas); (3) that which is created, yet does not create (temporal things); (4) that which is uncreated and uncreating (God). Since the first and last divisions are synonymous with each other, and since the second and third are linked inextricably together by their createdness, we really have two basic divisions—God and his creatures.

Creation (the universe) expresses itself in three orders: (1) the invisible and corporeal (angels), (2) visible and corporeal yet embodying the incorporeal and spiritual (man), (3) material. God constantly participates in all these levels and therefore is present in them. Finally, all is drawn back up again into God, who has no more been diminished through his giving of himself than has the sun through manifesting itself in its innumerable sunbeams.

The same love which caused the expression of being in all its hierarchies will recall it to perfect unity in the divine life. The plurality of being in disharmony; disagreement, and consequent suffering was due to man's fall. Reunion takes place in four stages: (1) death, release from the bondage and corruption of materiality, a return to the point of beginning when the soul entered the temporal order; (2) resurrection, reconstituting of the body, abolition of the sexes, perfection of body as it was before the fall; (3) reunion of body with its proper soul, giving it life, sense, reason and pure thought; (4) absorption of the body by the soul and its return to its cause or idea.

101

Everything, good and bad, will be thus deified and absorbed in the One. Yet the good will have added to this the beatific vision, the loss of pure idea in the contemplation of God. Each will be in God and yet himself too as idea in mind or a sunbeam in the sun.[59]

Eriugena was too sublime for his contemporaries to understand, much less to refute. He was an anachronism in the ninth century. Consequently he had no influence; his light was not diffused and did not dissipate in the slightest the darkness which was enveloping Western Europe; and, when philosophy re-emerged, it began at another point.[60]

VI. Alfred the Great

The spark which ignited on the continent of Europe what we have called the Carolingian Renaissance was itself struck on the hard flint of **British monastic learning** and **the erudition of the Irish establishments.** The Venerable Bede had been more than an historian. Around him had gathered scholars, so that his name had been associated with a whole school of disciples who continued his labors after he had gone. Out of that school of the North had come Alcuin of York himself.

Yet Britain fell on evil days. The Angles, the Saxons, and the Jutes, who had conquered the Celts, fell themselves a prey to the marauding **Scandinavians,** savage pliers of the sea, who harassed their coasts, pillaged their towns, and carried their children away into slavery. Three ships were seen afloat the waves in 787. They were Danish, and before they returned to their native harbors across the North Sea they had slain good English folk and left their marks of terror on West Saxon shores. Two years later another savage expedition wasted Northumberland, pillaged Lindesfarne abbey itself, and even slew its monks. By the ninth century marauders had become invaders; infrequent raids had been translated into steady conquests; and the land and people in more places than we care to enumerate had been vanquished.

These wars had a terrible effect on culture, civilization, and even religion. The great schools of the North, York itself, which had trained Alcuin, were extinct. Ignorance, superstition, fear were rampant. Monks and priests forgot the ideal of their calling and disgraced themselves in a manner similar to what we shall observe later in the Roman pornocracy.

Into such conditions came young Alfred. On the death of his brother Ethelred, who had been mortally wounded in battle with the Danes at

---

[59] MPL, CXXII, 441-1022. Cf. E. Gilson, *History of Christian Philosophy in the Middle Ages* (N. Y., 1955), pp. 113-28.

[60] For this entire period, A.D. 756-882, see Mourret, *op. cit.* III, 283-469, and E. Amann, *L'époque carolingienne* (1947), in *Histoire de l'église depuis les origines jusqu'à nos jours,* Vol. VI.

Merton (871), Alfred ascended the throne of Wessex. He was only twenty-three at the time. He ruled twenty-eight years, dying at the age of fifty-two, in 899.

Alfred is remembered for two superlative accomplishments—the one, military and political: he drove off the Danes and solidified the English people around his West Saxon crown, thereby creating a nation; the other, cultural and spiritual: he revived learning and scholarship among his people, reformed the morals of the clergy, restored ecclesiastical organization and discipline, and set religion again on the line of development it had got from Augustine and Theodore.

Though untutored and ignorant when he came to the throne, also emotionally handicapped, for he was an epileptic, he nonetheless became a scholar as well as a statesman, translating into Anglo-Saxon Boethius' *Consolation of Philosophy*, Gregory's *Pastoral Care*, Orosius' *Universal History*, and Bede's *Ecclesiastical History of England*. His greatest literary bequest was the *Anglo-Saxon Chronicle*, which he caused to be preserved and which gives us so much information about these times.

Alfred is considered by the British as their greatest Saxon ruler. He is the only sovereign in English history to have been accorded the title great. Though his field of operation was small, his theater of action diminutive and restricted compared with Charlemagne's, still in many ways he was a greater man than his continental counterpart. Not only did he encourage learning, but he became learned himself. Like Charlemagne, he inspired a Renaissance. What Charlemagne was on the continent at the beginning of this period, Alfred was in England at its close.[61]

[61] Asser of St. David, *Annals of the Reign of Alfred the Great* (ed. Stevenson, Oxford, 1904). *Anglo-Saxon Chronicle* (ed. Plummer, Oxford, 1892-1899), 2 vols., sub annis 853-901. *The Whole Works of King Alfred* (ed. J. A. Giles, London, 1858), 2 vols.

Chapter Five

Byzantine Christianity in the Eighth
and Ninth Centuries
(717-886)

THE EAST WAS AHEAD OF THE WEST IN ITS INTELLECTUAL AND HUMANISTIC accomplishments.

The word "renaissance," which is appropriate to describe the cultural aspects of the reign of Charlemagne, his son, and grandsons, is inappropriate as a designation of similar and more brilliant feats of the mind and spirit of the inhabitants of the Eastern empire during this same epoch of history. "Renaissance" by definition is a revival or renewal. The civilization of antiquity in the West had been wrecked by the barbarian invasions. Learning, where it had been able to exist at all, had existed in separated, almost isolated, establishments. Scholarship of necessity had been preservative rather than creative. Consequently the emergence of so many cathedral and monastic schools, the royal patronage of education, and the new productive scholarship which ensued was a renaissance in the nice meaning of the word, for the talents of the mind which had lain dormant for so long a time were revived to such a degree that the contour of Western society was for a brief time lifted and improved.

The continuity with the past had not been broken in the East. Though the eighth and ninth (especially the ninth) centuries were brilliant periods in Eastern history, they were not a renaissance. Nothing had been revived or renewed. These achievements were a part of a long series, a continuation, perhaps even development, of what had preceded them. There were never any Middle Ages in the East.

This does not preclude the fact that some epochs were more creative and famous than others. Such a great period in Eastern history was the 150 years when the empire was under the sway of the Isaurian dynasty (717-867). The accomplishments of this period laid the foundation for the power and prosperity of the Macedonian dynasty (867-1025), which followed it and during which the Eastern empire reached its political zenith.

What Charlemagne became to Christendom in the West—its political protector and even dictator—the Byzantine emperors had always been in the East. Indeed, the vigor and successful energy which the Frankish royal house exercised in the Latin church in the latter half of the eighth and first decade of the ninth century, Leo the Isaurian had already exercised in the Greek church in the first half of the eighth century, and his successors continued to exercise such strength long after Charlemagne's empire had become ineffective. The Eastern emperors always considered the church their patrimony, and many looked upon themselves as arbiters, perhaps even teachers and doctors, of theology.

I. The Controversy over Icons

Consequently the Iconoclastic Controversy was initiated by the emperor himself, Leo III (717-741); was continued by his son, Constantine V (741-775), and grandson, Leo IV (775-780); and was finally settled by an ecumenical conclave (787), though not without the aid, even the guiding influence, of the imperial throne. What earlier rulers had done, later rulers felt constrained to undo, and this within the same family, so that the Isaurians both precipitated and settled the Iconoclastic controversy.

Iconoclasm, which stands now in our general vocabulary as a synonym for destruction, the shattering of what is established to make room for something new and different, referred originally to a very particular and definite movement in the church—namely the effort to abolish images, pictures, or any material likeness of any sacred personage or event. The iconoclasts were the destroyers of icons, or sacred images. In contrast, there were those who found icons useful, even essential, to worship and who therefore venerated them. The iconoclasts looked on these people as iconolaters, worshipers of images.

Though 'the adoption of images in Christian worship and their use in beautifying cathedrals and churches had been a long and questionable process, a struggle upstream against the strong current of Judaic and primitive Christian conviction, nonetheless the acceptance of them was by now practically universal, and a church or religious house of any type without them in the East or West was unusual indeed. A custom which primitive Christianity looked upon as idolatry was common practice in the eighth century. Consequently what in ancient times had been an innovation was considered during this period as tradition. Those who opposed the use of images were looked upon as dangerous innovators who would destroy the established worship of Christendom. The icons were loved by the people.

It is difficult to understand what Leo III hoped to gain, either personally for himself or politically for his empire, when in 725 he issued his famous edict forbidding the use of images and ordering their discontinuance in services of worship and even their destruction. Immediately he was opposed by Germanus, patriarch of Constantinople (715-730).[1] Rebellions arose in Greece; in Italy the people were united under the leadership of the pope, and the hold of Constantinople through the Exarchate of Ravenna over the Italians was forever broken. Before the reform could really get under way Germanus had to be desposed. He was succeeded by his own chaplain, Anastasius (730-754), who supported the position of Leo III.

Perhaps it is difficult to understand the political motive behind Leo's action simply because politics did not influence his decision at all. Perhaps he did what he did for religious reasons entirely. As a soldier on the eastern frontier of the empire, he had come in contact with the Mohammedans and no doubt had been impressed with this feature of their worship. Constantine, bishop of Nacolia, persuaded him that the veneration of images is a stupid superstition and a flagrant violation of the second commandment.[2] In vain did the patriarch Germanus try to convince him that images show forth the Incarnation of the Son of God, that they are in keeping with and enforce upon the minds of the people our Lord's real humanity in contrast to the heresy of the Docetics.[3] Leo accepted iconoclasm as a divine mission he was ordained by God to perform. He was determined to eradicate image worship from his empire.

His opponents certainly rallied the masses to their support. A mob of housewives with no more than kitchen implements, mops, and brooms, beat to death some soldiers as they were removing their favorite icons from a public building. Leo's opponents likewise solicited the support of theologians and scholars. The most notable of these was **John Damascene,** who as his name implied resided in Damascus, an Arab city, and so was entirely out of the punitive reach of the emperor. On this subject he was free to write anything he pleased. In 727 he released his *First Oration in Defence of the Images,* followed two years later by the *Second Oration,* which added little or nothing to the first.[4] He made the point that the second commandment was abrogated by the Incarnation, in which God himself took the image of man. The iconoclasts kept of course the Holy Table of the Lord's Supper and such symbols as the cross. If, argued John, you adore the cross, why cannot you adore the figure of him who was hanged thereon? Images, like the Bible itself or even for that matter like the human nature of the Son of God, are material substances dedicated and sanctified to redemptive ends. The veneration we pay to images is not to the object as such but rather to the original they represent. After all, this veneration, even to the original when it is saint or prophet, is not more than honor and respect; it is not worship, which belongs only to God.

[1] Germanus, Ep. IV, MPG, XCVIII, 163-188.
[2] MPG, XCVIII, 144, 145.
[3] Germanus, Ep. II, MPG, XCVIII, 157 C.
[4] MPG, XCIVIII, 1231-1420.

John's position elicited immediate approval from the Eastern monks, from many bishops, and from the West, which showed no disposition whatever to support iconoclasm. Pope Gregory III (731-741) repudiated, as had his predecessor Pope Gregory II (715-731), the action of the emperor by convening at Rome a synod of ninety-three bishops, which excommunicated all who destroyed or defiled the images of Christ and his saints (731).[5] The scholars of Charlemagne's court and Charlemagne himself defended the use of images, but their writings, including even those of Hincmar of Rheims, add nothing to the classic statement of John Damascene. The West, as we have seen already, was now busy with its own affairs. Rome turned away from Constantinople and sought aid and protection from the Franks. The disagreement between the pope and Byzantine emperor on this subject but widened the gulf between Latin and Greek Catholicism. The West more readily than the East could accept the Damascene's verdict that the use of images "is a question for synods and not for emperors. It is not the right of emperors to legislate for the Church." [6]

What began as a genuinely religious concern of the emperor and a few strong-minded Eastern bishops soon became **the most vital of all political issues.** Since church and state were one, this was bound to happen; it was too good a cause not to be used by politicians who, then as now, exploited any opportunity to further their own appointed goals. There were four impressive political parties, which argued their tenets in the Hippodrome and on occasions rioted and stirred up all manner of social discontent. They were the Blues, the Greens, the Reds, and the Whites, the two most important of which were the Blues and the Greens. These latter two vied with each other for the control of the government by trying to win to their opinions the imperial house. Whenever the emperor was supported by one of these two parties, he inevitably had the other as his opponent. During the Trinitarian controversy and later during the debates on the Person and Nature of Christ, the Greens had generally tended to favor heretical opinions, while the Blues had been the strong supporters of orthodoxy. Now there developed over the issue of images among the population of Constantinople a party of die-hard extremists, unyielding conservatives, guided by the monks and ascetics, who saw in iconoclasm the destruction of Christianity itself; and also a party of liberals, radical in their desire for change, directed by the emperor, who looked on the use of images as crass superstition and idolatry; and fortunately a party of moderates, who desired the peace and unity of the church above all else.

Constantine V pursued the iconoclastic goal with more zeal, theological understanding, and fanatical cruelty than his father. Against the opinions of

---

[5] Mansi, XII, 299-300.
[6] πρὸς τοὺς διαβάλλοντας τὰς ἁγίας εικόνας, I, 27; II, 12.

the Damascene, his synod of 340 bishops, presided over by Theodosius of Ephesus and Pastillas of Perge (753), declared that pictures of Christ must be adjudged either Nestorian or Monophysite, since Nestorianism has an altogether human Jesus as the carrier of the Divine Christ, since Monophysitism by abrogating our Lord's humanity altogether likens Divinity itself to the form of a man. To use pictures of Christ cannot be orthodox, since it is impossible to represent divinity. The Holy Eucharist is the only proper representation of our Lord.[7] Even monasticism was proscribed, and monasteries were converted into barracks for the use of soldiers. The patriarch of Constantinople, Constantine II (754-766), who had been a monk, was forced to denounce his former state in his own church. Leo IV continued the iconoclastic policies of his father and grandfather.

However, when Leo IV died, his widow, the Empress Irene, who ruled as regent in the name of her ten-year-old son, Constantine VI (780-797), reversed the policies of the first three Isaurian emperors. She was a Greek, an accomplished lady from Athens, and a devout image worshiper. She deposed the iconoclastic patriarch, Paul IV (780-784), and put in his place a layman who was her secretary of state, Tarasius (784-806). He renewed relations with Rome, asked Pope Adrian I (772-795) for a council to declare invalid the iconoclastic canons of Constantine V, and to restore images to their proper place in Christendom.[8] It was under her regency that the famous Second Council of Nicaea (787) was held. It addressed itself successfully to the issue.[9] Yet even this conclave, in which both East and West were represented, did not settle immediately the controversy. It had now become too much a political issue for so quick a settlement. The army, for example, was largely iconoclastic.

Irene followed her theological victory with a victory over her son in the sphere of politics. Constantine VI, who became of age in 790, grew restive under the domination of his mother. He divorced his wife and married another. This antagonized the conservative group within the church, and it was to the conservatives that Irene owed her strength and favor.[10] This bold, ambitious woman went to the extremes of deposing her own son, having his eyes gouged out in the very bedroom in which she had borne him and given him suck, and proclaimed herself the first female empress in Roman history (797).[11] Her reign was short-lived. Within five years she was overthrown by one of her ministers, Nicephorus.

This period of anarchy (802-820) inaugurated a new period of iconoclasm

---

[7] Mansi, XIII, 251 A, 255 A, 256 D, 258 B, 259 B, 261-3, 283 C.
[8] Ibid., 985 B, 986 A.
[9] Ibid., XII, 951 ff.
[10] Theophanes, Chronographia (Bonn, 1839-41), I, 719.
[11] Ibid., 721-726.

(813-842). Though Nicephorus I (802-811) did not feel strongly one way or the other on the religious merits of this issue, he felt he must mildly support iconoclasm simply as a means of maintaining the supremacy of the state over the church. His patriarch, also named Nicephorus (806-815), gave him no trouble and defended him against the fanatical attacks of the monks, led by Theodore, abbot of the Studium (759-826). Indeed, Theodore appealed to Rome over the heads both of his patriarch and of his emperor. Michael I (811-813), who was defeated by the Bulgars and resigned, and Leo V, called the Armenian (813-820), pursued the policies of Nicephorus I, though without his mildness and judicious temper. When the Patriarch Nicephorus refused to reopen the issue of images, since he maintained it had been already settled by the Second Council of Nicaea, Leo V deposed him, set up the iconoclast, Theodotas I (815-821) in his stead, and called a synod which repudiated Second Nicaea and reaffirmed the findings of Constantine V's synod. Even the Isaurian, Michael II, known as the Stammerer (820-829), who regained the throne on the murder of Leo V, was an iconoclast, as was his son, Theophilus (829-842). Michael was tolerant enough to let people believe what they liked in private and use the icons to their heart's content, so long as they did not use them in public worship. Theophilus was a persecutor, having been persuaded to violence by his friend, John the Grammarian, whom he made patriarch as John VII (832-842). During his reign bishops were beaten, monks were tortured and jailed, and the use of images was a crime punished by exile.

It was left to a second woman, Theophilus' widow, **Theodora**, who ruled as regent for her three-year-old son, **to restore the images and to give peace to the church.** The abolition of images was no longer a religious concern. It was now entirely political, whereas the piety of the people demanded their use. Consequently, when Theodora, whose own piety required them, threw the weight of imperial politics in support of image worship, peace was restored to the church, and the controversy ended. She convoked a synod which deposed John VII and elevated Methodius I (842-846) in his stead. This synod likewise reaffirmed the findings and pronouncements of the Second Council of Nicaea.[12]

The Second Council of Nicaea proclaimed that images are right, proper, even necessary in worship. Its definition was that holy icons are to receive "greeting and reverential respect" but not worship in the sense of complete "adoration, which belongs only to God." This is the position of both Eastern and Western Catholicism to this day, for both parts of the church recognize the Second Council of Nicaea as the seventh ecumenical council.

This doctrine satisfied the same requirement as the doctrine of the localized

---

[12] Mansi, XIV, 787-788. L. Bréhier, La Querelle des images, VIII-IX siècles (1904), K. Schwarzlose, Des Bilderstreit (1890).

presence of Christ's body in the mass. The people in the East and the West demanded the tangible, the material, the sensible as an accompaniment of the purely spiritual.

II. John Damascene

This era of the Iconoclastic disputes produced **the greatest medieval theologian of the Eastern church.** Indeed John Damascene occupies a unique position among the Greek masters. Though he was not creative and daringly original like Origen, neither was he subjected to the indictment of heresy which the speculative genius of the Alexandrine scholar brought upon his works. Though he was not the proponent of any major dogma like that of the Trinity or the Person of Christ as were Athanasius, the Cappadocian Fathers, and Cyril of Alexandria, neither was his work as particularized and specialized as theirs. He achieved a comprehensiveness and theological breadth denied to his predecessors.

It is difficult to find his exact counterpart among the Western doctors. Augustine of course comes naturally to mind, for he summarized the dogmatic thinking of antiquity and laid the foundation of subsequent medieval developments. Yet Augustine was far more penetrating and deep than John. Even as he summarized, he was creative, so that old dogmas stood in a new light of understanding and meant far more than they had ever meant before, once they had been touched by his genius. Though John was not of his stature, it would be equally unfair to the Damascene to liken him to Pope Gregory I. John was no cheap popularizer; he at least understood what he was commenting upon; his interpretations became in many instances normative for Greek thought. There has been no significant development in Eastern theology since John Damascene.

The force of John's interpretative talents is felt in the areas of Christology and anthropology. In these particulars at least, he deserves to be accounted creative and deep.

First, as regards **Christology,** the important element is John's method. Once this is apprehended, the movement from one interpretative detail to the next is mechanical, like the application of a given laboratory technique in chemistry to many different substances. His method subsists in an undeviating concern for distinction; it is throughout scholastic, insisting upon nice categories and lines of demarcation and separation. Philosophically, John, in contrast to most of his Greek antecedents, is Aristotelian rather than Platonic, so that substance expressing form takes precedence in his thinking over essences and their many imperfect individuations. Since, according to Aristotle, the genus embraces all individuals, John teaches that the Second Person of the Trinity at the Incarnation did not unite himself with a particular man but rather took on himself the whole of human nature so that

110

he particularized it by assuming it. Consequently, since this human nature possessed no real hypostasis of its own—no principle of individuation, no person—it received its hypostasis, its person this is to say, from the Second Person of the Trinity. Yet at the same time it was so genuinely itself that it possessed independence in that Person to such a degree that it was not without hypostasis. This union in Jesus Christ of the divine and human was enhypostatic. Thus the hypostasis, or person, belongs to each nature, the human and the divine, and wholly to both of them. Therefore, though the humanity and divinity of Jesus are separated from each other, they interchange and share characteristics. The flesh, then, of Jesus actually became God; and the divinity of the Second Person of the Trinity actually became man and shared man's worst humiliation. The one hypostasis of Christ Jesus died for our redemption on the cross and rose again as our Savior on the third day. Nevertheless, since each nature remained separate and distinct from the other, the divinity was not affected in its substance by the humanity, even on the cross. As sunshine playing on a tree is uninjured as the axe cuts through it and fells the tree to the ground, even so the divine nature of our Lord was not mutilated or impaired as his human form writhed in pain and as his person expired on the cross. In the judgment of many, John interprets Chalcedonian Christology in such a way that Christ appears more like a "centaur" or "satyr" than a man. Some would claim that, after all, dreaded Apollinarianism has come because of him to be orthodoxy for the Eastern church.

Secondly, as regards **anthropology**, John shifts Eastern theological thinking away from the predeterminism of Augustine and stresses the significance of human freedom to a degree that the Synod of Orange (529) and the other post-Gregorian interpretations in the West were never quite able to reach. The image of God in man, which is a union of the visible (material) and invisible (spiritual), consists in power of thought and freedom of will. The spiritual part of man in his original state equipped him to love and praise his divine benefactor, while the material or corporeal part made it possible for him to be hurt, to suffer, and finally to be disciplined to the full appreciation of his spiritual privilege. What man was originally in his innocence was entirely a gift of grace. Yet, since nothing that is done under compulsion is really a virtue, and since corporeality of necessity lends even to the soul a streak of the irrational, genuine freedom was likewise a part of man's original endowment, so that he alone could submit himself to the rational and the good or to the irrational and the evil. Now man had from the start sufficient grace at his disposal to remain in the true state of his creation—rational and good. The forces of irrationality and evil were dormant in his nature. Yet freedom enabled man on his own to become unnatural—to be irrational and evil instead of rational and good. Tempted by the Devil, who had already

111

fallen, man deliberately turned away from the invisible and spiritual to the visible and material. He turned his concern entirely on himself rather than on God. Hence, since he was no longer good enough to live forever, death came as a result of his transgression. Christ had to come to him to teach him, to show him what he had been in his innocent state, to convince him of the superiority of the spiritual over the corporeal, and to offer him again the gracious benefit of immortality which he had been created to enjoy. What man does with this offer is his own decision. It is not proper to attribute everything to 'divine providence, "for that which is in our power is not the affair of providence but of our own free will."

The determinative element in man's salvation is for the Greek man's own freedom, in a way that has never been true for the Latin. This is due in no small measure to the convincing interpretative skill of the Damascene.

The particulars of John's view of creation are interesting but less important. God, out of his overflowing goodness, not willing to spend all eternity in contemplating himself, made everything that was made. Man was put in paradise—a place in the East, higher than the whole earth. Here he was to live in his body, while in his spirit he was to think about and to live with God. He was forbidden to eat of the Tree of Knowledge, because knowledge is bad for the imperfect, and makes him who has it prone to consider and contemplate himself. Adam was guilty of error in worrying over his body; if he had thought only about God, he would never have observed whether he was naked or not. Humanity was originally created only male. Woman was formed when God foresaw the fall, so that humanity might continue in spite of death. Sexual intercourse was a necessary result of sin.

The remainder of John's work is a summary of the findings of antiquity. In keeping with the thinking of the Areopagite, he teaches that God is above human comprehension, yet God has implanted in each of us the conviction that he is, and the natural order itself is a reflection of his majesty and power. He has revealed himself partially in the prophets, poets, and seers of the Old Testament and fully in Jesus Christ. Therefore we know that he is uncreated, unchangeable, uncompounded, incorporeal, impalpable, eternal, invisible, infinite, almighty, omniscient, omnipresent, and in control of all things which he has made. John follows the Cappadocian Fathers in thinking of God as existing in three separate and distinct individuals, all equal: Father, Son, and Holy Spirit. John's work on the Trinity as a whole and on each of the persons in it is altogether traditional according to the post-Athanasian interpretation. He adds nothing new whatever.

John's inordinate notion of the significance of man's freedom and of the creature's own responsibility for his salvation led him to lay little stress on the work of Christ. Consequently, apart from the restoration of immortality, we find no clear and definite theory of redemption. Christ is looked upon more as a teacher and exemplar inciting us to virtue than he is as a redeemer. But this treatment is in keeping with the East, where the person of Christ attracts the chief theological attention and little interest is shown in his redemptive work.

True to the temper of the East, John stresses the holy mysteries. He plainly and unequivocally teaches that in the Eucharist bread and wine are supernaturally translated into the body and blood of Jesus; and since divinity assumes completely human form it is proper to say they become the body and blood of God. God always uses plain, earthly objects like water in baptism and bread and wine in the Eucharist to convey his grace. This he does because the unusual is frightening and repellent to man. In the Eucharistic feast, they share Christ's body together, the communicants become one body in him. Thus it is very important that the wicked be excluded from this sacred act of worship.

He asserts the perpetual virginity of Mary, the Mother of God. He defines faith as right belief, thus equating error in dogma with immorality and sin. Once the dogmas of the church are accepted, faith becomes to the true worshiper the confidence that his prayers will be answered and God's promises will be fulfilled in his life. Good works always are essential to faith, as faith is also necessary if good works are to prove effective.

John is content to leave unnoticed either any elaborate and exhaustive treatment of salvation or any doctrine of the church. The penitential systems of the West are of no concern to him. His work exemplifies no inner unity of development or underlying motif of form, though externally it is well organized and systematic. But according to Eastern concerns and considerations no more was necessary, since each dogma is itself revelation and stands on divine authority as final truth about the subject or issue with which it deals.[13]

Very little is known about the life behind this doctrinal work. We do not even know the date of John's birth—somewhere between 670 and the end of the seventh century in the city of Damascus, probably around 676. He died well before the Second Council of Nicaea (787) met and gave dogmatic sanction to his doctrine in regard to images. Probably his death occurred around 745 or 750.

His family was a well-to-do Christian family in the Moslem city of Damascus. His father had a state position with the Saracenic government which John inherited. John was evidently a faithful minister, respected and trusted until Leo the Isaurian forged his signature to a plan to betray Damascus to the Christian armies of the empire. Leo sent this to John's sovereign, to wreak vengeance on John for his opposition to Leo's iconoclasm. John was

[13] MPG, Vols. XCIV-XCVI. Especially, De Fide Orthodoxa (Eng. trans. S. D. F. Salmond, 1899), XCIV, 790-1228.

tried as a traitor to the Saracenic state. The Moslem ruler had John's right hand cut off in punishment. The legend is that an angel of God restored it to prove to the infidel John's innocence.

John became a monk at the old Lavra of St. Sabas in Palestine. At first his superior forbade him to engage in any literary labors, but God in a dream showed this monk his mistake, and John was permitted to spend the rest of his days in study and writing. He was an exegete, theologian, poet, and hymnodist—no doubt the most learned man of his day and perhaps the most influential teacher in the Greek church.[14] Subsequent Eastern theology has been little more than commentaries on and interpretations of his work. If not in the quality of his thought, nonetheless in the position and outreach of his literary work, he deserves the appellative, "the Thomas Aquinas of the East."

III. Paulicianism and Monasticism

During the troubled years of Iconoclasm, the church in the East was likewise annoyed by a competing religion called Paulicianism.

The **origin** of this ideology is dubious. Its enemies claimed it sprang from Manichaeism, and its first proponents were a woman, Callinice, and her two sons, Paul and John. But the Paulicians themselves held as their founder a teacher named Constantine, who emerged in Kibossa, in Armenia Prima, shortly after the middle of the seventh century. They condemned Callinice and her offspring, together with Manes, founder of Manichaeism, as heretics. They boasted a history of persecution and suffering for their faith which they said was that of the apostle Paul himself. Constantine, who took the name of Sylvanus, was, after a ministry of twenty-seven years, put to death. So also was his successor, Simeon, who took the name of Titus, and whom the government brought to the stake under Justinian II in 690.

The Paulicians entered clearly into **history** as a religious body to be reckoned with when their leader Genesius was examined concerning his faith in Constantinople during the reign of Leo the Isaurian. He was so pleased evidently with what he saw and heard in the capital and especially with the iconoclasm of the government that he accommodated himself to the tenets of the church and became a devout communicant. Not so his followers. Genesius was immediately opposed by his younger brother, Theodore, who in the name of the Holy Spirit took over the leadership of the movement.

The great leader of the Paulicians was Sergius, called Tychicus, who began his public career one year after the opening of the ninth century. His followers spread rapidly in the eastern part of Asia Minor where the apostle Paul had so

[14] Vita by Michael of Antioch, trans. into Greek by John of Jerusalem, see M. Jugie, *La vie de Saint Jean Damascène*, in *Echos d' Orient* (Paris, 39 vols., 1897-1942), XXIII, 137-161). *Dictionnaire de théologie catholique* (Paris, 1903-1950), VIII, 663-751.

successfully prosecuted his early missions. The emperor Nicephorus, for example, had in his youth been greatly influenced by them and therefore encouraged them and facilitated their work. However, his successors dealt harshly with them. Leo the Armenian persecuted them vigorously, and Theodora bathed them in a bath of blood.

Consequently they were driven out of the empire into Saracenic territory. Their chief residences were Colossae and Laodicea. From these cities they formed military bands and carried on almost constantly guerrilla warfare with the soldiers of the empire. They remained vital and active, though not always united (Paulicianism itself divided into doctrinally differing groups, e.g., Thondrakians of Armenia), long after this period; and we find them in Thrace as troops of the empire, among the Bulgarians, and in Mesopotamia and Armenia.

The theological tenets of Paulicianism were: (1) God revealed himself in Christ for the first time. Consequently the God of the Old Testament is a Demiurge, from whose creative work man must be freed. (2) The church, together with its New Testament scripture, is the creation of the true God, revealed in Christ. All that went before it is null and void. (3) Mary is not recognized as the Mother of God, (4) neither is the Eucharist looked upon as the body and blood of the Savior. (5) Baptism is repudiated, for only Christ himself can be the cleansing water of eternal life. (6) A Docetic view of the Incarnation is maintained, for there was no real union between Divinity and human flesh.

Paulicianism likewise repudiated the entire hierarchical organization of the church, returning to the simple New Testament structure of apostolic preaching, with the knowledge of the New Testament for all the people.

With the Thondrakians, Gnostic and ancient Armenian and Persian ideas were infused with original Paulician tenets including the secret knowledge and rites of the initiates. Their chief propaganda was that prayers and devotions cannot avail for the forgiveness of sins. Only a good life, presented in terms of rigid asceticism, is pleasing to God.

Here in the Paulicians we have an example of another protesting and independent movement, witnessing again to the fact that the organic and doctrinal unity of Christendom was never a complete reality.[15]

Neither the Iconoclastic controversy nor Paulicianism impaired to any great extent the Eastern church or precluded the over-all effectiveness of Greek Christianity. This was due in no small degree to monasticism—the zeal, the determination, and the persistence of the monks. They were the real traditionalists, the unbending backbone of the conservative party. They bent the mind of the people to their opinions; they gave the impetus,

[15] MPG, CIV, 1239-1350; CXXX, 1189-1244; *Dictionnaire de theologie catholique*, XII (Pt. 1), 56-62.

fanatical though at times it was, to carry church and state alike to their own appointed ends. Though more than once outlawed, as we have seen, by the iconoclastic imperial government and actually disestablished as an ecclesiastical society and institution, monasticism in the end proved more durable than the dynasty which opposed it, and the monks enjoyed the popularity and favor of the people in a way that could only excite the envy and the hate of the emperors. Since the imperial government could not destroy or even subdue monasticism, it had in the end to embrace its cause if that government was itself to survive.

Monasticism was no different from that which we saw a century earlier under the Heraclians. Though it was deployed in separate and independent organizations, its theological interest was single and it could at will induce paralysis in the life of the empire.

The personification of the temper and spirit of monasticism during this period was Theodore of Studium. He taught that the monastic institution as such belongs as much to the holy mysteries of Christianity as baptism, the Eucharist, ordination, and the burial of the dead. It is itself sacramental like prayer, preaching, and the understanding of the Word of God. Monasticism means the disavowal of all earthly property as well as temporal desires. It fulfills itself in self-denying love—absolute renunciation.

Theodore came from the nobility. He was born in Constantinople in 759, ordained by the Patriarch Tarasius, and came to public recognition and prominence when he denounced Constantine VI for his divorce and second marriage and demanded that he be excluded from the communion of the faithful. Scourging, torture, exile, and imprisonment in a Thessalonian jail could not break down his opposition. Theodore was raised to honor by Irene, who depended on his support to hold her throne. Nicephorus and Leo the Armenian both found him an implacable foe. Once Nicephorus imprisoned him and all his monks. He died in exile on the island of St. Trypho in 826.

What John Damascene was theologically to the cause of the use of icons, Theodore of Studium was politically. His influence as leader of the monks was as effective as any other factor in the triumph of image worship.

Likewise, he was effective in the reform of monasticism itself. He found Studium dilapidated and its monks either indifferent or disconsolate. He gave his establishment a new rule based on the welfare of the community of monks rather than the desires of the individual. He insisted on education—knowledge of the church Fathers and Holy Scriptures—as well as skill in copying manuscripts. He developed the art of composing hymns.

What he insisted on for others he demonstrated himself. He was a gifted scholar and writer. He wrote theological treatises in support of images. He taught truth through his sermons, the collections of which are called the

Large and *Small Catechisms.* He wrote acrostics, epigrams, and hymns, and his voluminous letters afford excellent information concerning his times. In his organizational skill he was to Eastern monasticism what Benedict of Nursia had been to Western.[16]

It is interesting to observe during this period that monasteries, as well as churches and oratories, sought independence of bishops; they wanted where possible to be answerable only to the patriarch. Germanus, for example, had to rule that only those establishments were answerable directly to his patriarchate which had the patriarchal cross, with the date of their foundation behind the altar. Others must be answerable to the bishops in whose diocese they were.

No new double monasteries (for men and women together) could be established, though those already in existence were continued.

The spirit and disposition of the church-at-large was the piety of the monasteries—an exaggerated mysticism with stress upon the adoration of the saints, especially Mary the Mother of God. The hymns of the time, some written by John Damascene and his adoptive brother, Cosmas of Manjuma, are grandiloquent and given over to literary imagery. The legends of the saints are crowded with miracles; many saints end their lives by ascending into heaven.

IV. The Missions in Central Europe

The vitality of Eastern Christianity during this period was exemplified in the prosecution of the work of evangelism and the expansion of Christianity into new territories through the missionary enterprise. Already we have seen the concern which the church showed under the Heraclian dynasty for the Slavic peoples west and north of the empire. This registered itself especially in work among mercenary soldiers of this race in the imperial army. No doubt motives were mixed, since the government thought Christianity would be a means of cohesion and a device for inculcating loyalty to the state for which the troops were paid to fight. Then too the effects of this work reached beyond them to the peoples whence they came and who were almost constantly in arms against the empire. The ultimate aim of the government of course was conquest. What better way was there than peaceful conquest through Christianity?

The two chief instances of the expansion of Eastern Christianity into new territory during this period came in the ninth century. They were, chronologically at least, an aftermath of the Iconoclastic controversy and would appear therefore as the recovery of the church from the illness of heresy and division into the vigor of unity and expanding strength. There is little reason

---

[16] MPG, Vol. XCIX. *Orientalia Christiana* (1926) VI, 1-87. Krumbacher, *op. cit.,* 147-151, 712-715.

however for finding in them more than a shift of ecclesiastical concern or the normal response the church should always make to the needs of pagan peoples set down before its very doors. The Moravians, for example, solicited the gospel from the Greeks; and the Bulgarians showed some disposition toward Christian instruction before official missionary efforts were made in their behalf.

The Moravian mission is the first of these two instances of the expansion of Eastern Christianity to command our attention.

Moravia in the ninth century occupied the territory between Bavaria and the Drina River and the Danube and Styre River in southern Poland. It was the territory which today comprises Czechoslovakia. The race that lived in this country was Slavic and had not adjusted itself to the subjugation of Charlemagne or the Christianity he had exported to it in the Latin language. Consequently in 863 its King Ratislav petitioned the Greek emperor Michael the Drunkard (842-867) to send Christian missionaries to instruct his people.

Michael immediately took counsel with his advisors to know what to do. He was apprised that there was a military official in Thessalonica, Leon by name, who had two sons, Methodius (825-885) and Constantine (827-869), who knew Slavic and were therefore prepared in advance for the mission. Methodius and Constantine were summoned to Constantinople, given their assignment, and sent on their way with the blessings of church and empire.

The two brothers began to teach and to preach in the language of the people. They set up a school to train native sons for the priesthood. They spoke the service in the vernacular. This led them to the invention of the Slavic alphabet in order that they might put in writing the Bible and the liturgy. Here then is an example of what came to be the policy of the Eastern church—namely, to organize on racial and national lines leading in the end to a federation of autonomous churches with different usages but one doctrine and spirit. The Roman practice by contrast was to insist on the same liturgical language and customs.

Since Roman influence had already been exerted by missionaries from the see of Salzburg, to which Charlemagne had assigned ecclesiastical responsibility for this territory, there soon developed a clash of policies and interests. As a result, Methodius and Constantine sought recognition of their mission by Rome. This act illustrates again the unity of Christendom during this period and the desire of all the churches, in the East as well as the West, to stand in good graces with Rome.

In 868 the two brothers arrived in Rome, were consecrated to the episcopate by Pope Adrian II (867-872), and were authorized by him as a concession to the remarkable success of their mission, to carry on in Slavic. Constantine, who now called himself Cyril, died in Rome, February, 869; but Methodius returned to Moravia, became archbishop of Sirmium in Pannonia, and continued the work of organization and evangelism.

However, his episcopate was not a peaceful one. Disputes continued to arise concerning the use of Latin or Slavic. He was summoned again to Rome under Pope John VIII (872-882) ten years after his first visit. That pontiff modified the original concession to this extent. He said the service must first be read in Latin and then translated into Slavic.[17]

Evidently Christianity entered **Bohemia** from Moravia. Though fourteen Bohemian chiefs had been baptized at Regensburg on January 1, 845, their ruler had not. The Bohemian ruler Duke Borzivoi visited the Moravian king, Swatopluk, in 871. While Swatopluk and Methodius sat together at a raised table, Borzivoi and his retinue were served on the floor as heathens. Borzivoi asked Methodius what he might hope to gain by becoming a Christian. The Bishop replied, "A place higher than all kings and princes." He was baptized, together with his retinue of thirty; and his baptism was followed by his wife's. Later his house was raised above the Moravian, for in the tenth century Moravia ceased to exist as an independent state and became a part of Bohemia.

The latter years of Methodius' life were embittered by ecclesiastical strife. He died April 6, 885; later his disciples were expelled from the country; Latin took the place of Slavic in the churches; and his entire mission was absorbed into the organization of the Roman church.

The names of these two brothers, Constantine (Cyril) and Methodius, are outstanding in the history of missions. The former was philosopher, linguist, philologist, and disseminator of civilization. The latter was an organizer, administrator, and evangelist. Either might have been famous in his rights independent of the other, but together they performed a mission the luster of which shines down the ages to the present day.[18]

The 'second instance of the expansion of Eastern Christianity is the **Bulgarian mission.** Indeed, what took place in Moravia was duplicated, with variations of course, in **Bulgaria.** At practically the same time the Moravian Ratislav made his request to Michael the Drunkard, this same emperor received a petition from King Boris of Bulgaria asking for missionaries.

Boris had been prepared for the reception of Christianity by previous happenings in his realm just as Ratislav had been in his. Back in 813, after a successful military campaign against the empire, the Bulgarians had carried

---

[17] MPL, CXXVI, 904-905.
[18] CMH, IV, 215-229. Vita Constantini (original text and Latin translation by Ernst Dümmler and Franz Miklosich in *Denkschriften der kaiserlichen Akademie der Wissenchaften, philosophisch-historische Classe,* XIX, Vienna, 1870 pp. 205-248) and Vita Methodii (Latin translation by Ernst Dümmler in *Archiv fur Künde österreichischer Geschichts—Quellen,* XIII, Vienna, 1854, pp. 156-163). C. H. Robinson, *The Conversion of Europe* (N. Y., 1917), pp. 292-301.

as captives from Adrianople a number of Christians including a bishop. These captives had in the course of their witness won many Bulgarians to Christianity, though they themselves practically all were martyred.

Nearly fifty years later another captive, Constantine Cypharas, a monk from Constantinople, began to preach to his captors the gospel of Christ. In 861, as Constantine Cypharas was released to his native land, the king's own sister came home from Constantinople where she had been a hostage. She brought back with her a warm personal faith, having been baptized in Constantinople and made a member of the church. An enemy of the king's paganism was now a member of his own household. She persuaded her brother, in the midst of a dire famine, to solicit help for the relief of his people from the Christian God. The famine came to an end. Legend has it that she sent for a skillful Christian artist to decorate the royal palace. Instead of painting hunting scenes and scenes of battle, this artist adorned the walls with a picture of the Last Judgment. Evidently what he painted was so realistic that it frightened Boris into a decision. At least he accepted Christian baptism in 864 or 865.

Beneath these pious outward expressions there was undoubtedly a not altogether disinterested political concern. Boris, who had made an alliance with the Franks of the West, had, while his own armies were out of the country, sustained an invasion from the Eastern empire; and the price he had to pay for the return of his kingdom was the renunciation of his Western alliance and the acceptance of Christianity. He received a mission from the Patriarch Photius and was himself baptized with Emperor Michael the Drunkard as his godfather.

Yet astuteness in politics was not limited to the imperial party. Boris had ambitions of his own, made overtures to Rome, received apostolic emissaries from the Latin church, and might well have placed himself and his people in the Latin fold had the papacy constituted his realm into an archdiocese with a metropolitan comparable in prestige and power to the patriarchs of the East. Rome was too jealous of its own primacy for this to happen. It was therefore from the more territorially minded Greeks that the concession was obtained. In 870, in keeping with the sentiment of the Eighth Ecumenical Council, the Patriarch Ignatius of Constantinople consecrated a Bulgar archbishop of Bulgaria and sent him with ten bishops and many priests to his new see.

The rapid spread of Christianity among the Bulgarians came however when the missionaries of Methodius were expelled from Bohemia. Many of these missionaries were sold as slaves to the Venetian tradesmen, auctioned in the market places of Europe, bought by Eastern Christians, and sent back in their original role as preachers to the Bulgars. The Methodian methods of translating the ecclesiastical services into the native tongue was employed among the Bulgars, and the spread of the Slavic language kept apace with the spread of Christianity.

Boris himself surrendered his crown to his older son Vladimir and, after having educated his younger son Simeon as a monk, embraced the monastic habit himself. His peaceful devotions were violently interrupted when Vladimir apostatized and the nation with him. Thus Boris put aside the habits of the monk for his former vocation as a warrior, soundly defeated Vladimir in battle, had him blinded and imprisoned, placed the monk Simeon on the throne in his stead, and returned to his monastery to take up again the uninterrupted course of his prayers.

Bulgaria rather than Moravia or Bohemia became the center of Slavic Christianity. Simeon carried on with statesmanlike vigor the work of his father Boris, and, when he died in 927, the Bulgarian nation was in its entirety at least nominally Christian.[19]

V. The Photian Schisms and Byzantine Culture

The missionary and evangelistic labors of Greek Christianity were punctuated by two ugly schisms, and preparations were thereby made in both Constantinople and Rome for the final breach between Eastern and Western Catholicism.

Photius, the protagonist of these events, is a controversial figure whose immediate intentions, over-all purpose, basic motives, and individual deeds are all subject to diverse and contrary interpretations. Not only has he occasioned the undying disapproval of the West, in the archives of which so many of the records of his deeds are preserved, but also he has evoked abiding enmity among parties and groups within his own patriarchate. Much of the literature of the East is prejudicial to his character and cause.

But whatever attitude historians may take toward Photius, at one point they all agree. He was a man of extraordinary native talents; his industry and determination were Herculean; he succeeded amazingly well either for good or for ill; and the contour of Christendom was never the same again after he had wrought his mighty deeds. He seems to have had one of the most winsome, engaging, and captivating personalities in all history so that to come directly under the personal influence of the man was, as with the song of the Sirens, to be lured from the course of one's own convictions and to be imprisoned forever by the power of persuasion in the domain of his own aims and ends. The same emperor, for example, who deposed and exiled him called him back to live in the royal palace and to educate his own children and restored him to his patriarchal throne. Most of the very clergy who denounced his patriarchal advent as a brazen usurpation of unwarranted

[19] CMH, IV, 230-239. M. Spinka, *A History of Christianity in the Balkans* (Chicago, 1933), pp. 17-56.

power, when deprived of his leadership, either pined away into indifference or else became recalcitrant and divisive, so that vigor and unity were restored in the East only by recalling him to his see.

We know little of Photius' upbringing and early life. He was born into a Constantinopolitan family of affluence somewhere between the years 815 and 820. His parents had suffered misfortunes and outrages from the iconoclastic emperors and had died early, "adorned," to use Photius' own expression, "with the martyr's crown." Both they and he had been excommunicated by an iconoclastic synod. Yet the punishment of the government did not extend to the confiscation of wealth, for Photius seems never to have been deprived of material goods and the usual comforts which favor the life of the rich. While still a boy he began to collect a library; and before he had reached man's estate he had read and mastered the contents of both pagan and Christian antiquity and had acquired a breadth of understanding and learning which most scholars spend a lifetime and yet fail to acquire. He was without doubt the greatest intellect of his age; and, together with John Damascene, he was the chief luminary of Greek Christianity since the patristic period. He was the last doctor the influence of whose learning was to reach across the bleak and barren years of the Crusades and to provide the substance as well as the inspiration for the Greek heralds of the Renaissance before the fall of Constantinople.

Indeed, his *Bibliotheca* or *Myriobiblon*, which is a digest of 280 books which he had read and studied, is all that has remained of the works of such worthies as Ctesias, Memnon, Conan, and the lost writings of Diodorus Siculus and Arrian. It was prepared at the suggestion of the Patriarch Tarasius (784-806); contains within its pages writings by historians, grammarians, and physicists as well as by theologians and philosophers; and reviews the acts of ecclesiastical councils, martyrs, and saints. Fortunately less known works are treated in preference to better known works which evidently even in Photius' time were more readily accessible. Poetry alone is conspicuous by its absence. The *Bibliotheca* is not an anthology; it is a critique as well as a summary and stands as a classic in the field of literary criticism.[20]

This amazing man prepared for his most devoted disciple and truest friend, Amphilocius of Cyzicus, a book consisting of answers, mostly biblical and theological, to questions which Amphilocius had posed. This book, called the *Amphilocia*, was an effort to resolve the ambiguities of the Bible. Photius drew heavily on the Greek Fathers down even to John Damascene in his own century. Consequently the work is hardly original, yet it displays great industry on the part of its author and exemplifies, with the *Bibliotheca*, his amazing erudition.[21] In addition to these two works, he wrote sermons and

[20] *Bibliotheca* (ed. I. Bekker, Berlin, 1824), 2 vols.
[21] *Amphilocia* (ed. C. Oeconomus, Athens, 1858).

addresses, portions of which have been preserved, showing us the grandiloquence, floridity, and imaginative figures of speech of Eastern oratory in the ninth century; Bible commentaries; a lexicon, which is amazingly well done; poetry, consisting of three odes on Basil of Caesarea and nine on Christ; and innumerable letters, which are the best expressions of his real personality and character. Like those of Basil of Caesarea in the fourth century, these are incomparable sources for understanding the events of the times.[22]

Most important of all his writings are his **polemical works**, since they reveal the tenor of theological speculation in the East, discriminate between orthodoxy and heresy, and delineate the basic doctrinal difference between Greek and Latin Christianity. His dissertation entitled *On the Sprouting of the Manichaeans*,[23] for example, which is in four books, is perhaps the best source material for the origin and history of the Paulicians and certainly provides, on dogmatic and Biblical grounds, orthodoxy's best refutation of their doctrines. *Precise Conclusions and Proof*, in contrast, is a contribution to Eastern polity and discipline, since it is Photius' justification of his own patriarchal position against the attacks of Rome and draws heavily on conciliar documents and other historical material. Like the *Amphilocia*, it is in the form of questions and answers. It is interesting to observe its method: it never once refers directly to Photius' own case; indirectly by allusion and innuendo it accomplishes its purpose; hence its usefulness extends beyond its local setting to the whole field of Eastern episcopal supervision.[24]

Photius' theological masterpiece is his *Treatise on the Mystagogia of the Holy Spirit*, which gives with precision and finality the Eastern church's understanding of the procession of the Holy Spirit. It is a revival within the bounds of orthodoxy of the Origenistic concept of the primacy, if not the superiority, of the Father in the Trinity. To say that the Holy Spirit proceeds from the Father and the Son is an absurdity, since the outflow of all divine life is from the Father, while the other two Persons are recipients, not bestowers, of the life they express. The Holy Spirit is not therefore the product of the Son; to believe that He is destroys the unity of the Trinity and introduces gradations and degrees within the Godhead. Photius cites the authority of the Fathers, Western as well as Eastern, showing that the filioque of the Latin creed is a heretical innovation.[25]

In addition to his intellectual talents, which gave him very early a professorial chair in the Imperial School in Constantinople, Photius had "good connections" and soon was made, first, Captain of the Imperial Guard and then, First Secretary of State in the Eastern government. He was the brother-

[22] MPG, CI, 1189-1254.
[23] MPG, CII, 15 ff.
[24] MPG, CIV, 1219 ff.
[25] Edited by Hergenröther, Regensburg, 1857. MPG, CII, 279-400.

in-law of Bardas, uncle to the Emperor Michael the Drunkard and the real power behind the throne. Indeed it was as a strategic move on the part of Bardas to consolidate his gains and maintain himself in control of the government that Photius was raised to the patriarchal throne.

Political conditions in Constantinople at this time were very similar to what they had been after the overthrow of Irene a generation before. The dowager queen Theodora had given place to her son Michael III. She did this grudgingly, of necessity, and with the determination still to rule as his chief counsellor. She had been superseded, however, in his confidence by her own brother Bardas, who to gain support for himself favored the political party which she had opposed. Consequently in this instance, as previously, the internal affairs of the imperial household were the common property of the people, constituting the planks in the platforms of the chief political parties and furnishing issues for debate and struggle between the reactionaries and radicals, the conservatives and liberals, the extremists and moderates.

Theodora, in her efforts permanently to establish the use of images, had thrown herself into the arms of the extremists who were headed by the monks of Studium, and had raised to the Constantinopolitan patriarchate an ascetic called Ignatius, who himself was the son of a previous emperor and therefore combined the autocracy of royalty with the fanaticism of monkish piety and devotion. He had at best a mean understanding of people, was incapable of adjusting to a revolutionary situation, and always set an abstract principle above the effects it might have upon the welfare of those who had been entrusted to his pastoral keep. His own elevation to the patriarchate had been compromised by the manner in which it had been effected. Theodora had appointed him before nominations had been submitted to her by a synod. At his enthronement, he had shown his inflexible attitude by saying to Gregory Asbestos, bishop of Syracuse, who was a member of the opposition party of Moderates and a prominent candidate himself for the Constantinopolitan see, that he did not want to see him present at the ceremonies. Whereupon the fiery Asbestos had flung down the lighted taper he was holding, stalked out of the church, and exclaimed that instead of being blessed with a pastor the church had been put into the hands of a wolf.

Consequently, when the Moderates regained control of the government with the ousting of Theodora and the promotion of Bardas, Ignatius was altogether incapable of making the adjustment. In a nation accustomed to the unity of state and church, with the church as an auxiliary to the crown and the emperor as supreme head of ecclesiastical as well as civil affairs, an ambiguous situation was created by Ignatius' recalcitrance. His stubborn refusal to step into line set the church at odds with the crown. It amounted to insubordination—viewed through Eastern eyes—to little less than treason itself.

Ignatius refused publicly at the Feast of Epiphany (858) to administer Holy Communion to Bardas on purely moral grounds: he had divorced his wife to marry his daughter-in-law. Later in the autumn of that same year he flatly declined the request of the government to force the veil on Theodora and her daughters and thereby to remove them from public affairs. More than this it seemed to Michael III and Bardas that in almost every issue the patriarch sided with the opposition party and compromised the effectiveness of the government by impairing its unity at the very point where it counted most, for the church through its pulpit naturally exerted the greatest influence on the people. Rumor had it that Ignatius condoned, if he did not actually further, plots to overthow the government and recall Theodora to the purple in the place of her son.

The situation was impossible from the viewpoint of the government. Whether Ignatius saw this himself, and voluntarily resigned, is disputable. If he did, he soon was persuaded by the Studite monks and other extremists to change his mind, to behave as if he had not resigned but had been expelled, to harass his successor with fiery denunciation as a robber, usurper, and an adulterer of the purity of the church, and to feign the role of a persecuted saint and martyr for Christ's sake. The year 858 witnessed **Ignatius' deposition** and exile. He was examined by a synod which declared his election invalid. **Photius was elected** in his stead, and the opposition party was replaced in the chief sees by safer episcopal occupants. As a result Photius wrote the usual letters of enthronement which he sent to the other patriarchs including of course the bishop of Rome. With this letter to the pope went another from the emperor explaining the situation from his point of view and asking the pope to send legates to a synod in Constantinople to clear up entirely the Iconoclastic controversy.

Nicholas I received the Eastern emissaries in Rome in 860 and read the two epistles. He was impressed no doubt with Photius' seeming humility, for his letter protested the fact that he had been elected against his will and had assumed the patriarchal obligations from a sense of duty. He wrote out his doctrine which the pope found entirely orthodox. The emperor's letter however raised suspicions. It stated first that Ignatius had been deposed by a synod for neglect of his flock; later it referred to the fact that he had resigned.

Nicholas I, unconcerned really about the Iconoclastic matter, immediately dispatched as his emissaries Rhodoaldus, bishop of Portus, and Zacharias, bishop of Anagni, with orders to thoroughly investigate the situation and to report their findings directly to him so that he personally could adjudicate the whole affair. He wrote the emperor that he should have been consulted before any decision was reached, since Rome alone has the final say in the deposition of any bishop. Yet he implied he would be willing to accept matters as they now stood if Constantinople would surrender to his control the sees of Thessalonica and Syracuse and restore to his patrimony Calabria and all of Sicily. He censured Photius for accepting the patriarchate when he was only a layman but encouraged him to use his good offices in promoting his request of the emperor.

It is one thing to instruct a legate. It is quite another to arrange the conditions so that the legate's instructions can be carried out. Rhodoaldus of Portus and Zacharias of Anagni met stubborn resistance on the part of the Greeks to Latin interference with their patriarchate, and only a genuine concern for the unity of the church and a desire not to offend the papacy persuaded the Greeks to open the issue at all. To gain this concession the legates had to accede to a conciliar judgment on the validity of Photius' election. This was contrary to Nicholas' explicit instructions, for he reserved the right of final decision to himself. The synod of 861 decided in Photius' favor. The legates, whether bribed, coerced, or convinced, accepted its verdict and approved its proceedings. Neither Thessalonica nor Sicily was given to Rome. And the pope felt he had been both out-maneuvered and cheated throughout. Really, if he had only known it, he had lost a few territorial concessions but at the same time had achieved a vantage point from which to gain and to sustain an ultimate victory, for the Greeks had conceded to his see primacy of power in ecumenical supervision as well as of honor and prestige. Photius for example had not dared in his own name to refuse the concessions Nicholas had demanded of him, but had simply replied that this issue was not his to decide: it rested entirely with the emperor.

Nicholas was too perturbed over his present losses, which were evident enough, to realize the far-reaching possibilities which the situation afforded. He acted hastily, and therefore precipitated a crisis which neither he nor his opponents could resolve. In March, 862, he espoused the cause of Ignatius, denounced Photius, and issued his verdict, not only to the emperor and his patriarch, but also to Eastern Catholicism at large through letters to Alexandria, Antioch, and Jerusalem.

His declaration at first occasioned the worst of all humiliations—namely, that of indifference and neglect. Photius and the emperor ignored his verdict. In the meantime he received in Rome the monk Theognostus of Constantinople and got from him his first reports from the Ignatian side of the controversy. This led to Nicholas' excommunication of Photius at an official council in April, 863. Then, two years after his decision, August, 865, the emperor wrote him that his efforts in behalf of Ignatius were in vain and that he must reverse his decision and adjust himself to the situation as he found it. The emperor referred to Latin, the language of the West, as "a barbarian and

Scythian tongue," and the pope replied in kind by saying if the emperor felt that way about the speech of Rome it was ridiculous for him to style himself Roman emperor

The outcome was unfortunately more than a fit of temper: the pope anathematized Photius, and Photius excommunicated him (867). Schism undoubtedly would have been the outcome had not political events intervened to reverse the ecclesiastical situation. Basil of Macedonia first murdered Bardas (866) and then Michael III (867) and assumed the purple himself. Therefore, with his accession as Basil I (867-886), the forces which had elevated Photius to the patriarchate were entirely dissipated, and Ignatius was recalled from disgrace and exile to the honor of his patriarchal throne.

Yet the papacy found in Ignatius as great a barrier to its designs as it had found in Photius. He ignored the demands of Rome for the restoration of Bulgaria and the withdrawal of all Eastern missionaries from that kingdom. All in all his second patriarchate was ineffectual (867-878). Before he died Photius had been restored to favor (876), had become the emperor's chief ecclesiastical advisor, and in all but name was the real head of the Eastern church. Indeed, during Ignatius' last illness, Photius made regular pastoral calls on him, affording us a supreme illustration either of his power of persuasion which captured at last as friend his worst and most implacable enemy or else Ignatius' willingness to forgive which made him love the person who had inflicted on him his most abject misery. When Ignatius died on October 23, 878, Photius was reinstated only three days later, October 26, as patriarch.

The first schism, which had been outwardly healed by the deposition of Photius in 867, was followed by a second schism between Rome and Constantinople. To be sure, Pope John VIII (872-882) showed a gracious disposition to temporize. Not only was he willing to recognize Photius' legitimacy but also to drop the filioque from the creed and return to the purity of the Nicene usage. But then in return he expected from Constantinople the recognition of his supremacy and also the return of what Nicholas had claimed as the papal patrimony and ecclesiastical jurisdiction over Bulgaria as well. This was a hard bargain, and it clearly shows the subservience of doctrine to temporal success in the policies of Rome in this peculiar period of papal history. Evidently the East was even less willing to comply with Western demands than it had been in 867. Nonetheless, a synod which met in Constantinople from November, 879, to March, 880, confirmed Photius' reinstatement in his see, and the papal legates concurred. John VIII was as indignant at the proceedings as Nicholas had been at those of 861, and he disavowed the action of his legates in unconditionally accepting the elevation of Photius to the patriarchate. Whether or not he actually anathematized Photius and thus refused to have communion with his adherents (long assumed by historians) is now a disputed issue. If he did, Photius ignored it, and for eight years ruled as if he were pope himself. After all, the Eighth Ecumenical Council (869-870) had affirmed the autonomy of the see of Constantinople and had raised its patriarch to an equality with the pope of Rome.[26]

Photius' fall was in no wise connected with the West at all. In fact it was directly the result of politics, though as we have seen in the East political matters were generally always religious concerns as well. Basil's emotional balance had been disturbed by the death of his favorite son, Constantine; and Photius became chief minister of state as well as patriarch. For seven years, 879-886, he ruled in the East as an autocrat and like the Hasmoneans in Judea, created a theocratic state. He was accused of plotting to succeed Basil as emperor in name as well as fact. Whether this was true or not, we cannot say: certainly Basil's son and successor, Leo VI (886-912), believed it. Consequently **Photius was deposed,** forced to resign, and exiled in 886. Five years later (891) **he died** in a monastery, closing his career as he had begun it in study and meditation.

The two Photian schisms, if schisms they can be properly called, were more than the result of conflicts between strong personalities. They were the normal expressions in history of the variance of two opposite spirits— Western ecclesiastical autocracy with its insistence on unity, conformity, and subservience to Rome, and Eastern imperialism, where the church was an arm of the state and where the political and social aspirations of the people always reflected themselves in their worship. These differences were more political and social than doctrinal. After Photius, the break between East and West was inevitable.

Though the chief **luminaries** of the eighth and ninth centuries in the East were John Damascene and Photius, together with Theodore of Studium, there were others as well, who though less gifted and prominent, did their part in helping to make this era the brilliant period that it was in Byzantine history.

Like the preceding era it produced no histories, but a number of chronicles, written by Theophanes the Confessor, George Syncellus, Nicephorus, patriarch of Constantinople,[27] and the monk George Hamartolus. These provided abundant data out of which later histories were made. John the Grammarian, himself patriarch of Constantinople, made a profound impression because of the scope and variety of his learning; while Leo the Mathematician bridged the gulf separating Greek and Arab culture enabling each to influence the other. The greatest poetess in Byzantine history, Kaisa, lived and sang during

---

[26] J. Hergenröther, *Photius, sein Leben, seine Schriften, und das griechische Schisma* (Regensburg, 1867-1869), 3 vols. F. Dvornik, *The Photian Schism* (Cambridge, 1948).
[27] MPG, C, 41-160, 169-1068.

this period. She almost became the bride of Emperor Theophilus. She was selected as a candidate for his favor together with other beautiful women over the empire. As she stood in line with the rest, Theophilus paused before her and was about to hand her the golden apple—the token of his choice. But her wit and boldness in response to one of his questions turned him away, and he chose Theodora in her stead. The romance of *Barlaam and Josaphat*,[28] probably written by John Damascene, delighted the people of the empire and later, through translation, the people of the West. It was based on the life of Buddha and came from Indian sources.

Art was not as bleak as one might suspect due to the iconoclastic tendencies of many of the emperors. Rather Hellenistic models were revived, and the decorative talents of the Arabs were imitated. A few mosaics in Thessalonica testify to the skill of artists, and scenes from the common life of people adorn the palaces and public buildings instead of the staid religious pictures of earlier days. Unfortunately most of the relics of this period have been destroyed.

The eighth and ninth centuries were preparation for the second golden age of Byzantine civilization which was to succeed them.

[28] Trans. by G. R. Woodward and H. Mattingly, N. Y., 1914.

Chapter Six

The Separation of Eastern and Western Catholicism
(882-1081)

THE YEAR 1054 IS A PIVOTAL YEAR IN THE HISTORY OF CHRISTIANITY.
Until that time the majority of Christians had, despite differences in customs and languages, worshiped together in the same ecclesiastical family. Schisms, though they had occurred, had generally been either local and inconsequential or else, though broad and important, still only temporary. Even the second Photian schism between Rome and Constantinople had been outwardly healed in a matter of months after the deposition of the patriarch. "You did right to excommunicate Photius," [1] had been the Roman pontiff's reply to the Eastern emperor, who had carefully informed him in detail of the reasons for what he had done, showing on both sides, Latin and Greek, the recognition of one Catholic church. Decisions of doctrine and polity had been made jointly through ecumenical councils, called as in the days of Constantine by the Eastern emperors but always deferential to and concurred in by the Roman popes. One Lord had meant in East and West alike, not only one faith and one baptism, but one church as well.

After 1054 things were entirely different. The two bodies of Christendom, which had been drifting apart for so long, now recognized their differences openly, appraised them as important enough to warrant separation, and broke off communion with one another never again to re-establish permanent fellowship. Eastern and Western Catholicism became almost two distinct religions; for though they had both inherited enough from the past to have practically the same doctrine, still their cultic expressions of it were different, and they treated one another like enemies or like heathen in need of conversion to the true faith.

The century and a half immediately prior to the schism was a time of glaring contrast in Eastern and Western history.

[1] Mansi, XVI, 436 D.

In the West it was that period which can be properly styled the Dark Ages —when the lamp of learning flickered and almost went out, when ignorance and superstition were so common that an educated person was looked upon as a curiosity, and when a man's purview was no broader than his landlord's farm and no higher than the stone turrets of his protector's castle. Feudalism was more than a social system. It was a philosophy of life, a culture, even a civilization. The lower classes became serfs—that is, farmers and herdsmen bound to the soil on which they were born. The upper classes became the local nobility or gentry—that is, the lord or knight for whom the serf worked and whose prestige and influence reached as far as his strength and military prowess extended them. The kings to whom the lesser nobility and gentry owed allegiance were no more cosmopolitan than their subjects. Louis the Stammerer, Charles the Fat, and Charles the Simple—as their names imply—personified hesitation, laziness, and incompetence such as mark the breakdown of political stability and the dissolution of the social order.

In the East it was this period in the Middle Ages when the empire reached its zenith. The Macedonian dynasty (867-1025) gave to the Byzantine government a succession of wise and successful rulers, as able perhaps as any others in the entire range of history. The imperial frontiers were extended; travel was constant and commerce thrived; wars in Europe and Asia were won; wealth increased and cities grew; learning and culture adorned the life of the people. The glory of ancient Athens had returned to Constantinople.

The church, Latin and Greek, reflected as in a mirror the conditions and accomplishments of the times.

I. The Pornocracy

The sordid death of Pope John VIII was the portent of the ignominy and tragedy which were to afflict the papacy for almost a century (882-964). His own relatives, coveting his money, administered poison to him and when this did not act fast enough to suit their diabolical ends they beat his head in with a hammer.[2] Though the nice historical use of the term "Pornocracy" applies perhaps only to the sixty years between the elevation of Sergius III (904) and the death of John XII (964), when the occupants of the Roman see were themselves the personification of vice and corruption, the entire eighty-two years were blighted by incompetence and failure; and the papacy was little more than the plaything of the ruthless nobility who controlled it.

The nine years immediately following the death of John VIII saw three popes succeed one another in rapid succession, no one of whom had time enough, even if he had the energy and ability, for any worthwhile undertaking. Martin II (882-884), the first of the three, deserves notice—not for

_____
[2] *Annales Fuldenses,* a. 833, in MGH (1826).

131

anything that he himself accomplished—but simply because his elevation is the first instance in history of the translation of a bishop from another see to the see of Rome. Heretofore the pope had always been chosen from the lower ranks of the Roman clergy.

This triumvirate of failure was followed by the pontificate of **Formosus,** who had been the able papal legate to Bulgaria under Nicholas I and whom Boris had requested to be made his first patriarch.[3] Formosus, by temperament austere and forbidding, was in private life an ascetic but in public life a dangerous schemer, capable of treachery and sedition. He had been degraded and disgraced under John VIII [4] only to have been restored and honored under Martin II, who had destroyed the records of his trial and condemnation. He was the type person who could not take orders from anyone else but had himself to rule. Though he was never known to eat meat or drink wine and was constantly retiring in order to pray, his following consisted of brigands and assassins,[5] and in his ecclesiastical relationships he behaved as if the ends justified the means. Though a man of culture and possessed of both scholarship and understanding, he was too much of a politician to endear himself to his flock as their shepherd. He attempted through more than one council to check the intrusion of the laity into the affairs of the church [6] and to give peace and justice to Europe. But he himself crowned Lambert, duke of Spoleto, Holy Roman Emperor (894), only to repudiate his own choice by crowning Arnulf (896), king of Germany, in his stead. For this treachery he paid, though posthumously, a terrible price. The merciless Agiltrude, mother of the deposed Lambert, had his body exhumed, clothed again in the papal robes, and tried in public court. He was found guilty of treachery; the holy orders conferred by him and the decrees he promulgated were declared null and void; the three fingers he employed to bestow the papal blessing were cut off; his vestments and insignia were stripped from his dead body; and his corpse was dragged through the streets of Rome and thrown into the Tiber.[7] Consequently his five years as Supreme Pontiff (891-896), harassed as they had been by turmoil and dissension, were libeled by political accusers and public opinion as being criminal as well.

There began, wrote Hergenröther, with the death of Formosus "an era of deepest humiliation for the Holy See." [8] The years 896-904 witnessed ten popes on Peter's throne, one of whom ruled but four months, another one month, and still another twenty days. Then, with the advent of Sergius III

[3] LP, II, 185.
[4] MPL, CXXVI, 675-79.
[5] J. Regesta, 3041.
[6] Mansi, XVIII, 122, 126; Flodoard, *Historia Remensis,* IV, 2, in MPL, CXXXV, 267 ff.
[7] Mansi, XVIII, 108, 109, 222-23. J. Regesta, 3481, 3486, 3500, 3501; MPL, CXXXVI, 804; Mabillon, *Museum italicum, seu collectio veterum scriptorum* (1724), II, 86.
[8] J. Hergenröther, *Handbuch der allgemeinen Kirchengeschichte* (1924-1925), II, 202.

(June 9, 904) began the so-called "Pornocracy," when for approximately sixty years the papacy was tied to a woman's apron strings.[9] **Theodora and her two daughters, Theodora the Younger and Marozia,** through their charming and enticing harlotry **controlled Rome** and with it even **the church itself in the West.** These women sold their bodies for positions, titles, land—the stuff out of which power comes and by means of which great influence is exerted. Marozia, more clever if not more corrupt than her mother, numbered among her amorous relationships one with Pope Sergius III, and out of that illicit affair a son was born who later became Pope John XI.[10] Yet the seeds of such profligacy, sown by women who had regard for neither God nor man, grew to their own destruction.

Marozia converted Hadrian's Mausoleum, called the Castle of Sant' Angelo, into a residence for herself. She was called by the populace **Donna Senatrix,** "Madame Senator," and she ruled like an empress; she was finally overthrown by her own son. Indeed, at the very apex of her power, with her offspring John XI on the papal throne, she made her plans to have placed upon her head the imperial crown, thereby receiving recognition as supreme ruler of the West. To facilitate this she married Hugh of Provence, who was one of the claimants to the imperial title and possessed wealth and power. At this juncture her younger son Alberic intervened. He had been publicly insulted by his stepfather. In revenge he expelled Hugh of Provence from Rome, kidnapped and imprisoned his own mother, who soon died under mysterious circumstances, took into custody his half brother, the pope, and became a dictator himself. Though personally Alberic was of finer stuff than his mother and grandmother and though he reigned (932-954) in Rome with benevolence and justice, nonetheless he exercised absolute control over the papacy and at his death bequeathed to the church in the person of his son Octavian the worst legacy it could possibly have received. It seems that all of the vices of this wicked family, with no mitigating virtues whatever, were comprised in the person of the odious Octavian.

Before Alberic's death the clergy and people of Rome had, in solemn conclave in Saint Peter's Basilica, sworn on the demise of the reigning pontiff Agapetus II (946-955) to elect Octavian as his successor. This they did one year after Alberic's death, though Octavian was only sixteen years old at the time. The new pope took the name of **John XII** (955-964), which is the second instance in history of a pontiff's changing his baptismal name to another on the occasion of his enthronement. Yet that practice has persisted ever since, so that it is the invariable custom of a man on his elevation to the papacy to choose a new name.[11]

[9] MGH, *Scriptores,* III, 714.
[10] LP, II, 243.
[11] MGH, *Scriptores,* III, 342.

The pope's new name unfortunately did not designate a new character. As Octavian he had in a drunken orgy made a toast to the devil, and as John he continued to live the devil's life. John attended church only when he had a sacerdotal duty to perform, and his personal conduct, frequently on public display, was a scandal. However, so far as the records show, his pronouncements on matters of faith were faultless, and his moral teachings were a condemnation of everything for which he stood. At least there was one sin the guilt of which he cannot be accused. He did not seek to justify himself.

This young voluptuary, though he controlled to his own ends the Roman nobility about him, soon ran afoul of the rising German royalty in the north. Otto I (936-973), though aggressive and ambitious, was at the same time high-minded and decent; and the thought of a character so depraved as John hypocritically occupying the chief place in Christendom was altogether repugnant to him. Otto accepted coronation as emperor at John's hands (962), but then he insisted on the Carolingian right that no pope should in the future be consecrated without the emperor's consent.[12] No sooner had Otto vacated Rome than John, no more consistent in politics than in his personal life, repudiated his agreement, embraced the cause of Otto's bitterest enemy, Berengarius II, and thereby invited war and pillage from the Germans on Rome itself. Otto assembled a synod November 6, 963, in St. Peter's, heard witnesses who swore on oath to the irregularities of John's conduct, and ordered the pope to appear in person and answer the charges. This John refused to do: "We have learned," he wrote, "that you wish to elect another pope. If you do, we excommunicate you in the name of the Almighty, so that none of you may ordain or celebrate mass." [13] The Council deposed John and elected a layman Leo (Leo VIII) in his place. On February 26, 964, John convoked another synod in the same place and undid what Otto's synod had done.[14] Shortly thereafter, as Otto prepared to attack Rome, John XII died suddenly, probably assassinated by someone he had wronged.[15]

In this era of shame, degradation, and corruption, there shone a shaft of pure light, unblemished by any moral flaw or spiritual defect. Its source was Aquitaine in what is now central France. Though circumscribed and of no great range at first, before the end of the next century this beam was to illumine the whole of Western Europe with its reforming light. This was the **Abbey of Cluny,** founded by Duke William of Aquitaine to the glory of God and the salvation of his own soul. This generous act of piety and consecration took place in September, 909, during the debauchery of the pontificate of Sergius III (904-911). Its greatest abbot, Odo (879-942), was elected by

[12] J. M. Watterich, Pontificum romanorum vitae (1861), I, 52, 53.
[13] J. Regesta, 3696, 3697.
[14] Mansi, XVIII, 471.
[15] C. Baronius, Annales ecclesiastici, a. 964, n. 17. Mourret, op. cit., III, 432-63.

his brethren to preside over them as the successor to its first abbot, Berno, in 927, the very year when Marozia's power and evil influence were at their height. William stipulated that the monks of Cluny should have the right and liberty of electing their abbot according to the *Rule* of Benedict without any outside power interfering with that election. "By God, in God and all his saints, and under the threat of the Last Judgment, I beg and implore," wrote William, "that no secular prince or count or bishop will presume to place over the monks an abbot against their will." [16] This request was respected. Within a short span of time the properties of Cluny increased through gifts and bequests from neighboring lords and noblemen. The great of the earth as well as the humble, mighty warriors as well as peasants, laid down their arms to serve the Prince of Peace in meditation, prayer, and solitude within the walls of this abbey. The outside world sought advice and guidance from the monks. Odo for example settled the dispute between Hugh of Provence and Alberic, made no less than three pastoral visitations to Rome in Alberic's behalf, and became his spiritual confessor.

Yet Cluny was the exception, not the norm, of these times. The Church must have been something more than human to have survived the bestiality and depravity of its leaders and to have emerged from the depths of humiliation and disgrace into which the Roman pontiffs plunged her.

II. The Church Under the Aegis of the Empire

The German Imperial House introduced a new factor into ecclesiastical affairs and served, at first at least, as a salutary corrective to papal abuses. Otto I, though perhaps less than a saint himself, was altogether an admirable man and a dedicated Christian; and he had the good fortune of being married to a saint (Queen Adelaide), of having a saint as his mother (Matilda) and of being counseled by a brother (Bruno) who was a saint also. With the halo of holiness surrounding his own home, it was not likely that Otto would countenance for long the disparity between the religion exemplified in the daily lives of the members of his own family and that practiced by the curia in Rome. Otto II (973-983), though not the man either in character or in strength that his father was, still maintained the same attitude and policy toward the church. His son, the youthful dreamer and adventurer Otto III (983-1002), although he began his reign in his own right when he was only fourteen (994) and ended it before he was twenty-two, nonetheless in that short decade gave to the Medieval church two of its best popes.

The demise of John XII did not throw the papacy immediately into the hands of Otto I. Indeed, Rome's spontaneous reaction to Otto's interference

---

[16] *Recueil des chartres de l'abbaye de Cluny* (ed. Bruel, 1876), I, 124, 125. MPL, CXXXIII, 43-858. J. Regesta, I, 3598-3600, 3603, 3605.

was that of defiance, so that Benedict V (964-965) was elected without the emperor's knowledge or approval. This led Otto to attack Rome, the inhabitants of which surrendered the luckless Benedict to his enemy, who carried him away captive into Germany. Otto, therefore, established his designee Leo VIII in office. On the death of Leo a few months later Otto's own candidate, a cousin of the late John XII in fact, was duly elected and consecrated John XIII (965-972). John's pontificate of seven years, though it accomplished no momentous enterprise, was at least dignified and respectable, so that John earned for himself in death the epitaph of having been in life "a wise and watchful pastor." [17] Benedict VI (973-974), who was elected after a considerable delay, occasioned no doubt by negotiations between Rome and Germany, was pope when Otto I died (May 7, 973). He was the unfortunate victim of an Italian uprising against German imperial domination. Supported by the local party of Crescentius, who tried to revive the Roman dictatorship of Alberic in his own person, a certain Franco had himself enthroned as antipope under the name of Boniface VII. He was so arrogant and overbearing that the people themselves became indignant at him. As he passed through the streets, little children ridiculed him by calling him "Maleface"—"doer of evil," instead of his chosen designation of "Boniface"—"doer of good." [18] In the face of imperial force, Franco fled to Constantinople, carrying the Vatican treasury with him.[19]

Otto I, hailed by subsequent ages as Otto the Great, was not only the real founder of the German nation and one of its greatest rulers, but also, like Charlemagne before him, the strong protector of Christianity and the patron of its institutions and its culture. Though untutored himself and not able to use Latin at all, he followed with pride the literary labors of his brother, Bruno (925-965), who wrote *The Lives of the Saints* and commentaries on the Gospels and the books of Moses. His court sponsored the historical labors of Liutprand (ca. 922-972), whose *Antapodosis* narrates events in Italy since A.D. 888 down through Otto's time and whose *Vita Ottonis* and *Legatio Constantinopolitana*, though of mean quality, still abide as samples of the literary efforts of that day. We have in the writings of Bishop Ratherius (887-974) of Verona lively and odd accounts of the habits and happenings of these times, while in the *Res gestae saxonicae* of Widukind (d. 973) of New Corbie Abbey we receive a history of Saxony from its beginnings. While Otto traveled afar as a warrior and conqueror, fighting his battles in foreign parts, his brother Bruno stayed in Germany settling disputes, giving justice, and scattering alms to the poor with almost prodigal generosity. Empress Adelaide took

[17] LP, II, 254.
[18] LP, II, 257.
[19] J. Regesta, 3823.

into her home the orphaned children of Berengarius II, Otto's worst enemy, and reared them as her very own.[20]

Otto II's reign of ten years, though marred by political turmoil and rebellion and compromised by defects in the ruler's character, was, at least after the flight of Franco and the elevation of Pope Benedict VII (974-983), one of stability and progress in Roman ecclesiastical affairs. Benedict's catholic nature, which made him concerned about every interest of the church, and his pacifying gifts were useful and effective in this period of Italian reaction to the German autocracy of Otto I.[21] France and England, both reflecting in the life of the church the disrupting influences of feudalism, which was playing havoc with the state, found in Archbishop Adalbero of Rheims and Archbishop Dunstan of Canterbury stalwart barriers against the flood of diocesan anarchy, simoniacal corruption, nepotism, moral indifference, monastic laziness and self-indulgence, and other glaring abuses which seriously threatened Christianity in those nations.

When Otto II died, away from home in Rome, December 7, 983, his son and heir, **Otto III,** was only three and one half years old. There now ensued a regency of almost eleven years (983-994), characterized by a struggle for power between Henry the Wrangler and those loyal to the Saxon House.

During this time two important events occurred outside the empire. At this period the ownership of land meant everything, and the Carolingian House with its careless loss of property had also about lost its power to rule. The French nobility, with the approval and support of the church represented by the powerful and determined Adalbero of Rheims, elected Hugh Capet, count of Paris, king of France (987), at a national assembly at Compiègne, thus inaugurating the famous Capetian dynasty. Likewise, in 990, a treaty between King Ethelred of England and Duke Richard of Normandy inaugurated the Truce of God, which stipulated that in wars between Christian princes the property of the church and of the poor should not be damaged or destroyed, neither should clergymen, pilgrims, merchantmen, women, children or the poor be molested. Anyone guilty of violating the Truce of God was to be anathematized.[22] Inside the empire, Pope John XIV (983-984), reigning pontiff when Otto II died, was imprisoned and later assassinated by the antipope Boniface (Franco),[23] who returned from Constantinople, took over the papacy, and rented church property for his own gain (984-985).[24] John XV (985-996), who persuaded Ethelred and Richard to sign the treaty estab-

---

[20] MGH, *Scriptores,* III, 264-363, 312-314, 408-467; IV, 63-65, 69-70, 252-275; VI, 347-349, 352.

[21] LP, II, 258.

[22] MPL, CXXXVII, 843, 854-856.

[23] LP, II, 259.

[24] J. Regesta, 3825.

lishing the Truce of God, is an obscure figure, and most of what happened during his eleven years as pope is lost to history.

Otto III enjoys a unique and enviable position in ecclesiastical history; for it was he who, sensing the ecumenical nature of the papacy, translated the office itself into an international institution. Heretofore it had been held exclusively by Italian clergy, and until the time of Martin II entirely by Roman clergy. Hereafter it was to be occupied by men of other nations as well. Throughout the remainder of the Middle Ages Germans, Frenchmen, Greeks, one Englishman, and Spaniards as well as Italians and Romans rose to the occupancy of Peter's throne. Only with the end of universal dominion in the West—that is, with the Reformation itself—did this international principle die out and did the custom that none but an Italian should occupy the Apostolic throne again silently become law.

Otto III was one of the best-educated men of the Middle Ages. His teachers had been John of Calabria (Italian), Bernward of Hildesheim (German), and the famous Gerbert of Aurillac (French), so that his training itself had been from the start cosmopolitan and international. It is not strange then that he assumed the reins of government with a preconceived idea of the universal scope of both church and empire. In his thinking, two empires were incompatible with each other; therefore it was his resolve to bring East and West back together again under his own majestic rule. There could be no New Rome as long as the Old Rome was still in existence. Since his mother had been a Greek princess, there flowed in his veins the blood of both imperial houses anyway. Consequently he abandoned Germany for Italy, built his palace on the Aventine in Rome, refused the use of German manners and speech as barbaric, affected Roman dress, and likened himself to Constantine and Justinian.

Immediately upon the death of John XV, Otto's first visit of state to Rome saw, as a result of the German king's nomination, his youthful cousin, Bruno (only twenty-three years old but nonetheless seven years Otto's senior), elected and consecrated pope (May 3, 996).[25] Eighteen days later the new pope, who took the title of Gregory V, crowned Otto emperor. Both the empire and the papacy were now in the hands of men of the same nationality and members of the same family. Gregory V was the first German pope.

As was to be expected this innovation in ecclesiastical affairs provoked a rebellion. A certain Crescentius caused Gregory to flee Rome for Pavia, set up Philagathus of Piacenza, a Greek from Calabria, in his place; forced the emperor to return to Italy; and paid for his folly with his head. The poor misguided Philagathus, whom the pope and the emperor forgave, was seized by the populace, who blinded him, tore out his tongue, cut off his ears and

[25] MPL, CXXXVII, 880.

nose, and led him on the back of an ass through the streets of Rome.

Gregory's one positive accomplishment was the restoration of Arnulf to his see in Rheims, whence he had been uncanonically deposed, and the translation of the new occupant of Rheims, Gerbert, to the vacant see of Ravenna—thus settling a dispute of more than ten years' duration and pleasing the royal house of Capet.[26] Yet if Gregory pleased the Capetians in this, he displeased them by declaring null and void the marriage of Robert the Pious and his close relative Bertha and forcing them to do seven months of penance for their error. Gregory V died at the age of twenty-six, presumably of poison, after a short pontificate of less than three years (996-999).

The first German pope was succeeded by the first French pope, Gerbert of Aurillac, first archbishop of Rheims and later archbishop of Ravenna. He had been Otto's principal teacher; and, as an expression of his sympathy with Otto's dream of world domination through one empire—a dream which he no doubt had inspired—he took, appropriately enough, **Sylvester II as** his papal name. (Sylvester I had been the bishop of Rome at the time of Constantine.) Now that this new Constantine, Otto III, had got his French Sylvester, the Roman populace hated him the more. Likewise, Sylvester, one of the ablest of the pontiffs, was at the same time one of the most despised. This pope had always been as much of a politician and diplomat as he had been a churchman. He had helped Adalbero engineer the election of Hugh Capet as king of France. His companions were the secular rather than the spiritual princes.

He was a scientist as well as an ecclesiastic. He represented the earth by a wooden globe and placed the lines of the North and South Poles in an oblique direction in their relationship to the earth's rotation, as we do today. From tubes fastened together he made a usable telescope, thus anticipating the achievement of Galileo. He studied the art of medicine and described symptoms as well as cures for diseases. He concerned himself with the nature of steam to such an extent that his findings led to the invention of the steam organ. He invented for his private use a system of shorthand. In addition, Sylvester II wrote lyrics of hymns (though these have not survived), mastered and elucidated principles of music, and advanced his own theory of oratory which based public speaking on dialectics and poetry, contending that an effective address must be both persuasive and picturesque as well as logical, clear, and convincing.

The arts of civilization were again revived, though on a far less extensive scale, by Otto III and Sylvester as they had been by Charlemagne and Alcuin of York. The beautiful though fragile structures of the Carolingian period were replaced by stone edifices, thus beginning at the close of the tenth

[26] Hefele, *op. cit.* (Leclercq ed.), IV, 856-857, 884, 889.

century the Romanesque architecture with its vaulted stone roofs in place of roofs of wood. Great schools such as those of Rheims, Fleury, and especially Cluny abounded in students and produced a few scholars—though none of the merit and scope of Sylvester himself. The monk Richer, for example, wrote at Rheims his *Historiae*, the style of which is marked by color and vivacity, and which provides us with remarkable information about the tenth century. The most influential institution in Western Christendom was Cluny Abbey, presided over for fifty-five years (994-1049) by Odilo, who was the moral forerunner of Hildebrand and the tutor of later reformers. New chants, together with musical compositions, emerged under the influence of the followers of Notker the Stammerer, a musical genius who worked during the latter part of the ninth century at the monastery of St. Gall. Song and verse alike began now to be expressed in the popular languages.

In addition to his patronage of science and the arts, Sylvester II gave general statesmanlike direction to the affairs of the church. He counseled and encouraged those responsible for the expansion of Christianity in Poland, which had first been reached by Moravian missionaries who founded a church near Cracow in 949. The Polish ruler was baptized in 966. Sylvester sent Otto III to Poland in 1000 to venerate the relics of Adalbert and to constitute Gnesen into a metropolitan see. Otto at the same time freed the Duke of Poland from all terms of vassalage, so that his state visit was the origin of the Polish nation. Sylvester II, in obedience to a dream, withheld the crown of Hungary from Boleslaus and conferred it on Stephen instead, thus binding the rulers of Hungary to the papal see. This was a signal gain since the first princes of Hungary to embrace the gospel had been baptized at Constantinople (949), though Latin bishops had later worked among the Hungarian people. He regulated on three separate occasions the affairs of important sees in France including that of Rheims which he himself had been forced to vacate. He foresaw correctly the fate of Christians under the new Saracenic tyranny in the Holy Land and prematurely called Europe to a crusade. He entered into covenant with Otto III to restore in all its majesty the Roman empire, though this time under the aegis of the church with a Christian Caesar at its head.

Yet neither Sylvester nor Otto was appreciated. Both, in the face of uprisings and rebellions, abandoned Rome, and when they found Germany rent asunder by dissension, turned south again into Italy, hoping to find in the southern part of that peninsula loyalty from enough of the people to begin again. They were not given the time to accomplish their mission. Otto got only as far as Mt. Soracte near Rome. Wasted by disease and broken in spirit, he died on January 23, 1002. Glamorous and in ideal even great, he had wrought his accomplishments while still a boy. Otto was only twenty-one when he died.

Less than two years later, having returned to Rome, Sylvester followed his pupil and friend to the grave.[27] He governed the church for only four years and three months (999-1003), yet the quality of that government was such as to make his pontificate immortal. His learning was so vast and his understanding so keen that the common people looked on him as a necromancer and said that he must have sold his soul to the devil in exchange for so much knowledge. Subsequent ages have revered him as a bright light in a dark age.

The death of Otto III loosed temporarily the reins of the empire upon the papacy. The next three popes, John XVII (1003), John XVIII (1003-1009), and Sergius IV (1009-1012) were all placed in office by the Roman family of the Crescentii. Likewise, their three successors, Benedict VIII (1012-1024), John XIX (1024-1032) and Benedict IX (1032-1045), though brought into active relationship with the German Imperial House, owed their elevation to the papacy to the Italian family of Tusculum, of which they were members. These forty-two years of papal history largely reflect the rivalry between these two powerful Italian houses. Otto's successors, in contrast to him, were first German kings and only secondarily Roman emperors. Each of them, Henry II (1002-1024), Conrad II (1024-1039), and Henry III (1039-1056), was a capable and energetic ruler, devoted to the welfare of his nation and loyal to the church.

Indeed, this epoch of history sets forth the strange anomaly of piety and moral uprightness in both the private lives and public administrations of the chief secular rulers of the West and at the same time either, at best, time-serving mediocrity or, at worst, vice and corruption in both the personal habits and official actions of the Roman pontiffs. Outside the empire, for example, Robert Capet (996-1031) of France, better fitted no doubt for the monastery than the throne, nonetheless conscientiously tried to enforce the Peace of God; put down in Orleans a mysterious sect which denied the Old Testament, the real presence of Christ in the Eucharist, and the virginity of Mary, and which proclaimed the eternal coexistence of good and evil; and so conducted himself as to win the appellative of Robert the Pious. Casimir I of Poland abandoned the peace of monastic seclusion in order to save his country from anarchy and thus won for himself the title of Blessed. Inside the empire, Henry II, the patron of Cluny Abbey and the personification of Christian knighthood, became a saint. It is said that on his wedding night he took the vow of absolute continence and thereby resolved to live the life of a monk in marriage. His wife, Queen Cunigundis, denied the pleasures of her husband's bed, became a saint also.

In contrast, the papacy sank to the nadir of political and social ineffectiveness, moral degeneracy, unabashed vice, and spiritual impotence during the

[27] MPL, CXXXIX, 57-338; LP, II, 263-264; CMH, III, 209-214, 530-538.

pontificate of **Benedict IX** (1032-1045). When no more than a boy of twelve, he was elevated to the apostolic throne by the insatiable greed and ambition of his family and the criminal indifference of the Roman populace and the empire. Two of his predecessors were to a degree responsible for what took place. Benedict VIII (1012-1024) turned over all temporal responsibility to his brother Romanus, a layman; and on Benedict's demise, in order to save embarrassment both to his brother and to his successor, Romanus himself was elected pope as John XIX (1024-1032). It was only a step, then, in violation of canon law, from the acceptance of a layman as supreme pontiff to that of a degenerate boy. Benedict IX sustained himself against a rival, fought battles for his see, made the usual official pronouncements and decisions or had them made for him, and carried on his functions like a man in his majority. Yet at the same time he indulged himself in all his vices until, weary even of the pretense of rule, he sold the tiara to the highest bidder. John Gratian, who bought it, succeeded him as Gregory VI (1045-1046). The new pope was a gifted scholar and teacher, the patron of monks and reformers, yet himself guilty of simony. He was forced by Henry III to abdicate. The German Suidger, who took the name of Clement II (1046-1047), was put in his place. He was succeeded by Damasus II (1048), who reigned only a few months. Thus in two short years, five popes counting the antipope Sylvester III (1044-1045) occupied the Roman see.[28]

Yet despite Rome the Western church made some gains during this period. Though war was not outlawed, at least the effort was made to Christianize it in chivalry. The squire kept vigil all night before the high altar on the eve of his being dubbed a knight, and he swore allegiance to God as well as to his liege lord. Both Henry II of Germany and Robert the Pious of France promoted the welfare of the people. They met at Ivois (1023) to discuss means of reforming the clergy and securing peace. They attended mass together and ate at the same table. The Camaldolese Order arose under the inspiration and direction of Romuald (950-1027). At the age of twenty, as he witnessed a terrible duel between his own father and the opponent whom his father killed, Romuald gave himself to the monastic life, abstaining from meat and wine and wearing an untrimmed beard. This order did for Italy what Cluny did for France. The Camaldolese monk soon became a familiar figure, with his long beard, his bare feet, and his white robe.[29] One of this order, Guido of Arezzo (990-1050), the only artist of the age, fixed the musical staff in the Gregorian chants according to diatonic notation.[30]

The chief accomplishment was missionary. Henry I of Germany forced

[28] CMH, V, 1-23.
[29] MPL, CXLIV, 953 ff.
[30] MPL, CXLI, 375-444. Mourret, op. cit., IV, 18-125.

Gorm the Old of Denmark to restrain from persecuting the Danish Christians (934); in 972 Harald Bluetooth of Denmark and his entire army accepted baptism; and, after a pagan reaction under King Sweyn (ca. 986-1014), Canute (1019-1035) led the nation of Denmark to embrace the faith, ordering his subjects to learn the Lord's Prayer and to receive Holy Communion thrice a year. Christianity entered Norway from England with King Haakon (935-961), who had resided there for a time, but he compromised with paganism, and not until the conquest of Norway by Denmark (977) did Christianity really begin to spread among the people, and that largely by force. By the year 1000 the people were nominally Christian, yet their real training in Christianity came later (ca. 1016-1030) through missionaries from Hamburg, who revived the pacific labors of Ansgar. King Olaf Tryggvason (995-1000) was the artificer of institutional Christianity in Norway. The first Christian king of Sweden was Olof Skötkonung (993-1021), who was baptized at a well of Husaby near Skara by Bishop Sigfrid in 1008. Later, at least five bishops were consecrated in Bremen for Sweden, and before the end of the eleventh century this land belonged entirely to the Latin church. Two Icelanders, Gissur and Hinalti, returned home from Norway with a priest, Thormud, and succeeded among their people where previous missionaries had not. Gissur's son, Isleif, educated at Erfurt, became Iceland's first native bishop in 1056. Shortly thereafter all heathenism was extirpated from the land.[31]

III. Eastern Catholicism at Its Zenith

While the Western church was in the throes of perhaps its deepest humiliation, the Eastern church was at the pinnacle of its success. Doctrinal disputation, which in the East generally led either to warring factions vying with each other for control of the government or else to open schism, was at a minimum. The expansion of the empire led to the increase of the church. Monasticism, which more than any other social institution, represented the piety and devotion of Eastern Christianity, was at its greatest strength and influence. Missionary gains were both most numerous and territorially most extensive. Byzantine culture, itself the creation of the Byzantine church, was in its second golden age. Though the artistic and literary achievements of the Macedonian period were not as creative and original as those of Justinian's time, they were more widespread, and Constantinople combined the intellectual glory of ancient Athens with the political and military grandeur of ancient Rome. Even when the patriarch of Constantinople and the emperor were at odds with one another, the interests of the church were not allowed to suffer; for the cause of Christianity, even orthodoxy, was as

[31] CMH, III, 105-109; 215-339. K. S. Latourette, A History of the Expansion of Christianity (N. Y., 1938), II, 118-143. C. H. Robinson, op. cit., pp. 437-84.

much at the heart of the Byzantine rulers of state as it was at the heart of the prelates of the church. As trade flourished and wealth increased and people in general became more prosperous, the ecclesiastical organization became stronger, more influential, more powerful, and in artistic forms and expressions more glorious than at any other time in history.

As a result, orthodoxy was thought to be the only legitimate expression of Christianity. The Eastern church and empire therefore opposed the heresy of the Bogomiles, who were numerous in Bulgaria and were to a certain degree responsible for that nation's decline. They were a dualistic sect which had originated as a result of the teachings of Theophilus, who worked among the Bulgarians between 927 and 950. They believed in a Superior and an Inferior God. The Inferior God's name was Satanael, who had been driven out of heaven and who had created earth as a new sphere of influence. The Superior God intervened when Satanael created Adam by supplying Adam with a soul. Consequently there are two elements in man who belongs to the Superior God and to Satanael. The Superior God sent Jesus Christ to rescue man from his bondage to Satanael. After Jesus Christ conquered Satanael, he left the Holy Spirit as his agent in the world and himself returned to heaven. Man must be rescued by the Holy Spirit from corruption. Those rescued will be changed into ethereal bodies at death. The Bogomiles accepted as canonical only the New Testament and the Psalms. They rejected the Eucharist, marriage, baptism by water, infant baptism, and all formal prayers except the Lord's Prayer. They repudiated the hierarchy and were adoptionists in Christology. They weakened Bulgaria by undermining the church in that nation.[32]

At the same time cordial relations existed between the Armenian church and Constantinopolitan orthodoxy, for Armenia supplied the empire with its best soldiers; and, though Basil II twice entered Armenia with his armies (991 and 1021) to secure its garrisons against outside foes, he did not tamper with the people's faith. Though there is little evidence one way or the other, the Jacobites of Syria, always a small body, were no doubt treated either with indifference or with proselytizing concern which, rebuffed, led to policies of containment by the orthodox church after Syria had been regained for the empire. The Coptic church in Egypt, under the Shia sect of Islam, was tolerated and prospered to the extent that its patriarch, Ephraim (977-981), put down simony and concubinage among the clergy and engaged in a program of church extension. Its branch in Abyssinia, however, was torn asunder by two rivals for its chief see, each claiming the support of the patriarch of Alexandria. The Nestorians of Persia, likewise outside the empire, won (in 1009) twenty thousand Turks and Mongols to the Christian church.[33]

[32] D. Obolensky, The Bogomiles (1948).
[33] Barhebraeus, Chronicon Ecclesiasticum (ed. Abbeloos and Lamy Lovanii, 1872-1877, III, 280-282.

The Eastern church of Constantinople exercised sway in what is now Jugoslavia during this period. By 891 Serbia, Croatia, and Dalmatia, by what processes we do not know, were entirely orthodox lands. By giving the Slavs an alphabet Cyril and Methodius helped indirectly to give them Christianity too. Though the Serbs were under Bulgarian religious domination during the reign of the Bulgarian kings, Simeon (893-927) and Samuel (976-1014), they were under Byzantine control in between those two rulers and thereafter until the thirteenth century. The oscillation between Bulgarian and Byzantine influence made little difference anyway, since doctrinally and liturgically (except for language) the two churches were the same.

The successive Eastern emperors, more than the Constantinopolitan patriarchs, molded the policies of the church. On the second deposition of Photius (886), Leo VI (886-912) set up his younger brother Stephen (886-893) as patriarch, while fifty years later Romanus I (919-944) repeated this policy by elevating his own son, Theophylactus (933-956). These two acts illustrate the influence of Armenian Christianity on orthodoxy, for in Armenia the catholicus was a prince of the royal family.

The ablest Constantinopolitan patriarch between Photius and Michael Cerularius was **Nicholas Mysticus** (895-906). It was his difficult mission to appease the emperor. **Leo VI** the Wise had been married three times. He had lost each of his wives by death. He contemplated a fourth marriage; but when he discussed it with Nicholas, the patriarch was unalterably opposed because canon law forbade fourth marriages regardless of circumstances. Consequently Leo took a concubine who bore him a son, the future Constantine VII. In order for the infant Constantine to receive baptism Leo had to promise Nicholas that he would no longer live with his concubine. However, Leo later married his concubine, claiming thereby that he had kept his promise by making the concubine his legitimate wife. In doing this he had flagrantly violated canon law. Nicholas reciprocated by refusing to crown Zoë, the new wife, as empress. The emperor therefore took the imperial crown in his own hands and placed it on Zoë's head, thus provoking the patriarchal taunt that Leo was to Zoë "both groom and bishop." The patriarch forbade the emperor to enter the church. Leo circumvented the prohibition by entering by a side entrance after the service had started, provoking the amusement of the congregation.

Imperial prestige won the support of the other Eastern patriarchs. Nicholas Mysticus was deposed. Euthymius (906-911) was set up in his stead, and Euthymius complied with Leo's will on the grounds that public welfare demanded it. The people were not so responsive. There developed as a result two strong ecclesiastical parties—the Nicholatians and the Euthymites. Dissension spread from church to state. In the end Leo called Nicholas out of exile, deposed Euthymius, and reinstated his foe (911) on the patriarchal throne.

Zoë, on the death of her husband, became regent for her son; she stripped the patriarch of all his influence. Yet, when the regency changed hands, Nicholas regained his influence. He convened a synod in 920 which reasserted the illegality of fourth marriages. The pope of Rome, together with the other Eastern patriarchs, had supported Leo VI. The pope sent legates to this synod and through them disavowed his former stand, thus capitulating completely to the position of the Constantinopolitan patriarch. Nicholas served for nearly fourteen years after his reinstatement, dying in 925.[34]

The pendulum swung from ecclesiastical independence back to subservience to the state. The Emperor Romanus Lecapenus (919-944) gained control over the church.[35] Caesaropapism was exhibited in its most complete form, however, some years later in the reign of Nicephorus Phocas (963-969). Perhaps the emperor felt he was as well fitted to manage the church as any of its bishops. Personally he was so devout that he had considered becoming a monk himself. He had even worn the hair shirt and had kept vigils with fasting and prayer. As a general he had sponsored monks on Mount Athos. Yet his disposition altered when he married the young and beautiful Theophano, the widow of his predecessor, Romanus II (959-963).[36] One year after his coronation he issued the decree forbidding both the founding of new monasteries and the giving of new endowments to the upkeep of old ones. He likewise forbade any further gifts to ecclesiastical hospitals, hostelries, metropolitans, and bishops. He claimed he did this for religious reasons. The church, he thought, was inflicted with the disease of cupidity. He wanted to root out the "God-hated evil of ambition." There was no doubt a social reason as well.[37] He wanted, as a wise ruler, to protect as best he could free peasant holdings from the expanding monastic landownership. Public opinion was not ready for this reform, and the law had to be annulled by Basil II (976-1025). Basil expressed the true sentiments of the people when he styled this law as "outrageous and offensive not only to the churches and hospitals but to God himself." [38]

Nicephorus Phocas was in sentiment a true Greek. He forbade the use of the Latin rite in Apulia and Calabria, Greek territories in southern Italy. He wanted to venerate as Christian martyrs all soldiers who had fallen in the wars against infidels, but the patriarch of Constantinople thwarted his ambition in this regard.

Nicephorus Phocas and his successor John Tzimisces (969-976) were both

[34] MPG, CXI, 9-392. Vita Euthymii (ed. C. de Boor, 1888).
[35] MPG, CXVII, 635-926.
[36] G. Schlumberger, Un Empereur byzantin au dixième siècle. Nicéphore Phocas (Paris, 1890), 366. Leo the Deacon, Historiae, 453, in CSHB.
[37] K. E. Zachariä von Lingenthal, Collectio librorum juris graeco-romani ineditorum, Ecloga Leonis et Constantini (Leipzig, 1852), II, 292-296.
[38] Ibid., III, 303.

associated with the establishment of coenobitic monasticism on **Mount Athos,** which came to be the greatest center of ascetic piety and power in the Greek world. Mount Athos, a long rugged peninsula jutting southeast from Macedonia into the Aegean Sea, had been the refuge for hermits since the fourth century. During the iconoclastic disturbances many solitaries with their beloved icons had fled there from the persecuting emperors. Yet anchoritic asceticism prevailed. The hermits were individualists, and most of them lived alone. Therefore they were easy prey for Arab maritime marauders who carried many of them away as slave laborers in Moslem communities.

This situation was altered by a monk named Athanasius, who established a Coenobitic community after the regulations of Theodore of Studium and built the Great Lavra monastery in 963. There had been one earlier monastery, founded at Kolovou in 875. It lasted only a century, however, for it reversed its mission of protecting the hermits against the peasants and became the oppressor of both.

Athanasius, a rich man's son, was from Trebizond, a port of Asia Minor on the Black Sea. In 950 he migrated to Athos to become a mountain hermit like the rest of its inhabitants. He disguised himself and hid in a cave that he might be protected from the world. There he was discovered by a companion of his youth, the general Nicephorus Phocas, later to become emperor. Nicephorus asked him to pray for victory over the Saracens on Crete. Athanasius made Nicephorus promise if he won the battle, he would become a monk. Nicephorus after victory failed to keep his promise. He tried to buy release from his vow by providing Athanasius with resources for the building of the Great Lavra. Athanasius persuaded some monks to accept the coenobitic regulations of Studium. He constructed a permanent establishment out of stone, made harbors for boats, and imported oxen for hauling and plowing.

The hermits opposed him and his companions. They even appealed to Nicephorus Phocas' successor, John Tzimisces, to prevent Athanasius' work as a violation of the ancient customs of the Holy Mountain. Tzimisces decreed that both anchoritic and coenobitic monasticism could exist side by side on the Holy Mountain. Consequently following the establishment of the Great Lavra many other monasteries were founded. When Athanasius died (1000) there were more than three thousand monks on Athos.

The coenobitic rule required absolute obedience of the monks of each monastery to their abbot. The abbot was chosen for life by a vote of the monks of six years' standing in the monastery. He had to be at least forty years of age. However, since there were many monasteries in close proximity to one another on Athos, there was a council of abbots headed by a chairman called the *Protos,* or "First," among them. The council was called the *Protaton.*

Learning was encouraged in the monasteries of Athos. Before the end of the Macedonian era Mount Athos was the cultural center, not only of the

Byzantine empire, but also of the whole world. It was entirely a man's community. Presumably not since almost the beginning of the Christian era had any woman set foot on Athos. Now in the tenth century it was forbidden for any female thing to come to this Holy Mountain. The unseemly act of mating must not be allowed to offend pure souls bent on meditation and spiritual purification. Tradition held that the Virgin Mary, while still alive, had selected this peninsula as her garden and had excluded all other females from it. In the majestic grandeur of its mountains and the heavy woods on its hillsides and in its valleys, Athos was one of the most beautiful places in the world, a natural retreat for prayer and contemplation.[39]

The military prowess of the Eastern empire was everywhere felt. The Byzantine state re-established itself in southern Italy, gained control of the Mediterranean Sea, fought its way to victory in Syria, Armenia, and Iberia and thus fully regained its ancient territory in Asia Minor. It entered into favorable alliances with Venice, Naples, and other small Italian principalities in the West and with Russia to the North. Bulgaria, which formerly had striven with the empire as an equal and under its great king Simeon (893-927) had almost captured Constantinople itself, was now hopelessly defeated, its captives blinded, and its people reduced to vassalage. Byzantine political and military power reached its height during the long reign of Basil II (976-1025), which lasted forty-nine years.[40]

The sense of social responsibility and concern for the poor lifted imperial policy to a high level of humanitarianism during this epoch. Basil I began a restudy of the law. His son Leo the Wise produced the *Basilica*, the most complete collection of Byzantine legislation in history. Basil II revised an old law making the rich landowners responsible for the payment of the taxes levied against the poor and succeeded in putting it into effect. By this means he financed his expensive Bulgarian wars.[41] Unfortunately after Basil's time this policy was reversed, bringing about in the East serfdom, which was already a well-developed feature of social life in the West.

Art flourished during this period. There appeared now for the first time the imperial school of icon painters. Some of the loveliest icons in existence were created in Constantinople by the members of this school. So many of the fine chapels, churches, and monasteries on Mount Athos were built in the late tenth and eleventh centuries. The magnificent frescoes in the rock-hewn cone-shape chapels of Cappadocia were largely painted at this time. There seems to have been more variety and vitality in the art of this epoch than that of any other epoch in Byzantine history. This was due in part to a combination

[39] *Vie de Saint Athanase l'Athonite*, in *Analecta Bollandiana* (1906), XXV. P. Meyer, *Die Haupturkunden für die Geschichte der Athosklosters* (Leipzig, 1894), 1-153.
[40] CMH, IV, 49-118.
[41] CMH, IV, 712-725.

of the virile simplicity of the ancient Hellenic pattern with the color and ornateness of the Moslem designs. The royal palace of Basil I with its mosaics was one of the wonders of the civilized world.

What was achieved in art was likewise achieved in **literature**. The poems about a Greek hero in Asia Minor who fought bravely against the infidels on the eastern frontier became a Byzantine epic comparable to the *Song of Roland, Nibelungenlied*, and *Arthurian Legends* in the West. It was called *The Epic of Digenes Akrites*. It became the prototype of the *Arabian Nights*. Christopher of Mytilene, whose graceful style and charming wit expressed themselves largely in short poems addressed to prominent persons, wrote in the eleventh century. Geometres, a contemporary of Nicephorus Phocas, Tzimisces, and Basil II, left a collection of sundry poems containing a eulogy on asceticism and hymns in honor of the Holy Ghost. The famous *Lexicon of Suidas* was compiled during the reign of Constantine Porphyrogenitus (913-959). Arethas, metropolitan of Caesarea, wrote the first Byzantine commentary on the book of The Revelation as well as commentaries on Plato, Lucian, and Eusebius. Simeon Metaphrastes compiled his *Lives of the Saints*, while Constantine Kaphalas made a collection of short poems from pagan antiquity and Christian times known as the *Anthologia Palatina*. The reign of Constantine Porphyrogenitus also saw a work *On the Administration of the Empire* and *On the Ceremonies of the Byzantine Court*. Two emperors especially were creative in the field of letters: Leo the Wise and Constantine Porphyrogenitus.

History and geography flourished. Leo the Deacon memorialized the wars in his writing—especially the Bulgarian campaigns of Basil II. Constantine Psellus, the head of the school of philosophy in Constantinople, was perhaps the greatest historian Byzantine civilization produced. He was an incomparable scholar and writer. He was not so great as a man. He forsook his monastic vocation for a gay life at court. He became prime minister. So compromising and adjustable to changing conditions was this sycophantical courtier that he managed to hold his influence under nine successive emperors. He died in 1078.

The school of Constantinople embraced the advanced studies of law and philosophy beyond the basic discipline of the seven arts, thus anticipating in its work the Western universities of the thirteenth century. If not in name, nonetheless in fact, the Byzantine empire produced the first real university in history.[42]

IV. The Conversion of Russia

The supreme accomplishment of Greek Christianity during this period of its greatest might was the conversion of Russia.

[42] A. A. Vasiliev, *History of the Byzantine Empire* (1958), I, 361-374.

This huge **land** stretching from Scandinavia south to the Black Sea and from Poland east to the Caucasus mountains was controlled by a people called the Varangians—Scandinavian in origin—who made their capital first at Novgorod, inland from the Finnish Gulf in the north, and later-at Kiev in the Ukraine in the south. It was at Kiev that the first political and therefore significant contacts were made by these people with Christianity. Since Constantinople was the mercantile capital of the world and since the Varangian territory bordered on the Black Sea as did that of the Eastern empire, it was but natural that Greeks and Russians would be thrown together, and each would visit the other's capital for business purposes. Certainly by the middle of the tenth century there were a few Christians residing in Kiev.

The Russian **people** were especially suited for missionary propaganda and evangelism. Their forms of worship, their code of behavior, their adoration of nature in its multiple forms and expressions, their polytheism were all crude and primitive—a throwback to the barbarism of the invaders of the Western empire in the fourth and fifth centuries and comparable to the beliefs and practices of their kinsmen in Scandinavia, some of whom had already yielded and others of whom were now in the process of yielding to active Christianity.

The first person of consequence among the Russians to embrace Christianity was the dowager Queen Olga, who was the dominant political force in Kiev during the minority of her son. This remarkable woman had been influenced by the little Christian community in Kiev, which her husband Igor (913-945) had tolerated. After his death, when the reins of restraint were loosed, she followed the dictates of her own conscience and embraced the faith (954). She then requested the Western Emperor Otto I to send Latin missionaries to Kiev. Adalbert, consecrated for the purpose by the Archbishop of Mainz, came; but he had no success.

The real founder of Russian Christianity was Olga's young grandson **Vladimir.** Vladimir won the throne by murdering his older brother. During a good part of his life he was a libertine, perhaps even a debauchee, yet a grateful church has nonetheless conferred on him the title of saint, for he gave to his people Christianity and to Eastern Catholicism its strongest and most populous church.

Vladimir invited representatives of Islam, Roman Catholicism, Judaism, and Greek Catholicism to extol the merits of their religion. He was not greatly impressed by either Islam or Judaism. But he had great difficulty deciding between Latin and Greek Christianity. He sent emissaries to visit both Rome and Constantinople and to report to him what they found there. The splendor of Saint Sophia and the ordered beauty of the Eastern service decided the issue in favor of the Greeks. The Emperor Basil II himself had escorted the Russians to Saint Sophia, where clergy and courtiers alike bedecked themselves in ceremonial robes of splendor and where the music was like an angelic chorus and the ritual like the language of heaven. The report of the emissaries was rapturous: "We knew not whether we were in heaven or earth, for there is not any similar sight on earth nor is there such beauty. We cannot describe it, but we only know that it is there 'that God dwells with men.'" [43]

Vladimir did not want to accept the Greek religion as a suppliant. He thought he must win it by defeating the empire. Consequently he besieged Kherson, an imperial city in the Crimea, took it by cutting off its water supply, and made a treaty with Constantinople in which he consented to become a Christian and to marry the Emperor's sister, Anna. Anna was also the sister of Theophano, wife of Otto II and mother of Otto III. Vladimir was baptized in 988. Vladimir's twelve sons followed their father in his new religion. Indeed, so many of the Russian people accepted baptism that there were not priests enough to immerse them. Consequently they assembled beside the Dnieper at Kiev, heard the reading of the ceremony, and immersed themselves in the flowing water. Christianity spread, not without opposition, from Kiev to Novgorod, Rostoff, Tzernigov, and Bielgorod, which became Russia's chief sees. Vladimir wisely did not coerce his people into Christianity. He set up Christian schools, made education as nearly as possible compulsory, and so won over the young. Before he died in 1015 the majority of his people had become Christians.

His son **Yaroslav** (1019-1054) continued his work. It was he who had the Scriptures translated into Slavic and meditated on them day and night. He had his uncles who had died as heathens exhumed and their bones baptized into the Christian faith.

The famous Petchersky monastery near Kiev was founded in 1010 by the hermit Antony, who had spent some time on Mount Athos. That monastery is subterranean, its cells and chapel having been dug out under ground. Perhaps that is parabolic of what Russian piety became—a retreat from life, mystical, contemplative, concern for one's own sins not the reformation of the world.[44]

V. The Great Schism

By the middle of the eleventh century the expansion of Christianity into new territories practically stopped, since the principal countries of Europe had officially at least adopted the gospel as the faith of their inhabitants. The last to embrace the Latin expression of Christianity had been the Scandinavians, while the Russians had been the last to embrace the Eastern. Consequently

[43] *Chronique de Nestor* (Paris, 1884), 67-90.
[44] CMH, IV, 200-210. Latourette, *op. cit.*, II, 251-255.

the ecclesiastical map of Europe was fixed. The bounds of the Western church reached across Poland to stop at the steppes of Russia and the wheat fields of the Ukraine. The Eastern church was coterminus with the bounds of the Byzantine empire, and thus held sway over most of the Balkans and kept strong outposts in southern Italy.

However, both bodies were still in communion with each other. There was still one faith; and men everywhere, whether in Scandinavia or Russia, in Constantinople or Rome, thought of themselves as members of the holy universal church. During the pontificate of Pope John XVIII (1003-1009) the name of the pope was reinserted in the diptychs of the church of Constantinople (1004),[45] though as early as 920 all differences between Old and New Rome had been settled.[46] Outwardly at least, there was a singleness of spirit, which always is essential to organizational unity and administrative cooperation.

Yet this singleness of spirit was more apparent than real. The very fact that in the reign of a single emperor, Leo VI (886-912), a minor disciplinary dispute over whether a man could marry a fourth time or not, even though all three of his wives were dead, could cause patriarch and pope to break off communion with each other, is evidence of the superficial relationship that existed between the two branches of the church.[47] The religious reasons for the final separation, given by the two churches, are now in retrospect difficult to grasp. The truth is that the real reasons were scarcely religious at all. They were cultural, sociological, and political. To a certain extent they were personal. The occupants of the sees of Rome and Constantinople were perennially jealous of one another, and oftentimes priority of dignity and rights took precedence in their minds over everything else, even the unity of the church itself. Due to the difference in language, the liturgical practices of the Eastern and Western churches became increasingly different as the two rituals developed. Likewise, the Greeks adjusted themselves ecclesiastically to the nation in which their religion entered, translating their services into the language of the people. The Latins did not. Consequently the Greek expression of Christianity tended to become nationalistic and autocephalous, while the Latin remained international, unitary, and authoritarian. The Greeks were by tradition loyal to the government; more and more their church became a department of the state. The Latins were religiously independent, tended to make the ruler in any land dependent upon his priests and bishops and ultimately on the Roman pontiff himself.

The ecclesiastical happenings of the middle of the eleventh century were not so much basic causes of the schism as they were its precipitating events.

[45] Baronius, Annales, a. 1009.
[46] Mansi, XVIII, 331-342.
[47] MPG, CXI, 249 A.

The protagonists of the schism were the Roman Pope Leo IX (1049-1054) and the Constantinopolitan patriarch Michael Cerularius (1043-1058), both strong-willed individualists, able, and bent on the achievement of their own ends. Each had been in office a few years before the divisive issues were posed and had thereby gained the support of his own constituency.

Leo IX was before his elevation the bishop of Toul in Alsace, which see he had occupied for twenty years. Before that he had spent a residence of two years as imperial chaplain at the court of Conrad II. After his elevation he wandered, like a pilgrim, over Western Europe winning public opinion to the decisions of his Roman Synod (1049) condemning simony and incontinence. One simoniacal bishop, the occupant of the see of Sutri, who had planned to exonerate himself by lies, collapsed before Leo and, like Ananias, had to be carried from the courtroom. Likewise, he dealt successfully with the doctrinal deviation of Berengarius of Tours (999-1088), who denied the substantial change from bread and wine to body and blood in the Eucharist. At Leo's instigation Berengarius was tried at a synod at Tours (1054), in the presence of Leo's legates, Hildebrand and Gerard, and forced to recant. He opened the gates of monasticism, so that the monks might sally forth as soldiers in his campaign for moral reform, which encompassed Italy, Germany, France, England, and even Spain. Leo IX constantly engaged in good offices in behalf of rulers and their peoples. He journeyed to Hungary to avert a war between that nation and the forces of King Henry III of Germany. He secured from the Duchess of Tuscany and Mantua an amnesty for some guilty prelates who had turned a local synod into a bloody brawl. In Rome he received King Macbeth of Scotland as a penitent for his crimes and forgave him. He released Edward the Confessor of England from his vow to come on a pilgrimage to Rome and caused him in exchange to erect in honor of the apostle Peter what came later to be Westminster Abbey. Likewise, Leo IX led his troops in battle against the Normans in southern Italy; and, though he was defeated, the power of moral suasion was such that the Normans began to cease their brigandage and even to replace with their own men the troops out of Leo's army that had been killed. Leo IX was a great leader of men.[48]

No less accomplished was the Eastern patriarch, **Michael Cerularius.** Before his elevation he had been a learned professor and government official in Constantinople. So capable had he been at whatever had been assigned him that a faction in the government, unbeknown to him, had actually conspired against the emperor and the emperor's brother, the chancellor, to raise Cerularius himself to the throne. The conspiracy had been discovered and Cerularius exiled (1040). When Constantine X had overthrown the Paphla-

---

[48] *Analecta Bollandiana* (Paris and Brussels, 1882 ff.), XXV, 258, 297. Bruno de Segni, *Vita S. Leonis IX*, in MPL, CLXV, 1116 ff.

gonians, Cerularius had been recalled (1042). Constantine had been so impressed by the sight of Cerularius, whom he had not known personally, that he said, "That is the man to be patriarch." Cerularius' patriarchate, begun March, 1043, was marked by two concerns: to lift the Constantinopolitan patriarchate to equality with the papacy and to free the Eastern church from subservience to the imperial government. The first of these concerns involved a rupture with the West and the constitution of the patriarch of Constantinople as an independent head of the church in the East. Michael Cerularius knew this; he planned deliberately to take this step. The initiative in effecting the schism came from the Eastern patriarch. He instigated the publication of a manifesto by the Bulgarian archbishop, Leo of Ochrida, sent deliberately to the West and addressed as an open letter to "the bishops and priests of France, the monks, the peoples and the most reverend pope." This manifesto imputed four serious errors to the Latins: (1) the use of unleavened bread in the celebration of the Eucharist; (2) the habit of fasting on Saturdays (like Jews); (3) the use of the meat of strangled animals; (4) the practice of forbidding the singing of the Alleluia during Lent. The haughty document contained the inflammatory question of the West, "Why are you laboring at the reform of people? Labor to reform yourselves!" [49]

This was followed by an outcry from a monk of Studium, Nicetas Stethatos, whose name in Latin was Pectoratus, "the man with the big chest." He addressed himself to his fellow Greeks, though his words of course reached the Latin ear, and added two further complaints against the West: (1) The Latin church subscribes to heresy in amending the Nicene Creed to read that the Holy Spirit proceeds from the Father and the Son, whereas the Greeks believe the Holy Spirit proceeds from the Father through the Son. (2) The Latin church forbids its priests to marry, which violates the law of nature and makes them less than human.[50]

In support of his subordinates Michael Cerularius closed the Latin churches in Constantinople, ordered the Latin monasteries in his domain to adopt the Greek rites or, if they refused, to be anathematized, and allowed the host at the Latin Eucharist to be thrown to the ground and trodden under foot.

Leo IX raised his voice in violent protest, contending that the Roman church since its inception was the one and only church entitled to respect and obedience from all Christendom. So tolerant and understanding had this church always been, he affirmed, that it had permitted, even urged, Greek establishments in southern Italy to retain their own rites and customs. Nevertheless it had been and is and will always be indefectible in its doctrine.[51]

The war in southern Italy with the Normans, of almost as much concern

[49] MPG, CXX, 385-386; MPL, CXLIII, 929.
[50] MPG, CXX, 981.
[51] MPL, CXLIII, 764.

to the emperor as to the pope, interrupted the argument for a short time. The patriarch was forced by the emperor to send a conciliatory letter to the pope, who responded in kind. As a result, Leo IX sent three legates to Constantinople to settle all these difficulties which had arisen between the Latins and the Greeks. However, after the battle with the Normans had been lost, the emperor no longer needed the pope. The papal legates were received in Constantinople with insolence. Cerularius renewed his former accusations and, in pontifical fashion, ordered the patriarch of Alexandria to remove the pope's name from the diptychs.

Consequently in retaliation on July 16, 1054, the papal legates formally laid on the altar of Saint Sophia a sentence of anathema against Michael Cerularius and all those who followed him: "Let them be Anathema Maranatha, with Simoniacs, Valerians, Arians, Donatists, Nicholaitans, Severians, Pneumatomachi, Manichees, Nazarenes, and with all other heretics, yea with the devil and his angels. Amen. Amen. Amen."

Four days later (July 20, 1054) at the same place, Michael Cerularius responded in kind and excommunicated the pope and his followers.

The schism was now completely effected.

VI. The Aftermath In East and West

The immediate effect of the schism on East (1054-1081) and West (1054-1073) was the same. It reduced the activities of both churches to their own spheres of influence and limited them almost entirely to a concern for themselves. This concern in each instance registered itself in a strenuous effort on the part of the church to free itself from governmental restrictions and controls. Unfortunately, in the East this attempt proved abortive: its ecclesiastical concern scarcely became anything more than a concern; it was not possible to transform it into any real accomplishment. The attempt in the West was pregnant with success: the accomplishment, to be sure, was not wrought immediately, but the twenty years following the schism at least showed signs of promise, so that in retrospect they appear to us like heralds of what was to come.

Michael Cerularius survived the schism he had effected by only four years (1054-1058). Having rid himself of the papal yoke, he now addressed himself to the still more strenuous task of casting off the imperial yoke as well. At first it appeared as if he would succeed. He gave strong and effective aid to the conspiracy which dethroned Michael VI (1056-1057) and which raised Isaac Comnenus (1057-1059), a successful and popular general, to his place. In gratitude the new emperor transferred his own right to appoint the grand chancellor and treasurer of the church to the patriarch and put the entire administration of ecclesiastical affairs in Cerularius' hands. He even honored the patriarch as a father and sought his advice frequently. No doubt all would have gone well had Michael Cerularius been content with the management of ecclesiastical affairs. He presumed not merely to advise but also to command his emperor, whom he corrected as a father might a child and censured as a teacher a pupil. Once he lost his temper with his imperial master and scolded him by exclaiming in indignation, "It was I who gave you the empire. I too can take it from you!" Isaac Comnenus responded by taking from him his patriarchate and destroying his lordly freedom by arrest. Shortly thereafter, disappointed beyond recovery, Michael Cerularius died.

With him perished his ambition of liberating the church from imperial management. His three immediate successors in office, Constantine III (1059-1063), John VIII (1064-1075), and Cosmas I (1075-1081), no matter what their personal attainments were, are historically speaking of no account. The church reverted under their administration to a department of state and subsidiary of the government. The emperors, Constantine X (1059-1067), Romanus IV (1067-1071), Michael VII (1071-1078), and Nicephorus III (1078-1081), all favored the church to be sure, but they patronized it as well. This was the era when bureaucracy, always a potent factor in the imperial government yet never quite the equal of the autocracy of the emperor, became supreme. The conduct of affairs was in the hands of a "brain trust"—a company of literary dilettantes under whom the empire shrank in size. Taxes rose, governmental services declined, feudalism began to emerge, and anarchy increased.[52]

Michael Cerularius, though less talented than Photius, was very much like that earlier patriarch in his education, personal interests, and ambition; and both men stand together as the chief historical personages in bringing about the schism. Photius discerned the reasons for it, sowed its seeds and watered them; Michael Cerularius harvested the crop. The court official Psellus, who knew Michael personally, states that he announced in his boyhood what he wanted to become and all his life manifested a solitary spirit and brooded on his ambitions. He was an ascetic, but he knew how to manage men. He died in the midst of the prosecution the emperor had brought against him—in fact, without ever appearing in person before his judges. Yet so great was his influence, the emperor had to announce publicly his deep veneration for the dead man, to implore posthumously his forgiveness, and to weep in penitence and grief at his tomb. Within less than a year of Michael's demise, Isaac Comnenus mysteriously abdicated the throne.

Photius and Michael Cerularius are the two greatest patriarchs of the Eastern church in medieval history.

Leo IX did not survive the mission of his three legates to Constantinople

[52] CMH, IV, 318-326.

and consequently was spared the knowledge of the schism. He felt the previous exchange of kind letters between him and Cerularius would effect good results.

Hildebrand, his chief counsellor, was at the time of Leo's death in France carrying out his mission against Berengarius at the Synod of Tours. He returned immediately to Rome to avert a break between the Emperor Henry III and the Italian clergy and populace, who wanted one of their own as their pope. Though Henry succeeded in having another German elected, still he renounced his title as patrician of Rome and did not interfere in the election. Indeed, his own chancellor, whom he did not wish to release from his political post, was chosen as Victor II. He was Hildebrand's nominee, and Hildebrand was his most trusted advisor and the most influential person in the church.

Hildebrand and Peter Damian, both ascetics and reformers, inspired by the ideals of Cluny and its monks, had been raised to prominence by John Gratian during his brief pontificate as Gregory VI. Hildebrand had been his pupil and was his personal secretary and constant companion. Damian was a Camaldolese monk—fiery, zealous, impetuous, a crusader for reform at any cost. He, to use his own expression, became Hildebrand's thunderbolt.[53] He and Hildebrand complemented each other: Peter Damian was the agitator, Hildebrand the statesman and the diplomat. These two reformers, though they desired the liberation of the church from state control as much as did Cerularius, knew that if the church were to gain its independence, it had to be able properly to manage its own affairs. Consequently they sought for it internal moral reform and spiritual vitality.

Victor II (1055-1057), under their tutelage, exerted himself as did his predecessor in peregrinations over the land in behalf of reform. The Emperor Henry III died, repenting of his sins, in the Pope's arms (October 5, 1056); and for a brief time Victor reverted to his old role as chancellor and ruled the empire in the name of Henry's widow (Empress Agnes) and six-year-old boy (Henry IV). He died away from Rome, July 28, 1057.

Stephen IX, his successor, abbot of Monte Cassino, elected in Hildebrand's absence and without the knowledge of the German Imperial House, represented Italian reaction to outside influence. Since his pontificate lasted but eight months (1057-1058), there was scarcely any time to effect a breach with Germany. It is significant only for the origin of the Patari (peasants) of Milan —a league of common people organized to expel from their position all unworthy and scandalous clergymen. Had Stephen carried out his aim of conferring the imperial crown on his own brother, Duke Godfrey, it is difficult to

[53] MPL, CXLIV, 273.

surmise what the outcome might have been. Could Italy have united to sustain this honor against German aggression?

Nicholas II (1059-1061), the personal choice of Hildebrand, had to sustain himself in office against a rival, Benedict X, who in defeat retired to live with his mother near the Church of Mary Major in Rome. Peter Damian said of the antipope that he was too devoid of understanding to appreciate what was going on around him.[54] Nicholas II, under Hildebrand's counsel, set up the College of Cardinals to elect all subsequent popes according to the following procedures: (1) On the death of the pope the cardinals will elect his successor; the cardinal-clerics, the clergy, and the people will then give their consent to their choice. (2) If a suitable candidate can be found among them, the pope must be elected from the Roman clergy. (3) The election can, under necessity, take place wherever the cardinals deem desirable. (4) If his enthronement is delayed, the new pontiff nonetheless will exercise full jurisdiction and power. (5) Care will be exercised to secure the honor and respect due to King Henry IV and his successors.[55]

When Nicholas II died, his successor Alexander II (1061-1073) was properly elected according to these provisions by the cardinals. Though Henry IV reacted violently to the choice and had his own candidate elected one month later under the name of Honorius II, after three years (1064) a German synod acknowledged Alexander II, and the antipope was deposed.[56]

All these pontiffs were worthy men and zealous in their administrations for the reform of the church.

[54] MPL, CXLIV, 104, 291.
[55] Hefele, op. cit. (Leclercq), IV, 1139-1165.
[56] CMH, V, 31-50.

Chapter Seven

The Age of Mighty Warriors
(1073-1124)

THE FIFTY-ONE YEARS BETWEEN THE ACCESSION OF POPE GREGORY VII (1073) and the death of Pope Calixtus II (1124) in the West and the long reign of Alexius Comnenus, which lasted for thirty-seven years (1081-1118), in the East were vigorous and decisive years in the history of Christianity.

The Latin church took those first bold and deliberate steps which were to lead eventually to its domination over secular politics and the creation of an ecclesiastical empire. The Greek church, always the faithful custodian of the theological treasures of the past, became concerned over the West's deviation from the tradition of the Fathers and realized as never before the importance of making the witness of one generation conform to the witness of other generations that have gone before it. It appeared to the Greeks as if the Latins had lost all their memories, while the Latins looked upon the Greeks as quiescent, indifferent to contemporary problems, and substituting the recollections of a glorious past for the accomplishments that needed to be wrought in the present. Both bodies of Christendom were thrown into close proximity with each other. The Cerularian schism accentuated difference without effecting isolation. Consequently rivalry and, to a certain extent at least, envy and intense jealousy were inevitable.

The events of Latin history were enacted against the background of the political struggle of the papacy with the Holy Roman Empire, while Greek history in all its parts was affected by the First Crusade, which subjected religion as well as politics and society to its terrific impact.

These years belonged to the warriors, so that even the peaceful movements of society such as monasticism and the cathedral schools imbibed their aggressive spirit and domineering tendencies. Indeed, monasticism was the spiritual leaven in the dough of a reforming papacy, while scholarship was adventurous and courageous and effected an entire new method of thought. Anybody who counted at all in this period was in his own way a fighter.

159

I. The Gregorian Reformation

For twenty-five years the monk Hildebrand had governed the Western church. He had ruled as the chief adviser of six pontiffs, at least three of whom he had personally chosen for the papal office. To be sure, his power had been entirely that of moral suasion; it had not sprung from position, and its continuation always was problematical, depending upon the influence he was able to exert upon the reigning pope. Now with the death of Alexander II, the first pope elected to his position by the College of Cardinals, the eyes of Christendom were fixed upon this body to see who its second designee would be. As heretofore, Hildebrand himself stubbornly resisted consideration.

Before the College could officially act the impetuosity of the Roman populace took the decision out of its hands. Hildebrand conducted the funeral of Pope Alexander II. Thus the occasion for honoring the deceased pontiff was seized upon by the people as the opportunity to designate his successor. Despite his feverish protests of unworthiness, the impropriety of the manner of election, and the inopportuneness of the time, Hildebrand was constrained to accept the papal office, the people themselves insisting that he who exerted the power should hold responsibility in name for all that he did. Consequently, presumably on the very day that Alexander II was buried, Hildebrand was seized by the mob, carried into the Church of Saint Peter in Chains, and installed in his new office by coercion.[1] One month later to the day (May 22, 1073), he was ordained priest,[2] and on June 30 he was properly consecrated a bishop and enthroned in papal splendor in Saint Peter's.[3] Ironically he who, more than anyone else, had created the College of Cardinals to elect the pope was not himself elected by it; and the man who did most to give law and order to papacy and empire alike received his position in an irregular manner. Indeed, the very name he selected for himself and, more especially, the reason he gave for selecting it were hardly in keeping with the role he performed. **Hildebrand took the name of Gregory VII** in honor of his old teacher Gregory VI (John Gratian), who had bought the tiara from the unworthy Benedict IX and later had been deposed for simony.

The compromising circumstances of Gregory's election did not deter him in the least from the pursuit of an uncompromising course of action directed toward the **reformation of Christendom**. This expressed itself in two major concerns: first, the internal cleansing of the church by the eradication of incontinence and simony among the clergy; and, secondly, the release of the church from external secular power by freeing its sees, parishes, and other institutions from lay investiture—that is, from the selection and appointment

[1] MPL, CXLVIII, 283, 285, 291, 400, 439, 566.
[2] Bonizo of Sutri, *Liber ad amicum*, VII, in MGH, *Libelli de lite imperatorum et pontificum*, Vol. II.
[3] MGH, *Scriptores*, III, 203.

of bishops, priests, and abbots by kings and nobles within whose domain or on whose property these clerics were to serve. Lay investiture was, from the viewpoint of the church, the worst evil of feudalism. Since under the feudal form of society a spiritual lord inevitably had to exercise temporal responsibilities, it was of supreme importance to his prince that the occupant of a fief be a person whom he could control and who would be subservient to his best interests. Likewise, the welfare of the church required that all its officials be loyal to its purposes and ends. In the eleventh century, no less than in the first, a man could not serve two masters. A cleric could not serve both pope and emperor.

The chief allies of Gregory in his program of reformation were the monks. They were spared from lay interference. The charter establishing Cluny, for example, expressly stated that no outside power should attempt to coerce the monks in the choice of their abbot or to interfere with them in the management of their affairs according to the rules of the order. The monasteries by nature were retreats from the cares and strains of the world, and there was a sanctity about them which generally deterred even the most callous prince from lifting unholy hands against them.

Prominent among these monastic allies of the papacy were three new establishments: (1) the Abbey of Vallombrosa, near Florence in Italy, founded in 1039 by John Gualbert, a nobleman of Pistoia; (2) the Hirschau monastery in Germany, reoccupied and revived after fifty years of abandonment by twelve monks from Einsiedeln in 1066 and made famous by its great abbot William, who dotted the landscape of South Germany with its offspring and who reformed other older monasteries nearby; and (3) the Carthusian order, begun in 1084 by Bruno Hartenfaust at Chartreuse, near Grenoble in France, which, after the Eastern pattern, sought pure contemplation rather than activity, and promoted righteousness by prayer rather than by preaching reform. The Carthusian monk, even in company, was always the hermit, alone with his own 'thoughts and God.[4] Chief of all Pope Gregory's allies, however, was Cluny Abbey, under the guidance of its sixth abbot, Hugh, who had been elevated to his position by the unanimous vote of his brethren when he was only twenty-five years old. Tall in stature and eloquent in speech, he added to the magnificence of his presence the command over people which learning, wisdom, and unselfish piety alone can confer. These monks became the moral and spiritual executives of the pope's political will.

Gregory VII's first action was taken in the area of **clerical reform.** At the first synod (March 1074) he held, less than a year after his elevation to the pontificate, he decreed: (1) a cleric guilty of simony is by that very fact unsuited to perform any sacred office; (2) a clergyman who pays money for a

⁴ MPL., CLII, 420 ff.

parish by that unworthy act loses his parish; no man can be permitted either to buy or to sell an ecclesiastical position; (3) a priest guilty of fornication must relinquish immediately the sacerdotal functions; (4) the people shall themselves disavow the services of clergymen who refuse to obey the papal decrees against simony and incontinence.[5]

It is one thing to promulgate a decree. It is quite another to enforce it among people disinclined toward both its intent and its application. Gregory immediately ran athwart the common behavior of a sizable portion, perhaps even a majority, of the clergy of Western Europe. In France, the leaders of the church, at a synod held in Paris (1074), openly proclaimed the papal commands absurd and frankly said nobody could conform to them even if he wanted to.[6] The situation was the same in Germany. Though the young King Henry IV apparently received the decrees without objection when he first was apprised of them,[7] his clergy set themselves steadfastly against a reforming council, and local prelates who tried to obey Gregory's orders met with stiff opposition. The Scandinavian countries and Hungary were indifferent to his edict. Though Gregory VII thought William the Conqueror, ruler of Normandy and England, was in sympathy with his purposes, the archbishop of Rouen was stoned out of his cathedral when he transmitted the Roman edicts to his clergy; and Lanfranc at Winchester, wisely sensing public sentiment, did not reveal to his people the full scope of the papal command.[8] It was obvious that a different method of approach was necessary to the accomplishment of so demanding and sacrificial an end.

Turning from the contemptible habits of clerical simony and incontinence to what he thought to be the basic cause which produced them, Gregory addressed himself to the Herculean task of eradicating lay investiture from the ecclesiastical practices of Western Europe. Gregory reasoned that as long as immoral princes were able to appoint their kind to high ecclesiastical office, all moral and spiritual reformation would be frustrated. The only way to reform the church would be to fill its positions with reformers.

Now the use of the good offices of the papacy in diplomatic and political affairs was traditional among all the governments. Gregory's pontificate, like that of his predecessors, was characterized by negotiations with princes and influence upon the internal management of states. The pope established good relations with Denmark, for example, when he instructed its king constantly to defend widows, orphans, and the poor; and he encouraged Norway to have the sons of the nobility educated in Rome. Fearlessly he excommunicated Boleslaus II for murdering with his own hands Bishop Stanislaus of Cracow,

[5] MPL, CXLVIII, 752.
[6] Mansi, XX, 442.
[7] Mansi, XX, 459.
[8] MPL, CXLVIII, 382, 383, 878; Mansi, XX, 442, 459.

Poland. In Bohemia and Hungary he cemented the ties between those nations and the papacy, helping the latter to end a civil war.

In Spain he upheld the sacredness of marriage among the laity as well as celibacy among the clergy and encouraged the fight against Islam. He sent missioners to Dalmatia, which he enticed away from the Eastern empire and church, sent doctrinal counsel to distant Armenia, staged a mission to expand the faith in an Islamic principality of Africa, and even conceived of an expedition to fight the heathen Turks in the Holy Land.[9]

These projects however were of little avail in accomplishing the papal will in regard to lay investiture. Earlier than most of them, Gregory declared himself unequivocally on this issue in his famous Roman synod of February 24-28, 1075:

the cleric who in the future receives from a layman a bishopric or an abbey will not be looked upon as a bishop or abbot by the church. We forbid him communion with Blessed Peter. The same prohibition applies to the lower clerical offices. If an emperor, duke, marquis, or count, or any other lay person invests a person with an ecclesiastical office, he shall be subject to the same condemnation as the cleric who accepts it.[10]

This declaration was the axe which Gregory VII laid at the root of lay investiture throughout Christendom.

The three principal roots were England, France, and Germany. Germany, holding the imperial title under Henry III and his royal predecessors back to Otto I, was the main theater of conflict between government and papacy on this issue—certainly during the lifetime of Gregory VII. Relations between William the Conqueror of England and Gregory were strained because of William's adherence to the policy of lay investiture, yet no rupture occurred. The archbishop of Rheims in France, only weakly supported by his king, had to give in to papal pressure and for a time was suspended from office for simony. Henry IV of Germany was the chief objective of Gregory's campaign. No doubt the pontiff discerned that if he, the greatest offender and the most powerful ruler, fell under the church's righteous onslaught, then all lesser sovereigns would fall with him. Consequently the papal axe fell in relentless blows on young Henry and his court.

Conditions in Germany were favorable for the papal attack. The long minority of Henry IV (the boy was only six at his father's death) had played havoc with the interests of the crown. This royal heir had been wrung by force from the hands of his mother the Empress Agnes, whom Henry III had designated as his guardian and regent of the kingdom, and had been

---

[9] *Gregorii VII Registrum*, I, 18; II, 6-8, 53, 63, 70, 71, 73, 75; III, 18, 21; IV, 25; VI, 13; VII, 65, 203 ff.; in MGH, *Epistolae*, II (1920-23).
[10] MPL, CLIV, 277.

passed, like an inanimate pawn, from one powerful personage to the next, each of whom had ruled the land while the royal lad was in his custody. At the same time the relative equality of strength among the princes, spiritual and temporal, and the intense rivalry among them had heightened feudalism in the realm and had increased those disruptive and divisive forces which can break a nation into a confederation of small principalities. On the other hand, the Cluniac reforms had had widest acceptance among the German clergy. The powerful archiepiscopal sees of Cologne and Mainz were both occupied by partisans of Cluny, and after a century of sustained and effective labor under a succession of six saintly abbatial statesmen the abbey was bound to have communicated its principles to the ranks of the lesser clergy adjacent to its premises. The innumerable monastic offspring of Hirschau, itself Cluniac in inspiration and doctrine, were in addition to Cluny taking the conscience of South Germany by storm. Though there had been enough simoniacal and incontinent prelates in high places to resist the conference on internal ecclesiastical reform which Gregory VII had first proposed, still such leaders had no strong objection to the reformation of others; and, when the pressure was taken off them and put on the lay princes and the king, they felt no strong inclination to resist. King Henry IV, when he was no more than twenty years old, had been constrained by circumstances to put down by force of arms the uprisings of the feudal powers in Saxony, to restrict the free use of forests and moors, and to increase taxes to replenish a bankrupt treasury. The last uprising had been so bitter that he had paraded the Saxon populace, lords and people alike, barefooted and unarmed, before his victorious army, as a spectacle of complete subservience to his crown. Consequently the Saxon people hated him intensely.

At this juncture, the authoritarian edict of Gregory on lay investiture struck Henry's court like a bolt of lightning. The young king, surrounded as he was by a host of enemies, desperately needed the use of investiture to place loyal friends in the powerful ecclesiastical posts of the realm. Without such a privilege his own crown was in jeopardy. The decree of the Roman Synod of February, 1075, was sent to Germany in the form of a letter from Gregory VII to Henry IV, who had only recently filled the two Italian sees of Fermo and Spoleto unbeknown to the pope. Gregory chided him severely for this, instructed him to confess his sin immediately to a priest and to do penance, and warned him to remember the fate of King Saul, who disregarded the admonition of God through Samuel the prophet. Yet the pope was kind and fatherly, too; he assured Henry that he would help him mitigate any difficulties that might arise in the realm over these reforms.[11] Henry, who hoped to be crowned emperor by the pope, replied in a filial manner, but subsequent

---

[11] *Gregorii VII Registrum*, III, 10.

events proved he was not sincere. He made several more important ecclesiastical appointments including that of Tebaldo to the see of Milan, which was not even vacant at the time.[12] The pope himself was kidnapped on the night of Christmas (1075), and a strong supporter of Henry IV in Rome was responsible for the act. Consequently in January, 1076, Gregory VII sent three legates to Germany and ordered Henry to appear in person on February 22 in Rome and to answer to the pope and a synod for his misconduct. If he failed to comply, he was to be anathematized.[13]

The king tried to offset the course of events by changing the subject at issue. He launched a counterattack on the pope by calling into question the legitimacy of his election and by seeking his deposition. To effect this, he summoned a synod of his German bishops at Worms, January 24, 1076, where Gregory was condemned, ordered to relinquish his office, and anathematized. The greeting and conclusion of Henry's letter to Gregory are interesting: "To Hildebrand, a false monk . . . I, Henry, king, by the grace of God, with all my bishops, say to you, 'Come down from the papal throne and be damned through all ages.' " [14]

Gregory responded through a synod at the Lateran, which was in session when news of Henry's action and that of his twenty-six bishops reached him. Even though Henry's mother, the Empress Agnes, was present **the pope excommunicated Henry and released his subjects from fealty to him.** He made public his action through a bull.[15]

This papal decision rested upon a comprehensive political and ecclesiastical ideal, international in its scope, defining precisely the relationship between the supreme spiritual ruler and the secular heads of state. In both the delineation of its specific principles and the definitiveness of its aim, it was new. It represented Gregory's concept of church and state—an imperial theocracy which placed under God's vicegerent all the principalities of Christendom. Only the pope exercised universal sway over all governments, could use the imperial insignia, possessed the right to depose emperors, might annul the decree of any person or synod of persons, was entitled to judge everyone yet could himself be judged by no one, and held the power to absolve subjects from their oath of fealty to wicked rulers.[16] Gregory expected kings and princes symbolically to show their subservience to his will and obedience to his commands by kissing the papal foot. This is what King Henry would have been required to do had he obeyed Gregory's orders to come to Rome.

The action Gregory took in excommunicating Henry and in placing an in-

[12] Bonizo of Sutri, op. cit., VII.
[13] MGH, Scriptores, V, 241, 280, 431.
[14] Ibid., p. 352.
[15] Registrum, III, 6.
[16] Dictatus papae, in Registrum Gregorii VII.

terdict on his kingdom was revolutionary. Consequently the king and his advisers were totally unprepared for it. Services were suspended throughout the churches of the realm; the blessed Sacrament was denied to the enemies of God's church; the common people who took their religion seriously hissed at the king and pelted him with stones in the street; his castles were pillaged and his lands ravaged; Saxony revolted again; and the helpless monarch was, if still in possession of a throne, almost without subjects to sustain him on it. His own nobility assembled at Tribur (October, 1076), suspended Henry from the government of his realm, ordered him to live at Spires as a private person and not to enter a church, and set another council to meet later at Augsburg where he would be judged by Pope Gregory himself. If he did not give the pope such satisfaction that he might be admitted again to communion with the church, he would be deposed.[17] Here at Tribur the laity itself recognized the legitimacy of and capitulated to the papal action. The Roman Catholic Church was supreme.

The young King Henry was desperate. He could not face the possibility (and it was a real one) of deposition at Augsburg. Consequently he devised a strategy of his own to offset this aggressive campaign of papal autocracy. Unable to defeat the pope politically, he decided to employ the weapons of the spirit. Henry resolved to feign the role of the penitent and to cast himself for mercy and forgiveness at the pope's feet. Disregarding winter weather and the dangers of the journey, he crossed the Alps with his family and a small contingent of his subjects. He found Gregory VII at Canossa in Tuscany, the guest of the Countess Matilda. Fortunately for Henry his godfather Hugh of Cluny was also a guest there, and Henry knew that Hugh would use his influence to persuade the pope to forgive him. Three days, from morning until evening, Henry, barefooted and in the garb of a penitent, stood in the snow before Gregory's hostel and cried for mercy. What could the pope do? To forgive Henry would undo all the papal gains in Germany and set at nought the political victory the church had already won. It would invalidate Augsburg before the council had been held, for there would be nothing for which to try the king. Yet not to forgive him would impeach Gregory's own integrity as the chief pastor of Christians. The church could not shut its door in the face of a suppliant. It existed to forgive sinners.

Be it said to the credit of Gregory that he sacrificed his political victory for the obligations of his priestly office. Like any other confessor, he forgave his royal penitent, accepting his confession at face value. That was all that Henry needed. He had not been sincere. He had saved his throne. He now turned to the consolidation of his power and the ruination of him who had restored him. January 27, 1077, the day Henry was forgiven at Canossa, stands in history

[17] Mansi, XX, 379.

as the supreme moment both of papal magnanimity and mercy and of royal perfidy and contempt.

The eight years that followed were bitter and disastrous for the church. Though loyal friends of Cluny and of the papacy rose in indignant rebellion against Henry, their time of opportunity had passed at Canossa. Rudolph of Swabia, elected king in Henry's stead by a council of nobles at Forchheim (March 13, 1077), died of wounds he received in battle three years later (1080), and there was no one else left to contest with Henry his right to rule. Consequently at Brixen (June 25, 1080) Henry convened a council which deposed Gregory VII as pope and elected Guibert, archbishop of Ravenna, in his stead. Italy was invaded, Rome besieged and captured, and Gregory himself rescued by the Normans under Guiscard, who transported him to southern Italy as their guest, though in reality he was little better than their prisoner. Henry was crowned Holy Roman Emperor in his camp by the antipope Guibert, who had taken the name of Clement III. On May 25, 1085, Gregory died in sun-kissed Salerno, with this lament upon his tongue, "I have loved righteousness and hated iniquity; therefore I die in exile." [18]

In the sphere of international politics Gregory VII stands as the moral hero of the Middle Ages. He championed a cause which, though temporarily defeated, was destined ultimately to win. He was willing to fail himself in order to bequeath to those who came after him such a legacy that they were bound to succeed. More than anyone else, Gregory VII was the creator of the papal empire of the thirteenth century.

II. The First Crusade

The attention of Europe was directed from the debacle into which the war of investiture between Henry IV and Gregory VII had plunged the church by an aggressive military campaign of the Christian West against the Moslem East. Gregory VII had envisaged such a campaign and had planned to lead it himself. The act of its accomplishment was left to his successor, who wisely saw that the way to victory over Western principalities was an oblique one and that it led through the East.

The gains which the Macedonian dynasty had achieved for the Byzantine empire had been lost in the troubled times which had followed the reign of Basil II, and the twenty-five years from 1056 (death of Theodora) to 1081 (the establishment of the Comnenus dynasty) had seen an expansion of Islam comparable to its first great wave of conquest in the seventh and eighth centuries. Armenia had been lost in 1071 at Manzikert, where the Byzantine army was destroyed and the Emperor Romanus himself wounded and imprisoned. Raids into the heart of the empire as far as the Aegean coast had

---

[18] Watterich, *Pontificum romanorum vitae* (1861), I, 340.

been followed by the conquest of a great portion of Asia Minor, so that the bastions of Islam reached almost to Constantinople itself, for Nicaea was in enemy hands. The impetus for this new conquest had come, not from the Arabs, but from the Turks, who had originated in Central Asia and had been converted in the tenth century to Islam by the Samanids of Persia. Syria, including Palestine, was entirely in their hands (except for Aleppo under Arabic control), so that their power reached to the borders of Egypt, where the Fatimids ruled. Fortunately for the Eastern empire these Turks were not united; and the Arabs, their coreligionists, were not their friends. Travelers of the time were impressed that almost every city had a different master.[19]

Nonetheless **the changed condition of the East imposed heavy penalties upon the Christian pilgrims to the Holy Land.** The Turks were notorious as brigands and thieves. One could not cross Anatolia safely without an armed guard, and each town in Syria showed its hospitality to the stranger by levying a tax on him. It is surprising to us that anybody at all went from Christendom to the Moslem East, but those intrepid souls who did came back with horrible tales to tell and thereby fired the folk at home with a passionate desire to rid the Holy Land of this sacrilege. The Eastern Emperor Alexius Comnenus, who had come to power in 1081, though his wars against the Turks were faring well, nonetheless was in need of additional troops for his campaigns. Since he had found Western mercenaries, especially the Anglo-Saxons, good fighters, he turned West for new recruits. He made his appeal directly to the pope, hoping to use the religious issue as the means whereby to replenish his armies. To accomplish his purpose he sent Byzantine ambassadors to the papal court.

Pope Urban II (1088-1099), trained at Cluny and the loyal disciple of Pope Gregory VII, was better able than his master had been to use conditions such as now prevailed in the East for the advantage of the church in the West. In appearance he was tall, straight, and remarkably handsome in contrast to Gregory, who was small, corpulent, and had very short legs.[20] He commanded men's attention at once by his physical bearing and then by his manners, which were gracious and conciliatory. Indeed, he possessed in abundance that indefinable characteristic called charm. His voice was deep and rich; he had the instincts of an actor; his use of words was remarkable; in short, he was one of the most gifted preachers of history. He was diplomatic in all his ways.

Since the antipope Guibert occupied Rome, Urban became a wandering evangelist, visiting northern Italy and France, and winning friends and supporters wherever he went. He wisely discerned that the way to triumph over

---

[19] William of Tyre, *Historia Rerum in Partibus Transmarinis Gestorum*, I, 8.
[20] MGH, *Scriptores*, X, 474. L. Paulot, *Urbain II* (1903), 2-3.

his opponents was to have a cause bigger than either he or they. His cause from the outset was the deliverance of the Holy Land. His aim was to unite western Europe in a mighty crusade. If this could be achieved, the unity of Christendom about his see would follow as a matter of course.

Consequently he decreed, after years of careful preparation and much personal propaganda, a council at Clairmont in southern France to consider the plight of the East. Though the council sat for ten days, November 18 to November 28, 1095, it was on Tuesday, November 27, at a great public meeting, held in the open air on a field outside the town, that it reached its dramatic climax. Urban II on that occasion delivered one of the most effective sermons in all history, for his message initiated the First Crusade and set Western Europe upon a series of military migrations into the East which, though ultimately unsuccessful in the accomplishment of the purpose for which they were ordained, nonetheless marked and, to a degree at least, facilitated the shift of civilization from Byzantium to the West. "God wills it!" shouted the crowd in response to Urban's call for a crusade. Adhemar, bishop of Le Puy, who led those who made public profession of their commitment to the enterprise, was unanimously chosen as the ecclesiastical head of the holy expedition. Means were devised to inflame the conscience of Europe, so that people of all classes would support the movement. The Feast of the Assumption (August 15, 1096) was set as the date of departure and Constantinople designated as the meeting place of the armies for their march of conquest into the East. Pardons, indulgences, promises of relief from sin and guarantee of paradise were given in abundance, so that most people felt they had little to lose and much to gain by accepting the challenge.[21]

Though the pope himself wrote to many of the princes and nobles, and bishops dealt directly with the great within their dioceses, the masses were enlisted by popular preachers, the best known and most effective of whom was Peter the Hermit. Peter had been a pilgrim to the Holy Land; he therefore knew from experience conditions that prevailed there; and he had the remarkable gift of making others see what he saw and of feeling what he felt. He was a typical ascetic, abstaining from bread and meat as well as wine. He rode a little donkey; and his long, lean face made him look very much like the beast, which people came to revere almost as much as its master. He was short and swarthy, sweated profusely, never bathed or changed his clothes, and consequently had an odor as strong and impressive as his personality and his message. Yet amazingly enough he carried those he had enlisted with him —his army of recruits growing steadily larger as his migrations continued. When he entered the Rhine Valley on the last phase of his recruitment campaign, there must have been fifteen thousand folk in his train.

---

[21] Mansi, XX, 815-820.

Yet the flame of enthusiasm, unless it is continually refueled, soon burns out. The only way to hold the loyalty of those recruits was to let them march on to Constantinople. Out of this movement of popular preaching there arose five different armies, each of which set out separately for Constantinople. Only two, however, reached their destination intact. One went Jew hunting in the Rhine Valley, believing that it should destroy the infidels at home before hunting them down in foreign parts, and so was disbanded by its own folly. The two that arrived in Constantinople were led by Walter the Penniless and Peter the Hermit. They crossed the Bosphorus, engaged the Turks, and before the army of the princes arrived had utterly perished. A heap of whitening bones testified alike to their valor and their folly.

The **Crusade of the Princes** was more successful. The first of these to answer Pope Urban's summons was Hugh of Vermandois, younger son of Henry I of France and therefore brother of the reigning French monarch, Philip I. He was courtly and chivalrous and probably went for the adventure. The next was Godfrey of Bouillon, a descendant of Charlemagne and loyal vassal to Henry IV. He had supported his king against Pope Gregory VII. Now perhaps his conscience smote him. He would join the Crusade to compensate for his sins. Since he had to sell lands to raise money and since the expedition cost him so much, his motive in going must have been chiefly religious. His two brothers went with him: the elder, Eustace, who was unenthusiastic and always anxious to return home and the younger, Baldwin, intrepid, bold, but avowedly selfish. Since Baldwin was landless, he went East to win for himself a fief and the fame and fortune that went with it. His worldly ambition was matched only by that of Bohemund, the Norman of southern Italy, who was in a similar plight, and his nephew Tancred. They were third in the succession of these great leaders. Probably the first to pledge his support to the pope but fourth to set out on the march was Raymond of Toulouse, a mature man of almost sixty, who had fought for the cause of the church against the Moors in Spain, the friend and confidant of Adhemar of Le Puy. Raymond undoubtedly wanted to be the secular leader of the movement. Bohemund wanted to be leader also. Consequently he and Raymond were bitter rivals. The last great princes to go were Robert of Normandy, eldest son of William the Conqueror, and his brother-in-law, Stephen of Blois. Robert had been deeply moved by the preaching of the Crusade and went because he felt spiritually constrained to do so. Stephen of Blois was constrained to go, not by any feelings of his own, but by those of his wife.

The Eastern Emperor Alexius, who had appealed to the West only for mercenaries to augment his own forces, was alarmed when he got large and independent armies with their own leaders, methods of campaign, and purposes in coming. Consequently his concern was to keep them on the move and to guarantee the restoration to his empire of whatever cities and territories they captured from the Turks. Since the leaders and their forces did not all arrive at the same time, he negotiated with each as he came. Hugh of Vermandois set the precedent for the rest by taking on arrival the oath of vassalage to the Eastern emperor. Though the others demurred at first, they all acceded to this demand of Alexius. All, that is, but Raymond of Toulouse, who on an expedition such as this would swear vassalage only to Christ! Yet in the end Raymond was more loyal to the emperor than any of the others. He insisted that each city as it was taken be restored to its proper owner. As a result, he got little for himself except the satisfaction of the pilgrimage and the spiritual blessing of having accomplished the mission which the church had decreed.

The first city to fall was Nicaea (June 19, 1097), and this not to an assault by the crusaders but by surrender to the emperor after the crusaders had besieged it for thirty-four days. The march across Asia Minor led to the capture of Dorylaeum (July 1). Then, after traversing the Anatolian desert, Baldwin and Tancred separated from the main army to make some conquests of their own. The chief result of this was the gaining of Edessa (February 6, 1098) and Baldwin's establishment as the ruler of that city and its territory on the Euphrates. The objective of the main army was Antioch.

Stephen of Blois had written to his wife after the capture of Nicaea "In five weeks' time we shall be at Jerusalem; unless we are held up at Antioch." This second statement proved to be prophetic. Antioch without doubt was the worst battle of the war. The main army reached it at the Iron Bridge, where the highway to Aleppo joins another road to cross the river, on October 20, 1097—four months and one day after the fall of Nicaea. On June 2, 1098, the enemy was overcome, and before nightfall every Turk in the city except the few barricaded in the citadel on Mount Silpius had been slaughtered. In the meantime, during those horrible seven months between arrival and victory and eight months more of occupation and defense against a mighty enemy, the crusaders paid a terrible price. They were afflicted by pestilence and famine. They killed their own horses for meat and drank one another's urine to quench their thirst. Peter the Hermit, so gifted in inspiring others to deeds of valor, was a coward himself and tried to run away. Stephen of Blois did desert the cause on the eve of its greatest battle. The crusaders' ablest leader and wisest statesman, Adhemar of Le Puy, died. The breach between the Westerners and the Easterners was irrevocably fixed, so that the emperor no longer figured in the contest. The best military strategists, Raymond of Toulouse and Bohemund, were set at each other's throats and could no longer co-operate. A mighty army of perhaps 100,000 soldiers was reduced to straggling bands of warriors and pilgrims. Antioch had fallen only by the employment of treachery, and similarly the Turkish army of relief had been defeated only by religious fanaticism inspired by the hoax of Peter Bartholomew, who claimed to have discovered the Holy Lance which had pierced the side of Christ.

Yet Jerusalem was the crusaders' goal. The common soldiers were determined to reach it and forced the leaders to desist from their quarrel over who would rule Antioch so as to move on. Bohemund stayed behind in possession of the city. But Raymond of Toulouse, Godfrey of Bouillon, and the lesser princes took the highway, and on Tuesday, June 7, 1099, arrived before the walls of the Holy City, now in Fatimid hands. The building of two movable towers enabled the crusaders to scale the almost impregnable walls, which they did successfully on July 13 and 14. They bathed the inhabitants of the city, Jews as well as Moslems, in their own blood. Indeed, around the temple area, blood ran as high as a man's knees. This wanton slaughter of the infidels by the Christians was as horrible as any recorded in history. Three days after the purge they met in the Church of the Holy Sepulcher to give to the Holy Land a Christian king.

Raymond of Toulouse declined to be a king in the city where Christ received a crown of thorns. He knew however that none of the other great knights wanted him; and that if he were chosen, it would be almost impossible for him to rule. Godfrey of Bouillon, less able but more kindly disposed, was chosen in his stead. He gladly accepted the office without the title, using in its place Advocate of the Holy Sepulcher, as if that shrine needed any other advocate than him who had been raised from the dead.

Urban II died fourteen days after the capture of Jerusalem before news of his crusaders' victory could reach his ears. The Italian legate whom he appointed to succeed Adhemar proved unworthy of his confidence. His name was Diambert. Though he got the patriarchate of Jerusalem, he disgraced it by his worldliness, ambition, and cruelty. He imposed on Godfrey, who to keep peace had to become his vassal.

One by one the lesser princes except Tancred returned home. Bohemund was captured by the Turks and spirited away to a prison in Anatolia; while Raymond of Toulouse, landless still, went to Constantinople to visit the emperor. Then ironically at the untimely death of Godfrey (July 18, 1100), Baldwin of Edessa—that selfish prince who had come East only for self-aggrandizement, wealth, power, position, and prestige, and who had not even participated in the capture of either Antioch or Jerusalem—became king (November 11, 1100). Without any compunction he took the title with the office and began actually to rule.[22]

So what had begun as perhaps the greatest movement of the Middle Ages (certainly the largest in numbers) degenerated before it was over into just another kingdom of this world.

[22] S. Runciman, A History of the Crusades (Cambridge, 1953), Vol. I. Full bibliography, pp. 327-335, 342-360.

III. Christianity in the East

The impact of the First Crusade upon the East was both beneficial and detrimental to the Orthodox church.

It was beneficial where the crusaders merely captured cities and their surrounding territories and then moved on, leaving them to be occupied and controlled by the Greek citizens and their officials. At Nicaea the imperial flag had been unfurled just as the crusaders were about to launch their assault. The Turkish inhabitants of the place, realizing that the outcome of the impending battle meant for them certain defeat, had surrendered to the emperor in the night. Alexius had guaranteed to them the right to withdraw unmolested and had accorded to the Sultana and her train the honor and respect due royalty. He was by temperament and habit kind and gracious; and it was characteristic of the East, once a battle was won, to be merciful and generous to the vanquished in the expectation of receiving the same treatment in the future when the situation was reversed. Alexius knew the crusaders would go as they had come. The Turks he would always have with him.

At Dorylaeum the crusaders rested only two days after their victory. The Greeks then reconstituted the city after the old pattern, and the Orthodox church exercised the freedom and leadership of its accustomed past. Indeed, throughout all Asia Minor north of the Euphrates the First Crusade initiated a new advance against the Turks on the part of the empire. After the fall of Nicaea Alexius reconquered the entire coastline of Asia Minor as far as Antioch in the extreme south. After his victory at Philomelium he took advantage of the defeated Turks to impose upon them a peace which gave him time to reorganize his new conquests. By the end of his reign (1118) the empire possessed the southern coast of the Black Sea as far as Trebizond on the border of Armenia. Likewise, it held all the territory of Asia Minor from Sinope in the north to the Syrian border in the south—roughly speaking, what is now the western half of Turkey.

Alexius, faced with what might well have been an embarrassing threat to the independence of his empire in the armies of the crusading princes, used them as far as he could to his own ends and thereby converted a threat into a support. He was one of the most remarkable of the Byzantine rulers. He came to the purple when the empire had been seriously reduced in territory and wealth. He found the Balkans in the turmoil of revolt. The Normans had robbed the Greeks of their territories in Italy and had invaded Epirus in Greece and the island of Corfu. Added to these military difficulties was a commercial one, for across the Adriatic Sea Venice had awakened to its maritime opportunities and was a serious competitor with Constantinople in the marts of trade. The Bogomiles of Thrace, aided by the Petchenegs, were at war again. Yet he managed, despite all these reverses, to restore the credit of the empire.[23]

Alexius the man was a typical Greek. He was both short and broad. His skin was brown to match exactly the color of his big eyes. He had thick, curly, black hair and a long, black beard shining a little with the oil he kept constantly on it. Like Constantius, his predecessor of many centuries, he preferred since he was so short to be seen sitting either alone on his throne or on the back of a horse. His manner was oily like his person. He gave lavish compliments and gifts, but he took as well, and everything he did was for a purpose. Always his actions, personal as well as official, were designed to serve his imperial ends. He impressed the crusaders by his magnificence. Stephen of Blois wrote his wife, "Your father," meaning William the Conqueror, "made many great gifts, but he was almost nothing compared to this man." [24] He was not easily fooled. Bohemund, the handsome Norman with the beautiful yellow hair and certainly the greatest tactician of the First Crusade and perhaps even the greatest strategist as well, tried to flatter him into winning from him the appointment of imperial commander in chief of the expedition. Yet Alexius distrusted and despised him from the start; while Raymond of Toulouse, who refused the emperor homage, became his dependable ally and friend. Alexius was a true judge of men. He was a diplomatist and administrator as well as soldier. During his thirty-seven years on the throne (1081-1118) the empire and its church prospered at his hands.

To accomplish what he thought was for the good of the church as well as the empire, Alexius resorted to severe measures. For example, he ascertained exactly the number of clerics each monastery or establishment had a right to possess, and any more than that number were subjected to taxation like other citizens. Likewise he accorded a proportion of the income from rich monasteries to nobles whom he wanted to reward. He limited the number of clergy, secular and regular, by setting high standards of knowledge and conduct. Clerics had to pass rigid examinations. Not only did he reform clerical morals but he sought to put down heresy and ensure orthodoxy of belief. He entered into disputes with the Bogomiles and Armenians and condemned the teaching of Italus for its arid speculations and of Nilus for its Oriental adornments. He even wrote a theological treatise purporting to refute all heresies.[25]

The First Crusade was detrimental to the Orthodox church and other

[23] CMH, IV, 327-350.

[24] H. Hagenmeyer, *Die Kreuzzugsbriefe aus den Jahren 1088-1100* (Innsbruck, 1902) 138-140.

[25] Anna Comnena, *Alexiad* (ed. Reifferscheid, Leipzig, 1884), 2 vols. CMH. IV, 349-50.

Eastern ecclesiastical bodies in those cities and territories where the Westerners set up their own principalities and states.

Edessa is a typical example. Baldwin was invited by the Armenian population to become the ruler of the city. At first he was associated in the government with Thoros, the imperial governor of the city. He allowed himself to be adopted by Thoros in a quaint Eastern rite in which Thoros put a big shirt over himself and Baldwin, and the two men rubbed their naked bodies together as pledge of fidelity and love each to the other. Yet Baldwin betrayed Thoros to his enemies, soon replaced the native leadership by Westerners, and introduced his own Latin rites into competition with Orthodox and Armenian rites in the churches.

John the Oxite, patriarch of Antioch, was actually deposed and expelled from his see by Bohemund, who distrusted him (1100). A Latin prelate was put in his place.[26]

Since Simeon, patriarch of Jerusalem, did not live to quit his exile on Cyprus and return to his see, a Latin cleric, the disreputable Arnulf, was first elected to the vacancy and then was deposed to make room for the papal legate, Diambert. Furthermore, Latin rites replaced Greek in this ancient and revered seat of Christendom. As the Christian population of the new state increased, Orthodox, Nestorians, and Jacobites went over in wholesale numbers to the Latin church.[27]

It was out of the First Crusade that the various military orders were either reactivated or else actually emerged. These were a combination of monasticism and chivalry, a blend of the military vocation of the knight with his great prowess in combat and of the asceticism of the monk with his gift of prayer and self-denial. The occasion of their origin was the need to transport peaceful pilgrims in safety to the Holy Land and to lend them protective care during the days of their devotion.

The two great orders were the Knights of Saint John of Jerusalem called the Knights Hospitalers and the Knights of the Temple called the Templars, later named respectively the Knights of Rhodes and the Knights of Malta as they changed their places of abode. Both wore the armor of the soldier, over which the Hospitalers placed their black cloak with the white cross and the Templars their white cloak with the red cross.

The Hospitalers began before the First Crusade in 1048, when a hospital was opened by some Amalfi nobles and merchants in Jerusalem to care for Christian pilgrims and the sick. Gerard of Tenque gave to it a distinctive character by assigning to the members the task of defending the pilgrims against the infidel as well as affording them hospitality and charity. In 1113

[26] *Echos d'Orient*, XXXII, 286-298.
[27] L. Bréhier, *L'Eglise et l'Orient au Moyen Age* (1907), p. 100.

Pope Paschal II confirmed the order as Gerard had defined it and put it under the patronage of Rome.[28]

Five years later (1118) the Knights of the Temple arose under the inspiration of Hugh of Payens and Godfrey of St. Omer and six other chivalrous companions. Later they were joined by Hugh of Provence. In 1128 Bernard of Clairvaux gave them a constitution. They added to the three monkish vows of poverty, chastity, and obedience, a fourth vow—that of giving their life to the protection of the pilgrims. They swore never to leave the field of combat unless opposed by more than three infidels to one knight. They got their name Templars from the place of their establishment on the area of the Temple in Jerusalem.

Later other military orders arose such as the Teutonic Knights in Germany and the Knights of Calatrava and the Knights of St. James of the Sword in Spain.

Consequently the First Crusade introduced a foreign element into the East —aggressive Latin Christianity in vigorous competition with any form of ecclesiastical life which was different from it. Heretofore, the schism between East and West had not been generally known or recognized. John the Oxite of Antioch was still in communion with Rome when the crusaders arrived. So was Simeon of Jerusalem, who lent them active aid. But after the First Crusade the schism which had begun as a dispute between Rome and Constantinople was extended throughout the entire East. As Greeks and Latins came into proximity with each other, the observation of their differences accentuated their separateness. The Orthodox Christians wanted now to have as little to do with Rome as was possible. Where Latin churches were set up, the Greeks maintained their establishments also. In Antioch, for example, after the deposition of John the Oxite, there were both a Latin and a Greek patriarchate. Bohemund, Latin ruler of Antioch, actually attacked Constantinople itself, and the Emperor Alexius had to negotiate a peace.

Despite both the war with Islam and the establishment of Latin principalities on Greek soil, the **Empire** under Alexius Comnenus was still the **greatest state in Christendom,** and the **culture** of its inhabitants and the monuments and artistic treasures of its cities were unequaled anywhere else in the civilized world. The crusaders appalled the citizens of the empire by their ignorance and crudity, affording examples of the Western people whom Nicetas called "those dark and wandering tribes the greater part of which, if they did not receive birth from Constantinople, were at least reared and nourished by her, and among whom neither grace nor muse takes shelter." Sweet singing seems to them "the cry of vultures or the croak of crows." [29]

[28] MPL, CLXIII, 314.

[29] Nicetas Choniates, *Historia* (ed. I. Bekker, Bonn, 1835), 764, 791, in CSHB.

Alexius' reign saw a revival of interests in ancient Greek literature, so that the style of the time was an imitation of Hesiod, Homer, the dramatists, philosophers, and orators of the Periclean age. Such imitation produced artificiality. Strict adherence to Attic dialect made the written language dissimilar to the spoken language of the people. The emperor wrote in iambic meter, while his daughter Anna memorialized the splendid achievements of her father in an epic poem. Anna's writing is perhaps the noblest document of her father's reign and gives us vivid details of the men and movements of the time. Her husband, Nicephorus Bryennius, was also an historian as well as a statesman. He wrote a memoir giving an account of the rise of the family to power.

Alexius Comnenus opened the way for the transmission of Byzantine scholarship to the West by making possible direct contact between persons from Italy and his empire. Conversations, especially on theological and ecclesiastical matters, were held in Constantinople between representatives of the East and West. These were not only continued but became more frequent under his successors.[30]

IV. The Conflict over Investitures and Its Settlement

The First Crusade, though it directed the attention of the West from the struggle between the papacy and the empire and thereby lessened its intensity, did not halt it in its course of development, for the Crusade did not eradicate those issues out of which it had arisen. Neither did it affect directly the chief participants in the controversy. Both pope and emperor stayed at home, while only lesser princes, ecclesiastical and lay, took the cross and went East. All the crowned heads of the West remained steadfastly with their dominions. Indeed, this ugly contest between the spiritual and secular powers sapped the energy and wasted the strength of six successive pontificates, so that all the years between 1073 and 1122 were lived under its menacing shadow.

Perhaps Gregory VII's immediate successor divined what the lot of the pope would be, for he begged his fellow cardinals not to elect him; and, when they did despite his protest, he appealed to Providence for release and so escaped his burden of the pontificate through the merciful gift of death. The abbot of Monte Cassino, who received the name of Victor III, died after a reign of only four months and eights days (May 9-September 16, 1087).

It is interesting to observe that in the eleventh century the pope did not choose his own name. It was assigned to him either by the people or by the secular ruler, though often of course they asked him, as in the case of Gregory VII, what name he wanted.

Urban II's vigorous pontificate of almost eleven years (1088-1099), made

---

[30] Vasiliev, op. cit., II, 487-505.

glorious by the triumph of the First Crusade abroad, was dogged by the investiture struggle at home. The issues could no longer be confined to Germany and the empire. They broke out in other nations as well. They were aggravated by the plots and plans of the antipope Guibert, who called himself Clement III. Of all the rivals to the papal throne, none either before or since has prosecuted his cause with more zeal, tenacity, and brazen self-confidence than Guibert, who was the ecclesiastical tool of Henry IV. He took Rome three times, maltreated his opponents (one had his eyes plucked out, while another was stoned to death), held synods and issued decrees as if he had been the canonical pope. He outlasted Urban by one year, stubborn and unyielding, "taking his anathemas with him into eternity." [31] His movement was strong enough to give him a successor. Theodoric was elected in his place but did not receive the support of the empire and was soon dethroned. The Guibertist faction proved as stubborn as its founder and elected Albert to take Theodoric's place. He lasted only three months, one of his own friends then surrendering him to the Holy See.

What Urban II set out to accomplish had to be continued by his three immediate successors. Paschal II (1099-1118), Gelasius II (1118-1119), and Calixtus II (1119-1124) were all occupied with the investiture issue and its subsidiary expressions. Therefore, in regard to the controversy and its settlement, these four pontificates coalesce into a single pattern.

Philip I of France, who as a child of seven had solemnly sworn, on the instruction of his father, Henry I, in the presence of the French hierarchy in the cathedral of Rheims "to maintain the canonical privileges for each of you and for the churches entrusted to you," [32] stubbornly opposed ecclesiastical reform in his realm, practiced simony, and added personal scandal and immorality to the corruption of his government. He divorced without cause his lawful wife, Bertha, and married Bertrade, who had actually solicited his affections and invited him to commit the sin. As a result Philip I was excommunicated along with Henry IV. The next ten years in Philip's life were bitter. The pleasures of his adulterous bed were more than offset by the pains of public censure and exclusion from the privileges of the church. Wherever he went in his realm all religious functions were discontinued at his approach. One evening as he was leaving a town which had been as quiet as death while he was in it, he heard the church bells ring merrily forth. The disconsolate king turned to his queen and said, "Bertrade, do you hear how these people are driving us out?" [33] During the time of his excommunication Philip did not wear his crown or put on his purple robe or even take part in a public

[31] MPL, CXLVIII, 1018.
[32] *Historiens des Gaules,* XI, 32.
[33] William of Malmesbury, *De gestis pontificum Anglorum,* V, 404, in MPL, CLXXIX, 1360.

178

festival. Indeed he dared not lest the people hiss at him or try to stone him. He and Bertrade finally made their peace with the church on December 2, 1104, by yielding their personal desires to its law.[34]

The investiture struggle in France was never as intense and ugly as it was in Germany. For one thing, the French ecclesiastical fiefs were not so rich and powerful as the German, and therefore the control over them did not appear so necessary to a secular prince. Then too they were more diversified—that is, in the hands of more of the lesser nobility than in Germany. The king of France did not feel constrained to defend the rights of lay nobles, which were often in conflict with his own. But more important still Cluny Abbey was in France; its principles were highly respected there; and the people were able to discern more clearly the distinction between the rights temporal and the duties spiritual. The issue soon resolved itself. Without participation in the voting by either the laity or the lower clergy, the cathedral chapters elected their own bishops, who were merely confirmed by the king. The bishop was the appointee of the church, yet he acted as a loyal subject of his king.

In England William the Conqueror, though he had tenaciously held to his privileges of controlling the principal ecclesiastical sees while favoring clerical reforms, was succeeded by his second son, William Rufus, who was brazen in his defiance of the papacy and ruthless in dealing with any who opposed his will. At first his haughty disposition and violent temper had been softened and controlled by the influence of the saintly Lanfranc, whom his father had made archbishop of Canterbury. Yet with Lanfranc's death, the autocratic passions of King William Rufus burst forth with the violence of an erupting volcano. The object of his fury was the mild and gentle Anselm, Lanfranc's pupil and successor. William Rufus' policy had been to keep as many sees vacant as long as he could in order to turn their revenues to the usage of the state. Among them had been the see of Canterbury itself. But once, while grievously ill and expecting any minute to die, the king had been persuaded to accept Anselm, the nominee of the clergy, to the vacant see. Anselm had consented on three conditions: (1) that the king confess fully all his sins; (2) that he promise to amend his life; (3) and that he put into immediate effect the ecclesiastical reforms recommended by the bishops. William Rufus consented, and all might have gone well if after his consent he had expired. The trouble was that he got well and regretted what he had done. He refused to make a choice for England between Urban II and the antipope Guibert. He forced Anselm into exile and refused to fill any ecclesiastical vacancies. Yet Anselm protected his sovereign from excommunication and saved Britain from an interdict. William Rufus' brother, Henry I, ac-

[34] MPL, CLXXXVIII, 617.

tually confiscated the revenues of Canterbury, though Anselm was still alive and titular occupant of the see. Nonetheless, due to public pressure, especially from the laity, and to the good offices of Matilda, Henry's queen, a concordat was concluded between the king and the pope, called the Concordat of London (August 1, 1107). A person elected to an ecclesiastical see was required to take the oath of fealty to the king before he could be consecrated. Nevertheless the church was allowed to make the original choice.[35] As a result the dispute between the king and his archbishop was settled. The king sought the counsel of pious people. He even put the administration of his kingdom in Anselm's hands while he was away on a protracted visit to Normandy. Anselm, "that weak old sheep," as he had called himself, "had ended by prevailing over the ungovernable bulls yoked with him to the plough of the English church." [36]

Germany, where the papacy had begun the struggle over investiture, was the last to lay down arms by reaching an agreement mutually acceptable to church and state. Henry IV, who had brought down Gregory VII in sorrow to his grave, was himself brought down by a perfidious and conniving son, Henry V. Like Absalom, he wanted before his time what would have been eventually his by inheritance. To gain his end he invited his father to a parley, overcame and imprisoned him, and then began to reign in his stead. The old king escaped and wandered through his own realm like an outcast. He was entertained and befriended only by those Rhenish cities and towns he had favored. Finally he died on the eve of a battle with the usurper. After the death of Henry IV (1106), Henry V (1106-1125), whose older brother Conrad, the favorite of the church, had already died, became king by right and continued the ecclesiastical policies of his father with equal force and far greater cunning. Determined to settle once and for all the investiture controversy, Henry demanded that Pope Paschal II come in person to Germany to preside over a conference convened for that purpose. But the pope, knowing too well the character of the king and realizing what to expect from a conclave in his realm, chose France instead and set Châlons as the site. When the pope resolutely sustained the position of his illustrious predecessor, Gregory VII, and when the bishops did not accede to Henry's demands, the royal representative, Welf of Bavaria, said with swaggering bluster, "Not here but at Rome and with the sword must the quarrel be settled." The pope was equally firm: "The Church, redeemed by the blood of Christ, cannot become a servant. Such it would become if its pastors could not take possession of their offices without the assent of the king." [37]

[35] Mansi, XX, 1227.
[36] Montalembert, *Monks of the West* (Gasquet trans., London, 1896), VI, 217.
[37] MPL, CLXXXVI, 1269.

Four years elapsed before King Henry was in a position to make good the threat of his spokesman. Then, in 1110, he entered Italy with his troops to deal personally with the pope. His agents contended that, since the church's fiefs were in the domain of the empire, to the emperor belonged the right to give investiture to them. The papal legates said that the church would surrender all regalian rights and live only on the tithe and offerings of the faithful. In other words, the church would give up all feudal rights and responsibilities, so that princely bishops and abbots would be obliterated. "We forbid any bishop or abbot, under pain of anathema, to hold any of these temporalities," wrote Paschal II, "that is, cities, duchies, marks, counties, rights of mining, markets or tolls, offices of advocate or of hundredsman, estates which belong to the empire, with any of their appurtenances, the right to hold castles or to do military service . . ." This appeared like the surrender of everything. It went too far even for Henry, who had no objection to the princely rights of bishops so long as they were his appointees. "The king would not allow such a violence to be done the church. He will not tolerate this theft," protested his agents. Yet this principle was embodied in the Concordat of Sutri, which Henry ratified.

King Henry V came then to Rome to be crowned Holy Roman Emperor. On February 12, 1111, the day set for his coronation, the terms of the Treaty were announced. The clergy, seeing their power as princes vanish, burst into an uproar. The Gregorians accused Pope Paschal of criminal inconsistency. He was forcing bishops to renounce their temporal rights, but he was retaining his own sovereignty as head of the states of the church. The weak Pope, torn with indecision, refused to complete the rite of Henry's coronation. As a result, Henry kidnapped the pope and cardinals and carried them out of the city.

Two months' imprisonment forced Paschal to renounce the papal right of investiture altogether (April 12, 1111) and to declare that affairs stood as they had been before the Gregorian Reformation or the question of church reform and lay investiture had ever arisen. This document of papal capitulation to royal power is known as the *Privilegium*. "For the deliverance of the church," wailed Paschal, "I yield to force. I do what I have wanted to avoid even at the price of my blood."

But no one can set back the clock of history. Even a pope could not successfully repudiate the entire Cluniac program of the pasty sixty years. Though Paschal crowned Henry Holy Roman Emperor (April 13, 1111) in the Basilica of St. Peter, as soon as Henry was out of Italy he renounced what he had done and volunteered to abdicate as penance for his shameful weakness. He was dissuaded from this second proposal, and one year later at a council at the Lateran (March 18, 1112), the *Privilegium* was officially withdrawn.[38]

It took another ten years before this controversy was resolved by an amicable agreement. German prelates refused to accept the solution of Sutri. Finally, at Worms (September 23, 1122) a concordat was approved which did for the empire what the Concordat of London had done for Britain. The emperor gave up investiture by crozier and ring and promised faithfully to allow the church to choose freely its prelates—bishops, abbots, and other high dignitaries. At the same time the church accorded to the emperor the right to preside at such elections and to invest the candidate with the scepter as the sign of his political responsibility.[39]

This is generally reckoned a compromise. And such it could well be made. For example, if a candidate was unacceptable to the emperor, he had merely to refuse to invest him; or if the church would not elect the person the emperor wanted, he could circumvent any choice merely by refusing to hold the election. On the other hand the vote itself was in the hands of the church; its function was to propose the candidate; the emperor could not impose his own man. Over the long years, the Concordat worked in favor of the church. Public opinion would not long countenance the imperial veto of a worthy cleric put up by his brothers for sacred office.

The trials in Germany, France, and England were spared to the papacy in other lands. Under papal tutelage the Spanish provinces of Aragon and Castile were fighting to shake off the Moslem yoke; while Sicily, after thirty-two years of warfare between the Normans and the Moslems (1060-1092), was brought back to the Christian fold. The pope sent to the Normans the flag of St. Peter (1063), and he reorganized the church in Spain around the primatial see of Toledo (1088). Spain and Sicily, in gratitude, lent strong support to the papacy.

All in all, the Gregorian principles had triumphed. Gregory VII had found the church a handmaiden, but his successors, loyal to the program of emancipation he had laid down, set her free.

V. The Flowering of Monasticism

The investiture controversy and the Crusade for the liberation from the infidel of the Holy Land are not the whole history of Christianity during this period. Beneath the steel breastplate of the galloping knight on his charger, there was the heartbeat of piety and faith which sent him on his mission. Behind the march of an aggressive papacy against the citadels of secular power and privilege, there was the simple devotion of Christian people registered in their habits of worship and standards of conduct and life. The last quarter

[38] Mansi, XXI, 49-67.
[39] MGH, *Leges*, XI, 75, 76.

of the eleventh century and the first quarter of the twelfth saw a renewal of piety in Western Europe and consequently a flowering of monasticism, which in every period of the Middle Ages was the chief vehicle of religious expression and the channel through which piety flowed to the various classes of society.

Scarcely had the Hirschau establishments in Germany begun their program of expansion than families sought guidance and strength in their religious life by affiliating with the monastery and by trying to introduce monastic practices into the home. This was the origin of the Third Order. To the monks and to the nuns were now added the family. Those who, because of obligations at home, could not themselves enter a monastery nonetheless determined to live within the family as the coenobites lived in their retreat and to regulate their household according to the monastic rule. Pope Urban II recognized at once the legitimacy of this aspiration and therefore endorsed and encouraged it, while Henry IV of Germany saw in it a dangerous threat to his ecclesiastical program and tried to stamp it out with relentless cruelty.

At the same time that this family movement was originating in Germany, two significant movements were taking place in France.

One was strictly monastic and eventuated in two new establishments. Robert of Arbrissel, who had given up his chair of theology at Angers and was living the life of a hermit in Craon forest close to Anjou, was ordered by Pope Urban II to begin itinerant preaching. He went as an itinerant throughout Touraine, Anjou, Brittany, and Normandy preaching and organizing the people who could not go on the First Crusade into companies of penitents to pray for the success of the expedition. He assembled his converts together at **Fontevrault** in Poitiers, where men and women lived separately in improvised huts (1096) until the wealthy neighboring nobility built them a double monastery (1106). Likewise, Robert of Champagne with twenty companions left one of the establishments of Cluny because he felt its monks were not austere enough in their devotion and founded a new monastery (1098) near Dijon. It was called **Citeaux** because of the many springs in the region.[40] This was the origin of the famous Cistercian Order, not new in the principles of its rule, for like Cluny it was Benedictine, but rather distinctive in the severity of its discipline and its zeal for righteousness. More than anything else it was the resurrection of what Cluny had been sixty years before but what Robert of Champagne felt it no longer was.

The other French movement was concerned with **canon law**; and, though its chief spokesman was the archbishop of Chartres, it was nonetheless monastic in spirit, for canon law in this period had as its norm the monkish ideal. **Ivo of Chartres** (1040-1116) set down the principle that laws must be in

[40] MPL, CLVII, 1269-1294.

harmony with the time and place of their operation, for they are not ends in themselves but merely means to assure the living of the Christian life and the salvation of souls. "If the strict law were to be applied everywhere, the priests of the church would have to abandon their office and retire from the world." In the years 1094 and 1095 Ivo of Chartres made his famous collections of canon law, divided into three separate bodies of material, the third of which, the *Panormia*, became the most widely used work of its kind in Medieval Europe, the legal counterpart to the *Summa* of Thomas Aquinas in theology. Ivo of Chartres gave legal support to the papacy in the investiture struggle. Of all the occupants of the see of Chartres none has been more illustrious through the works he has bequeathed to posterity than he.[41]

The flowering of monasticism may properly be said to have taken place in the opening years of the twelfth century, when many developments occurred in such close temporal proximity to one another almost to have been simultaneous.

For example, William of Champeaux established the **Canons Regular of St. Victor** in Paris in 1113, while Norbert of Xanten founded the Prémonstratensian Order near Laon eight years later in 1121. Only a year elapsed before Peter the Venerable initiated his great work of reformation and revival at Cluny (1122). Previous to all three of these remarkable advances, young Bernard had attached himself to the Cistercian Order (1112). So within a single decade four of the greatest movements in the spiritual life of the Middle Ages had been launched.

Neither the **Victorines** (Canons of St. Victor) nor **Prémonstratensians** were in the strict sense of the words monastic orders. Both found their constituency among the secular clergy, especially canons of the cathedrals. Indeed, the avowed purpose of the founders of both orders was to bring a select group of secular priests under monastic discipline, hoping thereby to imbue them with the highest spirit of Christianity. These two orders may properly be compared to the military order of the Knights Templars, where monastic principles were fused with those of chivalry, and the warrior was taught to behave like a monk for Christ's sake. William of Champeaux and Norbert of Xanten felt that nothing could be gained for the secular clergy by encouraging their envy of the regular clergy. If monasticism had been more successful in the promulgation of Christianity than the priesthood, then it was obvious that it had something the priesthood needed. Their mission was to give to the secular the advantages of the regular.

William of Champeaux was called to his new vocation from the chair of philosophy and dialectics at the cathedral school in Paris in 1108. He took as

41 MPL, CLXI, CLXII.

his new abode the little chapel of St. Victor near the Seine, where first students and then others came to him for guidance in the life of prayer. Though he himself relinquished his retreat for the bishopric of Châlon in 1113, he obtained a charter for his order from King Louis the Fat. The chief duties of the Victorines were liturgical and scholarly, punctuated by manual labor. They celebrated the canonical hours night and day, and they copied in exquisite style and decoration some of the more precious manuscripts of antiquity. Out of their order arose a famous school of mystical theology.[42]

Norbert of Xanten was the cousin and chaplain of Henry V of Germany. Though a cleric, he had been dissolute and worldly, the type a king might sometimes invest in a strong ecclesiastical post to effect his own ends. Norbert's ambition in life was to become chancellor of the empire. But then one day, as he was riding on a mission, a bolt of lightning uprooted a tree nearby, frightened his horse so that the beast threw him, and shocked Norbert himself into a stupor. As he lay on the ground, he smelled the sulphurous fumes of hell and heard a voice saying, "Norbert, Norbert, why persecutest thou me?" That experience marked his conversion to true godliness. At first he became a monk, wore a hair shirt, and engaged in long vigils and assiduous fasts. Pope Gelasius II sent him on his preaching missions, out of which came the establishment at **Prémontré**, its first inmates being clergy from the diocese of Laon. He allowed lay people and families to become affiliated with his order, believing as he did that the secular clergy should never give up their chief vocation, which is the care of souls. The distinctive feature of the **Prémonstratensian Order** was its observance of silence. The Prémonstratensian brother was able to remain completely silent even in the midst of a noisy crowd. Within thirty years the parent house at Prémontré had thirty offspring in the form of other houses under the same rule.[43]

The work of Peter the Venerable was entirely reformatory in character. **Cluny**, which had inspired the Gregorian Reformation and had given an unbroken succession of abbatial saints to the church from the days of its inception in the early tenth century to the time of Hugh, the contemporary of Gregory VII and Urban II, had itself fallen on evil days. Its abbot Pons de Melgueil, who in 1100 received the abbatial crosier of perhaps the greatest, certainly the most influential, abbey of Christendom, was more concerned with the prestige of his office and the honor done his person than the ideals of the order. He had a retinue of sixty horses and appeared more like a governor of a province than a director of men's souls. When his personal conduct became a scandal to his brethren, Pope Calixtus II constrained him to resign and do

---

[42] F. Bonnard, *Histoire des chanoines réguliers de Saint-Victor* (1906), I, ch. 1.
[43] MGH, *Scriptores*, XII, 663-706.

penance by going to the Holy Land. Some years later, just as Peter the Venerable was re-establishing order at Cluny, the wicked Pons returned, forced entry to Cluny with soldiers, and scattered its monks. For three months many atrocities were committed at Cluny. But Pons was excommunicated and died in separation from the church fourteen years after becoming too princely an abbot.

Peter had then to introduce at Cluny the severest discipline. He forbade the wearing of rich apparel, the use of fine food, and the right to leave the establishment at will. The principles by which he governed Cluny were as rigid as those that prevailed at Citeaux, so Peter was accused of aping the Cistercians. Peter himself was a man of great strength and talent. He was compared for his fine style to Cicero, for his verse to Virgil, for his logic to Aristotle, for his tenderness to Gregory the Great, and for his comprehensiveness to Ambrose. In depth of thought he was likened to Augustine.[44] History, however, has limited its commendation to his role as a monastic reformer.

Bernard of Clairvaux was the greatest of these four monastic teachers, as indeed he stands along with Benedict of Nursia as one of the greatest figures in the entire history of monasticism. The Cistercian Order, though high in principle and pure in practice, was not attracting many people to its ranks. Stephen Harding, an Englishman, was its abbot. He was discouraged and felt like laying aside his office in recognition of the failure of his leadership. There then appeared at the gate of his abbey a young nobleman from Fontaines in Burgundy, who came, not only seeking admission for himself, but bringing thirty companions with him. That day in the spring of 1112 was the Pentecost of Citeaux as indeed it was of the whole of Western monasticism.

Citeaux's regimen was diet of fresh or dried vegetables, oil, salt, and water. In a common dormitory, lighted at all times by candle light, its inmates slept fully clad, always ready for duty. Its schedule of public prayers took six hours a day to perform. Hitherto all this had appeared unreasonable and impractical. But the acceptance of it by Bernard and his companions changed an unattainable ideal into a challenge. Citeaux swarmed with new inmates. Three new monasteries sprang up almost immediately. The Cistercian Order, unlike that of Cluny which kept the supreme authority in the mother abbey, gave autonomy to each of its offspring. On December 23, 1119, Pope Calixtus II approved a Charter of Union which set forth the Cistercian pattern.[45]

The impact of monastic piety upon Western society was tremendous. It gave effective support to the strengthening of the hierarchical structure and the papacy. Norbert of Xanten, Peter the Venerable, and Bernard were states-

---

[44] MPL, CLXXXIX, 61-1054. J. H. Pignot, *Histoire de l'ordre de Cluny depuis la foundation de l'abbaye jusqu' à la mort de Pierre-le-Vénérable* (1868), III, 47-609.
[45] *Vita prima*, MPL, CLXXXV, 225-455; *Vita secunda*, MPL, CLXXXV, 469-524. AS, II, 109. P. Guignard, *Les Monuments primitifs de la Règle cistercienne* (1878), p. 82.

men as well as monks. An example of obedience to the papacy was the readiness of bishops to swear under oath at the Lateran Council of 1102 that they would approve or condemn whatever the Roman church approved or condemned. Again, on March 18, 1123, under Calixtus II, at another council at the Lateran which was attended by more than three hundred bishops, the principles of the Gregorian Reformation were solemnly ratified and approved. Both simony and clerical concubinage were unqualifiedly condemned. The pope was now regularly chosen by the College of Cardinals, which numbered six bishops, twenty-eight priests, and eighteen deacons. Generally the pope chose his legates for various missions from these cardinals. Metropolitans, though they consecrated bishops, investigated disputed elections, and exercised custody over vacant sees, still were forbidden to appoint bishops, and every bishop had the right of appeal to Rome. The bishops supervised all the parishes in their dioceses and exercised final authority over the disposition of the tithe. The bishop himself was elected by the cathedral chapter of the diocese. Either he appointed the canons of the cathedral or the chapter elected members to fill vacancies. Always the chapter elected its own dean. Most cathedrals were governed either by the Order of St. Victor or the Prémonstratensian Order. Priests from collegiate chapters supplied parishes in contrast to the members of the cathedral chapters who remained at the cathedral to conduct its worship and perform its pastoral obligations.

The use of the ordeal to determine a person's innocence or guilt was condemned by the papacy as crass superstition,[46] while indulgences were made more plentiful. In 1116 the first general indulgence in ecclesiastical history was granted by Pope Paschal II, though Urban II had given to the Church of Saint Nicholas in Angers, France, the right to issue an indulgence to any person who at any time visited its shrine. The formula of absolution was changed from a petition to a direct assertion. The priest now said to the penitent, "I absolve you from your sins."

Even the temporal interests of the common people were furthered by the monastic spirit. Parishes were organized by priests to enforce the Truce of God. When two noblemen started a combat, appeal could be made to the bishop or abbot to stop them and to cause them to observe a forty-day truce until he could arbitrate. If they refused, the people themselves could restrain their violence by force. It was only another step, short at that, from organization to enforce the Truce of God to a society to support the interests of the common people. Consequently the confraternities of the eleventh century were really communal orders for the good of their members. Monasticism had the outreach of a social gospel, and its revolutionary implications in the end helped to destroy the feudalistic system itself of which it was a part.

[46] Hefele, op. cit. (Leclercq), V, 480.

VI. The Rise of Scholasticism

No less important than the revival of monasticism, though for different reasons, was the rise of a new philosophy called scholasticism and the influence it exerted upon the development of theology and the formulation or explication of Christian doctrines. It began as pure methodology. It ended as an architectonic structure which subsumed within its scope the whole of time and existence. The human mind, awakened from the slumber in which the Dark Ages had lulled it, exerted itself at first like an athlete getting into trim, stretching and exercising the muscles before applying them skillfully against an opponent in the game. Its first issues were dialectical, had to do with logic, and sought the proper way in which to think rather than what to think about.

The early concern of these dialecticians was a problem bequeathed to them by Boethius—namely, what is real, the particular or the general, the individual entity or the larger class to which it belongs? What comes first, the whole or the various parts which constitute it? Those who held to the reality of the general, insisting that particulars derived their being as well as their definition from the general category in which they were comprised were called **realists.** Those who contended that only particulars have status in reality and that generals are nothing apart from the entities which make them up were known as **nominalists.**

The most celebrated exponent of extreme nominalism was Roscellinus, a priest of Brittany and a scholar of such robust forthrightness that he attracted students in large numbers. He taught that humanity is a notion of the mind derived from our observation of particulars and our association together of likes in groups. Genera and species are merely words; there is nothing in reality to correspond to them. Consequently God is just a concept; the divine reality is three persons: Father, Son, and Holy Spirit. He was accused of and condemned for tritheism, and that by his own words: "The three divine persons are three separate beings, like three angels; if custom permitted the expression, we might say they are three gods." [47] He was condemned for heresy at the Synod of Soissons in 1092.

Since extremes in one direction generally produce the reaction of extremes in the other direction, realism received its most pronounced expression in the position of William of Champeaux, founder of the Order of St. Victor and teacher of great renown in the Cathedral School of Paris. He taught that full and complete reality, even in this world of sensate things, exists only in the class. The reality of the individual is derivative; it could not be at all unless the particular participated in and was a part of the class which

[47] MPL, CLXXVIII, 357-372.

defines it and gives it the status that it has. First there is humanity; then there is man. God is; Father, Son, and Holy Spirit are because they participate in and share together God. Class is a unitary substance. Particulars and individuals are characteristics, aspects of that substance.[48]

The mediation between and yet at the same time the repudiation of both extremes found expression in the thought of Peter Abelard, who had studied under Roscellinus and William of Champeaux. He asserted that realism, unmodified, leads to pantheism, while nominalism breaks down all basic conceptions and destroys the relationship of thought. Certainly we think in terms of universals, else how do we distinguish a man from a horse or a piece of earth from a drop of water? The fact that there is a necessary link between perception and intellect means that similarity among things, the quality of their identity, is itself real. Universals exist as ideas in the mind of God before things are made. They then stand out in the particular as likenesses or as characteristic similarities. Finally they exist as concepts in our minds as we behold these similarities and group particulars together into classes and groups.

Since such speculation emerged in the church and since philosophy appeared foreign and even demonic to certain simpler minds, it was only natural that some folk should associate error and falsehood with the church itself and seek Christianity apart from the Christian institution. Such were Tanchelm and Peter of Bruys. Peter condemned prayers for the dead and ridiculed the mass and the effectiveness of good works. Tanchelm repudiated the hierarchy and the sacraments. Both men had a wide following among common folk— Tanchelm in the north of France in what is now Belgium, and Peter of Bruys in the south of France. Their movements however were short-lived. The Prémonstratensians overcame the former, while the latter was conquered by the monks of Cluny.

Intellectualism was here to stay. The application of dialectics to theology was made with the gift of genius by **Anselm** in the last quarter of the eleventh century and by Peter Abelard in the first quarter of the twelfth. In their zeal for reason both men were equal, and each employed it unsparingly in his understanding and interpretation of religion. Their results however were not the same. The use Anselm made of reason earned him the title of Father of Scholastic Theology, while Abelard's rationalizing processes brought him condemnation as a heretic.

Anselm, whatever we may think of his particular interpretations, deserves recognition for having saved Christianity from irrationalism and the absurdity of illogical and self-contradictory suppositions. For example there were Christian spokesmen who, obsessed with the notion of God's unlimited power,

[48] MPL, CLXIII, 1039-1072.

said he could do anything, such as change the past, make a square circle, or fashion a finite stick without ends. No less prominent and formidable a figure than Peter Damian expressed such opinions.

Anselm, in contrast, though he said we must first believe in order later to understand what we believe, nonetheless contended that the basic propositions of faith are capable of demonstrative proof by reason.

He began with God, showing in the *Monologium* by a devious and circuitous method that grades of goodness imply by necessity one perfect Good against the norm of which they are judged and likewise degrees of reality necessitate one Reality in which they all exist. To say that several natures equal in perfection occupy the peak of existence is to admit that their equality lies in what they have in common. If this thing in common is their nature, then they are the same, for they have the same nature. If it is something other than their nature, then this common element is itself another nature superior to them and is itself the peak of perfection. Somewhere the chain of degrees or levels of goodness must reach an end. Likewise, the universe cannot be derived from several causes. These several causes either would cause one another or else exist by themselves. It is logically impossible for a thing which does not exist to be made by something which is itself nonexistent. Neither can things exist by themselves, for to do this would mean that what they have in common is the element of self-existence, and this fundamental element would itself be their causal principle. When we see anything good, we are able to compare it with something better, so that we judge it by the degree in which it measures up to the best. The greatest of all goods is that in which lesser goods must participate in order to have any worth at all. Thus in the *Monologium* Anselm combines in a threefold way the cosmological and teleological arguments in order to demonstrate God's existence.

From the existence of a Perfect Good which is God it is a simple matter by the process of deduction to arrive at his attributes. Creation is derivative of such a being. Either God made all that is out of nothing, or else what is exists as a part of God. We cannot admit the latter, since the imperfections of creation would introduce imperfection into the nature of the divine being of which they are a part. Consequently pantheism is precluded. Since the universe was made by God, God alone is real in the fullest sense of that word, and everything else is contingent—that is, is a derivative of his creative power.

In relation to a particular, truth is conformity of report to the object reported, yet in its basic expression truth is the general all-pervasive rectitude which is God, the one truth of all. Man is made with a will which inclines him in his actions to what he deems useful and beneficial. When he was originally created, he saw this as justice and uprightness. He still possesses freedom in the sense that he is at liberty to do this or not to do that, but since his fall he does not use this freedom for its created end. He makes specific choices, but these are contrary to justice and uprightness. Only after he is redeemed is he free to make choices that serve the ends of God and are therefore right and good.

Redemption is the answer to Anselm's basic question: Why was God incarnated, or why the God-man? Man was made in the image of God. He owed his creator everything, and to merit God's favor he had to live a perfect life altogether pleasing to his maker. This he did not do. Since he failed in his obligation, he incurred an infinite penalty. The penalty was commensurate with the honor and worth of the person sinned against. Only a man could repay a man's debt. Yet only God could merit by that payment the forgiveness of God. Therefore, God himself became a man in order to give satisfaction for the infinite sin and guilt which man had incurred. This is the classic expression of the satisfaction theory of the atonement which Anselm gave to the church.

His other great contribution to theology was the ontological proof of God's existence. God by definition, he said, is a being greater than whom no other can be conceived. Yet such a concept with real existence is greater than the same concept merely as a concept in the mind without real existence. Therefore, the greater than whom no other can be conceived does exist, and this is God.

Gaunilo, a contemporary of Anselm, replied that simply because a man conceives of the Blessed Isle, lost in the ocean, yet full of riches and more perfect than any other island, this does not mean it has reality. Likewise, in regard to God, one cannot rely on thought to prove existence outside of thought. Anselm responded that the only thought which necessitates the translation from concept to reality is the thought of the greatest and best of which it is possible to conceive. This position of Anselm is the supreme example of dialectic operating solely in a definition. The force of being is so great when in alliance with perfection that it compels him who contemplates it to affirm its existence.[49]

Anselm's theological philosophy rests upon the same realism—that is, belief in and use of universals—as characterized the thought of William of Champeaux.

The difference between the thinking of Anselm and that of **Abelard** is generally brought into focus at the point of the atonement and the two different attitudes toward God expressed in the contrary theories proposed. Both are alike in rejecting the ransom theory of Gregory the Great as giving too much prominence to the devil, who is only a creature like everything else that God made. But whereas Anselm insisted that divine justice and honor had to be satisfied and taught that the death of Christ was required for man's re-

---

[49] MPL, Vols. CLVIII and CLIX.

demption, Abelard said the death of Christ did nothing to God since God by nature is always forgiving and requires no historical act to prompt him to be merciful. The death of Christ incites man to goodness, prompts him to seek forgiveness and to love God with all his heart. This is the classic statement of the moral influence theory of the atonement.

This theory of the atonement is a clue to the understanding of Abelard's ethics. Sin and guilt as well as good and merit lie, not in a deed, but in the intention or motive behind the deed. To be sure, a man can think evil and not be guilty of sin until he expresses that thought in act, all the same once an act is done, the evaluation of it lies entirely in the motive or intention of the doer. The pagan persecutors of the Christian martyrs did not sin if their motive for killing the Christians was good. Even the slayers of our Lord escaped guilt if they sincerely thought Christ was evil. It is not surprising then that Abelard included among the saved many pagan philosophers and seers whose motives and deeds were worthy.

His view of God was that of a perfect, all-wise, all-powerful, benevolent person; and his doctrine of the Trinity, condemned at Soissons in 1121, was that God is a unitary being expressed triunely as Power (Father), Wisdom (Son), and Benevolence (Holy Spirit). This is a form of Sabellianism, though Abelard testifies that many of his examiners thought it was tritheism. That was due no doubt to the fact that Roscellinus had been condemned for tritheism; and since Abelard had rejected the realism of William of Champeaux, his opponents felt he must be a nominalist who would naturally conform to the individual expressions of God rather than to the universal essence which set them forth. However, there is no more complete an example of Sabellianism in Medieval history than Abelard's treatment of the Trinity.

As one might readily suppose, Abelard gave primary importance to human reason in dealing with the issues of theology. It is good to doubt, for doubt leads to inquiry and inquiry to understanding and understanding to genuine conviction. His book Sic et non states 158 propositions and shows disagreements among the Fathers of the church in regard to them. We are not, therefore, blindly to follow the Fathers. Each of us must reason for himself, taking Scripture itself as his basic authority.

Abelard's view of the inspiration of Scripture went far beyond the thinking of his age. God did not impart truth to men from without. Rather he enlightened men's minds, so that they discovered truth themselves. The writers of the Bible did not have a monopoly on such inspiration. Many of the Greeks were inspired too.

Abelard's theological treatise entitled Introduction to Theology divides the subject into three parts: Faith, Charity, the Sacraments. He defines faith as an opinion or judgment on things unseen. He contends that charity as the love of God, and through him the love of his creatures and one's self, is the sole motive for everything the Christian does, and he defines the sacraments as the visible signs of the invisible grace of God. True faith must be won through knowledge and understanding. "He that believes quickly is light-minded." [50]

Consequently Abelard championed man's right to free inquiry. He insisted that it is not a sin to be mistaken. He did not believe that anyone, even the most pronounced heretic, should be coerced into an orthodox opinion. He himself, however, was forced to consign his work on the Trinity to the flames.

As far as their productive years were concerned. Anselm was ahead of Abelard by one generation. Abelard reached his twenty-first year just as the twelfth century began, while Anselm died before the opening decade of that century closed (April 21, 1109). Both were Frenchmen, the older man from Normandy and the younger from Brittany. Anselm moved to England and became archbishop of Canterbury, having already distinguished himself as Lanfranc's best pupil and his successor to the abbey of Bec. Abelard moved to Paris, where he ousted his master William of Champeaux from his intellectual leadership at the Cathedral School and took his place as the most popular and well-known teacher in Europe. Each relied upon reason in dealing with the issues of faith. Yet Anselm used reason only to prove or to confirm what he already believed by faith, while Abelard subjected the contents of faith itself to the scrutiny and appraisal of reason. The older man was modest and self-effacing, never thinking of himself more highly than he ought to think. The younger man was arrogant and ruthless in dealing with the feelings of other people. He would make his point on a matter regardless of what it did to the reputation of others. He had absolute confidence in his own ability and only contempt for the ability of his rivals. He called the most celebrated theologian of his day (Anselm of Laon) a man of many words and few thoughts. Anselm died regretting that he had not had time to finish a work on the origin of the soul. Abelard lived with such careless self-confidence that soon he wrecked his own career. Yet both men, each in his own way, heralded the renaissance of the twelfth century.

[50] MPL, Vol. CLXXVIII.

Chapter Eight

The Twelfth Century
(1124-1198)

THE SEVENTY-FIVE YEARS, MORE OR LESS, WHICH FORM THE CORE OF THE TWELFTH
century are best described perhaps as years of transition. The Byzantine empire, despite the grandeur of its outward appearance, was beginning to weaken.
Likewise, the Greek church, still superior in culture to the Latin, became
more apparent in its distaste for Western innovations and more insistent on
undeviating loyalty to ancient traditions. The West by contrast was pre-
occupied with a living and therefore changing society and civilization. It was
now wide-awake from the long night of the Dark Ages. It was experiencing
both a political and intellectual renaissance anticipatory to its greatest unified
civilization in the succeeding century.

I. Eastern Christendom Under the Comneni

The Eastern church and empire were, in the twelfth century, afflicted by
two more crusades from the West. As they had got more than they had bar-
gained for in the First Crusade, the Second and Third Crusades came upon
them without their solicitation. They were Western expeditions to aid the
Latin states in the East, which states the Eastern empire had not wanted and
had no disposition to preserve. Pope Eugenius III (1145-1153) had permitted
Armenian deputies to complain to him about the Greeks,[1] and it had been
the announcement of the fall of Latin Edessa to the Turks which had fired
his crusading blood.[2]

Previous negotiations between Eastern and Western Catholicism for
reunion, undertaken by Pope Paschal II (1099-1118) and Emperor Alexius
Comnenus (1081-1118), had failed. Though Alexius had offered to relieve
the pope of his embarrassing maltreatment at the hands of Henry V by coming to Rome and accepting the crown of the Holy Roman Empire himself,
still Paschal had made as a condition of reunion the abject subjection of the

[1] Hefele, op. cit. (Leclercq), V, 797.
[2] Otto of Freising, Chronicon, VII, 28.

194

Eastern church to Rome, which the unyielding spirit of the Greek clergy had not permitted. The matter had been discussed in public debates between the archbishop of Milan, on the Latin side, and the metropolitan of Nicaea, on the Greek side, but it had not got beyond debate. This had taken place in the years 1112 and 1113.[3]

Such was the fate of succeeding attempts at reunion during the twelfth century. John Comnenus (1118-1143) had no better fortune with Calixtus II (1119-1124) and Honorius II (1124-1130) than his able predecessor had had with Paschal. Negotiations between Constantinople and Rome were continued for over a decade (1124-1136), ending only in a mutually recriminatory controversy between Anselm of Havelberg and Nicetas of Nicomedia.[4] Though circumstances appeared more propitious for agreement twenty-three years later, when negotiations were renewed by Pope Alexander III and the Emperor Manuel Comnenus (1159), the outcome after eleven years was no different. At the beginning the pope needed the Eastern emperor to aid him against Frederick Barbarossa;[5] but as that threat passed the pontiff's interests in reunion became less intense. The Eastern proposal for reunion with the West in exchange for the crown of the Holy Roman Empire (1166)[6] was met by the Roman counter proposal that the emperor come West to live and transfer his residence to Rome.[7] The year 1170 marked Manuel's final effort. He and the pope maintained cordial relations with each other to the end, but the Greek clergy distrusted the Latin, and the Patriarch Michael Anchialus exerted himself vehemently to frustrate the schemes of his sovereign (1169-1177).

Negotiations for reunion came to a terrible conclusion when the usurper Andronicus Comnenus (1183-1185), reacting against everything his predecessors had done, allowed popular feelings to express themselves in fury. Already one year before the usurpation, while the widow of Manuel ruled for her twelve-year-old son, the Greeks massacred the greater portion of the Latin population in Constantinople (1182). This unpardonable act led inevitably to open hostility between Western and Eastern Christendom, involving the political and military power of one state after another. William II of Sicily sacked Thessalonica in 1189. Frederick Barbarossa marched eastward one year later in 1190. And Richard the Lion-Hearted of England took Cyprus in 1191. At the same time the Eastern emperor entered into an alliance with the Moslem Saladin (1189) against the West.[8]

[3] CMH, IV, 600.
[4] L. d' Achery, *Spicilegium sive collectio veterum aliquot scriptorum* (Paris, 1655-1677), I, 161.
[5] LP, II, 403.
[6] LP, II, 415.
[7] Cinnamus, VI, 4, CSHB, p. 262.
[8] CMH, IV, 603.

It was the motives behind these negotiations on the part of both the contracting parties which caused failure from the outset. Neither East nor West wanted reunion merely for the sake of reunion itself. Reunion was desired as the means to an end, which in the West was the restoration of the Holy Places to Christian hands and the exaltation of the Roman episcopate as the supreme governing agency of the church, and which in the East was the security and prosperity of the empire and the recovery of all its ancient territories. The accentuation of theological differences was never really important either. Even the popes recognized the inalienable right of the Greeks to preserve their own traditions and ritualistic practices; while on occasion agreement was reached on such divergent issues as the procession of the Holy Ghost, the use of leavened or unleavened bread, and dissimilar views on the pains of purgatory. Nothing is more repetitious and profitless than the doctrinal essays on these subjects on occasions when it seemed politic to emphasize differences. Even Anselm of Canterbury fell a victim to such a disputation, while the Greek theologians spent most of their time and energy on it. The real divisive factor was not theological at all. It was the Greek love of independence and political adaptability in contrast to the Latin insistence on uniformity, papal absolutism, and the deliverance of the church from the control of any secular power. The Greek tendency was in the direction of local autonomy in alliance with the government; the Latin, of universality with patronage toward the government.[9] As a result many in the West, including such notables as Bernard of Clairvaux and Suger, advocated ecclesiastical unity by force.

It is no surprise then that the **Second Crusade**, launched by Bernard's oratory on Easter, 1146, was very different from the First. The Eastern emperor proved its enemy rather than its ally. The two great Western armies, each one of which was composed of seventy thousand knights and an innumerable throng of footmen, received a hostile reception from the Christians of the East. In fact, the German army, which had wasted Thrace on its march eastward, was resisted and defeated by imperial forces at Adrianople. It became an undisciplined mob which the Turks easily overcame and routed at Iconium. The king of France avoided such risks and took his men along the coast of Asia Minor through Smyrna, Ephesus, and Laodicea, but what he escaped from the Greeks he got in full measure from the Turks and almost lost his life before he reached Jerusalem. The recapture of Edessa, which was the object of the Crusade, proved impossible, and the two kings met in Jerusalem only to depart for home again, their proud efforts a miserable failure.[10] Louis VII of France, while he had been the guest of the Greek Emperor Manuel Comnenus in Constantinople, awaiting transportation to Smyrna,

[9] CMH, IV, 594-597.
[10] CMH, IV, 366-368.

had been advised by the bishop of Langres to open the Crusade by capturing Constantinople, but this he had refused to do.[11] Roger II of Sicily was less conscientious. When he learned that the empire had been weakened by the Crusade, he planned an expedition again. Already he had launched naval attacks on Greek cities and had temporarily held Corfu. His expedition did not materialize.[12] The Second Crusade (1147-1149) was a military and ecclesiastical fiasco.

The twelfth century was a period of enthusiastic literary and artistic activity within the Byzantine empire. The Greeks provided the Latins with much of the material which occasioned the revival of philosophy, theology, and the arts in Western Europe.

The imperial palace of Blachernae was erected at the end of the Golden Horn in Constantinople. Many churches, including the exquisite Pantocrator of the capital, where John and Manuel Comneni were both buried, were built. Pottery and glass, seals and metal work, finely carved gems and ivory, and above all else mosaics and frescoes of captivating beauty were produced during this period from Cappadocia in the east to Kiev and Novgorod in Russia to the northwest. The Cathedral of St. Mark in Venice (1095) was a Byzantine implantation on Western soil. It was built according to the plan of the Church of the Apostles in Constantinople, and its Byzantine mosaics were the wonder of the Western world.[13]

Manuel Comnenus wrote a defense of astrology against the criticisms of that science by the church. His sister-in-law Irene exercised her talents for verse. Theodore Prodromus and Constantine Manasses wrote their poetry under her patronage and much of it in her honor. The reigns of John and Manuel were preserved in the able history of John Cinnamus, who wrote in the style of Herodotus and Xenophon; while almost the whole of the twelfth century was brought into panoramic view by the greatest Byzantine historian of the Comneni era, Nicetas Acominitas, or Choniates.[14] The life of the common people was described vividly and with humor by the author of the Timarion, whose portrayal of a fair at Thessalonica is unforgettable. John Tzetzes' commentaries on Homer and on himself, as well as his history, show, together with the philology of his brother Isaac, great industry if little talent.

The quality of achievement during this period cannot be compared with that of the Macedonian era. In much of the literature of the twelfth century there is "a pitiful poverty of themes"; while the art, though splendid, is a reproduction of the forms of the past. Especially is this true in theology. Michael Acominitas, the brother of the historian Nicetas, was more than

[11] MGH, Scriptores, XXVI, 16.
[12] CMH, IV, 368, 369, 601.
[13] C. Diehl, Manuel d'art byzantin (Paris, 1925-26), II, 561-563.
[14] Nicetas Choniates, Historia (ed. I. Bekker), in CSHB.

thirty years the archbishop of Athens. His sermons and orations were so artificial and crowded with allusions to the past that they must have been incom-
prehensible to his auditors. The best theological work was that of Theophylactus,[15] the Greek archbishop of Bulgaria, entitled *On the Error of the Latins*.
This book was both critical and appreciative of Latin Catholicism; it pointed
out objections, while at the same time it was conciliatory.

The Comneni emperors were inveterate dabblers in theology and, like
Justinian, loquacious in doctrinal disputation, zealous to express their opinions
and thereby to form the thought of their time. Their opinions were of little
account.

The Greek church, proud of its orthodoxy and basking in the sunny memory
of the great councils of its past, was not constrained to supplement its dogmatic heritage with new ideas, nor was it eager to reform its liturgy or amend
its organization. Consequently its history was made, not by the power of an
internal spirit or creative impulse of its own, but rather by external events
which thrust themselves upon it and set the pattern of its affairs. Always it
resisted change and tried to remain true to what it had been. Manuel Comnenus insisted that the patriarch of Antioch, now in Western hands, come
from the Constantinopolitan clergy.[16]

The Russian patriarch was a Greek exported to his see from the Byzantine
capital. Yet the **church in Russia** was thoroughly regional and catered to the
whims of the ruling dynasty just as completely as the church in the empire
fulfilled the will of the emperor. If not in age and veneration the equal of the
ancient sees, certainly in the extent of its influence and the pomp of its office, the Russian patriarchate was gradually becoming a considerable factor
in Eastern Christianity. Even though the Grand Princedom of Kiev was beginning to decline and the Russian population, migratory in nature, was beginning to shift in three directions all at once—northeast, northwest, and
southwest—the hold of the church over the people was strong and secure.
Ecclesiastical power migrated with the political. The closing years of the
twelfth century witnessed the end of the domination of Kiev, yet it did not
see Russian power established in Moscow. Civil liberty was considerable
among the peoples of this recently won Christian nation. The population of
Novgorod, for example, was summoned to register its opinion by the great
bell of the Cathedral of Saint Sophia. There in the open square the people
indicated by loud shouts approval or disapproval of issues before them.

Neither Russia nor any other part of its ecclesiastical body was to save
Greek Catholicism from the ignominy and deprivations which its alliance to
the Byzantine state occasioned. The last fifteen years of the twelfth century
initiated its disastrous decline. In 1185 Andronicus, the last male of the

---

[15] MPG, Vol. CXXVI.
[16] Nicetas, *Historia*, I, 11.

Comnenus House, was succeeded by Isaac, the first ruler of the House of Angelus. This man was a debauchee with the tastes of a buffoon. He even took a nap on his throne as he presided over affairs of state. He rewarded a lying prophet and sycophant with the patriarchate of Constantinople and allowed his all too credulous brain to imagine conquests from Mount Libanus to the Euphrates River. Instead he lost Bulgaria, which re-established its independence after 170 years of servitude to the empire and which at the same time severed its connections with the Greek church. In Isaac's incompetent hands the Eastern empire began to grovel in the dust, and with it the Greek church as well.

II. Western Christendom Under Bernard of Clairvaux

Western Christendom, in contrast to Eastern, stood in the twelfth century on the verge of its greatest attainments throughout the whole range of the Middle Ages. In the vanguard of this forward march was the Cistercian monk, Bernard, abbot of Clairvaux, and for at least twenty-three years (1130-1153) virtual dictator of ecclesiastical affairs in the West. At least four of the five occupants of Peter's throne in Rome between 1124-1153 were either his abject dependents or else, though strong enough to act on their own, so enamoured of his wisdom as to accept his advice as the counsel of God. One of them had actually been his pupil. The Earl of Warwick was known as the "king-maker" to the English, but Bernard was much more than this. He was the "pope-maker" of the Roman Catholic Church.

He came to power during the troubled times after the death of Honorius II (1124-1130), when the papal office was being contested by Innocent II and Anacletus II. Honorius' own elevation, to say the least, had been unusual. He had not been the first choice of the cardinals; but the man they had chosen, Celestine II, had graciously stepped aside in his favor to secure peace when Robert of Frangipani, the leader of a powerful Italian family, had snatched the papal mantle from his shoulders and placed it on the shoulders of his rival. Though Honorius' election had been won by coercion, he had given the church good government for six years, sustained Lothaire of Supplinburg in the office to which he had been elected as ruler of Germany, secured from Count Roger of Sicily the oath of vassalage of Benevento, established accord between Louis the Fat and his clergy in France, and resolved the differences between the archiepiscopal sees of Canterbury and York in England.

The cardinals had provided that a quorum of eight of their number should have plenary power to choose the new pope immediately on Honorius' death. Fourteen had been present at the time, and they had elected by unanimous vote Innocent II. On the same afternoon twenty of their colleagues had chosen Anacletus II at the instigation of the Pierleoni family, who were the rivals of the Frangipani. The Roman people, bribed by Pierleoni gold, had supported Anacletus II, and Innocent II had fled for refuge to Louis the Fat in France.

Bernard of Clairvaux stepped into the midst of this situation which concerned the whole of Western Europe. The king convoked a council at Etampes, and its members immediately, by unanimous vote, put the settlement of the disputed election entirely in Bernard's hands. In other words, it voluntarily surrendered the mission for which it had been convened to him whose piety and judgment were the amazement as well as the pride of all the Christians of France.

Bernard resolved the issue on the basis of three considerations: (1) Who was the better of the two men? (2) Who had been chosen by the more worthy members of the electoral body? (3) Who had been elected in the more regular fashion? He decided in favor of Innocent II; opposed and contained his rival's powerful French supporter, Bishop Gerard of Angoulême; and accompanied the king of Germany into Italy to establish Pope Innocent in the Roman See.[17] It was as a preacher, not as a soldier, that Bernard won to the cause of Innocent II so many of the people of southern Italy. His was the animating voice of the Council of Pisa, which inaugurated the movement which led to Innocent's complete re-establishment and the ending of the schism. The glorious outcome was the Lateran Council of 1139, where almost one thousand prelates gathered to do homage to the pope. "You know," said Innocent II, "that the Roman Church is the head of the world. But you also know that its whole intention is to reconcile those that are divided." Yet Bernard practiced this in a way that the pope either was not able or else not willing to do. Innocent took revenge on his former foes, deposing some who had already been reconciled to him, for which Bernard shamed him, though without results.

There were others besides Bernard who made sizeable contributions to the progress of Christianity. The Irish monk **Malachy** (c. 1094-1148), considered by his compatriots the greatest of their religious leaders since Patrick, extirpated from his native land the competition between bishops and their suffragans called chorepiscopi, the passing of sees from one generation to the next in the same family, and lay control of clerical establishments. Bernard himself looked upon Malachy as the ideal bishop, for he tied the churches of Ireland to Rome and he established ecclesiastical discipline in the Irish church.[18] Bernard's fellow countryman, **Suger** (ca. 1081-1151), who was

---

[17] LP, II, 327; J. Regesta, 7413; Bernard, Epp., 45, 46, 47, 124; Mansi, XXI, 333; Hefele, op. cit. (Leclercq), V, 676-680, 681 n.1.; Historiens des Gaules, XII, 366-368, 395-397.
[18] MPL, CLXXXII, 1073-1118; CLXXXIII, 481-490.

converted by reading the Abbot of Clairvaux's *Apologia* and who became abbot of St. Denis, still did not abandon the affairs of state to less consecrated persons, but continued in public office as chief counsellor under Louis VI and Louis VII. At the same time he wrote Louis VI's biography and left to posterity the picture of himself as the friend of the poor and the great emancipator of the downtrodden of Paris. Bernard thought of him as the church's greatest servant and the glory of France. Louis VII actually gave him the title, "Father of our Country." [19] **Gratian** (d. 1179), a Camaldolese monk who taught law at Bologna, released sometime between 1140 and 1150 a collection of canon law which was revolutionary. It introduced the study of canon law as an independent discipline in the curriculum, and it gave to the church a more legal character and exactness. The work had three main divisions: part one dealt with law in general, part two with ecclesiastical cases, part three with rites of the church. This book became the standard text upon which all subsequent lectures on and studies of canon law were built.[20]

Bernard's times were disturbed by **revolutionary movements**, the most notable of which was that associated with the name of **Arnold of Brescia**. Italy had never become feudalized to the extent that the rest of Europe had. It still had large cities, some of which, especially in the North, developed into petty states. In such places, the common people became self-conscious and insistent upon their rights and privileges. Consequently there emerged a struggle between "the fat people" (rich) and "the thin people" (the poor). This struggle was not entirely absent from Rome itself. Arnold of Brescia gave to it a religious turn. He insisted that clerical vice and corruption were the result of temporal responsibility. No clergyman or monk should own land; indeed if he did—so Arnold taught—he could not be saved. Therefore the church, constituted as it was around the principle of wealth and power, was not the true church; and the people should not receive its sacraments but should confess their sins to one another and support one another in trying to live the good life. Arnold of Brescia wandered about France, lent his support to Abelard, and came finally to Rome, where he joined in a civic revolt against the papacy which precipitated a struggle that lasted for forty years. In the early months of 1146 shortly after Pope Eugenius III had returned to Rome, having been earlier expelled by the revolutionaries, Arnold of Brescia set up a competitive rule in the same city which lasted for almost a decade. He was overcome and arrested by Frederick Barbarossa, hanged, his body burned, and his ashes thrown into the Tiber (1155). As long as Bernard lived, he gave constant opposition to all revolutionary tendencies. He was the bulwark of

[19] Suger, *Oeuvres Complètes* (ed. A. Lecoy de La Marche, 1867).
[20] MPL, Vol. CLXXXVII.

social, political, and ecclesiastical conservatism. He preserved in church and state the status quo.[21]

Bernard's conservatism was most pronounced in the realm of theology, and his personal piety did not prevent him from hunting heretics to their ruin. In his sermons he attacked the Cologne heretics, precursors of the Anabaptists, for they admitted only the Bible as the rule of faith and rejected both infant baptism and belief in the communion of the saints. He urged the civil authorities to suppress the promulgation of their tenets by Peter of Bruys in southern France.[22] The Bishop of Poitiers, the brilliant Gilbert de la Porrée, embarrassed the French church by carrying realism to its extreme. He made a distinction between God and the Divinity of his nature in the same way that he discriminated between man and the humanity in which man participates.[23] His teaching was condemned at Rheims (1148), and Gilbert recanted in the presence of Pope Eugenius III, to whom he said, "If you believe otherwise, then I will believe as you do." [24] Yet Bernard encouraged the nun Hildegard who claimed to have perceived directly the Trinity, so that as a result of personal revelation she could explain God's nature, creation, and redemption. When she died in 1179, she left to posterity three volumes of her revelations.[25] He brought down to condemnation for heresy the renowned Peter Abelard, whose scintillating mind, though it had vanquished others, could not withstand the orthodoxy of his rival.

Bernard at the height of his career, aged fifty-six, set the Second Crusade in motion by the inspiration of his preaching.[26] Then, when its splendid armies were defeated and scattered and its two mighty leaders, the kings of Germany and France, came home vanquished and broken, he turned military defeat into spiritual victory by persuading the people that what had happened to the crusaders was an instance of the justice and judgment of God.[27]

In all things Bernard was a moral reformer, believing that the health of the church meant at the same time the health of society as a whole and that whatever afflicted the church injured the totality of life. Pope Innocent II (1130-1143) looked upon Bernard as his deliverer; Celestine II (1143-1144), Abelard's pupil, had a reign of only five months and had no opportunity to disturb Bernard's leadership if he had so desired; Lucius II (1144-1145), a former papal legate to Germany, considered Bernard a sagacious and effective counsellor; and Eugenius III (1145-1153), Bernard's own pupil, revered his

[21] Otto of Freising, Chronicon, VIII, 27; J. Regesta, 8807, 8808; LP, II, 387.
[22] MPL, CLXXXII, 293-295, 361-365, 434-436.
[23] MPL, LXIV, 1255-1412.
[24] Hefele, op. cit., V, 838.
[25] MPL, Vol. CXCVII.
[26] Otto of Freising, Gesta Frederici, I, 34.
[27] Bernard, De consideratione, II, 1.

old teacher as a master and father. The two men died within one month of each other, the younger preceding the elder to the grave.

Bernard disavowed all interest in temporal concerns. Yet no man had more success in controlling what he professed to despise. This little monk, personally shy and retiring, a poet at heart and a recluse by desire and temperament, became under the pressure of events a consummate master of men and virtual dictator over all he surveyed. Without armies or money he exercised, by the sheer influence of his person and the persuasiveness of his convictions, a power equaled by few monarchs and enough to fire with envy the most ruthless tyrants of mankind.

III. The Contests Between the Church and the Crown

The beneficent yet effective dictatorship of Bernard of Clairvaux, who had controlled kings as well as popes and had consolidated Europe around the policies of the church, was succeeded by the absolutism of two monarchs who sought to undo all that he had accomplished. Both monarchs were worthy men. They honestly feared the encroachment of ecclesiastical power and influence in the political domain. Each was bent on the exaltation of his own office and the control of all that went on in the domain of his rule.

One was the German Frederick I, called **Frederick Barbarossa**, or "Red Beard"; the other was the English King **Henry II**. In appearance the two men presented striking contrasts. Frederick was tall, thin, and extraordinarily handsome. He stood above six feet, wore a neatly trimmed red beard, was extremely careful about his person, had exquisite manners, and conducted himself on state occasions with that dignity which commands public respect. In a sense, he was the supreme personification of German imperial power in the Middle Ages—the precursor of such later heroes as Frederick the Great and Bismark. Henry was short, heavy, and extremely muscular. He had the head and neck of a bulldog. His hands were thick and callous like those of a peasant. He was untidy, careless in dress, and seldom bathed or changed his clothes. He was indifferent to manners, boorish, and coarse; no one could have cared less about his conduct at state functions. Both were men of great physical prowess and athletic skill. Frederick had the appearance of a runner or discus thrower; Henry, that of a wrestler. Each was crafty, cunning, shrewd—an accomplished diplomat, a gifted administrator, a consummate statesman. Whereas the German's stage of activity was the continent of Western Europe, since he was Holy Roman Emperor as well as king, the Englishman's was only his own realm. Consequently, Henry disturbed a single archiepiscopal see; Frederick disturbed the papacy itself.

The occupant of Peter's see at the time Frederick made his first visit to Italy was **Adrian IV**, an unusual man whose former name had been Nicholas

Breakspear, the only Englishman ever to attain the papacy. Adrian had come up the hard way. His childhood and youth had been impaired by abject poverty. He had migrated from England to France, where he had begun his career as a beggar and had ended it as the abbot of St. Rufus in the city of Avignon.[28] Indeed, he had left France for Rome to defend himself before Pope Eugenius III against charges of maladministration. Not only had he been exonerated but he had made such a good impression that he had been kept permanently in the employment of Rome. After the short and ineffective pontificate of Anastasius IV (July, 1153-December, 1154), he was unanimously elected pope. He had caught the public eye because of the quality of his work as papal legate to Scandinavia, where he had established the archiepiscopal see of Norway at Trondheim and had made Upsala the primatial see of Sweden. Evidently on his election he had grasped the difficulty of his task as pope, for he had exclaimed, "I know that my path is strewn with thorns, and this papal mantle which is placed upon me, although much tattered, is still heavy enough to weigh down even the strongest." [29]

Driven out of Rome by the revolutionaries under Arnold of Brescia, Pope Adrian met Frederick at Sutri, where signs of the conflict between them were apparent from the first. Frederick hesitated to hold the pope's horse and to assist him to mount and dismount. Likewise, the pope refrained from giving the emperor the kiss of peace. But each bethought himself, and these ancient courtesies were exchanged between them. As a result Frederick drove the revolutionaries from Rome and obtained from the pope the imperial crown (July 18, 1156).[30]

Subsequent relations between them were not happy. Adrian entered into negotiation with King William of Sicily to the displeasure of Frederick, who planned to take William's lands in Italy as his own; while Frederick gave papal lands to his own supporters and disregarded in his appointment of ecclesiastics the provisions of the Concordat of Worms. Unfortunately, the mission of Adrian's first two legates to Germany had been a failure, and they had been expelled by Frederick. One of these legates was Cardinal Roland Bandinelli. The occasion of the rupture was the mistranslation of a Latin word into German. Adrian had written to Frederick about the favors the church had conferred on him, and the word had been translated as fiefs. This made it appear that the Frederick was dependent upon Adrian for his lands. When Roland Bandinelli had said, not himself understanding the mistranslation, "From whom then does the emperor hold his imperial dignity if not from the pope?", the emperor had replied, "If we were not in church, you would learn

[28] LP, II, 388.
[29] John of Salisbury, Policraticus, Book VIII (ed. Webb, Oxford, 2 vols., 1909).
[30] Otto of Freising, op. cit., II, 22.

how heavy the German swords are." One of the royal retinue had wanted to decapitate Roland on the spot.[31]

Frederick employed legal tactics to win his case. He turned to the school at Bologna, famous for the study of law, and the legates, disregarding centuries of Christian usage, revised in his favor the laws of the ancient Roman empire. The outcome was the Code of Roncaglia (1158), which stipulated that all rights and powers connected with territorial sovereignty are in the emperor's hands.[32] This meant that the entire empire, including the church and the semi-independent Italian cities, was at the free disposition of the emperor, who could do with it what his discretion prompted.

The Code of Roncaglia was Frederick's undoing. At the death of Adrian IV (1159) at Anagni, the cardinals in an act of defiance elected Roland Bandinelli as his successor under the name of Alexander III (1159-1181). Though at the very time of his election Frederick's supporter among the cardinals, Octavian, snatched the papal mantle from Bandinelli's shoulders and put it around his own, and though for seventeen years war raged between him and the emperor (six of which [1160-1166] were a series of uninterrupted failures for the papal cause), in the end Alexander III vanquished Frederick I.

This he did by stirring up local pride and the desire on the part of cities for autonomy and independence. Consequently, the League of Verona and the Lombard League were too much even for Frederick. France too was afraid of her powerful neighbor to the east, suspected German aggression in her direction, and lent her support to the papacy. Though Frederick supported three antipopes in succession, Victor IV (Octavian), Paschal III (Guido of Crema), and Calixtus III (John of Struma), he was not joined by any other major sovereign, and his efforts against Alexander were to no avail. To be sure, he captured Rome, laid waste the cities of northern Italy, and engaged in barbarism as hideous as any which has stained the annals of history. He put little children—hostages he had taken from the cities—in the front of his war machines, so that they would be the first killed by their own parents in the siege. But after the taking of Rome (November 23, 1165) and the flight of Alexander from his own city in the disguise of a pilgrim, the plague did for the pope what his armies had not been able to do. It wasted Frederick's men by the thousands. At the same time it gave courage to his enemies, who believed it to be the judgment of God against him for his crimes. Consequently the soldiers of the Lombard League finished what the plague had started, and Frederick was forced to make his peace with Alexander III on Alexander's own terms (Treaty of Venice, August 1, 1177) and to placate the Lombard League as well (Constance, June, 1183).[33] The German emperor ended his long

[31] Mansi, XXI, 709-710, 789-790.
[32] MGH, Scriptores, XX, 449.
[33] Mansi, XXII, 122.

reign (1152-1190) of thirty-eight years by going on the Third Crusade.

What happened between Frederick I and Alexander III on the continent of Europe was repeated between **Henry II (1154-1189) and the archbishop of Canterbury, Thomas à Becket, in England.**

Henry was only twenty-two years old when he began to reign. He found in a young deacon at Canterbury all that he needed and desired in a counsellor and executive of his plans and therefore translated Thomas from duties in the church to grave responsibilities of state. Young as Thomas was (he was only a few years Henry's senior), he soon became Lord High Chancellor of the Realm. All might have gone well had Thomas stayed a civil official the remainder of his days. He was one of those honest characters who are absolutely loyal to the institutions they serve. Evidently Henry did not realize this trait in the character of his friend, for he secured his election as archbishop of Canterbury (June 3, 1162), believing thereby that he could consolidate the interests of the church and crown. In other words, Henry wished to govern the church with the same absolutism with which he governed his state.

The English church needed the strong hand of the king. Its discipline was lax; its affairs were loosely, even poorly, handled; its courts were a menace to public law and order. Indeed, for crimes for which an ordinary person was sent to the gibbet, a cleric was subjected to a period of fasting and prayer and then allowed to go free—even to resume his sacerdotal duties without compromise.

Therefore, King Henry decreed that when a priest or monk was found guilty of a crime by the ecclesiastical court he should be turned over to the civil court for judgment, and he insisted that a civil judge sit in on the proceedings of the ecclesiastical court (October 1, 1163). Thomas protested against this action with all the power at his disposal, and there ensued a five-year-long contest between Henry and his archbishop. The pope at first supported Thomas, making him papal legate over England (1166). Yet he withdrew this support (1168) and even suspended the archbishop's jurisdiction. The king boasted that he could buy any cardinal for a price and he had the pope in the palm of his hand.

The contest ended with the murder of the archbishop by four knights (December, 1170), who thought they were executing the king's will. Thomas' death was at the same time his greatest victory. So far-reaching and aggravated was the sentiment of the people against their ruler, that in 1174, four years after Thomas' death, Henry had to go as a penitent to his tomb, bare his own breast and back, and receive the cut of the cat-o'-nine-tails on his own flesh. Like Frederick of Germany, Henry of England had to bow to the will of the church.[34]

[34] J. C. Robert, *Materials for the History of Thomas à Becket* (1875-1885), 9 vols.

Alexander III signalized the glories of his pontificate by convoking at the Lateran an ecumenical council (March 5-19, 1179). In Western Christendom it is numbered the eleventh of the General Councils. This Council legislated that a two-thirds vote of the cardinals is necessary to elect a pope. A free school was to be set up at every cathedral, renewing thereby the neglected legislation of Charlemagne; priests were set aside for work among lepers; the church was called upon to rally against the heretics within Christendom and the Saracen infidels without. Almost one thousand prelates attended this conference at which the pope presided. Alexander reserved for the papacy the right of canonization, since already, before this conclave, he had canonized Thomas à Becket (1173) and Bernard of Clairvaux (1174), the English martyr having been raised to the ranks of the saints one year before his world-famous French predecessor.[35]

The five successors to Alexander III during the remaining years of the twelfth century—Lucius III, Urban III, Gregory VIII, Clement III, and Celestine III (1181-1198)—were far less able than he. Two of them, Lucius III and Celestine III, the first and the fifth, were extremely old at the time of their elevation. Yet Alexander's work had been so solidly laid that it could not be greatly disturbed. The papacy had to contend with the marital problems occasioned by the infidelity of Philip Augustus (1180-1223) of France and his devout Danish wife, who, though she could not speak French, cried as her appeal, "Roma! Roma!" The young German King Henry VI (1190-1197) disturbed Rome by trying to succeed where his father Frederick I had failed. Even Alfonso IX of Leon annoyed the pope by twice marrying close relatives. Yet these incidents were minor compared to what the papacy had suffered and in the end subdued. The papacy of the twelfth century opened successfully the gates of the secular kingdoms to the victorious ecclesiastical army of the thirteenth century.

IV. The Cathari and the Inauguration of the Inquisition

The church was also harassed within by heresy. There seems to have been no age in which there was absolute unanimity of doctrinal opinion. Especially in the late eleventh and early twelfth century, when the mind was reawakening out of a long intellectual slumber, there was a wide variety of religious interpretations, so that even within the range of orthodoxy such divergent interpretations of Christianity as mysticism and scholasticism existed side by side. It was only natural that heresy should arise also.

The most widespread and damaging form of heresy was that of the Cathari, a medieval expression of ancient Manichaeism and the Paulicianism of the Eastern empire. Its basic contention was that there are two coequal principles in operation in the universe and life—the principles of good and evil —each cosmic in its proportions and eternal in its cause. Neither good nor evil takes precedence over the other, for both are timeless. The superiority of the one to the other does not lie in the power of brute force or conquest but rather in the superior quality of life which the one engenders and the other does not. To choose the good is to become good, and goodness is its own reward.

Consequently among the Cathari there was a wide divergence between the status of those who were mere hearers and that of the perfected whose conduct imitated the source of pure good in which they believed. Theirs was the life of complete self-denial, of refraining from all sensual expressions, of avoiding any contact with flesh. For example, a wife was so rigid in this practice that she would not so much as handle her husband's body even on his death bed. It was forbidden to the Cathari to eat meat, milk, eggs, butter, cheese, or any other product which was connected with animal procreation. These people were vegetarians. They did oddly enough eat fish, evidently ignorant of the fish's origin in an act of sexual union.

Weird stories were told of these people similar to those told of the early Christians whose strange rites lent themselves to pagan misunderstanding and exaggeration. Since marriage was not encouraged for the perfect, rumors spread, with little or no justification, that the Cathari were promiscuous to the degree that they blew out the lights and engaged in free sexual orgies. It was said that their Eucharist was made of burned offal, and that whoever ate it was poisoned into a docile submission to Catharist tenets and practices. Such rumors were absurd. So far as we are able to judge, the morals of this group were ascetic and pure, going beyond the most rigid monasticism in attempts at self-denial. The more intense the pain the more abundant was the spiritual reward. To die a martyr was the greatest of all gains. Consequently sons and daughters frequently accommodated their aged parents by smothering them; sometimes a person would inflict death upon himself.

There were four orders in the Catharist ministry: (1) Bishop, (2) Filius Major, (3) Filius Minor, and (4) Deacon. The Deacon was an administrative helper to one of the other orders. Filii Minores were church visitors. Filii Majores, elected to office by the congregation, were the pastors, while Bishops were administrative heads, their ranks filled from among the Filii Majores as vacancies occurred. Adherents joined the Cathari by the sacrament of consolamentum—the laying on of hands. The Eucharist was a simple meal of the breaking of bread by the Filius Major as people stood together around a table and said aloud the Lord's Prayer.

The Cathari were antisacerdotal. Their members boycotted the church and did all they could to disrupt organized Christianity. Their movement spread rapidly in the twelfth century. Toward the close of the century the Cathari were scattered in sizeable groups in Germany, England, Italy, and especially in southern France. They were too numerous not to be noticed. To ignore them was dangerous to the progress of organized Christianity.[36]

It was in opposition to the Cathari that the **Inquisition** arose. This was an institution of the church both to discover and to eliminate heresy.

The effort to eradicate heresy by destroying the heretic did not begin with the ecclesiastical authorities. It began with the violence of mobs and the passion of groups so furious that they could not be restrained or controlled. In indignation against the extremists, mobs would catch individual Cathari, tear their limbs from their bodies, and burn, drown, or lynch them.

The church at first had disapproved and forbidden the use of violence in stamping out heresy. Bernard himself had counselled that heretics can be won by preaching, never by the sword.

But with such a rapid spread of the Cathari and the fact that by their conversions and propaganda they endangered the welfare of others, the church consented to the popular demand and inaugurated the inquisition, a department of every diocese where it was needful to stamp out heresy and insure orthodoxy. This was known as the episcopal inquisition. Prior to its establishment several councils, including the great Lateran Council of 1179, had authorized the suppression of heresy by the princes with the sword.[37] The act of the inquisition was established by Pope Lucius III on November 4, 1184, in which he made it mandatory for bishops of suspected areas to examine their flock at least once a year, requiring every member under oath to declare his orthodoxy. Likewise, the faithful under oath were to inform on those they knew to be heretics. Anyone who in any way protected a heretic was guilty of heresy along with him and must be excommunicated.[38]

V. The Third Crusade

The concern of the church for the integrity of its doctrine and the unity of its organization, together with its strenuous contests with the royal power in both Germany and England, had provided it with little time or energy for the affairs of the Christian states in the East. It is all too likely that Western Christendom took their perpetuity for granted, having very soon forgotten the travail and sacrifice paid for their creation in the First Crusade. Pilgrims arriving home from the Holy Land gave glamorous and enticing accounts of life there. What they said was enough to make the proudest Western poten-

---

[36] Rainer Sacconi, *Summa de Catharis et Leonistis*, in *Thesaurus Novus Anecdotorum* (Paris, 1717), V, collections, 1759-1776. S. Runciman, *The Medieval Manichee* (1947), pp. 116-170.

[37] Mansi, XXI, 532, 718; XXII, 209-468.

[38] Hefele, op. cit., V, 1124.

tate green with envy. While he was constrained daily to superintend his serfs, direct his vassals, fight his competitor for power, repair his castles, and pay his obligations to the church, his counterpart in the East, having exchanged the heavy mail of a knight-errant for the light silks of an emir, dined sumptuously and enjoyed all the luxurious extravagances of the East. To be sure Edessa had fallen, and the Second Crusade had failed to retrieve it. But nonetheless Acre, Tyre, Tripoli, and Antioch were intact; and Jerusalem "was builded as a city compact together"; it would endure in Christian hands for ever.

The shock to the West can be well imagined when it heard the unbelievable news that the **Holy City itself had fallen to the infidels** (October 2, 1187). The united armies of the Christian principalities had been defeated in a major battle at the Horns of Hittin near the Sea of Galilee, and there had been no strength left to exert in saving Jerusalem. When the report reached King William II of Sicily, that hardened warrior whose navies were endangering the security of the Byzantine empire at the time, shook on his throne and wept like a child. He vowed that all he had would be spent in the service of his faith. The news was too much for the aged Pontiff Gregory VIII. It reached him on the eve of his election to the highest office of Christendom (October 20, 1187); it fell over his enthronement like a shroud; it set the purpose of his reign; it brought him, broken-hearted, to his grave (December 17, 1187), not even having given him the time to begin the fulfillment of that purpose. When Henry II of England and Philip Augustus of France got the report, they knew immediately their obligation. Though habitual enemies and constantly at war with each other, they concluded a truce under the elm of Gisors and exchanged the kiss of peace (January 21, 1188). Even the old, though still virile, Emperor Frederick I, who all his reign had carried on a perpetual warfare with the papacy and its allies, put the welfare of Christendom above that of his empire in this time of dire emergency and swore to God that he would march.

Properly, as the West's greatest and most powerful prince, Frederick was the first to go. He led into the East perhaps the largest and best equipped army ever assembled. He negotiated in advance with the king of Hungary, the Byzantine emperor, and the Seljuk sultan to secure its peaceful march through their territories. Consequently, though there was some friction with the Greeks and though the sultan did not keep his bargain at all, the army was held intact and kept its full strength for the purpose of its expedition. Possibly this one force could have easily accomplished its mission, restored Jerusalem to Christian hands, and buttressed the little kingdom for a long life in the midst of its Moslem neighbors. Yet it was prevented by an untoward accident. The old emperor riding at the head of his troops was drowned in a stream near Selifke, just a little to the west of Tarsus (June 10, 1190). His young son Philip of Swabia took command, but he was not the crown prince, lacked experience and judgment, and many of his soldiers, bereft of confidence, returned home. The boy tried desperately to succeed. He carried his father's body, pickled in vinegar, with the troops. It disintegrated as did the expedition, and what was left was buried in the cathedral at Antioch.

Consequently, the burden of the Crusade fell on the **English and the French.** Richard I (1189-1199) of England and Philip Augustus of France (1180-1223) were the leaders. Richard was thirty-three years old at the time; Philip was eight years his junior, yet he had been on the throne of France almost a decade before Richard began to reign. In experience, maturity of judgment, cunning, administrative skill, and statecraft, he was by all odds Richard's superior. Philip Augustus was a well-built, vigorous enough man. But Richard was unsurpassed as an athlete and a warrior. He was tall, massive, and extraordinarily handsome. Consequently Philip was not his equal. The Frenchman was dwarfed by the Englishman's size and was afraid of him. Philip was a mean, selfish, dishonest, unscrupulous, ruthless person, but a great king; while Richard was a gay, charming, forthright, attractive person, but a poor king.

The French and English did not arrive ready for battle until four years after the fall of Jerusalem. They had stopped in Sicily, where Richard had given trouble to the successor of King William II. The English had tarried again at Cyprus, where Richard had displaced the Greek ruler, Isaac Comnenus, pretender to the throne of the Byzantine empire. Their first major engagement against the Moslems was the siege of Acre.

Though Acre fell to Christian hands on July 31, 1191, the Crusade did not accomplish its mission. Philip Augustus, ill since the day of his arrival and not sincerely committed to the cause, sailed home. Richard stayed until October 9, 1192; but he was soldier enough to see that even if he took Jerusalem, those who stayed behind could not keep it.

Consequently, before leaving he negotiated a peace with Saladin (September 2, 1192), the Moslem sultan, in which he gained permission for the Christians to worship at the sacred shrines and secured their cities and territories from Antioch down the coastline south to Jaffa. The Christian principality, still called the Kingdom of Jerusalem, was ten miles wide and ninety miles long. Richard put in the place of the incompetent Guy of Lusignan, to whom he sold Cyprus, his own nephew, Henry of Champagne, as king of Jerusalem.

The opponent of the crusaders was the wise and beneficent **Saladin,** thought of in the West as the antiChrist, but in reality a just and god-fearing man whose integrity put to shame the conniving deceit of many of his Christian enemies. In all his engagements, he was never known to go back on his word or fail in the fulfillment of his promises. After negotiating his peace with

Richard, he returned from the army camp to his capital in Damascus in order to set his affairs in order for a visit to Egypt and a pilgrimage to Mecca. He never made either. Worn out by war, he died before his time. He was only fifty-five years old. On Wednesday, March 3, 1193, as the Cadi of Damascus was reading the Koran at the passage, "There is no god but Allah; in him do I trust," Saladin opened his eyes and smiled and breathed his last.

Richard survived him another six years. He went back to Italy by sea and started across southern Germany in disguise. He was recognized at a tavern near Vienna, arrested, and handed over first to the Duke of Austria and later to Henry VI of Germany, who kept him a prisoner for a year. On payment of a huge ransom he was released in March, 1194. No sooner had he arrived home and settled affairs with his brother John than he began campaigning again against the king of France. He was struck by an arrow shot at random and died, in his early forties, on March 26, 1199. Though a gallant and gifted soldier, Richard was a disloyal son to his father Henry II, an indifferent and careless husband, and a poor king. He lives on as the personification of the Third Crusade, which, like him, was glamorous and heroic but a failure.[39]

VI. Speculation and Mysticism

Above and beyond the transience of crusading armies and more enduring than the policies of popes and emperors was the speculation of the philosophers and theologians. Remote though that speculation appears in restrospect, it was once wide enough in its appeal to create schools and to solicit as scholars the best minds of the time and so to open the way for the great philosophical systems of the thirteenth century. Both Anselm and Abelard had their followers, not in the sense perhaps that students designated themselves as their disciples, but rather in the deeper sense that the basic presuppositions and methodology which bent their thinking influenced the thinking and set the concerns of others as well.

Anslem, for example, was a realist. So too were the masters of the cathedral School of Chartres, brought to fame by Bernard of Chartres (d. ca. 1130), whose basic concepts were Platonic. Plato of course was not known firsthand either to him or to his disciples. He was known through a translation of fragments of the *Timaeus* and a commentary upon the same by Chalcidius and through the writings of Boethius.

The first figure of stature in the School of Chartres was **Gilbert de la Porrée.** He differentiated accessory forms (place, time, situation, habit, action, and passion) from inherent forms (substance, quantity, quality, and relation), stating that the latter belonged essentially to the nature of any entity under consideration, while the former had to do with its changing relationships.

[39] S. Runciman, A History of the Crusades, III, 3-75. Best bibliography, ibid., 493-503.

Though it is basic to the nature of any entity to have a relationship, what its relationship is depends to a degree on where it is at a definite time. Both accessory and inherent factors are forms, however; they are not mere categories, as Abelard would have affirmed. Gilbert's Platonic realism is even more pronounced in his interpretation of substance as an actually existing individual entity with specific accidents in contrast to subsistence which is only the abstract property which, in being what it is, has no need of accidents. Genera and species, for example, are subsistences, since they have no need of accidents in order to be. Mankind is mankind without qualification, yet a man, in contrast, is that which stands under and supports specific accidents or qualifications; he is a substance. Consequently a substance must of necessity be a subsistence, but a subsistence need not be a substance. When specific things come to be, three factors enter into their making: (1) unformed matter; (2) the worker with his being; (3) the idea of the thing to be made. The idea never itself descends concretely into matter. Only the model of the idea shapes and enters into the specific entity making it what it is. Thus forms are always subsistences by virtue of which substances come to be. Likewise, the former are always plural, since each individual is determined by a generic subsistence involving all individuals of its kind as well as specific substance with its accidents. By abstraction the intellect is capable of considering what is given as a whole in reality and finding similarities of the whole in other specific entities. John of Salisbury said of Gilbert de la Porrée, "He attributes universality to engendered forms, and he labors over their conformity." In all created things it is possible to distinguish between the thing which is and the principle which causes it to be what it is. Only in God do the two coincide; he is absolutely simple being. What God is and the principle by which God is (divinity) are the same.[40]

Thierry (d. ca. 1155), Bernard's younger brother and Gilbert's successor at Chartres, was a queer genius whose specialty was cosmogony. His bent was Platonic realism also, for he insisted that only unity is eternal since it is absolutely stable and immovable. Change belongs to time and is the domain of creation. God then as absolute unity is the only perfect and complete being; likewise, he is truth itself. God is the form of all things since everything that exists exists through him. Thierry set about to explain the first chapter of Genesis. There are four basic causes: (1) The efficient cause of creation is God; (2) the formal cause is the Wisdom, or Word, of God; (3) the material cause is basic matter in the four elements of fire, air, earth, and water; and (4) the final cause is benevolence—God made everything for man, so man could share in his benevolence. Thierry uses fire as the primary element, giving the light of the first day of creation and producing the heat to make the

40 MPL, LXIV, 1255-1412.

water into a vapor to compose the firmament. With that he curiously explains one by one the objects created in the sequential order of their creation. He shows us that a medieval Platonist could be a mechanist as well.[41]

Clarenbaud of Arras began at the point his master Thierry left off. He explained the meaning of God as the form of all things. Matter exists as potentiality. God, perfect form, is pure act needing no vehicle outside itself to express itself. When we see blackness or whiteness, we know the form of black or white is there. Yet wherever anything is, the form of being is. God is that form of being, and God in essence is everywhere. This working form is the prime entity that causes everything else. He also categorized philosophy into three parts: (1) theoretical, or speculative; (2) practical; (3) logical. Theoretical philosophy has three divisions also: (1) physics, which deals with forms in matter; (2) mathematics, which deals with physical properties of objects apart from those objects; (3) theology, which deals with forms separated from matter.[42]

Less exact in his findings, but more far-reaching in his appeal and charming and delightful in his expression was the last member of the School of Chartres, an Englishman, like the eighth-century Alcuin of York, who migrated to France, **John of Salisbury** (1125-1180). He said he could conceive five possible solutions to the problem of universals: (1) Universals are qualities that exist only in particulars; (2) universals are forms separated from particulars like mathematical units; (3) universals are just words, no more; (4) universals are general concepts; (5) universals are real in themselves, and particulars exist only as they participate in them. Since all these views make sense, it is best to suspend judgment and say we do not know what universals are. Indeed there are many problems we have not solved, and in regard to them the only attitude we can take is that of humble agnosticism. It is not a sin to say, "I do not know." We should reserve judgment, for example, on the origin of the soul, the infinity of numbers, divisibility and indivisibility, chance, free will, and a host of other issues. At the same time we should accept what our senses teach us, what we can discover through reason, and above all else, what we know by faith. Since God alone is true wisdom, true philosophy is the love of God. It is only a step then from John of Salisbury to the mystics.

Before taking that step however it is necessary to pause briefly to consider Abelard's disciples. Since Abelard had been convicted as a heretic, his influence had of necessity to be largely that of method rather than of substance. Pope Alexander III was his pupil, and before his elevation to the papacy he had done a good deal of study in philosophy. He used, for example, his

---

[41] *De Sex Dierum Operibus* (ed. B. Hauréau) in *Notices et extraits des manuscrits de la Bibliothèque Nationale* (1888) XXXII, 167-186.

[42] *De Trinitate*, in W. Jansen, *Der Kommentar des Clarenbaldus von Arras zu Boethius De Trinitate* (Breslau, 1926).

teacher's threefold division of theology (faith, love, and the sacraments), reversing the last two (the sacraments and love) on the grounds, properly so, that love is the product of faith and the sacraments.[43]

However, the most influential of these pupils of Abelard was **Peter the Lombard** (1100-1160), whose *Sentences* became the standard theological text of the Middle Ages. The Lombard was not concerned at all with psychological, dialectical, or even purely philosophical problems. He did not so much as treat the meaning of faith, its relation to reason, or the bounds of natural theology in contrast to revelation. His concern was merely to set forth one by one the traditional doctrines, quote what the Fathers and others said about them, and give his own explication. Yet his work was so complete, so well arranged, so easy to use that people abandoned the study of the sources and used *The Sentences* of the Lombard in their stead. Peter began by drawing the distinction between signs and things. The latter are ends in themselves, while the former point beyond themselves to something else different from them and more ultimate. The sacraments, for example, are signs. Peter the Lombard fixed them at seven, and so is responsible for the definite number traditionally accepted by the Roman Catholic Church. Augustine had said that they were innumerable, being all things that conveyed grace. Abelard had numbered them at ten. The Lombard, following the example of the Greek, John of Damascus, divided *The Sentences* into four parts: (1) Trinity, which dealt with (a) the knowledge of God, (b) providence, (c) predestination; (2) Creation, which included (a) angels, (b) men, (c) the fall, (d) grace, (e) free will; (3) the Incarnation, which treated (a) the person of Christ, (b) the work of Christ, (c) faith, hope, and love, (d) virtue and vice; and (4) the sacraments and eschatology. This fourfold division has marked the form of systematic theology ever since.[44]

Both Alexander III and Peter the Lombard, who became the bishop of Paris, naturally incorporated many of Abelard's ideas into their works, so that the thinking of him who was branded a heretic worked its way into the doctrines of the church.

At the same time the mystical strain was pronounced in the thought of the twelfth century. **Bernard of Clairvaux**, for example, delighted in the mystery of the faith, contemplating truths the very majesty of which lay for him in their inaccessibility to the reach of reason. He was content merely to believe what the church told him to believe and had little interest in whether its doctrines could be proved or not. Yet religion as union of the soul with God, not perhaps in a neoplatonic or pantheistic sense of individual absorption into the divine unity, but rather in the more vital sense of emotional, moral, and spiritual oneness where the knowledge of God led to the imitation of God's

[43] MPL, CXCIX, 1-1040.
[44] MPL, Vols. CXCI, CXCII.

character, was the passion of his life. Love for him was synonymous with Christianity. There are four stages in this love: (1) we love ourselves; (2) we love God because of our love of self—that is, we love God for the benefits that love confers on us; (3) we love God for himself alone; (4) we love ourselves for God's sake, for what we can do for him in fulfilling the end for which we were made. Such love enables us to have no enemies among the children of faith. We love our Christian neighbors as ourselves. Yet those who are not Christian we love in hope that they may become Christian. However, if they continue to thwart God's purposes, they become our enemies because they are his enemies, and we hate them for his sake. Bernard gave the logical justification for his attitude toward Abelard.[45]

Bernard of Clairvaux was not a theologian in the nice meaning of that word, but his younger contemporary **Hugo of St. Victor** (1196-1141) was. Hugo delineated faith as a joint activity of the intellect and the will, its contents being less than exact knowledge and yet more than mere opinion. It leads not to the assertion of a conviction only but also to the commitment of one's self to a person. Consequently there are three stages of faith: (1) the stage when we accept the teachings of the church without ever thinking about them, (2) the stage when we reason upon our beliefs, (3) the stage when we go beyond reason to mystical union with him in whom we believe. This is ecstasy. There are therefore three eyes: the eye of flesh which sees the external world, the eye of reason which sees the internal world, and the eye of faith which sees God and the things of God. The use of the third eye is given only to him who has given himself to God. Hugo was a philosopher and as such surveyed from the Christian viewpoint the whole range of existence. He wrote a prolegomena to all studies—agriculture and navigation as well as mathematics and logic. Yet his chief claim to fame was his skill as a theologian. He set forth the doctrine of redemption as the unifying principle of theology. In his book on the *Sacraments of the Christian Faith* (like Augustine, he made all of life a sacrament), he divided theology into two parts—that which deals with general living, with providence before the Incarnation (creation, general knowledge of God, angels, man, the fall, sin, restoration, faith, natural law and the decalogue, sacraments of general providence), and that which deals with Christian living, with redemption after the Incarnation (church, clergy, rites, ethics, forgiveness, eschatology). In this second part Hugo discusses practical matters which we would look upon as polity or ecclesiology. He used the Bible itself as his source rather than the Fathers. Though his theme always is man's redemption, he must show how man fell and his condition before the fall before he can treat his restoration. Man's spirit was made for God, his body for his

[45] MPL, Vols. CLXXXII-CLXXXV.

spirit, and the world for his body. All things were made by God for man in order that man might love and enjoy God.[46]

Richard of St. Victor (d. 1173) is remembered because of his unique interpretation of the Trinity in terms of love which is the quintessence of twelfth-century mysticism. To love only one's self is egoism, while to love only another is scarcely more than a projection of the love of self. In order really to love one must include a third person in the experience. Two people not only love each other, but they permit each other to love a third person who in turn loves each of them. This can be seen best in the family. Husband loves wife, and wife loves husband, yet both love the children who in turn love them. The nature of love itself implies a trinity.[47]

Adam of St. Victor, together with Bernard of Clairvaux, was the poet of mysticism. Fifty of his hymns are still extant, and many of them are in use. It was he who introduced the rhyme into the chants of the church. He was more than a poet; he was a musician as well, providing the melodies for his own lyrics.[48]

Mysticism could not but spill over into philosophy which led to a twelfth-century version of Plotinus, though without the benefit of the original as either model or point of departure. Bernard of Clairvaux, who had disparaged and ignored philosophy, could not prevent its intrusion into the Cistercian order, for the exponent of mystical theology was the Cistercian Humbert, who did his work in the second half of the twelfth century after Bernard had gone. Had Bernard lived, he would certainly have condemned him, especially for his views on the Trinity as an expanding Monad.

Humbert, or Alan of Lille, was the first apologist of Christianity against Islam. He was not crusader and could not perform miracles, so could not convert the Moslems by a catastrophic act. He would, then, convince them on the basis of reason. Consequently he made logical deductions from axioms and postulates which he took to be self-evident, thus constructing a theology after the pattern of Euclidian geometry: (1) The cause of a cause is bound to be at the same time the cause of its effect; (2) naturally the cause of a substance is the cause of that substance's accidents as well; (3) nothing can make itself—that is, cause its own existence; (4) no matter can exist without a form, neither can a form exist without matter; (5) composition of form and matter is therefore the cause of a substance. This last postulate is a demonstration: (a) since matter and form compose a substance, matter and form are together its cause; (b) yet since matter and form need each other to exist, therefore both have actual existence because of their composition; (c) conse-

[46] MPL, Vols. CLXXV-CLXXVI.
[47] MPL, CXCVI, 1-1378.
[48] L. Gautier, *Ouevres poétiques d'Adam de Saint-Victor* (Paris, 1858), 2 vols.

quently their composition is the cause of their existence; (d) but then their existence is the cause of the substance; (e) therefore since the cause of the cause is the cause of the effect, the composition of form with matter is the cause of the substance. Alan insisted that though nature and theology are approached in different ways, they never contradict each other. Nature proceeds from reason to faith; theology, from faith to reason; yet, their conclusions in the end are the same. God is unity. From this unity proceeds plurality or otherness. There are then three descending orders of being: (1) supercelestial order —God; (2) celestial order—angels, who are capable of mutability; (3) subcelestial order—bodies marked by plurality. There is of course some unity everywhere there is being. The restoration of unity is the end of creation. As we receive grace we are restored to unity with God. Here in Alan of Lille mysticism coalesces with the Platonic concerns of the School of Chartres without losing the intellectual daring and independence of Abelard, yet the philosophical outcome is different from anything any of these imagined.[49]

The **curriculum** of the Middle Ages consisting of the trivium (grammar, rhetoric, and dialectics) and the quadrivium (arithmetic, geometry, astronomy, and music) was well established by the middle of the twelfth century, and texts by which to teach each one of these seven liberal arts had been selected and were in use at the various cathedral and monastic schools. Chartres, for example, employed the texts of Donatus and Priscian for grammar; Cicero and Marcianus Capella for rhetoric, and Boethius and a part of Aristotle's *Organum* for dialectics. Superior to the arts was theology itself, beginning now to be dominated by the *Sentences* of Peter the Lombard.

The twelfth century also witnessed the flowering of **symbolic usage.** In the interpretation of scripture words and events were looked upon not for what they said or were in themselves but as signs of something esoteric. Symbolism is also seen in monuments and buildings. Gothic architecture was the instrument of the church. Every adornment, every curve, and every straight line had a meaning. The things of sense pointed to things of the spirit. The concrete was a representation of him who was and is without concretion.

All the ingredients for the making of the Christian culture of the thirteenth century with the exception of the finding of Aristotle and the benefits of Araby were in hand in the twelfth century.[50]

---

[49] MPL, CCX, 111-118; 305-482; 485-576; 621-684.
[50] E. Gilson, *History of Christian Philosophy in the Middle Ages* (N. Y., 1955), pp. 139-53, 164-78.

Chapter Nine

The Church Militant on Earth
(1198-1303)

THE THIRTEENTH CENTURY WAS A PERIOD OF MARKED CONTRASTS AND SHARP diversities. In the West it was, all in all, the greatest of the medieval centuries, while in the East it was the meanest in the long millennium of Byzantine history. The Roman papacy achieved its apex of political influence and power in Europe; the Greek church sank with the Eastern empire to the nadir of its effectiveness while still existing as the most venerable institution within an independent Christian state. The chief agents in the destruction of the Byzantine empire and the impairment of the Greek church were the Western crusaders not the Moslem infidels. Christians warred against Christians, and the wreckage of the Greek monuments of antiquity was entirely the doing of Latin troops. Consequently the Crusades petered out into nothingness. Islam had its greatest resurgence of power and influence. The grandeur of institutional Christianity was entirely in the West. Politically the church militant on earth, judged by the success of its undertakings, was almost exclusively the Roman papacy.

I. The Pontificate of Innocent III

In the papal election of 1198 the pendulum swung from age to youth. Celestine III had been eighty-five years old when he was elected pope. His successor was only thirty-seven, too young many thought to be a cardinal, much less a pope. Innocent III, for that was the papal name Giovanni Lotario de' Conti di Segni of the noble house of Scotii assumed, had been well educated at Rome, Paris, and Bologna, and in his case knowledge was synonymous with wisdom. It is said that as a student he had been uniformly proficient in all his studies, as adept at literature as at law, as skilled in science as in philosophy and theology. This is symptomatic of his pontificate; his activity belonged to the whole church; the catholicity of his concerns met with almost universal success the varied and multitudinous demands of his office. Indeed even in those incidents like the Fourth Crusade, for example, where his directives were not carried out and his original plan was radically altered, still he was able to use what he got and to make it subservient to his ultimate end. The adaptation, in this case perhaps, was more effective than the original plan, and, whatever else might have happened, the Roman church was exalted. Innocent was a master of circumstance. He seems always to have been the right man at the right place at the right time.

His physical **appearance** was in keeping with his role in public life. He was short, stocky, almost square. Perhaps he personified bodily the fourfold mission of his pontificate. He had a firm jaw and strong chin expressing determination. His nose was straight like the undeviating course of his actions. His mouth, small and tight-lipped, indicated the economy as well as the effectiveness of his commands; he waited to give orders until he knew he had the power to carry them out. His eyes were big like an owl's expressing the breadth and farsightedness of his vision. Innocent was pleasing enough in appearance as well as manner, and he showed from the start of his pontificate that he was a man with a plan and that he had the energy and the wisdom to carry it out.

His mission was fourfold: (1) to rule the papal states personally and directly by freeing them from the compromises of both internal and external interference; (2) to organize society, especially the Holy Roman Empire, around the policies of the Roman church and to bring governments as well as peoples under the tutelage and guidance of the Holy See; (3) to combat heresy and to guarantee the integrity of pure doctrine and proper ecclesiastical practices; (4) and to prosecute the cause of Christianity against the encroachments of the Moslem infidels. For nineteen years Innocent addressed himself and all the energies of his administration to this mission. In each particular he had remarkable success. The total accomplishment of his reign gave to the church its most powerful era in the temporal affairs of mankind.

Circumstances were ripe at the time of his enthronement for Innocent to take personal charge of the **government of the papal states** and to rule them with the authority of a monarch. A bitter contest was in progress in Germany between two rival candidates for the kingship, and the prefect (representative of the German king) did not know which one to represent in the government of Rome. The populace of Rome was without a leader, since Arnold of Brescia had been overthrown and no man of comparable stature had arisen to take his place. The nobility was divided among itself, and Innocent's own family was a powerful factor among them. Consequently Innocent began by bestowing gifts and favors on the people at large. He won the people; and the other two factions, the prefect and the nobility, followed as a matter of self-interest and safety. Though temporarily driven out of Rome in 1203 and 1204, Innocent re-established order around himself, secured the kingdom of the two Sicilies under the control of the widow of Henry VI, herself a Sicilian, and freed northern Italy from German domination. By 1208 Innocent was in complete charge of Italy.

Likewise, the pope entered aggressively into **German affairs.** Though he admitted that this nation, through its elective body, had a right to select its own ruler, still the person chosen had to be acceptable to the Holy See if he expected to rule over the Holy Roman Empire. Historically this empire had been created by the pope when he crowned Charlemagne; and, before the pope could approve a man to reign by crowning him, he had to examine and, after examining, to accept or to reject the candidate proposed. Since the emperor was the defender of the papacy, the pope was obligated to see to it that such a person was worthy of his office.

Innocent decided in favor of Otto IV over Philip of Swabia, who was later murdered on June 21, 1208. However, when Otto IV tried to rule in Italy, attempted to annex the Sicilies to his domain, violated the provisions of the Concordat of Worms, and was disobedient to the Pope, Innocent III excommunicated him (1210) and relieved his subjects of allegiance to him. France was called upon to wage war against him. In the end, Germany was defeated; Otto fled from the field of conquest; the dragon banner of the Holy Roman Empire was dragged in the dust; and young Frederick II, the ward of the pope, was elected to rule in his stead (1212). Though Otto continued desperately to struggle to regain his position until his death (1218), he was an ineffective force. The papacy had completely defeated him.

In **France** Philip Augustus, orthodox in belief and in public affairs loyal to Rome, nonetheless in his domestic life was a constant problem to the papacy. He could not be happy with his Danish wife Ingeburg. Yet when the problem was brought before a synod for adjudication (Soissons, March 2, 1201) and Philip saw the handwriting on the wall, he complied in advance with what he knew the verdict would be and rode off on horseback with Ingeburg before the assembly could meet. Later he imprisoned her. Only the death of his mistress and an impending war with England brought him to comply with the papal decision; then for ten years he honored her as his queen (1213-1223). Here again Innocent had had his way.

Sustained by Innocent's prayers and acknowledging his headship, the **Spanish rulers** of Castile, Navarre, Aragon, and Portugal won a great victory over the Moslems (July 16, 1212), which not only helped to unify Spain but also to bring her principalities closer to the Roman See.

Hungary, harassed by civil war and almost torn asunder by the strife among her nobility and the contest between two brothers for the throne, continually demanded papal concern and intervention. However, Innocent managed to preserve the unity of that nation. Innocent also was able to sever the Slavs of the Balkans from their Greek ecclesiastical associates. In fact the papal legate, John of Casamaris, actually became king of Bulgaria, and Innocent consecrated all the higher clergy of that nation. The kingdoms of Serbia and Galicia—one through civil strife, and the other in a war of independence from Polish and Russian interference—came under Roman ecclesiastical domination.

Even **England,** traditionally isolationist and independent, when excommunication struck her ruler and an interdict fell like a shadow over her, actually gave up her sovereign freedom and became a vassal of the Holy See. King John, May 15, 1213, placed his crown into the hands of the papal legate and exchanged his entire kingdom for the restoration of his soul. Consequently England and Ireland became parts of the patrimony of the apostle Peter and paid a tax of one thousand pounds sterling annually to Rome. Out of this unhappy time came Magna Carta (1215), which asserted that no tax could be levied without the consent of the Common Council of the Realm (twenty-five lords and the king) and which gave to every freeborn Englishman trial by a jury of his peers. This the church did not confer; Magna Carta came as a result of the demands of the English barons, who had risen in revolt against King John. Innocent did not approve the actions and declared Magna Carta null and void (August 24, 1215).

The other two major endeavors of this strenuous pontificate were both crusades, one a crusade against heresy at home, the other an extended crusade against the Islamic menace abroad. The first eventuated in a ruthless persecution, so that the papacy which inaugurated it tried desperately to terminate its barbarity, while the second got off its course and turned out to be a war of Christians against Christians.

Catharist tenets found wide acceptance in southern France through the **Albigensian movement.** It got its name simply from the fact that its followers were particularly numerous in Albi, where they were sponsored by Roger Trencaval, the viscount of Béziers.

Another heresy, likewise persecuted by the church, was the Waldensian. The tenets of this sect were entirely different from those of the Albigensian. The **Waldensians,** named from Peter Waldo their leader, had arisen in Lyons (1170), where they had been called the "Poor Men of Lyons." They were untainted by the dualism of the Catharist-Albigensian heresy. In fact they were simply New Testament purists rejecting the medieval doctrines of purgatory and transubstantiation and opposed to the hierarchy, the priesthood, and the veneration of saints. They wanted to purify Catholicism by simplifying it; the church naturally felt that such simplification meant in reality transformation to the point of destruction. Since the Waldensians had moved into southern France, territories adjacent to and also partly inhabited by the Albigensians, the crusade designed to extirpate Albigensianism played havoc also with Waldensianism.

The most important sponsor of the Albigensians was Raymond of Toulouse, the descendant of the famous First Crusader by the same name. He harbored them, honored them, and encouraged them.

Efforts to overcome them had been at first missionary and evangelistic. Dominic had preached to them in an evangelistic campaign in 1203. Even Innocent III tried to handle Raymond of Toulouse by persuasion, then by intimidation, and by threats. But Raymond had responded by warning the papal legate, Peter of Castelnau, "Take heed; wherever you go by land or by sea, I will keep my eye on you." Five days later Peter of Castelnau was murdered (Feb. 16, 1208), and all the evidence indicated that Raymond had instigated the deed.

Then it was that Innocent took military measures against the Albigensians and their supporters. After Innocent's first military effort had been successful (1209), Simon de Montfort took possession of Roger Trencaval's lands and warred on Raymond of Toulouse. Simon was a fanatical and intolerant champion of orthodoxy as well as a selfish and ambitious person. From 1209 to 1212 he conquered most of Languedoc. Only Toulouse itself and Montauban held out against him. Raymond of Toulouse in the end capitulated completely to papal dictates. Yet Simon had gone too far to be stopped. The orthodox King Peter II of Aragon had to come to Raymond's aid (1212). Even Innocent had to write to one of his bishops, "Discontinue stirring Christian people to the war against heresy" (1212).

The papal effort in the Albigensian Crusade was too successful. The suppression of heresy led to mass destruction including the innocent as well as the guilty. It went on for sixteen more years, twelve beyond the termination of Innocent's pontificate.[1]

The **Fourth Crusade** was also misdirected. Instigated by Innocent and his orators including Foulques of Neuilly, Peter the Chanter, and Peter Voracious, who read and knew so many books, this unhappy campaign was diverted by the Venetians. They transported the crusaders first to the port of Zara on the Dalmatian coast to destroy a competitor and later to Constantinople, there to unseat an emperor and enthrone his rival only to unseat him in turn and replace the Byzantine rule with Western. This was the beginning of the Latin empire in the East. Innocent, who had not planned this course of events, attempted to use them to accomplish the reunion of the Eastern and Western churches. He succeeded only in displacing Eastern rites in the lands of his conquests. The Moslem menace was unaffected by the Fourth Crusade. It continued unabated.[2]

---

[1] C. Douais, *Les sources de l' histoire de l' inquisition dans le midi de la France* (1881); *Documents pour servir à l'histoire de' l' inquisition dans Languedoc* (1900), 2 vols.

[2] S. Runciman, *A History of the Crusades*, II, 107-131.

This strenuous pontificate was concluded by an ecumenical council, the twelfth according to Western reckoning, and called the **Fourth Lateran Council** (1215). This condemned the Albigensian doctrines, gave approval to the hierarchical organization of Christendom around the papacy, and established the disciplinary procedures for the governance of the church which have continued in operation to this day.[3]

Innocent died (July 16, 1216) quite unexpectedly shortly after the close of the council. He was only fifty-six years of age at the time. Yet in his eighteen-and-a-half-year-long pontificate he realized all the aims of Gregory VII and combined in his person the duties of an emperor with those of the servant of the servants of God.[4]

II. The Mendicant Orders

What was most significant during the pontificate of Innocent III was not of Innocent's doing at all. It was not a part of his over-all plan of strategy, neither did it emerge as a tactical maneuver of his to meet some sudden emergency. The mendicant orders were the response of the church itself to the moral and spiritual needs of society at large. The desperate plight of the people, divided by heresy, animated either by the desire for material security or by the inordinate greed for wealth and power, and corrupted by sin, demanded a radical remedy. This was provided by the preaching of men who renounced the world only to possess it again for Jesus Christ, who gave up all comfort for themselves in order to provide others with the comfort of grace which they could not obtain apart from God. The creators of these orders were not popes or cardinals. They belonged to the lowly in spirit, if not born at least naturalized citizens of the classes they sought to help.

The Crusades themselves inspired the origination of at least one of these orders. Two men, Felix of Valois and John of Matha, inaugurated the **Order of the Holy Trinity**, the aim of which was to ransom Christian soldiers who had gone on the Crusade and had been captured. Their garb was a white woolen tunic marked by a blue or red cross. They were zealous, too, to perform good works and to combat heresy at home as well as infidelity abroad. This Order of the Holy Trinity won the endorsement of Pope Innocent III.[5]

The **Poor Catholics** were the offspring of Durán de Huesca, who got for them papal recognition from Innocent III. They set their poverty against the poverty of the Waldensians, whom they tried to win back to the church. These people renounced everything, slept on boards, refused gifts of silver and gold, and literally took no thought of the morrow. They started in 1207,

[3] Mansi, XXII, 903 ff.; supplem. II, 861 ff.
[4] MPL, Vols. CCXIV-CCXVII. A. Luchaire, *Innocent III* (Paris, 1904-1908), 6 vols. CMH, VI, 1-79, 219-251, 285-296, 393-413, 422-472.
[5] Potthast, *Regesta pontificum romanorum*, III, 483.

and by 1209 had communities in Aragon, Narbonne, Béziers, Uzès, Carcassonne, and Nîmes. Unfortunately the movement was short lived. The worldly prelates were suspicious of it. The crusading knights were impatient of it. Why take so much time, thought the knights, to convert heretics when it is so much quicker and simpler to exterminate them with the sword? The effectiveness of the Poor Catholics seems to have vanished overnight. In 1237 they were ordered by the papacy to select and to live by some monastic rule already in operation. And in 1247 they were restrained from preaching altogether. The Poor Catholics were the precursors of the Dominicans and the Franciscans.[6]

The **Dominicans** were the projection of the spirit and character of one man, the Spaniard Domingo de Guzman, known more familiarly as Dominic. He was born in Old Castile in 1170. Well educated in the arts and theology at the schools of Pelencia, he early displayed the spirit of sacrificial kindness. When he was only twenty-one a famine depleted the country and he sold all he had, including his books, to feed the poor. A decade or more later he accompanied his bishop north of the Pyrenees Mountains into Languedoc in southern France to help convert the Albigenses. He happened by chance while in Toulouse to lodge in the house of a heretic. He sat up all the night through trying to convert his host to Catholic orthodoxy. We know Dominic stayed in Languedoc even after his bishop, Diego, had gone home to Spain to die. It was on this mission which lasted almost half a dozen years that he founded the monastery of Prouille (1206) and counteracted thereby the influence of heretical convents founded to help poor girls to get an education. He knew, as the Albigensians did also, that whatever doctrine sways the home will go far to determine the future of society.[7] Fortunately a contemporary has left us the portrait of the young Dominic during those days: "His height was medium, but his face was beautiful. His hair and beard were light blond. He was always radiant and pleasant, except when he felt moved with compassion by some affliction of his neighbor." [8] He wore no shoes or sandals; he preached on the roadside and at corners of the street in the towns; he begged bread as a beggar. Though people made fun of him and even threatened him with dire calamities, he went on with his work until his peaceful means were superseded at Innocent's orders by a crusade in 1208. After 1208 he sank out of history for several years.

Then in 1214, a man forty-four years of age with nothing outstanding behind him to indicate the importance of his future, Dominic secured for himself as his companion in missionary and evangelistic labor a rich citizen of

---

[6] Innocent III, Regesta, XI, 98; XII, 67, 69; XIII, 63, 78, 94; XV, 90-93, 96, 137, 146. Berger, Régistres d'Innocent IV, No. 2752.
[7] Innocent III, Regesta, IX, 185. N. de Trivette, Chronicon, a. 1205.
[8] J. B. Lacordaire, Vie de S. Dominique (1888), p. 219.

Toulouse named Pierre Cella. Cella provided for their work a mansion near Chateau Narbonnais. There other like-minded and zealous souls gathered, and a little fraternity was organized. The bishop, Foulques of Toulouse, favorably impressed by them and agitated to the point of fanaticism by the Albigensian heresy, which he wanted to overcome, assigned for their maintenance one sixth of the tithes in his diocese. These men adopted preaching as their mission, believing that the proclamation of the Word alone would convert heretics and heathen alike. Consequently in addition to their maintenance Bishop Foulques undertook to provide them with books as well. Now that the sword of Simon de Montfort had laid waste the power of the Albigensians, Dominic and his companions undertook their conversion and instruction in the truths of Christian faith. Like all true evangelists the Dominicans employed only the techniques of love, sympathy, and service.

Foulques of Toulouse, recognizing the importance of these few Dominicans and their plans, carried Dominic with him to Rome to the Lateran Council to seek papal endorsement for his work. But the Lateran Council decreed that no new orders could be established. This meant of course that Dominic had to accept for his company the rules of an order already in existence. He therefore took the Rule of Augustine, which was the order he had entered in his youth in Spain and which had sent him north on his mission into Languedoc in southern France. It is said that Pope Innocent III, already disappointed by the failures of the followers of Durán de Huesca called the Poor Catholics, showed no disposition to receive Dominic at all. However some say as the result of a dream he did finally endorse the mission, and his successor, Honorius III, formally sanctioned it (December 21, 1216) as an organ of the whole church.

Dominic returned immediately to Toulouse. There he put into operation his gigantic missionary plan by carefully deploying his disciples at strategic points so that they might win, train, and send others to preach and teach as they themselves. The first brethren he assembled at Prouille were marvelously suited to a world-wide mission. Theirs was a cosmopolitan society from the start: Castile, Navarre, Normandy, France, Languedoc, Germany, and even England were represented among them. Yet their total number was only sixteen. They elected, in keeping with the provisions of Saint Augustine's Rule, one of their number as abbot, Matthieu le Gaulois. This was not as important a position as it might seem, since the order was really mobile and Dominic was its master. Later its format of organization was completely refashioned so that Matthieu le Gaulois has the distinction of having been the first, last, and only abbot of the order.

The little band dispersed for its work; some went to Paris, others to Spain, still others to Bologna, while Dominic himself went to Rome. The whole scheme looked stupid at first. How could sixteen men evangelize Western Europe by preaching? But, then, twelve men and the apostle Paul had essayed the conversion of the Roman empire twelve centuries earlier. Could not the renewal of the Gospel be as effective as its original or initial proclamation? In four years this new order had become organized in eight different countries and territories—Spain, Provence, France, England, Germany, Hungary, Lombardy, and the papal states. It boasted sixty converts all its own.

Dominic's plan of organization was remarkable. He divided the order into provinces, each with a provincial prior at its head. Its supreme head (under the pope of course and answerable to him) was the general master. These offices were obtained by election, and tenure was permanent on good behavior. Every friar owed absolute obedience to his superior. The group was entirely mobile, like an army; its members could be deployed wherever a need arose. In fact, these members looked on themselves as the soldiers of Christ. They lived like monks but not in a monastery. Their field of activity was the world of men. They studied and read, and many of them became great scholars—but always for a practical purpose. That purpose was to preach effective sermons and thereby win people to Jesus Christ.

They got their name seemingly by accident. Innocent III addressed a note to Dominic and his companions. Though the pope started to say, "To Brother Dominic and the preachers with him," he changed it to read, "To Master Dominic and the brethren preachers." This title commended itself to them, and they began at once to call themselves Friar Preachers.

Though Dominic died soon after the establishment of his order (1221), his machine was so perfectly built that it was to run on indefinitely. Soon the strongest intellects of the age were donning the habits of the Dominicans. By 1243, only twenty-two years after Dominic's demise, one of the order, the learned Hugh of Vienna, was made a cardinal; while in 1276, just a little over half a century after Dominic, Brother Peter of Tarentaise ascended the papal throne as Alexander V. The respect and veneration in which the order was held by the people was both great and universal. Yet Dominic's own canonization came slowly. Though Francis of Assisi was canonized within two years of his death (1228), Dominic lay in his grave thirteen years before the act of recognizing his sanctity was promulgated (July 3, 1234). The man died in Bologna in a borrowed bed and even a borrowed gown, but countless thousands in his own time and a host innumerable through subsequent ages received from him their rights to the kingdom of Heaven.

The Dominicans were the first order of the Middle Ages which had learning as its foundation. Every one of its established houses had a doctor at its head to teach the membership and prepare its sons to convince men of the truth of Christianity by the preaching of the Word.[9]

Quite a different reason for existence lay behind the foundation of the Franciscan order. "Grant me, O Jesus," prayed its founder, "that I may never possess under heaven anything of my own, and sustain the flesh sparely by the use of the things of others." [10]

The rule which Francis prepared for his disciples and which he refused to alter by changing a single word or phrase—even at the request of Pope Honorius III—on the grounds that he had received it from Christ himself— is, when one reads it, simple enough. It requires of each friar only that he live by the gospel and that he possess nothing at all. The person seeking admission to the order had to sell all that he had and give it to the poor before his case could even be considered. He was allowed a change of clothes, but the texture of these two gowns must be coarse and cheap—vile was Francis' word for it—and he defined its meaning concretely, for his own clothes were a home for vermin. The only mode of transportation for Franciscans was walking; no friar was allowed to receive any money except for the care of the sick and for clothing in certain rigorous climates. Hard work was to be rewarded only in the form of the necessaries of life like food and a place in which to sleep. The brethren went about from place to place begging alms.

Since the order at first disparaged preaching and decried learning, its methods of evangelism had to be more exemplary than hortatory. Francis and his followers went about from place to place doing work for the people where aid was needed. Their own radiant spirit and complete happiness in having nothing material to be happy about were parabolic that the kingdom of God is the only thing that is worth seeking. When it is had, all else is added that is needed, which is really nothing at all since that kingdom itself is everything. "The perfection of gladness," according to Francis, "consists not in working miracles, in curing the sick, expelling devils, or raising the dead; nor in learning and knowledge of all things; nor in eloquence to convert the world; but in bearing all ills and injuries and injustice and despiteful treatment with patience and humility." Absolute poverty is the sole means to that perfection which is synonymous with Christianity.

As the Dominicans had arisen to do something—namely to understand through study the Word of God and to evangelize and reform the people by effectively preaching it—the Franciscans arose not to do anything at all. Their

[9] F. Balme and P. Lelaidier, Cartulaire ou histoire diplomatique de St. Dominique (1891-1901), 3 vols. M. H. Laurent, Monumenta Historica S. P. N. Dominici in Monumenta Ordinis Fratrum Praedicatorum Historica, vol. XV (1933) and vol. XVI (1935). P. Mandonnet, St. Dominique (1937), 2 vols.

[10] Francis, Collat. Monast., 5.

end in existing was merely to be what they were, the disciples of poverty and the exemplars of the conviction that to gain life is voluntarily to lose it.

Francis' personal life was the personification of the ideals of his order. Born the son of an Italian father and French mother (1182) and reared in the abundance of a middle-class mercantile home, he renounced his inheritance, broke completely with his father, and went out on the highways of the world with nothing on his back but a borrowed cloak, singing, "I am the son of a king." Like Dominic at the time of the Lateran Council he too sought papal recognition for his work; but the mighty Innocent was repelled by the sight and scent of this filthy beggar. Only as he was warned in a dream did he come to bless Francis' mission. It is reported that he saw the Church of St. John Lateran about to collapse and its central pillars resting for their support solely upon a little beggar, and he knew instinctively that Francis was God's own man for a divinely appointed mission. He blessed the little poor man and sent him away with his companions to fulfill their mission.

Yet Francis struck with a more immediate and far-reaching impact than Dominic. Though he appears in retrospect like a fool—so exaggerated were his habits of poverty, so utterly fantastic his behavior—yet the contrast between him and his disciples and the rest of society about them was so great that their very difference was the power of their appeal. Commensurate with their demand was the response the people gave to it. If God was really God, then the only demand he could be expected to make would be everything, and that is precisely what the Franciscans announced.

They called themselves "the Little Brothers"—the Friars Minor. Like their founder they ate with lepers, attended their sores, and gave them love. By the time of Francis' death (1226) his followers were everywhere. The founder's own exaggerated lust for poverty made him strip himself naked just before he died, so that he might meet his Maker without anything. Yet he gave the world so much in kindness and love that within two years after his demise, his name had been enshrined forever on the calendar of the church's saints (1228).

Before his death Francis had organized his order for women on the same principles as the Friars Minor. Little sisters as well as little brothers had the right through poverty to receive in their fulness the riches of the kingdom of God. Francis had met and convinced a young woman named Clara of the wisdom and desirability of the life of poverty. Her flight from home against the wishes of her parents in the hours between Palm Sunday and Holy Monday, 1212, had precipitated his decision and caused his action. Francis cut off Clara's hair, robbed her of all feminine adornments, and laid on her the same heavy regimen of self-denial he had imposed on the men. When her sister

Agnes joined her, and other women as well, the Sisters as a separate order was launched.[11]

Both Francis and Dominic employed the plan of the Third Order, initiated as we saw in connection with monasticism in the preceding century. Thereby laymen who did not abandon their families and secular responsibilities could become associated with the two orders. Their ideals and spirit were more readily disseminated into the domestic areas of life. The Brothers and Sisters of Penitence (approved in 1221) was the Franciscan Third Order; while the Militia Jesu Christi, or Soldiery of Christ, was the Dominican counterpart. Thus laymen were brought to share some of the responsibilities and blessings of the clerics. Louis IX of France became a member of the first of these orders.

In addition to the Dominicans and Franciscans there were the **Carmelites**[12] **and the Friar Hermits of Saint Augustine.**[13] The former was an importation to the West of an eremitical society established in the Crusader Kingdom of Jerusalem in 1210. Its rule was that of Basil. However, when it was transplanted to the West, the strictly contemplative character was modified along Franciscan lines. Its brothers were allowed to preach and to beg. The latter was a union of many already existing groups of hermits. The interests of the Austin Friars were practical rather than theoretical. They made literary contributions to ethics and politics. Both orders were formalized during the pontificate of Innocent IV and so benefited from Dominican and Franciscan patterns. The four great orders, popularly characterized by their garb, were (1) the Black Friars (Dominicans), (2) the Grey Friars (Franciscans), (3) the White Friars (Carmelites), and (4) the Austin Friars.[14]

The mendicant orders were revolutionary. Indeed they introduced into monasticism an entirely new principle. The self-abnegation of the monk had come to be a means of self-salvation. He had left the world because he could not save himself within the world. The lust of the flesh and the pride of life had proved too much for him. But the mendicant was of different metal. He brought the spirit and discipline of monasticism into the market place. He entered the world positively and courageously to save it.

The mendicant orders—that is the Dominican and Franciscans—were the most salutary social movements of the thirteenth century, perhaps even of the entire Middle Ages.

---

[11] *Analekten zur Geschichte des Franciscus von Assisi* (ed. H. Boehmer, 1904). Paul Sabatier, *Francis of Assisi* (Eng. transl., 1894).

[12] *Ordinaire de l'ordre de Notre-Dame du Mont-Carmel par Sibert de Beka, vers. 1312* (ed. B. Zimmerman, Paris, 1910).

[13] *Bullarium Ordinis Eremitarum S. Augustini* (ed. Empoli, Rome, 1628).

[14] CMH, VI, 727-762.

III. The Crusades

Innocent III, as we have seen, had been frustrated in his plans for the Fourth Crusade. The Venetian merchants had outwitted him; and, though he had at first appeared elated over the prospects of church union which the capture of Constantinople might afford, still he had learned to his bitter disappointment that mercantile greed and military prowess are not conducive to spirituality, and that the mistreatment the Greeks had received from the Latins made them hate the Western church all the more. His gallant knights had become too busy with their new Byzantine fiefs to give any further thought to the Holy Land.

This proved fortunate for the Christian state in Palestine. It enjoyed a profitable truce with its Moslem neighbors, got a new and able king by marriage in John of Brienne, a man of sixty who took to wife the seventeen-year-old queen of Jerusalem and continued to rule after she died in childbirth, having given him a daughter. All might have gone well with the little principality except for the West's now unbreakable habit of launching crusades.

Innocent himself was a determined man. He could not bear frustration. Consequently what he had failed to accomplish in 1204, he was bound to undertake again at a more propitious time. Unfortunately that time never came for him. The movement was ordered and planned by the Fourth Lateran Council; but Innocent had died as he went north to settle a dispute between Genoa and Pisa, so that they might co-operate in supplying ships to transport his crusaders abroad.

Yet Innocent's continuous agitation of a crusade during his pontificate had produced the abortive efforts of the **Children's Crusades,** several idealistic adventures of youth all of which had ended in disaster. One day in May, 1212, King Philip Augustus of France had been approached by a shepherd boy, Stephen, no more than twelve years old, who had brought him a letter alleged to be from Christ ordering a crusade. The boy had been dismissed by the king, but his contemporaries who heard him believed his assurance that they would succeed where their elders had failed, followed him in the number of twenty thousand, and ended as slaves in Saracenic cities or in watery graves of the Mediterranean Sea. The Marseilles merchants who had offered them free transportation to the Holy Land had sold them to the infidels of Egypt at a lucrative price. Another crusade of German youth had marched to Rome, where Innocent had received them, thanked them for their zeal, and ordered them home again.

The **Fifth Crusade,** which Innocent had planned but which was actually launched by his successor, the aged Honorius III, divided really into two separate expeditions. King Andrew of Hungary and Duke Leopold of Austria, aided by King Hugh of Cyprus, achieved nothing. Their armies wandered aimlessly through Galilee (1217); King Hugh, though young, died suddenly; King Andrew returned home after he had added to his relic collection one of the water jugs Jesus had used in performing his first miracle at Cana of Galilee and also the head of Stephen, the first Christian martyr. The second expedition, headed by the papal legate Pelagius and King John of Jerusalem, directed its energies against Egypt, took the city of Damietta, and might have captured Cairo itself had the soldiers had more confidence in their leaders and had Pelagius and King John been able to agree. Francis of Assisi was a peaceful observer of this expedition and tried to win the sultan of Egypt to the gospel and thereby insure a Christian peace. The sultan thought he was mad, yet delightfully so, and was charmed by his manner and his speech. He was not interested however in embracing his faith. When the crusade left Egypt, the sultan offered to give the Christians the true cross. Unfortunately, it got misplaced and could nowhere be found.

All throughout the Fifth Crusade the fighting forces of Christians in Egypt had been promised the aid of the German armies under the leadership of their young emperor, Frederick II. After all, he had been the ward of the late pope, Innocent III, who had secured him on the throne of Sicily and had championed his cause in the empire. The reigning pontiff, Honorius III, had been his teacher. But Frederick had never come, and one of the principal causes of the failure of the Fifth Crusade had been its leaders' expectation of aid they never got. Had they forged ahead on their own strength immediately after the fall of Damietta, when the enemy was disorganized and famine wasted the Nile Valley, their story might have been different, but they had delayed expecting the superior imperial army. Frederick alone could have given the unity their command lacked and inspired the confidence of all the soldiers. There was nothing he could have possibly gained for himself out of the Fifth Crusade. Later however circumstances were altered so that his own interests constrained him to take the cross. The **Sixth Crusade was Frederick's.**

King John of Jerusalem, who was actually only regent for his daughter since he had gained the crown by marriage, decided to return for a visit to Europe (1222) in order to find a suitable husband for his eleven-year-old daughter, Isabella, popularly known as Yolanda. John was now better than seventy, and he knew that younger and stronger arms were needed in the East. When he got to Rome, he found Frederick a widower in mourning. His wife had died four months before. John was overjoyed when Frederick consented to become Yolanda's husband. His little daughter was to be married to the mightiest prince in Christendom. John went on to France to visit his old patron and friend—the man who had secured for him his throne—King Philip Augustus. Of course Philip was not pleased over the German marriage as he felt that John should have turned to his native France for a son-in-law.

All the same he was glad to see his old friend again and remembered him and his Jerusalemite kingdom handsomely in his will.

The wedding of Frederick, Holy Roman emperor, and Isabella (Yolanda), child queen of the Kingdom of Jerusalem, took place in the Cathedral of Brindisi, November 9, 1225: Frederick was thirty-one; Yolanda was only fourteen. Misfortune befell her immediately. On the day after the wedding Frederick unceremoniously left Brindisi with his bride; and when her father pursued and overtook them, his weeping daughter reported that her husband of one day had spent their first night seducing one of her cousins. John was outraged. Frederick responded by relieving him of his regency and taking from him the legacy Philip Augustus of France had left him. John fled to Rome to report the outrage to the pope, but Honorius III found it difficult to believe his former pupil guilty of such conduct. Yolanda was placed in the imperial harem at Palermo, Sicily, where after giving birth to a son she died three years later at the age of seventeen. Her father's services were solicited and received by the Latins of Constantinople who needed him as regent for their little emperor, Baldwin II. He had married the sister of King Ferdinand III of Castile, and they had a little four-year-old daughter, whom he betrothed to the child-emperor Baldwin II. In fact, John himself took and held the title of emperor until he died (1237).

Frederick's crusade reflected the nature of his character. There was nothing altruistic about it. He went simply because policy demanded it, not for piety at all. He sailed, not with the benediction of the church, as all his predecessors had in the long march East, but with its malediction instead. Honorius III, who died in March, 1227, was succeeded by a Roman pharaoh who knew not this German Joseph—or perhaps he knew him too well. Gregory IX was incapable of being tricked and deceived by Frederick as Honorius had been. The emperor had sailed on September 8, 1227; but a terrible malady had seized the party; Louis of Thuringia had died; and Frederick had returned to the spa of Pozzuoli to recuperate. Gregory had not believed his alibi and had excommunicated him. Thus when he did embark on June 28, 1228, his status was unique: he went to champion the Christian cause in the East without being considered a Christian himself.

His crusade was one of diplomacy not of battle. Since he had grown up in Sicily he knew the Arabs well; consequently he was quite adept in managing them. He managed to negotiate a treaty which restored Jerusalem itself to the Christians. But it was like a castle surrounded by a Moslem moat with one little narrow strip of land connecting it to the Christian territories along the sea coast. Its position militarily was indefensible. Frederick had no legitimate claims to the kingship of the Christian state; he was merely the father of Yolanda's son and heir Conrad. Yet he accepted the crown of Jerusalem from the altar of Calvary in the Church of the Holy Sepulcher (Sunday, March 18, 1229). Since he was excommunicated from the church, there was no bishop or priest to officiate at the ceremony. He crowned himself, the event being witnessed by his own soldiers. His actions shocked and divided the Christian principalities in the Holy Land. The result of his crusade, which ended with his return to Europe (1229), was a terrible period of anarchy. One petty ruling family was set against another, and the nobility were constantly at war among themselves and with the imperial agents. Frederick's departure from Acre, where, as he walked down the street of the Butchers, the people spat on him and pelted him with entrails and dung, is illustrative of the legacy of his crusade—for Christians now fought Christians, and Jerusalem, the Holy City, lay under the curse of a papal interdict.

Yet Gregory IX, restless and energetic like his cousin, the late Pope Innocent III, did not help matters when he initiated another crusade of his own. Though he could not persuade any of the great kings to take the cross, he nonetheless rallied the lesser lords, comparable in rank to the leaders of the First Crusade. The First Crusade after all had been the most successful of all the expeditions to the East. If it could just be repeated, then the pope's highest hopes would be fulfilled. His response came from France. At the head of the expedition was Tibald of Champagne, the king of Navarre; and with him went the duke of Burgundy and the counts of Brittany, Bar, Nevers, Montfort, Joigny, and Sancerre, and many lesser lords. All they did however was disturb the peace which Frederick had arranged; though they regained Beaufort, Safed, and Ascalon, their perfidy convinced the Moslems that treaties with them were futile and that Christian rule of any type in the East was a menace. Their crusade, begun in 1239 and terminated in 1240, was followed by another of Richard of Cornwall, who arrived at Acre in 1241 and set up a satisfactory rule in the name of the emperor. This unfortunately did not survive his departure and within three years Jerusalem was lost to the terrible Khwarismian horsemen, who massacred its priests, exhumed the bodies of its kings, and burned the Church of the Holy Sepulcher to a hollow shell (1244). Three years later (1247) Ascalon was lost to the Egyptian army, and the Christian state was reduced to what it had been at the end of the Third Crusade.

The last great effort on the part of the West to aid the Latin states in the Holy Land to break the Saracenic power that threatened them was the Crusade of Louis IX, king of France. It was modeled after the Fifth Crusade, and its military course followed almost exactly the course of that earlier expedition. Louis felt that it was useless merely to strike at the outposts of Saracenic power, to take a city here and there, even if it be Jerusalem itself, and at the same time to leave the enemy with the power to strike again. He selected as his objective Cairo, which was the capital of the Ayubite sultanate. On August 12, 1248, he left Paris to go to the battlefields of the East. Not until May 13, 1249, did his battle fleet of 120 large vessels, together with innumerable smaller ones, collect at Cyprus for the expedition. On June 4 King Louis and squadron arrived off the coast of Damietta, Egypt. The sultan, expecting the war to originate in Palestine, had been away in Syria consolidating his possessions and dealing with enemies. He hastened home, a man sick with tuberculosis, and put his aged vizier, Fakhr-ad-Din, in command of Damietta. The king's landing on June 5 was an easy victory; Damietta was evacuated and possessed by the Franks; and by December the crusading army was on the march south to Cairo.

Everything seemed to favor the success of King Louis. The sultan died; his widow tried to keep the news from the people until his son could arrive from Diabekir to succeed him, so she forged a document in his name appointing herself as regent during his illness and Fakhr-ad-Din as commander in chief of the army. The Saracenic forces were encamped outside Mansourah to intercept the Frankish march. They were separated from the Christians by a huge canal. They did not expect battle until the Frankish army could be transported over. However the rash younger brother of Louis, Robert of Artois, feeling that the greatest advantage lay in surprise, fell upon the infidels as soon as his contingents had crossed over. The Templars followed him. The enemy was unprepared for battle, their aged leader was slain, and the crusaders swept into Mansourah itself. Robert of Artois overplayed his hand. Had he awaited Louis after his victory all might have gone well. But the Moslems rallied; in the narrow streets of the town the crusaders could not maneuver; they were routed; only five out of two hundred and ninety of their knights survived; Robert of Artois was killed (1250). This greatly depleted Louis' strength.

There was little Louis could do. For eight weeks he maintained his camp outside Mansourah, hoping vainly that a revolution at court might dissipate the Moslem strength. The hoped-for revolution came, but it was too late for Louis. Disease and famine wasted his troops. He tried to negotiate an exchange of Damietta for Jerusalem, but the Moslems saw time was on their side. They knew sickness and exhaustion would win the battle for them. Nothing was left for Louis to do but to retreat to Damietta.

On his march back disaster befell him. He became seriously ill. While Philip of Monfort in Louis' name was trying to negotiate a truce with the enemy, a traitor, named Marcel, with only the rank of a sergeant, went through the camp giving the false news that Louis had accepted unconditional surrender. Thus the whole majestic army was taken. Louis was thrown in prison with almost an impossible ransom put on his head. The greater nobility were kept alive by the Moslems for the same use. But the infidels, being embarrassed by the enormous size of the crusading army and finding it too demanding of time and energy to guard so many, killed all the sick, infirm, and useless on the spot, and every evening for a week decapitated three hundred soldiers at a time. That was as many as they could conveniently behead in one evening.

Louis was ransomed by his queen and the Templars. Queen Margaret, in childbirth at the time, conducted herself heroically at Damietta. The luckless king and queen quit Egypt for Acre, where they remained another four years trying to reorganize and strengthen the Christian kingdom and to facilitate the release of the remaining Frankish prisoners in Egypt.

Louis returned to France, not because he wanted to, but because the needs of his kingdom were such that he had to. He had been away six years. Yet his heart remained in the East. Sixteen years later, he set out on a second crusade. His ambitious brother Charles of Anjou diverted him by persuading him to capture Tunis in North Africa on his way. There he died (August, 1270) with these last words upon his lips, "Jerusalem, Jerusalem."

Louis was in motive and life the noblest crusader of them all. He had all the daring and bravery of Richard the Lion-Hearted with a Christian character that Richard never possessed. But Louis' crusade was a failure too.

Two causes allied themselves to enervate all subsequent military efforts on behalf of the Latin states of the East. One was theological: If God had failed Louis of France, whom among the princes of the West could he be expected to help? Other crusaders might justly have failed because of their unworthy motives and their sins. Louis had been a saint. Perhaps God did not want the Christian control of the Holy Land, after all. If He did not, no effort, no matter how pure and powerful, could withstand or change the sway of his omnipotence. The other cause was political: The Mongols, who had given temporary relief from further Moslem conquest by conquering Syria, had been defeated by the Arab Mameluk of Egypt (1260), and a new era in Arab history had begun. Sultan Baibars, who seized the throne by murdering his master, was one of the most successful Moslem conquerors in all history. During his seventeen-year reign (1260-1277) the Latin kingdom was reduced to six coastal cities: Acre, Tyre, Sidon, Tripoli, Jebail, and Tortosa. The bastard sons of King James I of Aragon had proved so weak in their expedition that the cities of Acre had felt constrained to help them rather than to receive their help. Prince Edward of England had been stabbed with a poisoned dagger and had had to return home unsuccessful. Pope Gregory IX at a council in Lyons had gotten only the promise of crusading help, not its fulfillment. It was only then a matter of a short time until Baibars' work, even in less able hands, would be posthumously carried to successful fulfillment. The end of the Latin kingdom of Jerusalem came with the fall of Acre on May 18,

1291. Even the town itself was systematically destroyed. The Templars maintained one island fortress off the coast near Tortosa, but all the territory on the mainland, together with the cities, was by August 14 entirely in Moslem hands. Latin Christianity was destroyed by the flight or execution of the Latin people. The native Christians—Greek, Coptic, Jacobite, and Nestorian —were treated little better than slaves.[15]

The Crusades, begun so gloriously in 1095, ended two centuries later, in 1291, as if they had never been at all, for the Holy Land, without any concessions to the West, now belonged entirely to Islam. In Syria and Palestine the Cross had been decisively defeated by the Crescent.

IV. The Rival Empires in the East

The Fourth Crusade was the finish of the Byzantine empire. Likewise it was a crushing blow to the Greek Church. After it, what had been the most powerful and civilized political organization of the Middle Ages survived only in the form of a small nationalistic principality—a mere shadow of its former glory; while the Constantinopolitan patriarchate, the occupants of which had, since the beginning of the Middle Ages, styled themselves "ecumenical patriarchs," was superseded in power, if not in honor, by the patriarchate of Moscow, which became the third Rome.

Isaac Angelus had been deposed (1195) by his brother Alexius III, who had blinded him and thrown him into prison. But his son, the Prince Alexius, nephew to the usurper, had visited the crowned heads of Europe (1201-1202) and persuaded the leaders of the crusade to restore him to his throne. When Constantinople had opened its gates to them, the crusaders had found that the usurper Alexius III had fled and that the old emperor Isaac was seated again on his throne (1203). The Greeks had retrieved him to obviate a major war and to save their city from sack and ruin. But Isaac's son, Alexius IV, had been unable to live up to his bargain with the crusaders. He had succeeded neither in effecting a union with Latin Catholicism nor in paying the indemnity the crusaders had levied on him for their aid. His heavy taxes and sycophantic behavior toward the Latins had inflamed his own people, and they had deposed him in favor of one of the sons-in-law of Alexius III, Alexius V, called Mourtzouphlos. Alexius IV had been thrown into a dungeon and strangled; his father, Isaac, too blind to rule, had wiled away time with astrologers who prophesied doom; and when he had learned of his son's tragic end had out of grief promptly followed him to the grave. The crusaders had used these events as the occasion to declare war on the Greeks and to take Constantinople for themselves (1204).[16]

---

[15] MPL, CCXV, 699-702. S. Runciman, A History of the Crusades, III, 132-423, 493-503.
[16] CMH, IV, 415-420.

The sack of the city which followed was one of the worst atrocities in history. Constantinople had stood as Christendom's greatest city for nine hundred years. But in the space of a few days the ignorant and crude Franks looted its palaces and art galleries, destroyed its monuments, raped its women, and slaughtered its men and children. The Christian emperors were dug up from their tombs in the Church of the Holy Apostles in order that soldiers might strip them of their ornaments, and drunken troops pulled down the silken draperies of St. Sophia, while a harlot sang indecent love ditties from the patriarchal throne. The high altar was desecrated. At the end of three days the great and glorious capital of civilization was in shambles.[17]

The sack of Constantinople was the prelude to the establishment of the **Latin empire in the East.** The crusading nobles had decided in advance on a tripartite division of their conquests: (1) one fourth of the Byzantine empire was to go to a Latin emperor whom the crusaders would choose; the remaining three fourths would be divided equally between (2) the Venetians and (3) the crusading knights as fiefs.[18] A panel of six Franks and six Venetians would elect the emperor and patriarch. Though the leader of the Fourth Crusade had been Boniface of Montferrat, who was the ablest of the lot, Baldwin, Count of Flanders, was chosen emperor; and, as a consolation prize, Boniface was given the kingdom of Macedonia with his capital at Thessalonica. They professed that all that they had done was for the "honor of God, the Pope, and the Empire."

On May 16, 1204, Baldwin was crowned emperor in St. Sophia by Thomas Morosini, the newly elected Venetian patriarch. On October 1 the emperor held his court and gave fiefs to approximately six hundred knights who became his vassals. Yet Baldwin was deprived of the effective autocracy of the Greek emperors he had displaced. He had to rule under a constitution which made him little more than the presiding officer of a group of peers. His principality was less an empire than an importation from the West into the East of a confederation of fiefs. The new state was more baronial than imperial. Even the army was directed by the governing group called tenants-in-chief, which could countermand any of the emperor's orders.[19]

Such a state was short-lived. Its entire history was scarcely more than half a century. It produced one really capable and effective ruler, Henry of Flanders (1206-1216), but his decade on the throne was not time enough to do anything lasting. In 1222 the Latin kingdom of Thessalonica succumbed to the Greeks of Epirus, who in turn were consolidated with those of Nicaea in 1246. The Latin territory in Anatolia had already shrunk out of existence

[17] Nicetas Acominatus, *Historia*, CSHB, 757-763. Villehardouin, *La Conquête de Constantinople* (éd. Faral, Paris, 1938-39), II-52-58.
[18] Villehardouin, *op. cit.*, II, 34-36.
[19] *Ibid.*, 66-68.

(1224), and the Greek islands one by one had been put under the domination of Nicaea. Only the Venetian fleet kept Constantinople in Western hands. Once while it had temporarily sailed away from the Golden Horn to attack a neighboring town the Greek general, Alexius Strategopulus, took the city (July 25, 1261) with practically no resistance. His emperor entered it (August 15) and was crowned again in St. Sophia. Baldwin II, accompanied by his Latin patriarch, had already fled.[20]

No ecclesiastical history, save the substitution of Latin for Greek clergymen and thereby the titular acknowledgment of the supremacy of Rome, was written by the events of this little empire. Its single accomplishment was the wreckage of Byzantium both as an empire and even as a long continuing civilization. The Greeks, though strong enough to recover from and later to overcome their Latin invaders, did not possess the power to stand against more numerous and more powerful adversaries. All the Latins did was prepare the way for and weaken the Greeks' resistance to the Turkish infidels. Likewise they removed Western Europe's only effective barrier against them. The Latin conquest of the Eastern empire was one of the most stupid blunders in all history.

After the fall of Constantinople (1204), the Byzantine empire survived under three separate, competitive, and at times warring states, each of which called itself an empire. In Europe a bastard son of the Angeli set up a government at **Epirus** which became strong enough, as we have seen, to extinguish the Latin kingdom of Macedonia. In eastern Anatolia, two grandsons of the last Comnenus emperor, Andronicus, set up a government at **Trebizond** on the Black Sea. At **Nicaea** there arose the third government under Theodore Lascaris, the second son-in-law of Alexius III. When Mourtzouphlos, his brother-in-law, had fled from Constantinople, he had been elected emperor in his stead but had flatly refused the dubious honor though he had tried to rally the despondent Greeks to fight by taking command of their army. He waited until he had proved his worth as a leader before being crowned at Nicaea (1206). This walled city, the home of the first ecumenical council of the church, the former capital of the Seljuk empire, and the first city won from the infidels by the crusaders of the eleventh century, was an ideal place to reorganize the government. It had the advantages of the sea without the disadvantages of being directly on it. Its lake of Askania was useful as well as beautiful, and the fertile plains of Bithynia supplied it with corn and wine in abundance. In the words of a contemporary, it "lacked neither safety nor grace." [21] Like a magnet, it drew support and sympathy from Greeks everywhere. As we have seen, it overcame and absorbed its western competitor at

---

[20] CMH, IV, 421-431.
[21] Theodorus Metochites, *Nikaeus*, in K. N. Sathas, *Mesaionike Bibliothece, Bibliotheca graeca medii aevi* (Venice and Paris, 1872-1894), I, 140.

Epirus; and though the eastern state of Trebizond survived it by eight years, still that survival was by sufferance—not by independent strength—for the emperors at Trebizond became the vassals first of the Seljuk sultans (1240) and then of the Mongols (1253), awaiting final conquest and annihilation as a state by the Ottoman Turks (1461).[22] The only real successor to Constantinople was Nicaea, which destroyed its Latin rival and reoccupied Constantinople in 1261.

The first years of the Nicene empire were unpropitious. Greeks fought against Greeks, and all might have gone up in the clouds of battle had not the Bulgars in Europe relieved Latin pressure on the Greeks in Asia Minor by making war on the Franks of Constantinople. Lascaris' own father-in-law, Alexius III, returned and besought aid of the Seljuk sultan to regain his throne. When the sultan was defeated and killed, Alexius was captured, blinded by Lascaris, and died in prison.[23] In the end he got the same treatment he had given his brother, Isaac II, who before that had so horribly mutilated and killed his predecessor, Andronicus, the last of the Comneni.[24] It seems there was a chain reaction of violence in connection with the occupancy of the imperial throne. Lascaris (1206-1222) was an astute ruler. He encouraged the arts and was a patron of culture. Philosophy once again raised its head in pride with Demetrius Karykes in Smyrna, who lectured expertly on logic, while poetry and rhetoric flourished. Yet this emperor had enough common sense not to encourage theology, which, with the Greek speculative mind, was all too often divisive and factional.[25]

His successor John Vatatzes (1222-1254) made an alliance with the Bulgarian Tsar, John Asen II, and the price he paid was the recognition of the independence of the church of Trnovo and its separation from the jurisdiction of his own ecumenical patriarch, who now resided at Nicaea. Pope Gregory IX, who coveted the Bulgarians for his Roman fold, denounced Vatatzes as "the enemy of God and the Church." [26] Vatatzes likewise contended unsuccessfully with a schism in the Greek church between Epirus and Nicaea. This was healed only with the consolidation of the two states, illustrating the extreme national character of Greek Christianity and the church's dependence upon whatever secular government happened to be in power. Epirus continued to be independent of its patriarch even after political union. Since the Serbian and Bulgarian churches were autocephalous, the extent of the jurisdiction of the ecumenical patriarch was restricted indeed. Vatatzes lavished upon monasteries and churches wealth and architectural magnificence and con-

[22] CMH, IV, 514-516.
[23] CMH, IV, 484.
[24] CMH, IV, 384.
[25] CMH, IV, 486.
[26] Les Régistres de Grégoire IX (éd. Auvray, Paris, 1896-1910), II, 217.

240

ducted himself in "the presence of an archbishop almost as if he were in the presence of God himself." He favored learning so that a school of historians arose during his reign, and in a scholarly competition between Greeks and Latins the Greeks won. A century later Vatatzes was canonized by the Greek church. One finds in the literary legacy of his son, whose ineffectual reign lasted only four years, a strange assortment of intellectual interests, ranging from mathematics to philosophy. His learning unfortunately did not bestow upon him wisdom so that Theodore II (1254-1258) does not count for much in Greek history.[27]

However, his successor Michael Palaeologus (1261-1282) does. He was one of Theodore's generals and came to his post because of the dissatisfaction of the public with George Muzalon, the regent under Theodore's eight-year-old son. Theodore, only thirty-six at the time, had died in the garb of a monk imploring forgiveness for his sins and those of his sycophantic patriarch, the Bishop of Mitylene.[28] Muzalon was hewed to pieces, together with his brothers, in church at the hour of worship; and though Michael Palaeologus professed devotion to the boy John IV (1258-1261), he later had him imprisoned and blinded, which by now was the customary treatment for rivals. Yet outwardly, even in the heat of a controversy with his patriarch, Arsenius, Michael favored the church, followed with many genuflections the icon of the Pathfinding Virgin into the recaptured city of Constantinople, and earned undying fame from the ecclesiastical as well as the political East by restoring the capital to its rightful owners.[29] The empire over which he presided was greatly diminished in size, wealth, and influence from that over which his predecessors had ruled before the Latin conquest. In Asia it held most of western Anatolia, since the Turks had got only the Pisidian coast in the south including the seaport Attalia, and the coast of Paphlagonia in the north including Sinope on the Black Sea. In Europe it held only Thrace and the southern part of Macedonia including the great city of Thessalonica and the islands of Rhodes, Lesbos, Samothrace, and Imbros. Michael's strength was that of bargaining and intrigue. He was not a soldier, and he weakened the empire by employing foreign mercenaries, even in positions of command, for his armies rather than native troops.

His son Andronicus II (1282-1328), the first part of whose long reign fell within the thirteenth century and therefore within our purview, seems to have spent most of his time making and unmaking patriarchs, no less than nine having occupied the Constantinopolitan see while he was emperor. Theological and doctrinal disputation was his vocation when it should have been

[27] *Byzantinische Zeitschrift* (Leipzig, 1892 ff.) XIV, 217-232.
[28] CMH, IV, 501-506.
[29] CMH, IV, 507-513.

governing men, and Byzantium might have been better off had he spent his days in a monastery.

The chief ecclesiastical activity of the Greek emperors during the thirteenth century was a series of efforts at the reunion of Greek and Latin Catholicism. The motive on the part of the Greeks from start to finish was almost entirely political. Consequently such imperial efforts won little support among people and clergy.

Alexius IV, for example, had promised both union and a crusade in order to get back his throne. He had been unable to deliver either. The Latin empire had not accomplished union but only the substitution of Western clergymen in Eastern churches. The Greek ecclesiastical leaders among the moderates had wisely informed Innocent III (1213) that they would consider conciliation between the two churches but only at an ecumenical council and that no violence would be employed in securing unity. Yet Innocent's legate in Constantinople, the Cardinal Pelagius, whom we have seen already in the Fifth Crusade, had not facilitated the success of free discussion between Greeks and Latins. To be sure he had held a conference and received with honor the delegate of the Nicene empire, Nicholas Mesarites, metropolitan of Ephesus. But he had been so haughty, demanding, and overbearing that the discussions had terminated in one week with no results. Consequently the declaration of the Lateran Council that the Greeks had come once more under jurisdiction of the Holy See was hardly accurate. Such union, only within the subjugated Latin empire, had been that of coercion; and the Greek clergy who had remained in their churches continued to rebaptize infants whom the Latin clergy had baptized and to purify their altars after Latin usage.

The first positive effort toward reunion was exerted by the Greeks. Theodore Lascaris (1219), through a letter from his patriarch to the metropolitan of Naupactus, suggested calling, as his forebears had done, an ecumenical council at Nicaea to end the schism. Unfortunately he could not get his clergy to support him. In 1232 Manuel, the Greek despot of Epirus, who had taken Thessalonica as well, fearing his Nicene rival, had actually made submission to Pope Gregory IX. John Vatatzes, as the price for the reoccupation of Constantinople and the restoration by the Latins to the Greeks of all their churches, offered to recognize the primacy of the pope, to have the Greek clergy take an oath of obedience to him, to put his name again on the diptychs, and to allow him to call councils. At this juncture both John Vatatzes and Pope Innocent IV died (1254). Since papal policy was more uniform and stable than imperial, Pope Alexander IV, honoring the work of his predecessor, sent a legate to Thessalonica to arrange with Theodore II for Greek clerics to come to Rome for a council (1256), but Theodore was not prepared to continue negotiations.

The nearest union ever got to real success was during the long reign of Michael Palaeologus. Not that Michael any more than any of his predecessors desired it for its own sake, but circumstances were such that union favored imperial policy then more than ever before. It was Michael's only means of staying the expanding power of the new king of Sicily, Charles of Anjou, against his empire and of preventing another Latin crusade against the Greeks. After several abortive attempts between Michael and his papal predecessors, Pope Gregory X saw the union formally ratified at the Council of Lyons on July 6, 1274. The Greek clergy agreed to the primacy of the pope, the restoration of his name to the diptychs, and the right of appeal to Rome. When the expatriarch, Germanus, announced this at Lyons, the pope broke forth with the Te Deum. Bulgaria and Serbia likewise joined in the action of the Byzantines.

The union did not last long. Michael, emperor though he was, could not force many of the Greek clergy to swear fealty to Rome. When Nicholas III demanded the insertion of the filioque in the Greek creed and also the right to regulate Greek customs, harmony immediately lapsed back into disharmony and schism.

Immediately on Michael's death his son Andronicus II repudiated the union, deposed John Beccus in order to reinstate Joseph as patriarch—his father's strongest enemy on this issue—and turned to the monks who had rather lose the empire than modify the faith.[30]

The thirteenth century, when the Greek empire and church were so weak, gave Greek Catholicism in other nations the opportunity to develop along national lines. Especially was this true of the church in Bulgaria and Serbia. The Russian church, which later was to be the largest and greatest exponent of Greek Christianity, suffered with the Russian people under the warring migrations of the Mongols, or Tartars. Kiev was still the chief see until 1281; after that Vladimir held ecclesiastical pre-eminence until after the turn of the fourteenth century.

The papacy tried to wean Antioch away from Nicaea and later from Constantinople by offering its Greek patriarch all his liturgical forms and ecclesiastical privileges if he would only recognize Roman primacy. The Patriarch David was invited to send an embassy to Rome at papal expense, but this was no more profitable in the end than the negotiations with Constantinople.[31]

The Greek spirit was undaunted by the dismemberment of the empire. Literary and cultural achievements were wrought in Epirus and Nicaea, while the Greek subjects of the Latin empire continued to think and write as Greeks. The chief literary personages were ecclesiastics, witnessing in this

[30] CMH, IV, 607-614.
[31] Regesta Honorii Papae III, 5567-5570.

century of the dispossession of Constantinople to the fact that Byzantine culture was still Christian.

The metropolitan of Naupactus, John Apocaucus, through his letters, epigrams, and canonical writings, and the metropolitan of Corcyra, George Bardanes, through his Ecclesiastical Annals, left to posterity in elegant style the record of the Despotat of Epirus. Demetrius Chomatianus, the Bulgarian archbishop, did the same for the short-lived principality of Thessalonica. The Greeks in the Latin empire produced the romance Belthandros and Chrysantza, the Byzantine counterpart of the songs of the troubadours and national epics of the West in the thirteenth century.

Nicaea superseded Constantinople as the chief center of literary activity during the period of the rival empires. John Mesarites wrote an able commentary on the Psalms as well as theological tracts setting forth the Eastern point of view in the ecclesiastical negotiations with the West, while his brother Nicholas wrote a description of the Church of the Holy Apostles in Constantinople which has given us what knowledge we have of one of the noble edifices of Christendom. The Emperor Theodore Lascaris wrote numerous letters, some panegyrics, and a few treatises on ecclesiastical, theological, and philosophical themes, all of which display a remarkable knowledge of mathematics and the natural sciences. This ruler in culture and breadth of learning was the Byzantine counterpart of the Western ruler Frederick II. Georgius Acropolita wrote the history of the empire of Nicaea from the fall of Constantinople (1204) to its restoration (1261). Nicetas Acominatus, the historian of the Comneni era, after he had abandoned Constantinople for Nicaea, gave up history for theology and wrote A Treasury of Orthodoxy. The greatest writer of this period was Nicephorus Blemmydes. He produced two autobiographical works, giving interesting details of the times; a political treatise entitled The Imperial Statute, counsel after the style of Plato's Republic for the government of the empire; two textbooks on geography, and two philosophical treatises entitled Logic and Physics. Blemmydes was a monk though he departed frequently from monastic retirement to live at court and to travel on imperial missions abroad. Theologically he was a strong defender of orthodox doctrine.[32]

V. The Papal Empire in the West

The vicissitudes of the Latin Church were almost a complete contrast to those of the Greek. The century of a divided and imperiled Christendom in the East was the century of the Western church's greatest vigor and power.

Innocent III, still in his prime, died, quite unexpectedly, while on a trip away from home. Since he had been a very young man at the time of his

---

[32] Vasiliev, op. cit., II, 548-563.

election, the pendulum swung back away from youth to age. His two immediate successors were elderly men.

The first one, **Honorius III** (1216-1227), though he had a reputation for urbanity of character and a broad and shrewd knowledge of the world and men, did not live up to his reputation as pope. He was too kindly disposed and easygoing to do much. Fortunately, though he did not push the gains of his illustrious predecessor, neither did he lose them. His pontificate may be said to have marked a dignified standstill. The reason for this is not hard to discern. The chief obstacle to papal policy in West and East was the Emperor Frederick II. Until decisive action was taken in regard to him, the church could do very little. Honorius III, who had been his teacher, was incapable of believing anything bad about him, so for eleven years Frederick was able to pull the wool over the eyes of his ecclesiastical rival by masquerading as his most faithful son and ally. All the time he was harassing the pope's subjects in Italy, oppressing the Sicilians over whom he ruled and who were Rome's vassals as well, and terrorizing the region around Naples by means of a colony of Moslems he had planted near the city. All the same Honorius crowned him Holy Roman Emperor (September 22, 1220).[33]

Gregory IX (1227-1241), an octogenarian when elected pope, was nonetheless one of the most energetic and active pontiffs in history. He chose the title "Gregory" to denote his mission, for he looked on Frederick II as another Henry IV and consequently on himself as a Hildebrand. He was determined, no matter what it cost him, to carry out the policies of Innocent III.

Frederick at this time was a man in his early thirties. He was not so tall and handsome as his grandfather Frederick Barbarossa had been. But, in his own way, he was equally commanding. He was of medium height yet unusually well built and muscular. He was ruddy like all the Hohenstaufens. His hair was beginning to recede; his features were smooth and regular, though he had a big mouth with red, thick, sensual lips. He tended to smile, so that his expression looked kindly enough until one noticed his eyes. They were cold and lifeless, and their green color cast a spell of terror on the observer, for the eyes symbolized the calculating selfishness and complete indifference of the emperor. The man was obviously brilliant. He used six languages fluently: German, French, Italian, and Arabic as well as the classical Greek and Latin. He had studied diligently philosophy and the sciences. His knowledge of natural history, medicine, and geography was amazing. He was astute in his understanding of theology. He prided himself on his open-mindedness, his ability to see good in and to utilize the tenets of other religions. No other Westerner knew the Saracenic mind and character better than he. He was not perturbed by the Eastern-Western schism. In fact it bothered him not at

[33] LP, II, 453. Hefele, *op. cit.* (Leclercq), V, 1409-1466. Watterich, *Pontificum romanorum vitae,* I, 71-84.

all that the Greeks did not recognize papal primacy. In his heart he did not either. He was too brilliant and outspoken in his ideas to be appreciated by the West. He was by birth half German, half Norman, but his environment had been Sicilian. The people he knew best were Greeks and Arabs. They made up the population of that island. Despite Frederick's amazing talents, he was not likeable—in fact, almost detestable. He was unreliable as a friend, while as an enemy he was ruthless and unforgiving.[34] Frederick was a dangerous man. Pope Gregory IX knew this.

Their break was immediate. Using as a pretext Frederick's delay in going on the Crusade, Gregory excommunicated him (1227). The real reason was Gregory's knowledge of his general unfitness as a Christian. The emperor's morals were so loose that he shocked even the peoples of the East, notorious themselves for loose morals. Indeed, he engaged in abnormal erotic pleasures which were attractive to him chiefly because they were unusual. He seems to have been ever restless to do something new and different. He liked to think of himself as the first in everything. In retaliation against the action of the pope, Frederick forced Gregory to quit Rome for Perugia (1228). Though the emperor was himself in the Holy Land, he persuaded several noble families of Rome, including the family of the Frangipani, to espouse his cause. Fortunately John of Brienne was in Italy at the time and led the papal armies to victory against the rebels. The Treaty of San Germano (1230) gave the church six years of peace, but in 1236 Frederick began once again to harass and to embarrass Rome. He invaded Sardinia and Lucca, though at the very time his armies entered papal territory his emissaries were with the pope professing their master's love and desire to give full satisfaction in everything. Gregory issued an encyclical against Frederick (June 20, 1239) urging the princes and kings of Europe to take up arms against him. Only the pope's own subjects lent him military aid. Nonetheless Gregory recovered Rome and summoned a council to deal with Frederick. In his mind Frederick was an agnostic as well as a morally depraved person. Had he not called Moses, Mohammed, and Christ—all three—impostors? Was he not overheard mockingly to say as he pointed to a priest carrying the host, "How long can this ridiculous comedy last?"[35] Frederick sealed up the passes into Italy to prevent the entrance of the delegates to the council. He captured ships conveying prelates on their mission. At this the king of France, who had judiciously refrained from taking action, demanded the liberation of the prisoners.

The long pontificate of the aged and venerable Gregory IX was relieved of the monotony of constant strife with the emperor by other positive and salutary accomplishments. The Moors, for example, were beaten back in Spain,

[34] E. Kantorowicz, *Frederick the Second* (London, 1931), 366-368.
[35] Hefele, *op. cit.* (Leclercq), V, 1590, 1591.

the King of Castile and Leon having taken by assault Cordova, Seville, and Cadiz and the King of Aragon having overcome Valencia and Majorca. The four famous Spanish military orders of Avis, St. James, Alcantara, and Calatrava formed an effective wall against Moslem expansion, while King Ferdinand III of Seville (1217-1252) gave to government as well as church the example of a saint. He passed through his domain hearing and settling disputes and championing the cause of the poor and oppressed. He confessed, "I have more dread of the curses of a poor woman than all the armies of the Moors." Before a battle Ferdinand spent the whole night before the altar of God in prayer. He wore a hair shirt like a monk. Though at his death he had reduced the Moors to the single city of Granada in Spain, still he professed as his sole aim in life, "Lord, thou art my witness that I seek only the development of faith in thee and not in perishable conquests." [36]

The saintliness of Ferdinand III in Spain was duplicated in the life of Louis IX, who was his first cousin, in France. Louis did not participate in the war between the empire and the papacy, as much as he loved the church, because his policy always was to reconcile foes rather than to profit by their strife. He did not desire the extension of an earthly kingdom but rather the expansion of faith in Jesus Christ. "Never did a man charged with the responsibility of governing men have more upright intentions. . . . He guided his steps by the light of two ideas: that of right and that of salvation." [37] Louis' long reign of forty-four years (1226-1270) was begun by a minority of ten years (1226-1236) in which the kingdom was ably managed by his gifted mother, Blanche of Castile. Louis ruled France with the help of his mother for twelve years (1236-1248) before turning the government back into her hands in order to conduct the crusade. He returned after six years to rule for another fifteen years (1254-1269) before launching another crusade on which he died (1270).

The legal structure of France was overhauled by Louis, who broke the juridical power of noble and bishop and put it in the royal hands through trained judges and jurists answerable directly to the crown. He destroyed private wars in France and took in the cause of humanity the greatest step away from feudalism toward nationalism in the form of absolute monarchy. His was the golden age. For sixteen years (1254-1270) France blossomed through peace into prosperity. The great Gothic cathedrals of Amiens, Bourges, and Beauvais were built, and out of his own money the king erected Sainte-Chapelle to house his priceless relic, Christ's crown of thorns. He was without rival the most popular person in Europe. France had not had so great a sovereign since Charlemagne, and indeed among all the rulers of the Middle

[36] J. Laurentie, *Saint Ferdinand* (1910), 51, 62.
[37] E. Lavisse, *Histoire de France* (1910-1911), III, ii, 37, 38.

Ages, taking into account all aspects of their reigns, there was perhaps none as great as he. He stands almost as the perfect personification of Christianity on the throne of a nation. "History is sometimes pitiless in its destruction of illusions, but in the case of St. Louis history and legend are one. The fame of the man was as wide and as high as his repute." [38]

If Gregory's pontificate was adorned by the lives and works of men like Ferdinand III and Louis IX, it was also marked by the shocking necessity of the inquisition. This energetic pontiff so consistently used and so thoroughly organized the inquisition that some historians have erroneously attributed its establishment to him. The Council of Toulouse (November, 1229), for example, laid down the precise procedure for the discovery and punishment of heretics. It set up the ecclesiastical tribunals of inquiry which functioned so mercilessly and so effectively in the coercion of conscience and the subjugation of the mind in subsequent centuries. Specially trained inquisitors were sent from Rome to France, Castile, Aragon, and other states which would receive them. In Rome where inquisitorial procedures were written into municipal law the Church had its own prisons. The arrangement between church and state concerning this institution was carefully delineated: the church discovered the heretics and proved them guilty of their doctrinal crimes; the state burned them at the stake. Certain orders sought inquisitorial rights and privileges in certain places and territories. The first such title given to any order to exercise the inquisition was the one Gregory gave to the Dominicans in Provence (April 20, 1232). Gregory IX did not ignite the first fire of the inquisition, but he fanned it into a raging flame which burned mercilessly across Europe for centuries. From 1229 to 1240 he employed a series of measures to repress heresy, thereby setting the style and providing the example for his successors. Though Gregory did not conceive the idea of the inquisition, at least he made it into the institution it actually became.

It was this same pontiff who modified the exaggerated demands for poverty bequeathed by Francis of Assisi to his followers, so that the Franciscan order might survive and function within the limitations imposed by nature upon all save a very select few even among ascetics. Gregory knew that some property was essential to the maintenance of the ideal of the poor. The poverty practiced by the brothers therefore had to be reconciled with the wealth given by benefactors to their order. He likewise ratified the work of Raymond of Penafort putting into a system the rules governing the Dominicans and approved by their own chapter in three stages: 1239, 1240, 1241.

But Gregory's concerns were not confined merely to the organizational efficiency of the church and the strengthening of its institutions. He had an understanding of philosophy and theology as well. It was he who approved

[38] J. W. Thompson, The Middle Ages (1932), I, 540.

the introduction of the new learning in the form of Aristotelian studies, took precautionary measures to make such knowledge conform to the teachings of the church and to support orthodoxy, and set by his office the supreme example of open-mindedness which recognizes that learning is the ally of religion and that earthly wisdom and heavenly truth are one. The way to overcome false science is not by ignorance but by greater understanding which produces the true science. It is not surprising that it was Gregory IX who issued the charter of the University of Paris (1231). Thus he offset the natural tendency of the time, which was to reject Aristotle as a pagan and to proscribe the Arabic commentaries on his works. The Council of Paris, for example, had forbidden in 1210 either the public or private reading of Aristotle's natural philosophy, and five years later the papal legate in France extended this prohibition to his metaphysics as well. The wiser handling of the issue by Gregory kept such master minds as Albertus Magnus and Thomas Aquinas in the service of the church.

This remarkable old man, who was called to the heaviest responsibilities of his life and of Christendom at the age when most men are either dead or senile, lived on to have a longer pontificate than Innocent III and one equally full of great accomplishments. Gregory IX proves that for some men "old age hath yet its honor and its toil" and joins the ranks of Leo I, Gregory I, Nicholas I, Leo IX, Gregory VII, and Innocent III as one of the seven greatest popes.

Gregory IX died while the armies of Frederick II, his constant enemy, menaced Rome.[39] The papal see, due to imperial interference, remained vacant for two years before **Innocent IV** (1243-1254) was elected and enthroned. He deserted Rome for the fair city of Lyons on the border of France where King Louis could protect him. In Lyons he convened the ecumenical council his predecessor had planned. There gathered in June, 1245, the chief prelates of the Latin church including among them the patriarchs of both Constantinople and Antioch, now in Latin hands. Frederick was excommunicated, a crusade was decreed (Louis IX's crusade), and dueling and jousting tournaments were proscribed. Frederick died on December 13, 1250; but immediately the pope resumed the war with his sons Conrad IV in Germany and Manfred in Sicily and Italy. The financial drain on the resources of the church to fight these wars was tremendous, yet Innocent persevered, levying special taxes and revenues, until death took first Conrad (May 29, 1254) and later the pope (December 7, 1254). Innocent IV had not been able to live up to his namesake Innocent III. An important step in the development of papal elections however had been taken in 1241. The cardinals initiated the custom

---

[39] *Les Régistres de Grégoire IX* (ed. Auvray, 1896-1910). J. Felten, *Papst Gregor IX* (1886).

of enclosing themselves in a certain room from which they do not emerge until they have elected a pope. This was called the conclave.[40]

The forty years following the death of Pope Innocent IV (1254-1294), though the most brilliant in intellectual and cultural accomplishments in the West during the whole of the Middle Ages, count for little in the history of the papacy. No man of any stature occupied Peter's throne. Then too the reigns of the successive pontiffs were short, punctuated by all too frequent interregnums. Practically the same diplomatic, political, and social problems we have seen already in the first half of the thirteenth century posed themselves again in the form of new persons and events. Though the German empire became exhausted and no longer possessed the strength seriously to hinder or to impair the designs of the papacy, the ambition of world domination and absolute power which had animated its rulers was revived in the heart and actions of Charles of Anjou, the new French king of Sicily. It was he who extinguished the Hohenstaufens by defeating and slaying Manfred at the battle of Benevento (February 27, 1266) and by trying and executing as a common criminal the young Conradin, the grandson of Frederick II, whose death was staged as a public spectacle in the square at Naples (October 29, 1268). He hoped to take by force of arms both Constantinople and Jerusalem and to establish himself as another Constantine, the master of an undivided world empire. But, like Otto III, Frederick I, and Frederick II, his ambition was as insubstantial as a dream, and the French attempt at world conquest was as unsuccessful as the German. The highest level of papal accomplishment during this period was during the pontificate of Gregory X (1271-1276), who held the Second General Council of Lyons (1274), effected with Michael Palaeologus the temporary healing of the 220-year-old schism between the East and West, established political peace between the Greeks and the Latins, and even laid plans for a joint crusade of the Byzantine empire and the West against the infidels. Unfortunately, none of Gregory's accomplishments survived him.

The twelve pontiffs between 1254 and 1294, like the kings and peoples they served, did not see beyond the duties of the moment; and they were carried along in the prosecution of their tasks by the momentum generated by their great predecessors, Innocent III and Gregory IX.

The last pope of the thirteenth century, Boniface VIII (1294-1303), was as vigorous, as enterprising, and as zealous for the integrity of his office as the first. Unfortunately he was not so successful. Times had begun to change. Imperial unity was giving way to uncontrolled nationalism. The center of conflict between church and state was shifting from Germany to France.

Philip the Fair, whether he deserves it or not, has been looked upon as the

[40] Hefele, op. cit. (Leclercq), V, 1613, n. 2; 1642-1678.

personification of rising nationalism in Europe. Employing the talents of the legists who substituted Roman law for the feudal and ecclesiastically oriented tenets of the Middle Ages, Philip insisted that the king rules directly under the sovereignty of God, that his power is not subject to the church's approval or disapproval, and that his subjects' supreme allegiance is as nationals to the head of their state, not to a universal institution like the church. Ownership resides within the nation; all national properties are at the disposal of the king.

In opposition to this Boniface VIII, who had displaced the good but inconsequential Celestine V, issued two famous bulls, which are the most perfect expressions of the concept of the medieval imperial church. The *Clericis Laicos* (February 25, 1296) forbade under pain of excommunication any lay person or power to impose or any ecclesiastical dignitary or institution to pay any tax, tribute, or gift to any secular institution, ruler, or state. The *Unam Sanctam* (1302) stated that in the custody of the church there are two swords—the spiritual and the temporal. The first is to be used by the church and resides solely in the hands of the priesthood. The latter resides in the hands of secular rulers but is subject to appraisal by the church. If the temporal power goes astray, it must be judged by the spiritual power. This power can be judged only by God. In order to secure salvation every creature must be subject to the Roman pontiff.

Boniface already had enforced his words by deeds. He had attempted to avert a European war by arbitrating between the kings of England and France, who were at strife with each other. Yet his actions, so similar to those of Innocent III, who had succeeded, seemed to please no one; and the authoritarianism which once had awed into submission the proudest prince now often antagonized the most humble subject as well as his sovereign. The outcome was the outrage of Anagni, when the pope was broken in upon by French ruffians who, despite his eighty-six years, handled him with abuse and even violence (September 7, 1303). He died one month later (October 11, 1303), and with him died the imperial papacy.[41]

[41] G. Digard, M. Faucon, A. Thomas, R. Fawtier, *Les Registres de Boniface VIII* (1904-1939), 4 vols. Potthast, *op. cit.*, 24291, 25189. Mourret, *op. cit.*, IV, 520-568; V, 20-53.

Chapter Ten

The Zenith of Medieval Christian Civilization
in the West
(1198-1321)

MORE ENDURING IN THE WEST THAN THE ECCLESIASTICAL EMPIRE AS A POLITICAL entity with the papacy at its head were the intellectual and spiritual creations which came about under its hegemony. Indeed, if the thirteenth was for Latin Christianity the greatest of the medieval centuries, it was because of the ideas and their artistic, literary, and cultural expressions which came to fruition during this time. They all had a common source. There was a unity in variety and likewise a variety in unity never before or since attained. This period in history therefore was unique. Culture in the West was dominated by Christianity. Civilization was the church's own creation.

I. The Culmination of Scholasticism

This is seen primarily in philosophy. In antiquity Christian theology had existed in competition with pagan concepts of reality. The dogmas of revelation were set against the doctrines of the natural mind to such an extent that the presuppositions of theology had to be recognized as of a different kind from those of philosophy. To be sure the Fathers of the church had accepted as well as given instruction. Paganism had made its imprint upon the Christianity which had converted it. All the same when theology had sought philosophical expression, it had been in borrowed categories—those of Stoicism, Platonism, or the Neoplatonic mysticism of Plotinus—and every such expression had been properly recognized as partial and solitary—that is, less than the total gospel had been revealed. Philosophy and theology had been carefully delineated.

After the twelfth century such a distinction vanished. To the thirteenth century masters theology and philosophy were for all practical purposes the same. This was because **Christianity created her own philosophy**, distinct and separate from any other, so that the scholastic systems of the thirteenth century belonged exclusively to the church. Anselm had been a philosopher in the eleventh century, but he had employed natural reason to prove the validity of a few specific beliefs; while Abelard in the twelfth century, together with his philosophical contemporaries, had hardly got beyond methodology. They constructed no really unified system of Christian thought at all.

The thirteenth century masters were system builders. They sought to give a full and complete view of reality from the vantage point of Christianity. They employed heathenish categories and borrowed, seemingly without any restriction, from the pre-Christian Greeks. However, what they borrowed they paid for by making it entirely their own. Like raw material in manufacturing, Greek concepts were recast to fit Christian usage, and the Aristotelian principles of causation became with Thomas Aquinas the reasons for believing in the existence of God.

This new philosophy was made possible by **the discovery of the real Aristotle.** For this, the West was indebted to the infidel. Aristotle came through the Arabians, along with their interpretations and commentaries. That is why the church was momentarily frightened by the discovery and why the works of the Stagirite were proscribed at Paris by the papal legate, as we have seen. Indeed all throughout the century there was intellectual warfare on this issue. There were those who condemned Aristotelianism as the intellectual foe of Christianity. There were those who welcomed this new insight along with its Arabic interpretations as a healthful relief from authoritarian doctrine and accepted it as a substitute for theology. Finally there were those who employed it with modifications to Christian purposes, thereby creating the synthesis between Aristotelianism and Christian theology which produced the greatest of the scholastic philosophical systems. Amaury of Bène and David of Dinant, who belonged to the second group, were condemned as heretics.

The ban on Aristotle, effected at Paris in 1210, was ignored at Toulouse, which openly recommended as necessary in order "to look into the very bosom of nature" the books on natural philosophy which were prohibited at Paris. Consequently Toulouse became the center of a school of translators, the most famous of whom was Michael the Scot (1180-1235), who translated Aristotle from the Arabic translations into Latin. Sicily improved upon Toulouse by producing translators who worked directly from the Greek. In addition to Michael the Scot, Hermann the German, Robert Grosseteste, and Alfred Sareshel made their contributions as translators. The most celebrated of all Aristotle's translators however was William of Moerbeke (1215-1286), a Flemish Dominican, who collaborated with Thomas Aquinas and gave him the sources of his monumental works.

The first men in the West really to confront Aristotle philosophically were William of Auvergne (1180-1249), the theologian, and Robert Grosseteste

(1175-1253), the scientist. The first was a Frenchman who against the opposition of Pope Gregory IX became bishop of Paris. The other was an English man who became chancellor of Oxford University and later bishop of Lincoln. William of Auvergne accepted Aristotle's view of causation and applied it to separate God from all mystical and Neoplatonic attachment to creation, thus destroying the hierarchical arrangement of intermediary causes. However, he modified Aristotle by Augustine, insisting on a theory of supernatural illuminism in knowledge. He stated "that the soul is like an horizon between two worlds. One of these worlds is that of sensible things to which it is closely connected by its body; but the other is the Creator, who is in himself like the model and the mirror in which are reflected the first forms." [1] Consequently the soul can be connected with nature only by divine grace, for spirit is too unlike matter to find any understandable affinity apart from God who made both.

Robert Grosseteste, the founder of the scientific method more brilliantly developed by his pupil Roger Bacon, showed the influence of Aristotle in the form of a stubborn reaction against the Greek's principles and methods. He knew Greek and therefore had direct access to Aristotle, many of whose writings he translated and upon which he wrote commentaries. Yet for himself he adopted Augustine's theory of knowledge[2] and advanced on his own the so-called "light metaphysics," which holds that light is the bearer of all matter and all form. By nature it diffuses itself in all directions. Thus light, being itself without magnitude, engenders a sphere which in turn acquires dimensions and becomes a material body extended in space. Grosseteste thus makes form, not matter, the foundation of being and finds naturally enough in mathematics—especially geometry and optics—the clue to the understanding of nature. Whereas the University of Paris under its masters was to give itself to the study largely of metaphysics, thus magnifying the trivium, Oxford University because of Grosseteste was to study science also, showing that the quadrivium was relevant.[3]

The discovery and use of Aristotle meant, as both William of Auvergne and Robert Grosseteste clearly illustrate, the revival of Augustine as well. The Christian mind was not willing to concede superiority to the Greek. There might be some good things in Aristotle; if there were these should be reconciled with the teachings of Augustine. However in no sense should Augustinianism be abandoned or the major bent of its system be perverted by alien Greek elements. There arose devotees of Augustinian theology in contrast to the proponents of Aristotelianism. These men differed with one another in

---

[1] William of Auvergne, De anima, V, 7, in Opera omnia (Paris, 1674).
[2] Robert Grosseteste, De veritate, CXXXV, 4, in Die philosophischen Werke des Robert Grosseteste, Bischof von Lincoln (ed. L. Baur, Münster, 1912).
[3] De luce, LI, 11.

particulars, but certain tenets governed their thinking: (1) The apperception of truth is invariably a matter of divine illumination. (2) Things exist by virtue of the forms which express themselves in them. Consequently the universe is a universe of forms. (3) The soul is a self-subsisting entity independent of the body. It is its own principle of individuation; it is not merely the body's form.[4]

Though Willam of Auvergne and Robert Grosseteste were both members of the secular priesthood, the most notable contributions to philosophy in the thirteenth century came from the mendicant orders. Indeed the teachers of Western Europe were the Franciscans and the Dominicans. The latter were avowedly so from the start, since learning had been a reason for their foundation. The former became so in contradiction to the intention of their founder, since the propagation of faith had proved impossible without knowledge. The friars invaded the universities. Soon the theological faculties were dominated by their influence.

The Franciscan School of thought was, at least in its first stages, consistently Augustinian. Its three great masters were all disinclined toward Aristotle though of course they were influenced by him. Alexander of Hales (ca. 1186-1245), an Englishman like Robert Grosseteste, nonetheless taught at Paris (1221-1245) and gave to the Franciscans their first theological master in that university when he joined the order in 1236, only seventeen years after the friars minor had established themselves there (1219). His ideas were preserved in a form similar to the Sic et non of Abelard and called Summa theologica. This was written by his pupils. Roger Bacon described it as "that great summa, heavier than a horse."

John de la Rochelle, William Meliton, and Bonaventura were all his pupils, the most gifted of whom was Bonaventura (1221-1274). He was second in both time and significance in the Franciscan triumvirate. He succeeded Alexander of Hales in the Franciscan chair of theology at Paris, wrote his masterpiece, Commentary on the Sentences of Peter the Lombard, when he was only thirty years old, and died as general of his order. The force of his position lies in the fact that he subordinated philosophy to theology by insisting that all rational thought springs directly from faith. Knowledge is divine illumination of the intellect. Truth by its very nature is revealed truth. "The idea in God, according to its reality, is divine truth, and in accordance with our mode of knowing, the resemblance of the thing known; this resemblance of the thing known is the direct cause of our knowing any object, universal or particular, though in itself it is no more universal or particular than God." [5] "How would

---

[4] G. Leff, Medieval Thought (Pelican, 1958), pp. 190-194.
[5] Bonaventura, Collationes in Hexaemeron (Quaracchi, 1934), XII, 11.

the intellect know that a being was deficient and incomplete if it had no knowledge of a being without any deficiency?" [6]

This is Augustinianism pure and simple, yet Bonaventura took into account Aristotle. Indeed his significance lies in the fact that he was able to make Augustine relevant to his own time. He gave answers to the questions posed by the new knowledge of Aristotle. Consequently he related intelligible reality to the sensible world. (1) Individual things are what they are because of their intelligible forms, not their material accidents. (2) Corporeal matter is itself both general and special. It is general in relation to the form of light which subsists in all things to cause them to be. Yet it is special in relation to the particular thing it is—that is, to its forms of particular composition. (3) Thus the soul is an independent composition in its own right with no dependence upon the body for its knowledge or its existence. It is the agent of perfecting the rational body. (4) The intellect examines sensible data and judges them in accordance with its innate ideas, for all knowledge is regulated by immutable and eternal rules which are eternal truth.[7]

Truth is of grace and is impressed upon the soul by God himself. Therefore the highest point of knowledge—contemplation—is reached by turning aside from all sensible data and fixing on God alone.[8] We move from our senses to pure intelligence. Christianity in its singularity is love. Bonaventura both acted and thought like a Franciscan. When the legates of Rome arrived at his establishment to inform him that the pope had made him a cardinal, he kept them waiting until he finished his chores in the kitchen; and, when he got his red hat, he hung it on a tree while he washed the brothers' clothes. Likewise, he taught the beginning of religion is faith; and its end, through the exercise of intelligence, is the mystic contemplation of God.

Duns Scotus (1266-1308), the third in the triumvirate, was the most brilliant Franciscan theologian and philosopher of the thirteenth century, yet his daring originality was less constructive than Bonaventura's more cautious approach. Unintentionally he began the process of undermining the scholastic synthesis. He accepted the problems Aristotle posed, as did his older contemporary Aquinas, but he gave to them entirely different answers. Indeed he separated reason from faith instead of using it either as its precursor, in the case of Aquinas, or as its follower, in the case of Bonaventura. Consequently philosophy and theology were two distinct disciplines, the one dealing with being limited to material and time and the other with God and eternity. Aristotle's so-called proofs of God's existence from movement or the passing of potency into act explain only the origin of temporal causes. The only proof there is of God by reason is that an infinite regress is unthinkable. Hence

---

[6] *Itinerarium mentis in Deum, Tria Opuscula* (Quaracchi, 1938), III, 3.
[7] *Commentaria* (Quaracchi, 1934 ff.), II, 3, 13, 17, 24.
[8] *De scientia Christi,* V, 23.

there must be a first cause. Likewise since it is impossible to think of infinite progression, there must be a final and perfect end. From the idea of first being which is the cause of everything else we are able to deduce all the attributes of God.

Duns emphasized God's will as the cause of all that is. Knowing everything in idea, God makes what it pleases him to make. Likewise in man the will is supreme over the intellect, and it can accept or reject what is brought to its attention. Yet the human intellect can know and the human will unaided can deal only with finite things. Hence God at his own initiative must make contact with man both to direct and to empower him. This he did through the Incarnation. Duns will ascribe no limits to God. God used the methods he did simply because he willed to do so. He might have done entirely dif- ferently if he had chosen. There is no predicting what he will do. From man's point of view at least, the divine freedom is altogether arbitrary. Hence most of God's actions are entirely outside the scope of human comprehension, and the sublime truths of Christianity are not at man's disposal at all.[9]

Quite in contrast to the position of Duns Scotus was that of the great **Dominican, Thomas Aquinas**. Indeed, from the start the theological ideas of the two mendicant orders were in keen competition with each other. The **Dominicans**, who preceded the entrance of the Franciscans into Paris by two years (1217), became the supporters of Aristotelianism in place of Augustinian Neoplatonism. This adoption of Aristotle was not immediate; at first the Dominicans were as frightened of him as any other group.

To Albertus Magnus (1206-1280), the teacher of Aquinas, must be given the credit for recognizing in Aristotle the greatest potential intellectual ally to Christianity. He devoted almost his entire life to making Aristotle "in- telligible to the Latin West." As a consequence most of his work was con- sumed in commentaries and expositions upon, together with the editing of, Aristotle's major works. He was a gifted observer and cataloguer of natural life, and he insisted on giving to natural phenomena a rationalistic explanation of being. Yet in his own philosophical constructions he was vague, even con- fused. Nowhere did he attain the nice balance he advocated. Indeed in his attempts to utilize Aristotle, he did not succeed in breaking entirely with the Augustinian Neoplatonism of his time.

The philosophical future belonged to his more brilliant pupil, Thomas Aquinas (1225-1274), who became to the Middle Ages what Augustine had been to antiquity—its clearest and deepest thinker and its most comprehen- sive teacher and guide. Aquinas accepted the method of Aristotle and used his basic principles and presuppositions in the construction of his own system

---

[9] Duns Scotus, *Quaestiones Quodlibetales*, in *Opera omnia* (Paris, 1891-1895), Vols. XXV-XXVI.

of thought. At the same time he introduced the orthodoxy of Christianity into Aristotelianism as a new and radical element. This new element, always and without exception, was both the guiding and determinative principle in Thomism. Wherever the reasoning of the Stagirite conflicted with the disclosures of faith, Aristotle had to give way to Christianity. Thomas' method of operation was like that of a school boy solving a problem in mathematics. The boy has the right answer given him in advance. Always he works toward that. When the answer he obtains does not conform to the one given, he knows his calculations are in error so he must begin afresh until he reaches the right answer. Truth was given to Thomas in Christian revelation. His task was to reach in as many areas as possible the same answer, employing the tool of unaided human reason. To be sure some areas would not yield an answer alone; they belonged entirely to faith and stood as sublime mysteries: creation in time, the Trinity, and Incarnation. Yet many areas were subject, so Thomas found, to reason's sway, and these he explored with the zeal of a scientist and the devotion of a saint.

To his own satisfaction he proved without the aid of revelation the existence of God: (1) Since motion is the reduction of something from potentiality to actuality, this must be done by something already in a state of actuality, like fire, for example, which turns dry wood into fire. A thing cannot be both actual and potential at the same time in the same way. Therefore a thing cannot be both mover and moved, so whatever is moved must be moved by another. Since this process of movement must have had a beginning, the first mover, unmoved by anything else, is God. (2) Likewise since every effect has its cause, there must have been a first cause not itself the effect of anything, and that first cause is God. (3) In nature we find that it is possible for things both to be and not to be. If it is possible for a thing not to be, then at one time it was not. Consequently at one time possibly all things were not. But, if this were so, they would not be now, for what is not does not exist. Therefore something had always to be (necessary being), and that necessary being, the cause of possible or contingent being, is God. (4) Since we observe grades and degrees found in things, there must be something perfect which lends to all other things their quality and degree of worth, and this perfect thing is God. (5) All things are made for a purpose or end toward which they move. This being which directs all natural things toward their end is God.[10] These five arguments he tied together by means of the third. Necessary being which causes all contingent beings is of necessity the first mover and cause and likewise provides the standard of value and appointed ends of all that it has made. Thus reason alone can deduce the attributes of perfect being and by analogy

[10] *Summa Theologica*, I, Q. 2, A. 3.

to the things made form some notion, inadequate though it is, of him who made them.[11]

Thomas' whole philosophy rests on the primacy of being, which means existence in concrete forms, that is, in actual entities, which are the objects of knowledge. As a result certain axioms govern all our thinking: (1) a thing cannot both be and not be at the same time; (2) if a thing does not exist by itself, it has its reason for existence in something else; (3) all that exists is substance and can be distinguished from its accidents or characteristics; (4) every contingent being has an efficient cause; (5) everything acts in relation to an end—that is, there is a purpose for it; (6) nothing exists in the intellect unless first in the senses. The form or pattern by which a thing is made gives it its being (humanity to a man, for example); but matter is the principle of individuation (particularizes and limits the form it contains by causing man to be the specific person he is).[12]

The difference between God and his creatures lies in the difference between potency and act; and Thomas' God, far from the mere "Thought of thought" of Aristotle, is the "I am that I am" of Moses, the infinite cause of all that is finite and the plenitude and perfection of all that is. Since the existence of temporal things presupposes an idea of them, all things were ideas in the mind of God before ever they came to have status in reality.[13]

God made angels as pure forms uncompromised by matter, but we do not see them; while man he made with a body and a soul, the latter of which must attain to first principles through sensible reality. Reason enables a man to choose freely and sets before the will the objects of its volition. Ordinarily therefore certain virtues like prudence and temperance are capable of native attainment, though the supernatural virtues of faith, hope, and charity are infused only by divine grace. Grace never abolishes nature; it only perfects it.[14]

The radical dichotomy between nature and grace established by Augustine is really set aside by Aquinas. Redemption seems more a supplementation of creation, not its transformed restoration. Reason and faith stand harmoniously together. Faith complements reason and goes far beyond it, but it never contradicts it. Thomas supplements his natural theology (philosophy) with a full-scale presentation of the body of revealed truth. The *Summa Theologica* is much longer than the *Contra Gentiles*. But it is in the same form: revelation is made as convincing as reason, for the native intellect is the tool utilized in the presentation of both.

The thirteenth century produced Thomas Aquinas. It did not thereby ap-

[11] *Ibid.*, I, Q. 5, A. 2.
[12] *Ibid.*, I, Q. 50, A. 4; Q. 15, A. 3.
[13] *Contra Gentiles*, IV, 13.
[14] *De veritate*, Q. 24, A. 2; *Summa Theologica*, II, Q. 82, A. 3.

prove him. In fact a **violent reaction** set in against his work, the effect of which reached to two opposite extremes.

On the one hand, the effect of Thomism was to stimulate radical elements in philosophy, for there were those such as Siger of Brabant (ca. 1240-ca. 1284) and Boetius of Dacia, who were eager to employ Aristotle together with his Arabian commentators in total disregard for any harmonious relationship between faith and reason. They taught the existence of astral powers and intelligences, the subjugation of the human will to them, and the eternity of the world and matter. They went as far as to imply double truth: truth which applied to philosophical speculation; and truth, entirely different and contradictory, which held sway in the realm of theology. Their works led to the Parisian condemnations of 1270 and 1277. These ecclesiastical censures at the same time cast a cloud of suspicion and doubt on the work of Thomas himself. They were a frank confession of the church's recognition of the failure of the attempt to prove Aristotle a worthy ally of Christianity, and betrayed a revulsion against the corruption of dogma by foreign elements from pagan philosophy.

On the other hand, the effect of Thomism was to arouse a conservative philosophical and theological defense of Augustinianism. This defense did not come entirely from the ranks of the Franciscans. Thomas' own brothers, the Dominicans, were divided in their appraisal of his worth. He had no more stubborn an opponent than Robert Kilwardby (d. 1279), the Dominican friar who held the chair of philosophy at Oxford and later became archbishop of Canterbury. The secular priest Henry of Ghent (d. 1293) likewise struck an Augustinian note on all the major issues; while the most influential Franciscans —Eustace of Arras (d. 1291), Walter of Bruges (d. 1307), John Peckham (1240-1292), Peter John Olivi (1248-1298), and the famous Raymond Lull (1235-1315)—formed a solid phalanx of opposition to Thomas and apologetics for Augustine. What little support Thomas got, like that from Richard of Middleton (d. ca. 1307) and William de la Mare (d. ca. 1285), among the Franciscans, and from Giles of Lessines (d. 1304), among the members of his own order, was too isolated to alter the main intellectual current of the time.

The objection the conservatives had to the philosophy of Thomas Aquinas was fourfold: (1) By denying to an individual object of creation its own form he had made matter, not spirit, the principle of individuation, thus necessitating its preservation throughout eternity. At the same time he had established soul as the form of body, determining thereby its general type, thus bringing matter and spirit into an inseparable relationship and making soul itself the act of a material body. (2) He had made a distinction between essence and existence in things which to their minds compromised the absolute distinction between God, who alone was considered as pure form, and the objects of his creation, which were composite beings. (3) He had rejected divine illumination in his theory of knowledge and had thereby made revelation itself dependent upon proper apprehension through sense experience. (4) He had made voluntarism a mere appendage of understanding, the will of man the effect of his intellect.[15]

Consequently Thomas' last days were harassed by controversy. Indeed he was on his way to Rome to defend the orthodoxy of his opinions when he died.

It is, therefore, proper to look on the year of his death (1274) as the culminating point in the development of scholasticism. After him the pendulum swung from emphasis on synthesis to separation, and the recognition of the abiding worth of perhaps the greatest intellect Western Christianity ever produced was delayed for centuries.

II. The Inauguration of Experimental Science

The scholastics dealt with the essence of existence and the reality in eternity beyond the real in time, while the scientists contented themselves with trying to explain what took place every day in things about them. They were quite mundane in an age the intellectual habit of which was to be sublime. Yet their ultimate purpose, at least so they claimed, was to further the progress of theology by learning more about God's activity through a proper observation of the things he had made. This movement can best be styled as experimental science, since it advanced the method of experiment and thereby established the basis on which all modern science rests.

The names of these thirteenth-century scientists are few and, with a single exception, obscure as well. Robert Grosseteste, Adam Marsh, a Pole by the name of Witelo, Peter de Maricourt, John Peckham, Richard of Middleton, and Roger Bacon constitute the list. Bacon tells us that Peter de Maricourt was the most successful among them and what the others like himself thought of as theoretically possible Peter had already demonstrated as working fact. It is a pity that we know little more about him than Bacon's opinion of him. Grosseteste is better known and, if a single individual has a right to such a claim, should be thought of as the founder of this new experimental method. He was one of the teachers of Roger Bacon. His surviving works in comparison with those of Bacon register a debt of pupil to master far more apparent than Aquinas' to Albertus Magnus.

These men oddly enough were more Augustinian than Aristotelian, associating thereby the science of the thirteenth century with the non-scientific Platonism of the Greeks rather than with Aristotle, who is looked upon as the father of science. There were perhaps two reasons for this. One was that the Aristotelians felt Aristotle had discovered all the answers, and there was no

[15] Leff, op. cit., pp 224-245.

need to do more than to accept his explanations. The other reason was less superficial; it was a metaphysical reason. These Augustinians, accepting as they did voluntarism and believing that God could do and did as he willed, ruled out a closed view of the universe and addressed themselves to natural phenomena in the light of changes which they expected to take place.

Roger Bacon (ca. 1214-ca. 1292), because of the survival and effectiveness of his literary works, is the most memorable representative of this new experimental school and, with Grosseteste, the pioneer philosopher in the development of modern science. Such giants, for example, as Copernicus, Galileo, and even the great Newton himself, ride securely upon the stout shoulders of Bacon's method so that without him, or someone else like him, their work would not have been possible. Like Grosseteste, Bacon was an Englishman, an Oxonian, and a Franciscan.

Bacon enumerates four basic and perennial causes of error: (1) authority, (2) custom, (3) common view of the crowd, (4) and ignorant pretense. What is worse than the triple argument: this has precedent; this is customary; this is the common view? Especially when such an argument is advanced to cover one's own ignorance and to give the appearance that one has wisdom he does not actually possess? Such attitudes close the mind to the acquisition of new information and stifle all efforts at experiment. Consequently the time of intellectuals is spent in rearranging the ideas and findings of those who have gone before them, and their writings display "ineffable falsity" couched in "superfluous verbiage" witnessing to their authors' "infinite puerile vanity." Bacon seems to have had only contempt for the labors of Albertus Magnus and Thomas Aquinas.

He lists seven vices which mark the study of theology itself. (1) Theology is dominated by philosophy to the extent that such sublime issues as the Trinity, the Incarnation, and the Sacraments are discussed through the authorities, arguments, and distinctions of philosophy. Philosophy has no right to a hearing outside its own province. (2) The best sciences, ancient languages, mathematics, optics, moral science, experimental science, and alchemy, which might aid theology by affording it a more adequate view of creation, are altogether neglected by theologians. (3) At the same time theologians are largely ignorant of the lower sciences which they attempt to use: Latin grammar, logic, natural philosophy in its baser part, and a certain type of metaphysics. (4) *The Sentences* of Peter the Lombard have been substituted for Scripture. (5) The text of Scripture is corrupt in the Vulgate, so that (6) its literal meaning in passages is uncertain and consequently (7) its spiritual message is compromised by doubt and error.

Bacon however was far more than a critic. He enumerated the errors of his time only to attempt to correct them. In place of false knowledge and slavish subservience to the mistakes of the past, he wanted to substitute an understanding of truth. This to his way of thinking meant a **new method,** an entirely different procedure for confirming the validity of propositions and assertions. Consequently he urged (1) the study of the ancient languages so that Scripture and other authoritative works could be read as they had been originally written; (2) the pursuit of the higher sciences of mathematics, optics (physics), and astrology; and (3) the diligent use of the discipline (itself a science) of experiment (*scientia experimentalis*).

Though Bacon's discussions of the relevance of mathematics, optics, and even astrology for the support of theology are quaint and interesting almost to the point of fascination, it is his delineation of the **experimental method** which gives him his place among the great. Indeed this *scientia experimentalis* is not only the best of the sciences but is one which either confirms or refutes the findings of the others and therefore is master of them all. It is not concerned with the arguments of logic. Rather it attempts to treat by observation and experiment the conclusions which the other sciences have drawn. Consequently it accepts nothing in the order of creation until it has tested and proved its data specifically in the sphere in which these data fall. One cannot say, for example, that a dog breathes like a man on any other authority than the observation of the respiratory processes of both creatures and an exhaustive comparison of the same. Bacon had little regard therefore for deductive logic. He felt we can take for granted that our thoughts naturally are logical, and the important thing is to have the right information to think about. As a result experiment was for him what logic was for Aristotle and the scholastics.

The true method of research, as Bacon outlines it, is

to study what properly comes first in any science, the easier before the more difficult, the general before the particular, the less before the greater. The student's business should lie in chosen and useful topics, because life is short; and these should be set forth with clearness and certitude, which is impossible without experiment. Although we know through three means, authority, reason, and experiment, yet authority is not wise unless its reason is given, nor does it give knowledge but belief. We believe but do not know from authority. Nor can reason distinguish between sophistry and demonstration unless we know the conclusion is attested by facts.

The purpose of all knowledge is utility. For Bacon this utility was theological: we learn in order better to serve God and please him. Science therefore in the thirteenth century was also a handmaid of theology.[16]

[16] Roger Bacon, *Compendium studii theologiae* (ed. H. Rashdall, Aberdeen, 1911); *Opus tertium* (ed. Little, Aberdeen, 1912); *Opus majus* (trans. Burke, Philadelphia, 1928).

III. The Molding of Theology

Bacon and his kind were not typical of the thought of their century, and the scientific method they espoused was less influential than the scholasticism, either Augustinian or Aristotelian, which opposed it. The chief sphere of intellectual concern was theology, which remained the queen of the sciences, that majestic discipline in the retinue of which both philosophy and science were glad to serve as handmaidens. Here the scholastic method was influential; the doctrines of the church were given a precision and clarity of expression by the schoolmen which was in keeping with the general habit of their mind.

Therefore, though the dogma of neither the Trinity nor of the Person of Christ was in any way modified; both received careful attention by the thirteenth-century theologians and were restated in the categories of the time. The Trinity was given, in keeping with the thought of Peter the Lombard, an Augustinian interpretation; [17] while the Incarnation was treated so abstractly that the Jesus of the Gospels was made to vanish away in empty phrases.[18] However, the nature of God did receive from the scholastics an interpretation which the ancient church, despite its formulation of the Trinity, had not been able to provide. Thomas, who thought of God as pure actuality without any potentiality in his nature at all, defined the divine activity as thought and will reaching their goal.[19] God's goal is God himself. Everything that occurs in the world must be referred to his goal, which, since it is God and is commensurate with his nature, must be pure love. God therefore uses the world and all that happens in it as a means of realizing his final goal. In other words, he loves the world as he loves himself.[20] Consequently the Aristotelian concept of God in Thomas' philosophy is complemented in his theology by the spiritual notion of a personal loving will, all good as well as all powerful. Anselm's thinking Spirit is in Thomas merciful and kind.

The interpretation of the work of Christ, that is, his redemptive mission, is a clear illustration of the nondogmatic treatment of the atonement. The doctrine of the death of Christ has always been left an open question by the church. So in the thirteenth century the objective interpretation of Anselm was combined with the subjective interpretation of Abelard, both being considered essential to a full understanding of redemption.[21] To these was added the concept of Christ as head of the church, which through the explication

[17] Hefele, op. cit., V, 880-881.
[18] Bonaventura, Commentaria in Quatuor Libros Sententiarum Magistri Petri Lombardi (Quaracchi, 1882), III, D. 5., A. 1, Q. 1; D. 6, A. 1, Q. 1. Thomas Aquinas, Summa Theologica, III, Q. 2, A. 2, A. 7; Q. 16, A. 6; Q. 17, A. 2; Q. 18; Q. 19.
[19] Thomas Aquinas, Summa Theologica, I, Q. 9, A. 1.
[20] Ibid., I, Q. 19, A. 2; Q. 20, A. 1; Q. 21, A. 1, A. 2.
[21] Alexander of Hales, Summa universae theologiae (Quaracchi, 1924-48) III, Q. 1, 4 ff; Q. 16, 3, 4; Bonaventura, Compendium breviloquium (Quaracchi, 1938), IV, 1, 9; Commentaria, III, D. 20, A. 1, Q. 3.

of the relationship between head and members fixed clearly the implied connection between the redemptive act and its effects in the lives of the redeemed. Always with the schoolmen what is done by God for man is considered in the light of what happens, morally and spiritually, in man.[22] Thomas Aquinas adds the further consideration that the death of Christ was not of inherent necessity the only possible means of our forgiveness. God freely chose it; he might have effected redemption in some other way.[23] Likewise, the suffering of Christ for us was voluntary, an act of obedience and love.[24]

This is not to say that the scholastics did not believe that **redemption** in some form or other was necessary. They gave God all the credit for the salvation of man even from the time of his creation. Alexander of Hales set the pattern of scholastic anthropology, which pattern Albertus Magnus and Thomas Aquinas as well as Bonaventura followed. They all taught that Adam before the fall, though his natural powers were in harmony with the will of God and he was untroubled by concupiscence,[25] was endowed even then by supernatural grace which enabled him to love God as God loved him and so to win eternal salvation.[26] In order clearly to distinguish this supernatural gift from original righteousness, Alexander of Hales, Bonaventura, and Albertus Magnus all taught that it is not conferred on man immediately at his creation but at some later time as if he should earn it by a merit of fitness.[27] Thomas Aquinas made it simultaneous with man's creation, but its distinction from original righteousness given at the same time lies in its supernatural end.[28] Its end is eternal life, the means of attaining which exceed the powers of human nature. Acts of merit to be valid before God must be performed by God. Hence even before the fall man was blessed by the infusion of divine love, "that universal habit shaping both the subject and all his powers and works, through which God, living in his saints, infuses the power by which they merit eternal life." [29] Grace alone, as much for the scholastics as for Augustine, makes a man acceptable to God.

Man since the fall is unacceptable to God. He has lost both original righteousness and supernatural grace, the one defined as lack or incompleteness, the other as the occasion of God's displeasure since without such grace man

[22] Bonaventura, *Breviloquium*, IV, 2, Thomas Aquinas, *Summa Theologica*, III, Q. 48, A. 1, Q. 57, A. 6.
[23] *Summa Theologica*, III, Q. 37, 44, 46, 47, 48, 49, 53, 55, 57.
[24] *Ibid.*, III, Q. 47, A. 2.
[25] Bonaventura, *Commentaria*, II, D. 19, A. 3, Q. 1; Thomas Aquinas, *Commentaria in Quatuor Libros Sententiarum Magistri Petri Lombardi*, II, D. 20, Q. 2, A. 3.
[26] Bonaventura, *Breviloquium*, II, 11; Thomas Aquinas, *Summa Theologica*, I, Q. 94, A. 3.
[27] Alexander of Hales, *Summa universae theologiae*, II, Q. 96, M. 1; Bonaventura, *Commentaria* II, D. 29, A. 2, Q. 2; Albertus Magnus, *Summa*, tr. 14, Q. 90, M. 1.
[28] Thomas Aquinas, *Commentaria*, II, D. 29, Q. 1, A. 2.
[29] Albertus Magnus, *Summa*, II, Tr. 16, Q. 98, M. 4.

is corrupted by concupiscence.[30] Since man was made from nothing, he was by such deficiency capable of falling, and his refusal of supernatural help through pride made such a fall inevitable.[31] Original sin then is a sickness of the soul expressing itself in the moral and spiritual corruption of man in all his parts. Man's natural endowments are in no sense impaired, but through their exercise he no longer seeks to please God. His acts therefore become positive acts of evil. Unbaptized infants, though guilty of original sin, are not able to do serious acts of evil and, when they die in their infancy, are not sent to hell with all its torments but to limbo, where they are denied the vision of God.[32] Since the scholastics believed that the soul of every man is created by God, not inherited from his parents, they were disposed to explain its tendency to evil through its intimate relationship to the body. Thomas Aquinas said, since the creation of the soul is simultaneous with the generation of its body, which is propagated in concupiscence, it, too, becomes sinful.[33]

Yet the total depravity of man, stressed so vigorously by Augustine, got weak and halfhearted support from the scholastics. **Human nature,** they felt, is not totally corrupted by sin; even in a state of corruption man is capable of great and splendid acts of good. As a sick man need not be totally disabled by his illness, so the natural man may in particular acts resemble in moral conduct the redeemed man. Indeed, he needs only a good dose of the medicine of grace to be made entirely fit again. Consequently the thirteenth-century divines looked on the salvation of man more as the correction and perfection of his old nature than as the creation of a new nature in Christ Jesus. Grace was given a mechanical interpretation: it is the infused power of God in human nature enabling man in disposition and deed to become well pleasing in God's sight and therefore to merit from God the rewards of heaven. The theologians attempted by such an interpretation both to ascribe to God the credit for man's redemption and at the same time to fix on man the responsibility for its attainment and the satisfaction of fulfilling its requirements. Hence the strenuous demands of monastic asceticism found both the divine initiative and the human sense of personal achievement and success in this doctrine. With Thomas Aquinas grace is allied more completely with the power and intelligence of God as the prime mover in creation than with his redemptive love as heavenly Father. With Duns Scotus, in contrast, the predominance of voluntarism gives to the divine will a fresh and in a sense a personal expression of itself in every redemptive act, so that the good deed ex-

---

[30] Alexander of Hales, *Summa,* II, Q. 122, M. 2, A. 1.
[31] Bonaventura, *Breviloquium,* III, 1, 9.
[32] Bonaventura, *Commentaria,* II, D. 33, A. 3, Q. 2; Thomas Aquinas, *Commentaria,* II, D. 33, Q. 2, A. 2.
[33] Thomas Aquinas, *Summa contra gentiles,* IV, 50, 4.

pressing the good will of the good man is more directly the gracious gift of a person than the effect of a cause. In this Duns more successfully delineates grace as outflowing love and free, undeserved mercy than his Dominican rival, but he does not escape from its materiality, for will is co-joined with habit, and the motive of man which causes his act is qualified by the habitus of the man himself. In his theology, as well as Aquinas', grace is infused, put quantitatively into human nature by the divine agency. It becomes therefore something man has which enables man to be and to do what he must to merit the favor and love of God.

Such grace is given to man through the sacraments, which are the means of his sanctification. These grace-infusing acts of the church are efficacious only when they are administered and received with the intention of accomplishing through them what Christ intended to be accomplished.[34] Thus the tangible things used, like water in baptism and bread and wine in the Eucharist, are the matter of the sacrament; while the words of institution read by the proper person are its form. There are seven sacraments, five of them corresponding to the development and care of the body, baptism to birth, confirmation to growth, Eucharist to nourishment, the means of development, and repentance and extreme unction to cleansing, daily and final; and two of them corresponding to social obligation, marriage to propagation and ordination to leadership.[35] Alexander of Hales and Bonaventura taught that only two sacraments, baptism and the Eucharist, had been instituted by Christ;[36] but Albertus Magnus, Thomas Aquinas, and even Duns Scotus traced all seven back to him.[37]

Thomas Aquinas undertook to demonstrate how a material object like a sacrament could contain, as medicine the power of healing, the supernatural grace of God. He said simply that God appointed such objects properly used to produce spiritual effects. The words of institution cause the object to become sacramentally what it is intended to be and thus to effect its divine purpose in the life of him who receives it. It is more, therefore, than a sign or symbol; it is an agent or cause; it is the vehicle for transmitting and infusing grace from and by God to and into men.[38]

Bonaventura was not willing to go so far. He said the sacraments are no more

[34] Bonaventura, Commentaria, IV, D. 6, P. 2, A. 2, Q. 1.
[35] The number was fixed by the Synod of London, in 1237. As late as the Third Lateran Council, 1179, the number had not been fixed. Hefele, op. cit., V, 713, 1056.
[36] Alexander of Hales, Summa, IV, Q. 8, M. 3, A. 2, S. 3; Bonaventura, Commentaria, IV, D. 23, A. 1, Q. 2.
[37] Albertus Magnus, Commentaria in Quatuor Libros Sententiarum Magistri Petri Lombardi, IV, D. 23, A. 13; Thomas Aquinas, Summa Theologica, III, Q. 64, A. 2; Duns Scotus, Commentaria Oxoniensia ad IV libros magistri Sententiarum, IV, D. 2, Q. 1, S. 4 and S. 5.
[38] Thomas Aquinas, Summa Theologica, III, Q. 26, A. 1, A. 4.

than signs which represent what God does directly and creatively on the human soul.[39] In this he was supported by Duns Scotus, who insisted that only a direct act of God—an immediate expression of the divine will—can effect man's salvation. In other words the sacrament is only an image of what God himself works in the human soul. However it is done, sacramental grace, all the doctors agree, is the means of making man worthy of salvation—that is, acceptable to God. These sacraments, if the intention which prompts their administration be that of the church, are effective regardless of the moral and spiritual character either of the celebrant or of the recipient. These gracious acts of God confer divine power in and of themselves.[40]

The individual sacraments received specific treatment by the schoolmen. Their chief contribution here was toward the understanding of the Eucharist, the problem of which was posed by transubstantiation. How could bread and wine still taste like bread and wine to the recipient after it had been transformed into the body and blood of Jesus Christ? The answer Thomas Aquinas gave was that its substance is transformed, but its accidents as a concession to the taste and digestion of the communicant remain the same.[41] Likewise, the entire body and blood of Christ is contained in either element, wine or bread, so that only bread need be given to the laity.[42] Christ exists locally with the Father in heaven yet substantially in the Eucharist in as many places and times as it is celebrated on earth. This sacrament applies directly to the individual the effects of the passion of Christ on the cross, and blots out his venial sins.

This sacrament is closely allied to that of penance where mortal sins are confessed to a priest, absolution is granted, and works of satisfaction assigned. Penitential discipline is extended into the unseen world through the doctrine of purgatory, where baptized Christians are given further opportunity to compensate for moral sins for which they had not had time to render satisfaction on earth. Likewise, the works of those alive profit greatly the dead when they are applied to them by means of supplication.[43]

Such a sacramental theory necessitated a conception of the church in keeping with it. The church was the temporal custodian of grace. At its head was the pope, whose authority as the vicegerent of Christ on earth, was delegated through archbishops and bishops to the priests who administered salvation to the people through the sacraments. Since the church was the custodian of the sacred and the sole guarantor of eternal life, the most servile priest was

[39] Bonaventura, *Commentaria*, IV, D. 1, P. 1, A. 1, Q. 2, Q. 3, Q. 4. *Breviloqum*, VI, 1.
[40] Alexander of Hales, *Summa*, IV, Q. 8, M. 4, A. 1; Albertus Magnus, *Commentaria*, IV, D. 1, A. 1; Bonaventura, *Commentaria*, IV, D. 1, P. 1, A. 1, Q. 5; Duns Scotus, *Commentaria*, IV, D. 1, Q. 1, S. 10.
[41] Thomas Aquinas, *Summa Theologica*, III, Q. 75, A. 5.
[42] Alexander of Hales, *Summa*, IV, Q. 40, M. 3, A. 5.
[43] Bonaventura, *Commentaria*, IV, D. 20, P. 2, A. 1, Q. 5.

in heavenly things mightier and more exalted than the mightiest and most exalted of temporal princes. The pope held the keys to the gates of heaven.

The thirteenth century was the century of great theological systems in the West. Medieval Latin theology reached the same fullness and completion of form with Aquinas and Scotus that Greek theology had reached with the Damascene in the eighth century.

IV. The Development of Art and Literature

The inward life of the church, represented by philosophy and theology, found outward expression in both art and literature. Not only were the ideas of the schoolmen preserved and taught in their terse, unadorned, question-and-answer method of speaking and writing, they were also given concrete embodiment in the exquisite productions of the artisans and artists of the thirteenth century. The Gothic cathedral with its stained glass windows and flying buttresses was a book in stone which everybody, ignorant as well as learned, could read and understand. Likewise, the miracle and morality plays, the stories of Reynard the Fox and the *Romance of the Rose*, together with the biographical sketches of the major saints in *The Golden Legend*, the songs of the troubadours and Meistersingers, and the sublime masterpiece of *The Divine Comedy*, captured the soul of the masses and fired their imagination with a zeal not experienced in the preceding centuries. It was almost as if Homer or Virgil had been reincarnated and the glory of Greece and grandeur of Rome, at least in their epic qualities, had been made to live again in this Latin civilization of the thirteenth century. The singularity of the time lay in its religion. Christanity was the motive and theme of these masterpieces of art and literature.

Gothic art reached its most perfect form in splendid churches and great cathedrals, many of which were completed during the opening years of this century. Gothic was essentially an adaptation and therefore transformation of the older Romanesque patterns to satisfy more completely the aspirations of the people for the supernatural. Consequently it applied the high, pointed arch, which signified the infinite, to the ribbed vaults, and removed the thrust of the nave vaults from the inside to the outside of the church in the form of flying buttresses. The style gave careful attention to artistic detail in stone and glass, so that builders had to be artists as well as artisans. It originated out of an effort to erect churches which were completely vaulted in stone, and it strove to find the most appropriate and exquisite ornamentation for these new structures.

At first, as an architectural pattern, it was entirely ecclesiastical. As time went on however it was adapted to other buildings as well, so that city halls, palaces, residences, even barns were erected in Gothic style. It displayed the qualities of growth, freedom, and sincerity. Freedom enabled it to be widely applied so that it could meet almost any architectural need; growth (it was appropriate in any size) gave it the look of incompletion as if its perfect fulfillment lay in the infinite future with God. And sincerity, its plain columns and straight lines, made people believe that it always meant what it seemed to them to say—that it was authentic and therefore everlasting.

It originated in northern France toward the close of the twelfth century, spread immediately to England and Germany, and soon dominated all Western Europe outside of Italy. Notre Dame in Paris and Lincoln Cathedral with its Angel Choir (so beautiful that men attributed its design to angelic architects and craftsmen) in northern England stand today as illustrations of the Latin proverb that he wins every point who mingles the useful with the beautiful. Chartres and Mont Saint Michel, the former inland, the latter high and lifted up on the rock-bound coast of the sea, together form a perfect ensemble in stone, each telling the complete story of man's hunger and thirst after righteousness and the satisfaction of all his needs in Jesus Christ. A most striking feature of Gothic art as it is displayed in the medieval cathedral is the stained glass windows. Some of these windows, like the celebrated "Prodigal Window" at Chartres, re-enact the stories of the Bible and the careers of the saints; while others, like "The Five Sisters" at York, which is a group of five lancet windows, tell no story at all but flood the cathedrals with dim religious light. The mixing of colors, the formation of design, the durability and utility as well as the exquisite loveliness portray an artistic skill in glass unsurpassed in all history.[44]

The most remarkable feature of the Gothic cathedral is not the massive grandeur of its over-all design, nor is it the delicate perfection of any one of its individual parts. Rather it is the manner of its creation, for the cathedral was a community project covering frequently a time span of several generations and in which everyone participated according to his capacity and interest. A king or nobleman gave the quarry whence the stone came, but the inhabitants of an entire town or province hauled the stones to the site, chiseled them to fit into place, and executed the designs which made them beautiful. This meant that each person had to be prepared for what he did. As a rule each workman was the designer as well as the actual maker of the particular work he was assigned to do. Perhaps he made some gargoyles or little angels, perchance only a single statue of a saint; whatever he did he knew would be a tangible memorial to his faith and devotion as long as the cathedral stood.

Consequently, judging from their products, the guilds, or technical schools where these artisans were trained as apprentices for their tasks must have been superlative. A town not only had to build its own cathedral but also to train

---

[44] E. Corryer, *L'architecture gothique* (1891); C. H. Moore, *The Development and Character of Gothic Architecture* (1904).

its workmen to finish it in all its parts. A boy who had an inclination toward a certain craft would present himself when he was no more than ten or eleven years old to a guild of workmen. If he should after a year's time show an aptness for that work he was allowed to remain as an apprentice. He was given room and board, no more, and he assisted the workmen at their jobs observing as best he could their skill and industry. After four or five years he became an accredited workman himself—at the lowest level—that of a journeyman, one who traveled from place to place doing different jobs and at the same time observing how others in foreign places worked and so perfecting his art. He won promotions in his guild by his skill alone, so that the most honored artisans were those who did the best work. The aim of every ambitious artisan was to become a master workman. Most skilled workers after their period as journeymen settled down in their native town as members of the guild of their particular craft, and so their talents were devoted to the service of their community. The majesty of Rheims Cathedral, for example, is testimony to the artistic talent and industry of the citizens of Rheims. Cities and provinces competed with one another, not alone in the prowess of lord and knight on the battlefield, but also in the brain and brawn of men who gave the first of their toil to God in stately temples of worship and praise.

Guilds were genuine fellowships where all able-bodied members supported those who were sick, where regulation prescribed that each person fulfill his religious obligations in full, and where each delighted to do his best for the good of the whole. Consequently the name of the individual worker was not carved on his work since he expected his work to survive only as it was blended into perfection in the work of others.[45]

A few names however broke through this cloud of anonymity which characterized the art of this century. Cimabue and Giotto, for example, punctuated the development of painting so that with them the frozen, artificial, stereotyped work of preceding ages gave way to the natural and lifelike. This development heralded the Renaissance. Cimabue, whose great work was accomplished in the second half of the century, found Giotto, an even greater genius, and started him on his course. The former artist's Madonna, carried in triumph by the grateful public from his studio to the Church of Santa Maria Novella in Florence, caused that section of the city where it was painted to be called the "ward of joy," while his mosaic in the apse of the cathedral at Pisa shows his fidelity to nature and to the tradition of classic art. Boccaccio said of the latter artist that everything he painted was so true to the object it portrayed that it appeared to be that object itself. Giotto was able successfully to introduce many different figures on the same canvas and to display them with such variety and freshness that each figure appears

45 W. E. Wilda, Das Gildenwesen im Mittelalter (Halle, 1831).

like a new picture. Pisa, Lucca, Arezzo, Padua, Milan as well as Assisi, Florence, and Rome all abound with his masterpieces.[46]

The Gothic art of the thirteenth century is majestic and triumphant. Suffering and grief are not portrayed at all except in the damned. The Savior always wears a regal expression: the *Beau Dieu d'Amiens*, as its name implies, makes Christ charming, winsome, attractive—inviting men to come unto him, love him, even enjoy him. The people of Amiens with "charming appropriateness" call this statue their beautiful God.

The religious instruction and inspiration provided the people in beautiful but inanimate form in Gothic art was translated into life and movement in the **mystery and morality plays** which they saw and in which many of them actually participated as actors. These plays had originated, probably in England, in the eleventh century, but they became a fixed popular institution in Western Europe in the thirteenth century, when out of the experience of trial and error their motif was fixed and their type perfected. A mystery play, strictly speaking, is the dramatization of an event from the Bible, such as the life of Abraham or the missionary career of the apostle Paul; while a morality play is an allegory in which abstract virtues and vices are personified and made into living characters telling and displaying the story of their deeds on the stage. A miracle play is differentiated from a mystery by being based on the life of a saint or some post-Biblical character or event. All three types are essentially religious in plot and purpose. Perhaps these earliest plays, written by the clergy, were in Latin; but, since they were for the people and soon were taken over by the guilds and performed by their members, their language became the popular vernacular. Their progress was speediest in France, where they laid the form and became the rough model of the later drama. The mystery plays followed most closely the ecclesiastical calendar and were generally performed during the season when the event they portrayed had occurred. They were performed inside the church, in the churchyards, and on the squares of villages and towns. The Franciscans popularized the mystery plays and made them effective dramatic auxiliaries to their proclamation of the gospel through preaching.[47]

The **prose writing** of the thirteenth century included history, biography, and travel as well as theology and philosophy.

Geoffrey of Villehardouin (ca. 1160-ca. 1213) wrote, as a witness of what he saw, the record of that crusade during the pontificate of Innocent III which eventuated in the capture by the Latins of Constantinople.[48] The de-

---

[46] J. Strzygowski, *Cimabue und Rom* (1888). Carlo Carra, *Giotto* (1925). Giorgio Vasari, *Lives of the Artists* (ed. Betty Burroughs, N. Y., 1946), 3-6, 16-22.

[47] K. Young, *The Drama of the Medieval Church* (Oxford, 1933); *Some Texts of Liturgical Plays* (1909).

[48] Best editions of Villehardouin's work are those of Natalis de Wailly (Paris, 1872-74) and E. Bouchet (Paris, 1891).

scription of the sailing of the fleet from its home base and of its arrival before the walls of Constantinople is comparable to some of the best passages in Herodotus and Thucydides. Villehardouin was the first historian to write in the popular vernacular in France and, for that matter, perhaps in all Europe.

Matthew Paris (d. 1259), an English monk of St. Albans, vies with the Venerable Bede for the place of highest honor among the monkish historians of his nation. As Bede was the first among them in time, so Matthew was the last, and his vehicle of expression was Latin. He was not as careful as he ought to have been in his use of documents. Still he seems to have been fair in his judgments and absolutely fearless in telling what he felt should be told. "The case," he testifies, "of historical writers is hard. If they tell the truth, they provoke men; and if they write what is false, they offend God." His *Chronica maiora* is a polemic neither for church nor for throne; it is genuine history voicing the true sentiments of the emerging English nation.[49]

Less impartial is Joinville's (1224-1317) biography of his friend, King Louis IX of France.[50] One cannot read the book without realizing at once that its author loved as well as admired his subject. Like Villehardouin, Joinville wrote in the vernacular. He has left us the best biography of a well-known figure written in the thirteenth century. Another biography, perhaps of superior worth from the literary point of view but of less renown because of the parochial accomplishments of its subject, is Jocelyn of Brakelond's life of Abbot Sampson. This is the British counterpart to the French biography of Louis IX. Its style is straightforward and simple, so that the career of the man it presents is given without any waste of words. Probably no more graphic and life-like portrait of a man had been given in all literature before Boswell's *Life of Samuel Johnson*.

Vincent of Beauvais heralded the pioneering work of the French encyclopedists of later times by writing a compendium of general information in the preparation of which he consulted all the authors whose works he knew, both sacred and profane.[51] This encyclopedia of information garnered from the past was matched by new information about the world and its inhabitants supplied by contemporary travelers and explorers who wrote about what they had seen and heard.

Marco Polo, whose accounts are so strange that his contemporaries thought them imaginary, described his long journey into Asia and his stay at the court of Cathay (China). The mariner's compass and gunpowder were to Western Europe in the thirteenth century what rockets and space travel are to us. Likewise, the flow of oil, which Marco saw in Armenia and which he said

[49] *Chronica maiora* (ed. H. R. Luard, 1872-83), 7 vols.
[50] Best editions of *Histoire de St. Louis* are those of Natalis de Wailly of 1868 and 1874.
[51] J. B. Bourgeat, *Études sur Vincent de Beauvais, théologien, philosophe, encylopédiste* (Paris, 1856).

would burn like wood and at the same time soothe the skin of camels, was sheer fantasy to his fellow countrymen. The travels of Marco Polo were written first in French by a Pisan named Rusticiano, to whom Marco related them while a military prisoner at Genoa.[52]

Other noteworthy travelers whose explorations have survived in literary form were Friar John of Carpini, who went as Innocent IV's emissary to the Tartars in northern Asia; Friar William of Rubruk, who traversed much of the same territory and for similar reasons at the behest of King Louis IX of France; and the monks, Odoric, a Franciscan missionary to the East, and Hayton, a Premonstratensian brother. Hayton was reared in Armenia, lived in France, and wrote for the West of conditions in the Near East as he knew them as a boy. Both these monks supplied much of the data for Sir John Mandeville's classic of the next century.

A literary work in prose of supreme excellence, belonging to neither hagiography nor travel, and yet not qualifying as theological or philosophical in the nice meaning of those terms, is William Durandus' *Significance of Divine Offices*, or more properly known as *The Symbolism of Churches and Church Ornaments*. Really this is, like the *Imitation of Christ*, devotional and inspirational. Its popularity in the late Middle Ages is registered by the fact that, when printing was invented, it was the first book to appear from the press (John Fust, 1459) after the printing of the Psalter (1457 and 1459).[53]

More remarkable than the prose of this century is the poetry. The lyric, which gives expression to the poet's own inner feelings, as well as the epic, which sets forth some great event, was developed with technical skill and the inspiration of genuine sentiment and understanding. Illustrating this are the Latin hymns of the thirteenth century, comprising in rhymed verse some of the best religious poetry ever produced. The *Stabat Mater* and the *Dies Irae*, considered by many critics the greatest hymn ever written, provide us with samples of the incomparable worth of Latin hymnody.

The *Dies Irae* is so powerful in its effect that as it is sung the auditors can almost hear the thunderous cataclysm of the end of the world, the creaking noise of opening graves, and the trumpet sound of the angel Gabriel calling to judgment the quick and the dead. At the same time we are made to see the "King of tremendous majesty" seated on his great white throne ready, in mercy and justice, to mete out everlasting rewards and punishments. The appeal of this poem lies not alone in its eschatological theme but more in the intense earnestness and pathos of its author, its stately meter and triple rhyme, and the majestic simplicity and musical solemnity of its language.

Next to it in worth no doubt is the *Stabat Mater*, written by a Franciscan

---

[52] *Marco Polo* (ed. Yule and Cordier, London, 1903).
[53] James J. Walsh, *The Thirteenth, Greatest of Centuries* (N. Y., 1952) chs. 6-8, 14, 15, 25, especially pp. 400-414.

monk, Jacopone da Todi, who transfers the sorrows and hope of his own heart to the heart of Mary the Mother of Our Lord as she stood watching her son's death on the cross.

> By the cross, on which suspended,
> With his bleeding hands extended,
>   Hung that Son she so adored,
> Stood the mournful Mother weeping,
> She whose heart, its silence keeping,
>   Grief had cleft as with a sword.
> —Tr. D. F. MacCarthy.

These medieval religious lyrics are more original than their classical fore-runners of the Augustan age, for the Romans aped in Latin the Greeks, while these thirteenth-century masters used an old language to express sentiments and ideas as much their own as if they had invented a new language for their expression. Ecclesiastical Latin is hardly the Latin of classical antiquity, though its grammar and syntax may be the same.

While Latin was being refined through hymnody, the popular languages were finding literary expression in the songs of the Meistersingers and the troubadours, many of whom could not read or write themselves yet whose oral gifts of lyricism were extraordinary. Walter von der Vogelweide, the most familiar of the Meistersingers, when he was asked where he discovered his melodies, replied that he was taught them by the birds. It is no wonder that children loved him, since he championed their cause:

> Children with rod ruling—
> 'Tis the worst of schooling.
> Who is honor made to know,
> Him a word seems as a blow.

Walter's contemporary, Hartmann von Aue, warmed the hearts of his fellow Germans by his pure romanticism, while Wolfram von Eschenbach, without formal education enough even to read or to write, created the Percival story around which Wagner built his opera.

Contemporary with the Meistersingers of the Rhineland and Bavarian hills were the troubadours of Provence and southern France. As the Meistersingers glorified nature, so the troubadours sang of love. Arnaud de Marveil, Bertrand de Born, and Peyrols, who wrote a lament over the death of Richard the Lion-Hearted, as well as William St. Gregory, who preferred the theme of war to love, are celebrated examples. Thomas Carlyle said that because of the Meistersingers and troubadours of the late twelfth and early thirteenth centuries "suddenly, as at sunset, the whole earth had grown vocal and musical."

There emerged during the twelfth and thirteenth centuries three great **national epics,** built around ballads which had been accumulating in the folk life of the common people for centuries: the *Cid* in Spain, which extols the valor and military accomplishments of the champion of Christianity against the Moors in the eleventh century; The *Nibelungenlied* in Germany, the cantos of which contain perhaps the best description of battles, savage and terrible, in poetic form in the history of world literature; and the Arthurian legends in England, in which the quest for the Holy Grail is presented as the chief concern of a king and his knights, and spiritual attainment is thereby made the supreme aim of a whole nation. In regard to each of these, perhaps one poetic genius put in finished form what his people had given him in their folk songs and ballads, as Homer must have done in his *Iliad* and *Odyssey*. Some attribute to Walter Map, a Briton (Englishman) and chaplain to Henry II, the honor of first refining the Arthurian legends, which captured the imagination in French and English alike. The author of *Cid*, if it were produced by one person, is unknown; while the *Nibelungen Lied* doubtless emerged after the famous meeting of the Meistersingers on the Wartburg, which probably took place in the year 1207. Here again one man no doubt produced the masterpiece. These epics have had far-reaching and enduring influence on the literature of Western Europe.

No one of them, however, was as popular in its own time as *Reynard the Fox*, a French collection of animal stories with morals for men and women, after the ageless pattern of *Aesop's Fables*; the *Golden Legend*, written by Jacobus de Voragine, a distinguished Dominican preacher whose working life spanned the second half of the thirteenth century, a book on the lives of all the major saints of the church since the time of Christ; and the *Romance of the Rose*, in which the happiness of the poor man is contrasted with the disappointment and pain caused by the ambition, greed, and selfishness which wealth so often imposes.[54]

Medieval literary art reached its zenith in **Dante** (1265-1321), the Florentine politician, the Italian advocate of the revival of the secular Roman empire of antiquity, and the world poet who summarized in unforgettable verse the whole of the Middle Ages. Dante's first expressions in verse were those of the troubadour, of the Italian model, to be sure, which refined the sensual love of French minstrels into a more dignified and enduring type of devotion. When he was only nine years old, he saw a beautiful little girl named Beatrice, who awakened in him an adolescent desire for the opposite sex. Nine years later at eighteen he saw her again; this time her exquisite beauty and gracefulness of manner fired him with the possessive passion of mature youth. Yet this passion was never gratified physically. Dante never had any social relationships with Beatrice, who shortly after the second meeting married a banker and one year later died. Dante married and became the father of

[54] *Ibid.*, chs. 10-13.

several children. Yet his passion for Beatrice, sublimated into poetry, was the driving force of his romantic life.

Dante supported the cause of the upper middle class in Florentine politics, was elected in 1300 to the city council (called Priory), and was so strong a factor in government that when the opposition gained control (1302) he was exiled. The year 1302 was the turning point in his life. Though he expected only a brief exile from his native town, and therefore left his wife and children behind, he never lived in Florence again. His book *De monarchia*, though it championed the political cause of the German emperor against the pope, was not influential enough to persuade Henry VII when he invaded Italy in 1310 to restore Dante to power in Florence. Indeed, it, together with the poet's letters and denunciations, provoked the Florentines to declare Dante forever exiled. Though six years later this exile was lifted on all political criminals if they would pay a fine, walk through the streets as penitents, and accept a brief imprisonment as punishment for what they had done, Dante proudly refused. He lived for awhile in Gubbio at the monastery of Santa Croce, later at Verona, and finally in Ravenna, where he died.

The Divine Comedy, so named because it ends well for those who pass through the pain of purgatory into the bliss of eternal life, consists of three parts: Hell, Purgatory, Heaven. Each part, called a canticle, has thirty-three cantos to correspond with the number of years Christ lived on earth. One canto is added to the first canticle to make an even hundred. The verse form is that of a three-line series, the second line of which rhymes with the first line and also with the third line of the verse triad which follows. Religious symbolism therefore is expressed in the structural pattern of the masterpiece. The poem has, after the manner of the medieval interpretation of Scripture, three meanings: the literal, the allegorical, and the mystical. Thus its literal theme is the state of the souls after death; its allegorical is man as divine justice rewards and punishes him according to his own virtues and sins; and its mystical is the inspiration which moves men away from the misery imposed by temporal self-indulgence to a state of happiness occasioned by the love of eternal things.

This book, which consumed the long years of Dante's exile and which was finished only three years before his death, summarized everything he knew and was. Since Dante was a catholic man, felt and thought like his contemporaries—though of course more creatively and intensely than they—and was marvelously skillful in comprehending all that went on about him, the *Divine Comedy* is a synthesis of the Middle Ages.

In it we see hell as the medieval man pictured it—a deep funnel reaching down to the very center of the earth. It contains oceans of fire filled with burning bodies, the pain of which is never relieved. Purgatory, bad enough from our point of view, is, in contrast to hell, a mountainous cone of nine levels, symbolizing man's ability to cleanse himself of sin and selfishness and gradually through the good offices of the holy church to mount upward to salvation. Heaven is pictured, in Ptolemaic form, as nine hollow crystal spheres which can expand to accommodate more souls and which revolve about the earth. Each sphere contains its own planet and a multitude of stars which are set like gems in a crown in the divine intelligence and sing the praises of the Creator. God's will is the directing force of everything in paradise; like a magnet it draws everything to itself. Heaven too has its gradations. There is the seventh heaven of pure delight.

The *Divine Comedy* is almost a revelation. Its concern is not with this world but the next. Its author was looked upon as one who had been to hell and then had come back to earth again to warn others by what he had seen. This book is the greatest writing of the Middle Ages; and its author ranks with Homer, Virgil, Shakespeare, and Milton as one of the greatest literary figures of all time.[55]

V. Organizations for Social Betterment

The predominant other-worldliness of the inhabitants of the thirteenth century, registered so clearly in their art and literature, did not render them indifferent to the problems and concerns occasioned by living in the present world. Their religion taught them that they were pilgrims and sojourners as in a strange land. Heaven was their home. Yet their eyes were not closed upon the terrain they traversed, nor were they in such a hurry that they could not stop to aid another on the way or leave some relic of their journey which would occasion a more comfortable passage for those who came after them.

The **hospital** as an institution to house the sick and to cure them of their disease originated in the thirteenth century. It began in Rome at the personal initiation of Pope Innocent III, who invited Guido of Montpellier, an observer of the medical success of the Arabs in southern Italy, to come to Rome, there to organize and manage its first hospital. It was situated near St. Peter's and named, appropriately enough, in honor of the Holy Ghost. More than one hundred similar institutions, inspired by this act, were instituted in Germany alone during the thirteenth century. It is reasonable to suppose that both England and France were equally vigorous in their response to this universal need. We know, for example, that Hôtel Dieu in Paris became fully endowed so that it could care by means of its own resources for the needs of its patients, while the Hospital of St. Louis was given all the money raised from a special tax on salt for its upkeep. St. Bartholomew's, probably the oldest hospital in

[55] *Oxford Dante* (ed. E. Moore and P. Toynbee, 1923). J. A. Symonds, *Introduction to the Study of Dante* (London, 1899). K. Vossler, *Medieval Culture; an Introduction to Dante and His Times* (N. Y., 1929), 2 vols.

Britain, and St. Thomas', both in London, became thriving institutions. London's notorious institution for the insane, Bedlam, the name of which has provided a common term for confusion, was originally Bethlehem, a hospital founded in the middle of the thirteenth century and later converted to the use of the insane. Lepers, who had wandered loose like animals throughout the earlier Middle Ages, terrifying all who happened to cross their path by the sound of their bells, were now cared for in isolated leprosaria. These institutions led in the next three centuries to the virtual eradication of this dreadful disease from Western Europe. These hospitals, either directly through the papacy, the episcopacy, the monastic and mendicant orders or else indirectly through a pious ruler like Louis IX of France, were altogether the offspring of the church.

Likewise Innocent III chartered through John of Matha and Felix of Valois the Trinitarian Order (1198), the purpose of which was to ransom persons kidnapped or captured by pirates and infidels. These two men, John and Felix, had on the same night an identical dream. Each learned of what had happened to the other through mutual acquaintances, and together they appealed to the pope for an interpretation. As a result Innocent commissioned them for this great mission of Christian charity. A similar order designated for the same purpose was founded by Peter of Nolasco and Raymond of Pena-fort, Frenchmen as were John and Felix, twenty years later (1218), called the Order of the Blessed Virgin of Mercy. These men vowed if necessary to sacrifice their lives in order to ransom Christian captives, and Peter of Nolasco made this sacrifice. Gregory IX was the pontiff who recognized this order.

Work in behalf of others did not prevent men from combining in behalf of themselves. The trade guilds furthered better working conditions among their members, and the emergence of cities and towns together with great commercial leagues such as the Hanseatic, led to the demand for political privileges. Eight hours of work, eight hours of recreation, and eight hours of rest is not the slogan of modernity alone; in the Middle Ages a work day as set by the guilds was frequently no more than seven hours long. Four o'clock always was closing time on Saturday and on the eve of a feast day. Members of the guilds were required to attend social as well as business functions and to bring their wives or sweethearts with them. When absent they were fined. Each member paid regular dues, so that guilds became some of the most wealthy and therefore most powerful institutions of society. Their major social contribution was the sustenance of a member and his family when he was disabled or his family was orphaned.

The cities, influenced by their guilds, insisted on having representation in the government. The German cities had their representatives in the imperial parliament; Spain too under Alfonso the Wise made democratic concessions;

while after Magna Carta parliamentary government began its long process of evolution in England. Outside the guilds and even the churches there were charities practiced by towns and communities. Tolls were levied, a portion of which went to the aid of the poor. Insurance against hazards such as fire and even shipwreck were common features of the guilds. Every parish was a school in good citizenship—roads and common lands were kept, police and fire protection given, and community enterprises executed on the local level under the direction or at least with the counsel of the priest. Graft and political corruption were far less common then than now. Pensions were provided on disability when a man had been a member of his guild for as many as seven years.

Commerce became more than local, provincial, or even national during the thirteenth century. The Hanseatic League was the most famous medieval agency of international trade. It embraced the merchants of more than seventy cities (largely German), had houses in the chief trading cities of Western Europe, controlled a fleet capable of blockading a whole nation (i.e. Denmark), and proved to be a cartel as strong and at times as ruthlessly dangerous as any of the great monopolies of modern times. In order to protect its trade secrets it required its members abroad to remain celibate, guarded its establishments at night with fierce dogs, and had members living on its business premises at all time. That its members might stand up against torture it adopted initiation rites which were fierce and cruel. For example, an initiate was suspended by a rope in a chimney above a fire burning refuse which gave off nauseous odors of the worst stench imaginable. Though the social influences of this league of merchants were not entirely beneficial, still Hansa, more than any other agency, established international commerce and by trade effected constant intercourse and understanding among European peoples.

Industrial mass production did not exist in the Middle Ages, and the manner of making things was the same in the thirteenth century as we have already described it in the days of Charlemagne. Monastery and abbey remained perhaps the principal "factories," while the village and town fairs were the chief outlets of distribution and trade. However a few inventions were made in the thirteenth century: spectacles, the alarm clock, the double-jointed compass, and above all else, writing paper which transformed manuscripts into books. Cartography and geography, the scientific allies of trade, received now more exact attention; the famous map in the cathedral at Hereford, England, is amazing, though its topography mixes allegory and myth with reality.

The thirteenth century saw the beginning of law as an institution of the people. Though the church had been governed by canon law almost since its inception and the Roman empire in the East had inherited and preserved the legal customs of antiquity, the West since Charlemagne's time had meted out what was alleged to be justice in the most arbitrary, haphazard, and frequently unjust fashion. The manner of ascertaining guilt and the punishment inflicted for the crime varied according to local custom and habit and the disposition of the individual magistrates in charge. During many years of the Middle Ages trial by ordeal was common practice almost everywhere, and it continued in practice in some places even after the enlightened conscience of the church moved against it.

The country where law as we understand it today originated as an institution of the people to protect themselves against themselves was England. This had begun to take place in the twelfth century when the laws of Essex, Mercia, Northumberland, and the other provinces gave way to "the law and custom of the realm"—a phrase first used with propriety by Ranulf de Glanville, who had helped no little to bring it about under Henry II (1154-1189). Henry's son John, grudgingly and of necessity, accepted the provisions of Magna Carta (1215) in which many of the principles that are basic in current legal practice were enunciated for the first time: (1) if a person dies intestate, his properties, under the supervision of the church, shall go to the nearest kin; (2) a man's first debts however shall be paid before the distribution is made; (3) the widow's portion is guaranteed; (4) the debts of a father shall not be paid if they impoverish his children who are under age at the time of his death; (5) a man's properties cannot be taken from him by government officials without the payment of money; (6) there shall be a fixed place for common pleas. Likewise, legal enactment dealt with circumstance and job as well as personal rights applicable to all. Weights, measures, and coins were standardized by the Assize of Measures (1197). The Statute of Merchants (1283) and the Merchants' Charter (1303) radically improved the regulation of trade and guaranteed the rights of the middle-class traders. Finally, the method of trial was determined. Trial by combat had given way to trial by court in the Assize of Clarendon (1166), and this latter method was common practice in England by the close of the thirteenth century. It consisted in the submission of a man's case to a jury of twelve knights appointed by the sheriff. Torture was proscribed in the examination of witnesses. What took place in England was not duplicated procedurally elsewhere in the West. All the same the thirteenth century gave birth to most of the national legal systems of the various states of Europe. This was pre-eminently true in France and Germany, i.e., the Institutes of Saint Louis and the Mirrors of Swabia and Saxony, published by Frederick II in Germany at the diet of Metz. It was also true in Hungary and Poland. Since God was dependable and managed the universe, not arbitrarily but according to the fixed pattern of his own nature, so men should be governed, not by the whim or caprice of kings and emperors, but according to constant justice established by law. The institution and use of law was a gradual but great gain for the people.[56]

VI. The Rise of Universities

Equally significant and beneficial, though less extensive in its immediate outreach, was the rise of the universities, marking a revolutionary stage in the development of higher education.

The university was a distinctly **medieval creation**. It was not therefore the revival of an institution of Greek and Roman antiquity which the Dark Ages had lost and which the twelfth and thirteenth centuries had rediscovered. Antiquity had had its schools, and Athens had continued as the capital of the learned world down to the reign of Justinian. Yet such ancient prototypes found their medieval counterparts in the monastic and cathedral schools which heralded the universities yet were substantially different from them. The disciplines of antiquity had not been organized into faculties with standardized curricula, programs of study, and the awarding of degrees. Likewise, the monastic and cathedral schools which kept aglow the light of learning throughout the Dark Ages were informal and restricted. The former especially were designed for a specific end—namely, the training of the postulants according to the demands of the order—and any instruction outside the order was incidental and in the main inconsequential. Indeed, to have had outside students in great numbers would have proved prejudicial to the order. The latter, less narrow in aim and management, since they were situated in the towns where the people lived, became the germs of the later universities. Only a very few of them actually emerged into universities, however, illustrating the parochialism of their nature and the fluctuating quality of their instruction. As late as 1215 a conciliar law had to be renewed forcing every cathedral to reserve at least one benefice for a schoolmaster. Rheims, Chartres, Laon, and Tours were famous cathedral schools; they passed into relative obscurity with the rise of the universities. Indeed, throughout most of the Middle Ages, the reputation of a given teacher determined entirely the worth of the school in which he taught. In most instances he was his school. Wherever he went his school and pupils migrated with him. The founding of the university gave security. Teachers gladly joined its faculty as students matriculated in its classes.

In **structure** the universities resembled the trade guilds. As a matter of fact they were the trade guild of teachers. As a worker remained an apprentice or journeyman until he was admitted into full membership in his guild, so a

[56] E. Jenks, Law and Politics in the Middle Ages (N. Y., 1898). W. S. McKechnie, Magna Carta, a Commentary on the Great Charta of King John (Glasgow, 1905). Hansische Geschichtsblätter (Halle and Leipzig, 1871-1908), 14 vols. J. J. Walsh, op. cit., ch. 21-24, 26.

pupil remained a student until he was licensed by his university as a master. Consequently the earliest form of academic degree was simply the license to teach. A master was nothing more or less than a qualified teacher of the arts. A Doctor of Theology or of Medicine was a person deemed competent to teach those sciences himself. The very word "university" was borrowed from the vocabulary of trade. Originally it meant guild or corporation in general. It came later to specify a learned society of masters and students.

The stages of higher education, then as now, were two: undergraduate and graduate. The curriculum of the first stage was the trivium and quadrivium—that is, general instruction in the arts. The subsequent graduate study which alone qualified a person to become a master or doctor was specialization in a given field: the arts and philosophy, medicine, or theology. To be licensed as a master a scholar had to pass a rigid examination including success in public disputation and lecturing. The guild of teachers became the most exclusive in Europe, for knowledge acquired by intelligence as well as industry was the most difficult to master of any trade.

In the north of Europe the corporate structure of this new social institution was organized about the teachers. Masters themselves came together, set up their school, distributed their duties, determined fees, and made the rules of procedure. In the south of Europe by contrast, students organized the guilds and hired masters to instruct them. In both instances the examinations were in the hands of the masters, and they alone decided who qualified to be admitted to their ranks.

Learning was dependent upon books, scarce in number and scattered among the various libraries of the West. Their cost was prohibitive for student or even professorial ownership. The cheapest book brought the equivalent of two hundred dollars in our currency, or the entire earning capacity of a teacher for one year. An entire Bible for example was worth ten thousand dollars; Priscian's grammar was bought at the price of a house and lot; while an entire vineyard was exchanged for a missal. It took a whole year for a hard-working copyist to make a Bible. Cluny Abbey, which boasted one of the best monastic libraries in Europe, had at the beginning of the thirteenth century only five hundred and seventy volumes; while Canterbury, probably the largest cathedral library, had but five thousand. This meant that standard texts had to be employed in learning the trivium and quadrivium. These were read aloud in class; the master made his comments; while the student took his notes on a slate; and memory was an indispensable tool of learning. Seldom did any library have more than one hundred volumes. The teachers and the graduate students read them in stalls, where the books were anchored in place by heavy chains.

Since lectures were of necessity the **method of pedagogy** in the medieval university, much depended upon the skill of the master in the art of public discourse and communication. At Paris, for example, he was required to lecture without notes. New students were advised by old to hear a man at least three times before registering for his course. Almost from the beginning of the university the complaint was made that the elective system was lowering the standard of education and that masters were making their courses easy in order to attract more students, gain more fees, and win popularity. It was from this method of instruction by lecture that the title of professor was added to that of master and doctor. It meant simply proclaimer. In Italy, where student control was predominant, the managers of the guild were rectors chosen by the students from their own ranks. These rectors saw to it that the masters followed the regulations laid down by the students through the guild. They had to begin and to end their lectures at a specific time. If they went over time, students were free to walk out. Every master had to make a monetary deposit at the beginning of the term from which fines imposed on him by the student rectors were paid. He had to receive permission from the students for a leave of absence even for one day. Student committees checked on the conduct and skill of the masters. By boycotting a man's classes in large numbers, students expelled unsatisfactory teachers from their posts.

The most famous university in the West was the University of Paris, which received its charter as a guild of teachers from Pope Innocent III in 1210. It had evolved from the Cathedral School of Notre Dame made famous in the twelfth century by William of Champeaux and Peter Abelard. By the middle of the thirteenth century it had faculties of renown in theology, canon law, medicine, and the arts. Each faculty had its dean. The students in the school of arts elected a rector as well, and he gradually became the head of the entire university. There were in the beginning no special buildings for the university. The cloisters of Notre Dame were used for classes as well as lecture halls rented by the teachers. Students secured guest houses called **Hospices** and lived according to nationalities. Consequently the student body divided itself into four great national groups: French, Norman, Picardese, and English, each with its own proctor, or supervisor.

Though in the number of students, the reputation of scholars, and the brilliancy of accomplishment no other educational institution was able to rival the University of Paris, still it was not the only university to emerge in the West in the twelfth and thirteenth centuries. Both Pavia and Bologna in Italy claim to be older, while at the opening of the thirteenth century Oxford in England had as many as three thousand students, and as the century progressed the kings of Castile, Leon, Catalonia, Baleares, and Portugal established by royal patronage universities on the Iberian peninsula. Cambridge too arose from an exodus of masters and pupils from Oxford in 1209. Salerno in southern Italy was famous for its medical faculty, influenced in the beginning by Arabic science. Bologna had the greatest law school. Toledo developed a faculty in Oriental studies. And Paris, dominated by the Dominicans and Franciscans, was the theological and philosophical center of the world. Oxford began to acquire colleges and revenue as well for their upkeep. That university had its own houses of instruction and dwellings for masters and students alike.

These universities seem to have been open to anybody who wanted to attend them, who knew Latin, and who could pay each master his modest fees. There were no entrance examinations. During the five years of undergraduate study in the trivium and quadrivium there were, at least during the thirteenth century, no formal examinations at all. Recitations and disputations, involving as they did all students in oral exercises, were enough to convince the incompetent of their incompetence. Thus students themselves thinned their own ranks, so that in the main only the scholastically fit survived. However, when a student stayed the full time and indicated his desire to become a master, he was subjected first, to a general examination on the contents of his entire course of studies and secondly, to a public disputation in which he defended a thesis against all comers. The master's degree itself came only after subsequent study under a particular master, apprenticeship as a teacher, and an exhaustive examination by a committee appointed by the head of the university in the field of the student's specialization. A master was not supposed to present his student for this graduate examination unless he felt he was thoroughly qualified and could readily pass.

Student life itself was rough and ready. Since artificial illumination was poor, daylight was used for reading and writing as well as for lectures and recitations. Consequently the nights were free. Since students frequently were as young as thirteen or as old as forty and since they were unmarried, the norm of their behavior was not the same as that of the families in the town about them. As a result there was frequent conflict between town and gown. At Oxford, for example, the bell of St. Mary's summoned the students, while the bell of St. Martin's summoned the townfolk to battle in the intermittent fights between them. In Paris, as late as 1269, a proclamation had to be issued against students for breaking into houses and stealing, for carrying off women, for raping virgins, and for beating and at times killing members of the population. The young clerics were no exception. The University of Paris had to require an oath of all students not to take vengeance on their examiners when they failed to pass their examinations. Houses of prostitution flourished to cater to the sexual demands of the students. Prostitutes in Paris were bold enough to wander the streets enticing men, even young clerics, into brothels. When they refused to enter, the whores jeered at them and called them homosexuals. Each national group in Paris was characterized by its behavior: the English as drunkards, the French as effeminate, the Germans as obscene, and the Flemish as fat and greedy and soft as butter. It seems that fear of hell did not deter even the young theologians from their pleasures. Sin was not excluded from the universities any more than it was from the other areas of life.

Regardless of what he did with his leisure hours, study was the main business of the student. Many bright boys were supported by their local communities, so proud were they of their sons' talents. Monasteries afforded free food and lodging to students as they traveled back and forth from home to university. In the thirteenth century the school term lasted eleven months with only a few days free at Christmas and Easter.[57]

The university seems to have become the most enduring social estate bequeathed by the Middle Ages to modernity. While most other medieval institutions have been entirely dissipated, this legacy from the past is still intact, with its capital funds increased a thousandfold and paying high and regular dividends. It, like every other institution of the thirteenth century, was the creation of the Christian church.

[57] Hastings Rashdall, The Universities of Europe in the Middle Ages (Powicke-Emden Ed., Oxford, 1936), 3 vols.

Chapter Eleven

Christendom Before the Fall of Constantinople

(1303-1453)

THE 150 YEARS BETWEEN THE DEATH OF BONIFACE VIII AND THE FALL OF CON-stantinople marked the end of the Middle Ages.

Social unity in the West under the hegemony of the papacy gave way to nationalism and the diversity of competing states. The Eastern empire, which had been in closest union with the Eastern church for a thousand years (since Constantine in the fourth century), collapsed before the oppressive arms of Turkish infidels. Islam now displaced Christianity, both politically and so-cially, in the area of its earliest expansion as it had already displaced it in the land of its birth. The Eastern churches under the crescent assumed once again their ancient role of the church under the grim shadow of the cross. Christianity in this period was, so it seems in retrospect, being prepared for a revolution. In the East it awaited disestablishment. In the West it antici-pated reformation and reconstitution in a new pattern of multiple denomina-tional and national parts.

I. Eastern Christianity in the Last Years of the Empire

The best days of the Greek church in the Middle Ages were behind it. The vicissitudes of its existence in the fourteenth and first half of the fifteenth century were characterized by either indecision leading to no action at all or else impulsiveness effecting hasty changes which themselves had to be changed. The emperors continued to speak as if their voice were that of the Orthodox Catholicism they considered themselves to personify. But their promulgations no longer were echoed quickly and distinctly as before in the response of their subjects. Eastern Christianity appeared more and more as the property of the monks and less and less as the patrimony of the emperors and the sycophantical patriarchs of Constantinople whom they caused to be elevated to their sees.

This is seen especially in the efforts toward the reunion of the Greek and Latin churches, which, in the East at least, constituted the chief ecclesiastical concern of this period. This concern was largely imperial. The Byzantine rulers who espoused the cause of union did so almost entirely for political reasons. They saw the impending disaster to their dominions from the rising power of the Turks. Consequently they were willing to pay the price of relinquishing religious autonomy in order to keep political independence. The people, together with the majority of their religious leaders, were either blind or indifferent to this eventuality. Consequently they viewed the matter of union entirely as an ecclesiastical issue. They preferred their own religious habits to those of the West. If a choice had to be made between union of the churches and capitulation to the Turks, many of them actually preferred the latter. They could not forget the subjugation of Constantinople by the Latins during the first part of the thirteenth century. The word "crusade" in their mind was synonymous with invasion and slavery.

Hence the union between Latin and Greek Catholicism which Michael Palaeologus had struggled to the end of his reign to uphold collapsed with his death (December 11, 1282). Michael had used it as an effective military shield against Angevin attacks from the West; and, since the power of Charles of Anjou had disappeared, the union was no longer needed as a political tool by the Eastern emperor. Consequently Andronicus II (1282-1328) reversed the policy of his predecessor. Michael's obedient patriarch, John Beccus, was exiled to Brusa, while those clergymen whom Michael had expelled or imprisoned were honored as martyrs of the faith. Riots broke out in Constantinople against unionists. A fanatical reign of terror ensued, and the monks became virtual dictators of Eastern religious policies. Indeed the subservience of Andronicus II to untutored public opinion prepared the way for the fall of the empire. He excited the West to attempt another crusade against the East (abortive to be sure) and allowed the Ottoman state to form almost without being noticed. Narrow nationalism and religious exclusiveness were the chief characteristics of the Greek social character throughout the remaining years of the Middle Ages. The damage to the empire by the forty-six-year reign of Andronicus II could not be repaired.

Andronicus III (1328-1341) became anxious over the situation and sent to the papal court at Avignon two emissaries in behalf of union, a Venetian by the name of Stephen Dandola and the celebrated Constantinopolitan humanist Barlaam. They argued in behalf of an ecumenical council to consider union. But Pope Benedict XII would not consent to this on the grounds that one had already been held at Lyons and the East had under Michael Palaeologus subscribed to its findings. The Greeks retorted that this council was unacceptable since their delegates had been appointed by the emperor and not by the patriarchs of the great sees. However, negotiations in behalf of union were continued by succeeding Eastern rulers. The regent Anne of Savoy acted in behalf of her son, John V Palaeologus (1341-1391), who later on his own account visited Rome and abjured the schism in the presence of the pope on the steps of St. Peter's (October 21, 1369). His rival John Cantacuzene (1347-1354) worked for a council, and Manuel II (1391-1425) visited the West in person to plead for aid against the Turks. Not however until the reign of John VIII Palaeologus (1425-1448) was the council achieved.

The Western Council of Basel sent an embassy in 1433 to Constantinople to inform the emperor that it was superior to the pope, that the Western Emperor Sigismund was its sponsor and protector, and that, if the Greeks would recognize it by sending delegates, the Eastern empire would receive money and men from the West to defend Constantinople. This offer received favorable response, and, after six years of wearisome negotiations, a council on union between the Eastern and Western churches was convened at Ferrara, April 9, 1438. The Eastern Emperor John VIII Palaeologus headed the Greek delegation, which consisted of the patriarch of Constantinople, Joseph, seventeen metropolitans, and innumerable bishops and scholars. Due to the ravages of the plague the council was transferred to Florence (January 10, 1439). Everyone was given the privilege of free discussion and debate. Yet in order to effect agreement public consideration of issues was discarded for committee consideration, where compromises were reached on the filioque phrase in the Western creed, the Eucharistic bread, the nature of the pains of purgatory, the words of the consecration of the host, and even the primacy of the pope. As a result, on July 6, 1439, **the decree of union**, ratified alike by the pope and the Eastern emperor, was read by Cardinal Julian Caesarini in Latin and Bishop Bessarion in Greek; the two spokesmen kissed each other; and the entire council with the Eastern emperor at its head bowed down before the pope. After the council the major Eastern churches subscribed to the union: Armenian Church (November 22, 1439), Jacobite (February 5, 1441), Ethiopian (February 25, 1443), and the Syrians, Chaldeans, and Maronites (April 26, 1442). It looked as if complete unity had been achieved.

But such unity was only apparent. It had been effected organizationally—not spiritually. The Eastern delegation was greeted on its return to Constantinople (February 1, 1440) by jeers and stones from the populace. Mark of Ephesus, who had opposed union at Florence, became the most popular ecclesiastic in the East. The emperor's own secretary deserted him and entered a monastery. Mount Athos became the center of opposition to the union. Though the union was solemnly proclaimed in St. Sophia (December 12, 1452) in the presence of the emperor, the former patriarch Gregory, and the papal legate Constantine, the people did not accept it. St. Sophia was almost abandoned as a place of worship, and Greeks said openly they would rather see in their midst the turban of a Turk than the red hat of a cardinal.[1] The patriarchs of Alexandria, Antioch, and Jerusalem repudiated the Council of Florence and declared their brother of Constantinople a heretic. Likewise, the schismatic groups which acknowledged Florence continued in polity and faith as they had before the council; their corporate life was already circumscribed and restricted by Islam, which had engulfed them in its conquests. The attitude of the faithful in Constantinople was the attitude of church people in all parts of the East, the Balkans and Russia alike. Each nation was content with ecclesiastical nationalism. Orthodoxy had adjusted itself socially and politically to the principality where it had to live. The dying words of the Emperor Manuel to his son John VIII had been prophetic, "The pride of the Latins and the obstinacy of the Greeks will never agree. By wishing to achieve the union, you will only strengthen the schism." [2]

Though politically the empire was shrinking almost to the vanishing point and though ecclesiastical developments were no more than negotiations—successful in conference but failing to achieve implementation by the people—Eastern Christendom had an **intellectual and cultural renaissance** reminiscent of its glorious era under the Macedonian dynasty. It seemed that "on the eve of her final ruin, all Hellas was reassembling her intellectual energy to cast a last splendid glow." [3]

The schools of Constantinople were the best in the world. They drew Greeks from Sparta in the west to Trebizond in the east. At the same time they attracted Latin scholars from Western Europe, especially Italy. They helped to spark the Italian Renaissance which was about to dawn. Thessalonica and Sparta, now called Mistra, joined with Constantinople in sharing in the remarkable cultural advance of the fourteenth and fifteenth centuries.

This epoch produced a company of talented historians, each of whom in his own way told the tragic tale of the demise of an empire. Nicephorus Gregoras, a man of encyclopedic learning, which ranged from theology and philosophy to history and astronomy as well as rhetoric and grammar, wrote a monumental history in thirty-seven books on the Latin and Nicene empires, while John Canamus, John Anagnostes and a group of four—Phrantzes, Ducas, Chalcocandyles, and Critobulus—described the events prior to and after the fall of Constantinople. Only one historian dealt with far-off events. Xanthopulos wrote an ecclesiastical history which stopped with the year 911.

Philosophy, grammar, rhetoric, and poetry as well as medicine and jurisprudence flourished during this period. Distinction was achieved by many writers, but no person of real genius in any one of these fields emerged.

[1] CMH, IV, 613-626.
[2] G. Phrantzes, *Annales*, II, 13, in CSHB (1839); MPG, CLVI, 784B.
[3] E. Lavisse and A. Rambaud, *Histoire générale du IV me siècle à nos jours* (Paris, 1893-1901), III, 819.

Poetry now found expression in the popular Greek of the people, but the Byzantine empire did not produce a Dante. The greatest figure was in philosophy. Gemistus Plethon, who died in Mistra (Sparta) in 1450, tried to do for Plato what the thirteenth-century scholastics had done for Aristotle. It was he who conceived the idea of the Platonic Academy at Florence.[4] Art beyond literature was confined mostly to icons and exquisitely illuminated manuscripts.

Theology in the East as well as in the West was the chief intellectual pursuit of this period. The theologians' one great concern was the ecclesiastical issue of reunion with the West, and their writings are polemics either in support of or in opposition to the union. The greater talent seems to have been in favor of the merger, though the less talented but more numerous theologians of the opposition had the ear of the people. Nicholas Cabasilas alone rose above this issue, duplicating for the Greeks the achievements of the Western mystics of the same epoch.[5]

Ecclesiastical activity, now restricted by the contraction of the empire itself to the territory around Constantinople, was intensified by a struggle within the church between the "zealots" and "politicians." The "zealots" wanted to free the church entirely from imperial control, while the "politicians" were willing to continue in the age-old pattern of co-operation between church and state. The leaders of the "zealots" were the monks, who gradually attained the ascendency. The defeat of the plan of reunion was their victory. The chief center of monkish piety and power was Mount Athos. The days of the election of the patriarch of Constantinople from the class of imperial courtiers or even secular clergy were rapidly passing. The fourteenth and fifteenth centuries began the custom of filling the highest positions of the church by monks, especially those of Mount Athos.

The fall of the Byzantine empire came in the spring of 1453. The West sent reinforcements to the East to meet the attacks upon Constantinople by the Turkish Sultan Mehmet II (1451-1481). Greeks and Latins, patriarch and cardinal, said mass together as a united church for the last time in St. Sophia on the night and early morning of May 28-29, 1453. The Emperor Constantine XI Dragases (1448-1453) went from that mass to his death. He died, sword in hand, at the Gate of St. Romanus, exclaiming, "I will die with my city! God forbid that I should live as emperor without the empire!" [6]

II. The Babylonian Captivity of the Papacy

The paralytic nostalgia for the past which marked Eastern Christianity

---

[4] *De Rebus Peloponnesiacis Orationes duae; Oratio prima,* in *Analekten der mittel-und neugriechischen Litteratur* (ed. A. Ellissen, 1860), IV, 2.
[5] MPG, CL, 367-726.
[6] M. Ducas, *Historia byzantina,* XLI, in CSHB (1834).

during this period and which gave it at least the appearance of respectability, if not of success, was counterbalanced in the West by an inordinate concern for the affairs of the present. A new order was being born in Western Europe. The fourteenth and fifteenth centuries were times of national self-consciousness and in places and to a degree even of self-realization. France and England, for example, became nations. This nationalism in the political sphere clashed violently with the internationalism of the medieval church, especially the papacy. As long as the papacy and the nation sought the same goal—supreme power for itself to the exclusion of its rival—the increase of one meant of necessity the decrease of the other. The rise of French nationalism and the swift decline of the papacy were simultaneous. Indeed, for seventy-three years the popes were scarcely more than minions of the French kings. Their government was an adjunct to that of France. Avignon on the Rhone, not Rome on the Tiber, was the ecclesiastical capital of the West. These seventy-three years (April 13, 1304—January 17, 1377) are known as the period of the Babylonian Captivity of the Papacy.

The tragedy of Anagni was more than a personal disaster which befell the reigning pontiff Boniface VIII. It signalized in its lugubrious spectacle of terror and violence the demise of the medieval papacy. On September 7, 1303, the murderous mercenaries of King Philip the Fair of France, with the legists William of Nogaret and Sciarra Colonna at their head, entered the public square of the town of Anagni where the pope was in residence at the time, and replaced the papal banner by the fleur-de-lis of France. The pope was kidnapped and personally abused. Though he was liberated two days later by the enraged inhabitants of the countryside, he survived the shock only long enough to return to Rome, where he died. His successor, Benedict XI, one of two cardinals who had stood steadfastly by his side on the occasion of his arrest, was forced on April 13, 1304, to abandon Rome for Perugia, where he was poisoned three months later by a young man disguised as a woman who brought him a present of newly ripened figs (July 7, 1304).

Clement V (1305-1314) was the first of the seven popes who resided at Avignon. He was elevated from the archiepiscopal see of Bordeaux when he was forty years old. By the time he was forty-five he was already an old man shattered by the constant, unrelenting pressure exerted on him by his neighbor across the Rhone, Philip the Fair of France. He died after a strenuous pontificate which lasted within one year and two months of a decade. It was inaugurated by Philip's efforts to condemn Boniface VIII posthumously, and Clement was intimidated into permitting a trial, the verdict of which fortunately was never reached. However, the evidence presented, false though most of it was, was extremely damaging to the papacy as well as to the memory of Boniface.

This unhappy pontiff also presided over the liquidation of the Order of Knights Templars, whose properties were coveted by the king of France. Though there were rumors of irregularities within the order and alleged debaucheries and unnatural expressions of lust and passion, still the motive for the trial was less moral than political, and the prosecutors were as venal and wicked as the defense. Technically the properties of the Knights Templars were assigned to the Knights Hospitalers; but, when Philip the Fair presented his bill of expenses incurred on account of the Templars, the Hospitalers found themselves impoverished rather than enriched by their legacy. Jacques de Molay, Grand Master of the Templars, was sent to the stake (March 12, 1314), protesting his innocence and appealing to God to settle his account with his accusers at the last day. One month later Pope Clement died (April 20) and had to face De Molay at the judgment.

Clement V was unfortunate in his relations with the rulers of Germany and England. He was plagued by the heresies of the Beghards, Beguines, and the Spiritual Brethren. The Beghards and Beguines contended that the perfect man is freed from all moral obedience and can enjoy immorality without compunction of conscience. The Spiritual Brethren, who held that poverty is mandatory, advanced also the notions that baptism only wipes out sin, that it does not confer virtue, and that the rational soul is not the form of the body and that Christ was still alive when pierced with the lance. These heresies, together with the crimes of the Templars, were condemned by the Council of Vienne (1313). Clement V's pontificate, though crowded with the doing of many things, was nonetheless negative and of mean worth.[7]

The second pope to reside at Avignon, in contrast to the first, was an able and successful ruler. The dilatory and procrastinating habits of his predecessor did not carry over into his manner of governing the church. John XXII was a compromise candidate who won the election after a two-year period during which the cardinals could not reach agreement. He was seventy-two at the time and lived on to govern the church for eighteen years (1316-1334), reaching his eighty-ninth birthday. Rumor had it that, when the cardinals could not obtain a majority for any one candidate, they turned to this aged member of their group and asked him to resolve the deadlock by naming a man whom they promised to accept as pope. Immediately he responded to their request by naming himself. This is probably apocryphal, but it illustrates clearly the confidence John always showed in himself. (1) He dealt with the Spiritual Brethren and their contention that poverty lifts a man above the level of secular clergy and pope and that the use of property is a concession to weak-

---

[7] *Regestum Clementis Papae V ex Vaticanis Archetypis* (Rome, 1885-1892), 7 vols. E. Baluze, *Vitae Paparum Avenionensium* (ed. G. Mollat, 1914-1927), I, 1-106; 551-566. Hefele, op. cit. (Leclercq), IX, 326-338, 345-358, 423-431. J. Gmelin, *Schuld oder Unschuld des Templerordens ?* (1893), 2 vols.

ness. (2) He condemned the *Defensor pacis* of Marsilius of Padua and John of Jandun, which declared that sovereignty resides in the people represented by their majority, and accordingly the supreme power of the church resides, not in the papacy or the episcopacy, but in the council, composed of clerical and lay delegates representing the people. (3) He opposed the political schemes of the German emperor, Louis of Bavaria, in whose service the proponents of the *Defensor pacis* worked. (4) From the antipope whom Louis and Sciarra Colonna raised up in Italy he won back the city of Rome. (5) He carried out the decision of the Council of Vienne to teach theologians the language of infidels so that the gospel might be spread to foreign lands. (6) He inspired a naval crusade to victory against the Turks. (7) He revived over the West the system of annates, whereby the living of a vacant benefice was taken over for one year, to bring new revenues to the declining economy of the church. John was also a vigorous preacher. Notwithstanding in a sermon on All Saints Day (1331) he espoused heresy by saying that the souls of the blessed dead do not enjoy the full sight of God until after the general resurrection. This little old man, said to have been ugly to the degree of being repulsive, nonetheless must be classified among the greatest of the popes.[8]

His greatest fault was the fault of omission: he made no effort to move the papacy back to Rome. Indeed John XXII, as well as his predecessor, Clement V, and his three immediate successors, was too much a Frenchman to be willing to abandon Avignon, protected as it was by the French crown, for the trials and tribulations of Rome. The College of Cardinals was controlled by the French, and the Italians and French looked on one another as bitter rivals. Rome was not considered a safe place for a French pope to live.

The accomplishments of John's successors in the papal office were not great: (1) Benedict XII (1334-1342) laid the foundation of the splendid papal residence at Avignon, as if he intended the papacy to remain there always; failed in his negotiations with the Greeks for union, in his attempt to end the dispute with Louis of Bavaria, and in his effort to launch a crusade; and turned down the invitation from the Romans to return home.[9] (2) Clement VI (1342-1352), relieved as he was of the conflict with the empire by the succession of Charles IV, who was called "The Priest's Emperor," was nonetheless embarrassed by the activities of a dictatorial fanatic, Cola di Rienzi, in Rome. He managed to turn a deaf ear to the pleadings of Brigid of Sweden that he restore the papacy to Rome.[10] (3) Innocent VI (1352-1362)

⁸ *Vatikanische Akten zur deutschen Geschichte in der Zeit Kaiser Ludwigs des Bayern* (ed. S. Riezler, 1891), pp. 1-577. *Acta Ioannis XXII*, in *Pontificia Commissio ad redigendum Codicem Iuris Canonici Orientalis Fontis*, Series III, Vol. VI, Tome II. Baluze, op. cit., I, 107-194.
⁹ LP, II, 486.
¹⁰ Baluze, op. cit., I, 241-308; II, 335-433.

restored order to Rome through the services of Cardinal Albornoz, who had the ability to win the hearts as well as the minds of men; reduced expenses by depriving the papal court of its luxury; and protested against the establishment of the electoral college (the seven privileged electors) to choose the emperor of Germany without consulting his will. (4) **Urban V** (1362-1370) re-established good relations between the papacy and Germany by crowning Charles IV Holy Roman Emperor, himself returned to Rome (October 16, 1367), and there on the steps of Saint Peter's accepted the Greek Emperor John Palaeologus' abjuration of the schism. Yet on September 5, 1370, he left Rome for France in an attempt to avert hostilities between that country and England. England renounced her vassalage to the Holy See, incurred by King John, and refused to pay any more tribute to the papacy. Urban died, disillusioned and brokenhearted, in France, thus losing the opportunity of re-establishing the papacy at Rome.[11]

This privilege was won by his successor **Gregory XI** (1370-1378), also a French prelate, who had the hardihood, despite personal preference, to move to Rome, there to die among a foreign people whose language he did not understand. This act was heralded by open war between Florence, Perugia, and Milan and the papacy. Yet Gregory himself was a man of peace. He settled, at least for a time, the strife between France and England and put an end to the war in Spain. Gregory's mentor and guide in gentle offices of kindness and restoration was Catherine of Siena, who deserves almost as much recognition as he for restoring the papacy to Rome. On January 17, 1377, as Gregory entered Rome, the days of the Babylonian captivity came to an end.[12]

III. The Western Schism and Its Aftermath

On September 20, 1378, less than two years after this welcome return from exile, an even worse calamity than the Babylonian captivity of the papacy befell the Western church. The schism began. Latin Christendom divided into **two ecclesiastical allegiances,** one with its capital at Rome, the other with its capital at Avignon. The diplomacy of the various nations determined their alignments. France naturally supported the Avignon papacy; and Scotland, southern Italy, and Spain followed her example. The Scandinavian countries, Poland, Hungary, Germany, England, and the greater part of Italy were loyal to the Roman pontiff.

This great split in the body of the Western church, if not the direct effect of patriotic nationalism in which the French could not get on with the Italians, was nonetheless influenced and conditioned by prejudices of land and language. Certainly no doctrinal, liturgical, or even administrative prin-

[11] Baluze, op. cit., I, 349-414.
[12] Baluze, op. cit., I, 415-467. Mourret, V, 54-144.

ciple divided the church. The schism arose over a papal election by the cardinals which many of them later came not only to regret, but also to repudiate. The first man they elected was Italian, the man they later chose in his stead was French.

Gregory XI died, muttering in his delirium terrible predictions concerning the future of the church. Could it be that this Frenchman really in his heart regretted having moved his see back to Rome? He warned his cardinals "to distrust men and women who, under the cover of religion, relate visions of their mind." He could have meant none other than Catherine of Siena, who sent him as by the finger of God from Avignon to Rome.

When the cardinals assembled in conclave at the Vatican (April 7, 1378), they were greeted by a threatening mob of people demanding an Italian, preferably a Roman, as their pope. Impatience was added to insistence so that after a day and night of waiting the people began to crowd into the Vatican itself. Then it was that on the motion of a Spanish cardinal, Pedro de Luna, Prignano, cardinal archbishop of Bari, was elected pope; he was an Italian, though not a Roman. When the people now cried in their excitement for a Roman, the cardinals tried to persuade the aged Tebaldeschi of St. Peter's to pretend he was pope. Instead he announced the election of Prignano, who was accepted by the people and enthroned on Easter Sunday, April 18, scarcely a week following the election. Presumably all the cardinals pledged him their loyalty and obedience. He took the name of Urban VI.[13]

Urban VI had a violent temper as well as an autocratic, over-bearing spirit. One day he complained publicly that there were too many Frenchmen in the College of Cardinals. He insulted two cardinals personally by calling one an imbecile and the other a libertine. He silenced a third in open consistory by ordering him to desist from stupid babbling.[14] It is little wonder that, with the heat of summer, one after another of the cardinals requested the privilege of a vacation. Soon the court of Urban VI was bereft of its foreign ecclesiastical princes, noticeably the French, who constituted the majority of the College at the time of his election.

The majority of the cardinals at their own initiative met in the old city of Anagni at the foot of the Apennines, declared the election of Urban VI null and void due to the coercion of the mob (August 9, 1378), and elected Robert of Geneva, a Frenchman, in his place (September 20).

Robert was a military man as well as a prince of the church. He had commanded the armies of Gregory XI in the war against Florence, Perugia, and Milan. He had ordered a horrible massacre at Cesena (February, 1377), and has been compared, quite properly, in his public career with Herod and Nero.[15]

[13] N. Valois, Le Pape et Le Concile (1909), I, 54-82.
[14] Hefele, op. cit., X, 39-41.
[15] Muratori, Rerum italicarum scriptores (1761), XVI, 526.

In his private life however he was exemplary; and after his elevation to the papacy he behaved more seemly, certainly with less violence, than his rival at Rome. Robert had been one of the cardinals who, with Pedro de Luna, had espoused the cause of Urban VI and had facilitated his election. On account of the French majority of which he was the undisputed leader, he might have had the office for himself at the time when Urban was elected. Consequently he and his colleagues now went back on their own original decision. They were in reality more French than Catholic. They re-established the papal headquarters at Avignon, and Robert took the name of the first Avignon pope and became Clement VII.

The Western church was now about evenly divided in its obedience. Though Urban's despotism alienated some of his own cardinals who transferred their allegiance to Clement and though he bathed Italy in the blood of his wars of revenge and hate, he nonetheless managed to remain a pope until his death (October 15, 1389) eleven years and one month after the schism. Clement survived him by five years (1394). The easiest way to have ended the schism would have been for Urban's cardinals to have elevated Clement to the papacy on Urban's death. This they did not do. Indeed, three men succeeded Urban in the Italian-Roman section of the church before the schism was healed: Boniface IX (1389-1404), Innocent VII (1404-1406), and Gregory XII (1406-1415). Likewise, Benedict XIII (1394-1422) followed Clement VII in the French-Avignon section of the church.

The schism was not healed by the papacy at all. In fact union was effected in spite of and even with the opposition of the papacy. Pedro de Luna, who became Benedict XIII, was an able lawyer as well as ecclesiastic, and he found fault with every proposal made for effecting unity. Though his Italian counterpart was less active and apparent in his opposition, he was nonetheless by his indifference just as effective. Plans of unity came from the universities, especially the University of Paris, and their theologians. It was effected finally by a general council of the Western church. To make this possible it was necessary to recognize in the church a power superior to the papacy.

The **conciliar theory,** propounded by Henry of Langenstein, chancellor of the University of Heidelberg in Germany, and Jean Gerson, chancellor of the University of Paris in France, and supported by Pierre d' Ailly and most of the secular rulers of the West, was that the church is subject to the same rules that regulate any other social institution. Its effectiveness must be judged in the light of the purpose for which it exists. It exists to secure the good order and peace of Christian people everywhere. This is not being accomplished through schism. Consequently the papacy, ineffective as it is, must be changed for the better by a general council. Providential events themselves prove the supremacy of council over pope. This was always the case in the ancient church.[16]

The cardinals, fourteen of the Roman and ten of the Avignon hierarchy, against the will of their respective pontiffs, called a general council which began its sessions on March 25, 1409, at Pisa.[17] Its attempt at union proved abortive. It fell under the management of a shrewd Italian politician and adventurer, Balthasar Cossa; and, instead of uniting Christendom under one supreme pontiff, it further divided it among three. It elevated, on Cossa's nomination, Pierre Philargis, a septuagenarian of scholarly achievements, to the papacy; and when he died one year later, Balthasar Cossa himself became pope as John XXIII (1410). Hence the major portion of Christendom fell under his government with its seat at Rome, which Gregory XII had vacated. Rumor ran that John XXIII had in his young manhood been a pirate on the Sicilian seas. Certainly his instinct always was predatory and selfish. His own interests seemed constantly to run athwart those of the church. Nothing he did therefore was beneficial and salutary. The conference he convoked in Rome was ineffective (1412-1413). It is said that when he invoked the Holy Ghost, an owl flew down and lighted on his shoulder. It had to be driven away with a stick.

This miserable pontificate dragged on until it was brought to an end by another council, this time under the auspices of the Holy Roman Emperor Sigismund, which was convened at Constance, November 1, 1414. All three popes were invited to its sessions, but only John XXIII dared to attend. Perhaps he imagined he would outsmart its delegates as he had those of Pisa five years earlier, for he swore in the devil's name as he journeyed thither that he would trap all the foxes who were out to trap him. This council was thoroughly representative; all the great nations of the West sent official delegates. There were twenty-nine cardinals, three patriarchs, thirty-three archbishops, one hundred and fifty bishops, more than one hundred abbots, and about three hundred theologians. More than three thousand harlots too were moved into Constance to take care of the physical needs of the delegates. Three men however dominated the assembly; they were theologians: Pierre d' Ailly, Zarabella, and Jean Gerson. Their ideas gained the ascendency: (1) the supreme authority of the church resides in the ecumenical council; (2) the supremacy of the pope is only accidental, useful, to be sure, in normal times, but subject always to the judgment and appraisal of the council; (3) popes can err and even become heretics; (4) popes are only the first officers of the church. They should be removed when they fail to serve.

This council therefore decreed the deposition of John XXIII and ordered

[16] Gersonius, Opera omnia (Antwerp, 1706), II, 54-73.
[17] Hefele, op. cit. (Leclecq), VII (Pt. 1.), 1-69.

him to be put in safe custody by the Emperor Sigismund. Gregory XII submitted his resignation, which was gladly accepted. Benedict XIII was abandoned by his prelates and fled in exile to Spain, where he survived for five more years on the rock of Pensicola. This council elected its own pope. Otto Colonna was chosen under the title of Pope Martin V (November 11, 1417). Consequently after a period of thirty-nine unhappy years the schism was healed.[18]

The Roman Catholic Church reckons Urban VI and his three Italian successors as the legitimate popes. Clement VII (Robert of Geneva) and his successors as well as John XXIII (Balthasar Cossa) are looked upon as schismatics. Consequently Gregory XII, in Roman Catholic opinion, made the election of Martin V valid by himself having first resigned.

Unfortunately the healing of the schism did not restore vitality and health to the church. It left more than an ugly scar on the outward ecclesiastical body. It dispossessed it inwardly in its regal spirit. Certainly the papacy did not become in the fifteenth century what it had been in the thirteenth. The single world of pope and emperor was a thing of the past in the West. As Europe was divided into nations, so the papal states became one of the many small Italian principalities, and in secular affairs the pope was found a petty despot like the doge of Venice, the king of Naples, or the prince of Ferrara.

Likewise in ecclesiastical affairs the pope was now the tool of the council. The Council of Constance decreed that another ecumenical council must be called five years after its adjournment. Thereafter an ecumenical council must be held every seven years. In other words it recognized itself and other bodies like it as the supreme government of the church. No matter what the pope thought about the council, public opinion throughout Christendom was all in its favor. Even the East saw some hope in these gatherings and consented to enter into their deliberations.

Perhaps the councils might have become the proper organs of reformation, restoration, and revival in Western Christendom. Such they did not prove themselves to be. They not only set themselves at odds with the papacy, but they degenerated into argumentative and antagonistic factions which split the main body asunder and caused a conciliar schism not radically different from the papal schism which the Council of Constance had overcome. The Council of Basel, for example, divided into the councils of Basel and Florence, the latter of which accepted the guiding influence of the pope while the former did not.

The three popes of this troublesome era were **Martin V** (1417-1431), **Eugenius IV** (1431-1447), and **Nicholas V** (1447-1455). Martin V, to whom

[18] *Ibid.*, VII (pt. 1) 71-584. Mansi, XXVII 519-1240; XXVIII, 1-958.

the very mention of the word "council" evoked terror,[19] tried to regulate affairs between his see and the various nations by means of concordats, or individual treaties. Nonetheless when the five years expired he called a council to meet at Pavia and because of pestilence moved it to Siena. Then almost immediately he disbanded it since war between France and Britain and the struggle in Spain against the Moors prevented most of the delegates from coming.[20] Seven years later, frightened by threats if he did not call another council, he summoned the delegates to meet at Basel and then conveniently died.[21]

His successor, Eugenius IV, who won the election by promising to subject himself and his office to the council and by agreeing that no declaration of war, political alliance, collection of tithes and other revenues, or even appointment of cardinal, bishop, or abbot could be made by the pope without a majority vote of the College of Cardinals,[22] nonetheless carried on a constant fight with the Council of Basel until he bypassed its deliberations by attending its rival, the Council of Florence. This latter body, as we have seen, effected at least temporarily the reunion of Christendom.

Nicholas V ignored the Council of Basel, which finally disbanded itself (April 25, 1449). He brought crowds to Rome to celebrate the jubilee of 1450, and encouraged secular art and literature to the degree that he has been called the Father of Humanism.[23]

The advent of nationalism and the extent of its power is witnessed in the fact that the most influential religious visionary of this period, Joan of Arc— who gave a supernatural reason for everything that she did—was committed entirely to the cause of her native France, which she equated with the cause of God. Though she was burned at the stake (Rouen, 1431) as a heretic, her chief accuser was the nation she opposed, England, making her death in reality political, not religious. Seven years after her death she had her way for, to use her own expression, the English "were kicked out of France." [24]

The church, especially the papacy, now needed saving as much as any other segment of society. By 1453 it was on the verge of reaching its nadir of effectiveness and strength.

IV. Interpretations of Christianity and the Church

The thought patterns of this period as well as the religious practices were of a piece with institutional developments. They all marked radical change.

---

[19] Monumenta Conciliorum generalium saeculi decimi quinti (Vienna, 1857-1896), I, 66.
[20] Valois, op. cit., I, 76-80.
[21] O. Raynaldi, Annales Ecclesiastici, 1198 to 1565 (1679), a. 1431, numbers 5-7.
[22] Valois, op. cit., I, 100.
[23] Rerum Italicarum Scriptores (ed. Muratori, Milan, 1734), III, cols. 907-960.
[24] W. P. Barrett, The Trial of Joan of Arc (1931). CMH, VIII, 232-272, Mourret, op. cit., V, 145-175.

The unity of the thirteenth century had been shattered into pieces intellectually as well as organizationally.

Mysticism flourished—especially in Germany. The herald or forerunner of this movement was Meister Eckhart, who died in 1327. Since he published nothing himself, we are dependent for our understanding of his teaching upon his disciples. He was condemned by Pope John XXII because he proclaimed that our external moral acts will not sanctify us and also because he taught that we are incapable of expressing what the attributes of God are. He conceived of religion as a marriage between the soul and God in which the soul is purified altogether of its sin and creatureliness and transformed by being entirely absorbed into God's uncreatedness. These ideas were further developed by John Ruysbroeck (1293-1381), John Tauler (d. 1361), and Henry Suso (1295-1366). Ruysbroeck, for example, described true religion as man's hunt, with the Holy Ghost as the hound, for the divine. Tauler insisted that man must give up all that is accidental and transitory, destroy his self-will, and abandon himself completely to the Holy Ghost. Suso's work is autobiographical: he portrayed his own sufferings and showed how they had led him into the exquisite love of God. The pattern laid down by all these mystics is a familiar one. Their three steps are (1) purification, (2) illumination, and (3) unification. Man attains perfection by renunciation of self. He must strive in thought, word, and deed to imitate God as he reveals himself in Jesus Christ. The end is ecstasy and the loss of self in the totality of the divine nature.[25]

One of the loveliest books of all time came out of this period. It bears the name *Imitation of Christ*, which is perhaps an accurate description also of its contents. Its environment was the Brothers of the Common Life, organized after the rule of Saint Augustine in 1395. Its author, Thomas à Kempis, is said to have been a member of the order. He put together in four parts the maxims or ideals practiced and cherished by the founder of the order, Gerard Groote, and recommended by him to his spiritual sons. Apart from the Bible itself probably no other book has had a greater influence on the devotional life of the church.

In contrast to mysticism, stressing as it did personal experience and the moral requirement of imitating the behavior of Jesus, there was at the same time the externalizing of religion through sacramentalism. The select few were mystics. The masses, including the vast majority of the clergy, were sacramentalists. Louis of Bavaria, the foe of Pope John XXII, proved his orthodoxy by repeating the Apostles' Creed and the Lord's Prayer. Saying the Ave Maria so many times was an easy substitute for keeping the Ten Command-

[25] Meister Eckhart, *Schriften und Predigten* (ed. H. Büttner, Leipzig, 1903-1909), 2 Vols. J. Ruysbroeck, *Werke* (ed. J. David, Ghent, 1858-1868), 6 Vols. J. Tauler, *Sermonweisende auf den nähesten waren Weg* (Leipzig, 1498). *Theologia Deutsch* (ed. F. Pfeiffer, Stuttgart, 1851). CMH, VII, 796-812.

ments. Consequently the sacrament of penance was inordinately stressed. A sinner must confess his sins to a priest, be forgiven, and do the necessary works of satisfaction. In penance fear of punishment (attrition) was enough to satisfy the church. This tended to displace genuine penitence (contrition) with deep sorrow for sin. Thus penance tended to depersonalize penitence. John of Platz put the matter bluntly when he wrote: "such attrition cannot be better defined in common speech than by the definition of 'gallows penitence,' because the attrite mourns that he has sinned out of fear of the infernal gallows." Even the works of satisfaction which normally follow confession and absolution proved too burdensome to some of the people of the fourteenth and fifteenth centuries, and an accommodating church provided easier substitutes for them. An indulgence was issued freeing a man of guilt and the temporal punishment entailed therein. The indulgence, which in reality included for the sinner the automatic operation and fulfillment of the entire sacramental act of penance, could be secured by money. Hence the desire to escape punishment, confession of sin to a priest, and the payment of a little money were all that was necessary to satisfy the religious demands of the Western church. What was sufficient for the living was also sufficient for the dead. Consequently relatives of the deceased bought indulgences for them. Special masses were said in their behalf, and their stay in purgatory was shortened as a result.

The individual **theologians** and **philosophers**, in contrast to those of the thirteenth century, employed reason, not as an ally to faith, but rather as its rival, illustrating in the intellectual sphere the competition between sacred and profane which we have already observed in the political sphere.

William of Occam (d. ca. 1350) was the most celebrated master. He introduced a radical nominalism, stating that nature exists as individual objects and the universal is merely an aspect of man's subjective understanding. Knowledge itself is made of sensory impressions, not things themselves. The data of dogma cannot be established as true by reason. Thus God might just as well have entered the world as an ass as a man. If the Second Person of the Trinity was born of Mary, why not the First or the Third also? On the basis of the communication of attributes in Christ's personality, it is proper to say, "God is the foot of Jesus." Consequently the doctrines of the Trinity, the Incarnation, and Transubstantiation were subjected to merciless irony by Occam as he examined them from the vantage point of reason alone. Philosophically for him they were absurd. Yet he said we must believe them on faith simply because the Roman church teaches they are true. "Whoever is a Catholic and believing Christian can easily believe anything which he could by no means by his natural reason accept." [26]

Others spelled out in terms of specific doctrines the implications of Occam's

[26] Occam, *Quodlibeta septem* (Paris, 1487), II, 3.

nominalism. John of Jandun, a master at the University of Paris, contended, in opposition to Thomism, that God knows nothing outside himself, that the active intellect in man is impersonal, and that the world is eternal. He stated outright the independence of and frequent antagonism between re-vealed and philosophical truth. It was only a step from John to Pietro Pom-ponazzi of Padua, who bluntly asserted theological truth is philosophical error, while the rational discoveries of philosophy are the denials of the tenets of faith. Ficino revived Plato in Plotinian form and anticipated much of modernity by combining Christianity with paganism in a universal type of religion. Nicholas of Cusa (1401-1464) defined God as the being in whom all other beings meet, unite, and are reconciled. God is the synthesis of all the antitheses in the universe. Nicholas attacked the geocentric theory of the universe and made the knowledge of God on the part of man an intuition of grace.

Despite this epistemological and metaphysical nominalism on the part of Occam and his disciples, and the pantheistic tendency of revived Platonism, the actual content of particular doctrines of Christianity was not altered. Au-gustinianism in its pure form was replaced by the interpretation of Duns Scotus in regard to fallen human nature. Man's freedom, they taught, is not impaired by sin.[27] Likewise, redemption and atonement were set forth ac-cording to the thought and form of the thirteenth-century masters. This was not Anselmian. Abelard's subjective view was combined with an objective view which made Christ's meritorious work the ground of our forgiveness. Man is free to believe or disbelieve the gospel. In coming to God man carries himself to the point of repentance through fear of punishment (attrition). After that God works automatically in his behalf through the sacraments. Both Duns Scotus and Occam wrote as if they were skeptical of transubstantia-tion, though they both stressed sacramentalism in effecting righteousness in the lives of men. Consequently, though man's freedom was stressed, the Catholic doctrine of grace was never repudiated. Predestination comes in the end as a reward of man's efforts which entitle him to election to life ever-lasting.

However, in regard to ecclesiology, especially the interpretation of the hierarchy, the thought of the fourteenth and fifteenth centuries was radically different from that of the thirteenth. The teaching of Boniface VIII was en-tirely repudiated. Indeed, in much current teaching the church was defined in terms of its constituents, its purity or impurity depending upon their faithful-ness in thought and life to the teachings of Scripture. Both pope and council can err. Bishops are no different, except in the function of their administrative

---

[27] Occam, *Super quatuor libros sententiarum subtillissimae quaestiones earumdemque decisiones* (Lugduni, 1495), IV, Q. 8.

office, from priests. The power of the pope is the power of the church at large, not of any one man in the church. Consequently the papacy is entirely functional, to be judged good or bad by the effect it has on the ecclesiastical body as a whole and to be modified or abolished as circumstances and conditions demand. It must be stripped of its temporal powers and made entirely a spiritual responsibility. Christ himself and all his apostles were in social and political affairs subject to the rulers of this world. Church and state are separate and distinct entities. In the conclaves of Christendom a layman has a voice as well as a priest.[28]

V. John Wycliffe and John Hus

The criticisms of institutional Christianity, doctrinal as well as organizational and disciplinary, registered by John Wycliffe of England and John Hus in Bohemia were, if less disturbing at the time, more far-reaching in their consequences than those of either the conciliarists or the mystics and radical nominalists.

John Wycliffe (ca. 1325-1384), Oxford scholar, sponsor of the first translation of the Bible into English, and the author of the major principles of Protestantism before Protestantism emerged as a new ecclesiastical organization, seems to have begun his illustrious career as little more than a **political agitator**, supported by the ruthless John of Gaunt in his quarrel with the English hierarchy. His appearance before Convocation in the Lady Chapel of St. Paul's was more like what we would expect from a politician working in a political convention seething with the hatred of various factions than from a priest attending a conclave of the church. John of Gaunt accompanied Wycliffe with a troop of soldiers, and the exchange between that nobleman and Bishop Courtenay, culminating in John's threat to drag the prelate out of the church by the hair of his head, precluded the success of the trial. Wycliffe refused to obey the summons of Pope Gregory XI to answer in person the accusations against him at the papal court and continued as the adviser of king and parliament on ecclesiastical matters.[29] His political position, so favorable to the court and secular realm, was simply that it was the moral responsibility of the government to confiscate all ecclesiastical endowments wrongly used and to employ them to relieve the poor and to accomplish any other worthy aims for the good of society.[30] It is difficult therefore to see any real connection between his theological doctrine of property and his pro-

---

[28] Occam, *Compendium errorum papae, Octo quaestiones de potestate papae,* in *Opera politica* (Manchester, 1940). Marsilius of Padua, *Defensor Pacis* (ed. C. W. Previté-Orton, Cambridge, 1928).

[29] *Chronicon Angliae* (ed. E. M. Thompson, 1874), 118 ff., 173 ff., 206-207.

[30] *Tractatus de Civili Dominio,* Books III-V of *Summa Theologiae* (ed. Poole and Loserth, London, 1885-1904).

gram of action. As doctrine, he advanced the notion that since God is the sole owner of everything and since God delegates the use of what is his only to those who are morally and spiritually worthy, the righteous alone have the right to temporal ownership and lordship and they should hold the goods of this world in common among themselves.[31] Wycliffe confessed this was the ideal of perfection. In an imperfect world he recognized the necessity of both political authority and individual ownership of property. He thought, in England at least, the state could do more good with the property of the realm than the church.

The beginning of the Western schism (1378) lifted Wycliffe from the role of mere political agitator against particular ecclesiastical abuses which he felt adversely affected England into that of **reformer of the church** itself. He began to seek to change basic institutions and doctrines.

This is seen most clearly in his teaching that the Bible and it alone is the source of religious authority. All truth, he contended, is contained in the Scriptures; and everything written therein is true. Consequently the Bible is the only law by which church and state should be governed. It is equally valid in all its parts. Its authority does not rest on church or even on the authors of its several books but rather on God himself, who used those authors as his secretaries. Knowledge of the Bible, acquired by reading its contents in humility, prayer, and under the guidance of the Holy Spirit, is essential to salvation. Obscure passages are to be explained by other passages that are clear and lucid. Without knowledge of the Bible one cannot know Jesus Christ. The reading and preaching of the Word are therefore more important than any sacrament. The Bible needs no accessories such as masses, fastings, prayers to saints, tradition, and papal decretals to make its message valid.[32] The natural outcome of this doctrine was the translation of the whole Bible into the Middle English of the common people. Heretofore only parts of it had been in translation in Anglo-Saxon and Norman French. Wycliffe engaged Nicholas de Hereford of Oxford and other scholars of that institution to translate the Old and New Testaments, using the old Biblical glossarists and commentators in order to establish the exact meaning of words and passages. The Wycliffe Bible is not therefore the Reformer's own translation but rather the work which he instigated and which was done by others.

The use of the Bible as basic authority led Wycliffe to the formulation of a doctrine of the church very similar to that of Augustine. He described it as existing in three great divisions: (1) church triumphant in heaven; (2) church militant on earth; (3) and church asleep in purgatory. Yet the sole basis of church membership, according to Wycliffe, is the predestination of God. Men

[31] *De Dominio Divino libri tres* (ed. Poole, London, 1890).
[32] *De Veritate Sacrae Scripturae*, Book VI of *Summa Theologiae* (ed. Buddensieg, London, 1905-1907).

are saved and incorporated into Christ's mystical body by grace alone. They have nothing whatever to do with their salvation, and on earth they never know whether they are saved or not. This applies to the pope and hierarchy as well as to the most humble laymen. Consequently the veneration of relics, pilgrimages, prayers to saints, indulgences, and other ecclesiastical paraphernalia do not avail anything at all in effecting salvation. Their abuse is a scandal to Christianity. God does not sell righteousness; to pretend to pardon sin for money is blasphemous. Membership in the church militant on earth is no criterion of membership in the church triumphant in heaven.[33]

The papacy therefore is an opportunity for service, not a primatial right or privilege. Peter's primacy rested on his spiritual leadership and Christian character. Election to an office will not confer such gifts on a man, only the grace of God. In the beginning the church was governed by a general council, not a pope. The power of the keys belongs to the priesthood and applies only to the earthly institution. Popes and bishops should forego all luxury and riches and live the simple life of ordinary people. Wycliffe thus castigated the historical papacy, showing how one pope had contradicted another. He even praised the schism for turning men's minds away from the trivialities of institutionalism to the significance of Biblical truth.[34]

Wycliffe repudiated the doctrine of transubstantiation. In its place he taught that the "host is only a sacrament, and not a part of Christ. But Christ is hidden insensibly in the sacrament." By this he meant that we do not eat Christ in a material manner but rather that we are sustained by him spiritually through our faith. Faith therefore apprehends Christ's body objectively. How this can be Wycliffe did not explain. He was content to call it a miracle.[35]

Even John of Gaunt could not guarantee Wycliffe's freedom to disseminate his eucharistic teaching. He went to Oxford and ordered his ward to desist. The rector of the University condemned Wycliffe's writings on this subject. But by this time the followers of Wycliffe were numerous all over the realm. For years he had been sending out poor priests to evangelize the masses— priests who held no benefices, were not commissioned by bishops, and itinerated. They won adherents by the quality of their lives.

However, this gospel movement was used by agitators of sedition and rebellion. Wycliffe's doctrine of property played into the hands of those who would reform the feudal system. Serfs demanded emancipation and specific payment for their labor on the farms. John Ball and Jack Straw instigated the Peasant's Rebellion (1381). Wycliffe condemned the sedition of the peasants as well as the greed and injustice of the landlords. A peasant army from Kent

---

[33] *Tractatus de Ecclesia*, Book VII of *Summa Theologiae* (ed. Loserth, London, 1886).

[34] *Tractatus de Potestate Papae*, Book IX of *Summa Theologiae* (ed. Loserth, London, 1907).

[35] *De Eucharistia Tractatus Maior* (ed. Loserth, London, 1892).

and Essex under Wat Tyler captured London and executed the archbishop of Canterbury, the Chancellor, and other dignitaries of the realm. Wycliffe survived this tragedy only three years. He died of apoplexy at his rectory in Lutterworth. His movement however continued to be effective and despite repression and even some persecution carried on the mission of its founder until it was swallowed up in the sixteenth-century reformation.[36]

Though John Wycliffe died in his own bed, his younger contemporary the Bohemian John Hus was less fortunate. The contrast in the degree of antipathy and violence with which the church reacted to the teachings of the two reformers is perhaps indicative of the strength and thoroughness of their respective movements. The Lollards never represented a majority or even a sizable minority in English Christianity. The revolt of the peasants (1381), though perhaps stimulated by their preaching, was certainly not their doing; and Wycliffe not only disassociated himself from this revolt, but also denounced its instigators as anarchists and traitors to the country. The Hussite movement was more extreme and extensive than the Lollard. Indeed, with the exception of Joan of Arc and her service to France it was the first example in the West after the conversion of the barbarians of the alliance of nationalism and religion: the upheaval of a people whose patriotism, racial self-consciousness, sense of autonomy and separation, and above all else hatred of the German foreigner found vent for expression in ecclesiastical deviation. The Bohemians had originally been converted by the Eastern church; they had never taken readily to Western ritualistic practices; theirs at best was a tangential adherence to Rome; their local leaders always represented to them the guiding authority in religion.

Most influential among these local leaders in the first half of the fifteenth century was John Hus (1373-1415). He was preceded by a group of talented and effective preachers in the fourteenth century, Conrad of Waldhausen, John Milic, and Matthew of Janov, all of whom labored for reformation of morals and manners. Hus himself in the first years of his ministry reproduced their type. He was a gifted teacher and became rector of the faculty of Arts at the Charles University in Prague in 1402. Though as early as 1403 he championed the right of Czech scholars and students to read and to study Wycliffe's writings, he did not personally espouse Wycliffe's opinions. As late as September 1, 1411, he categorically denied all allegations of heresy and stated specifically his orthodoxy on such doctrines as those of transubstantiation, the administration of the mass, and indulgences. These were years of controversy and misunderstanding, since the archbishop of Prague proscribed Wycliffe's writings and excommunicated their disseminators. But the Czech masters on the faculty of the University supported Hus almost to a man, some of them

[36] H. B. Workman, *John Wyclif* (Oxford, 1926), 2 Vols.

having actually been jailed in his behalf when they went as his deputies to Pope John XXIII at Bologna. During these eight years (1403-1411) he personified his nation, having the unqualified support of his sovereign and his peers.

His fortune began to shift a year later. For one thing, John Stokes, an Englishman on a royal mission abroad, declared that John Wycliffe was considered a heretic in England while his works were held in such high regard in Bohemia. John XXIII launched a broad campaign to raise money for his wars by means of selling indulgences. The indulgence trade began to thrive in Bohemia. In the face of such scandalous practices as the sale of indulgences occasioned, Hus was led from concern over abuses to open opposition to indulgences as such. At this point his activity as a practical reformer of morals and manners was translated into the prophetic role of reformer of the doctrines of the church itself. Now he began to alarm and even to alienate his former friends. The road of the prophet is lonely.

Hus' opinions about indulgences reached the ears of the pope. The papal agent sent to examine the case threatened Hus with excommunication if he did not recant in twenty-three days. Three stones were thrown against his dwelling as the sign of his curse, while every place that gave him hospitality was subject to interdict. Thus in October, 1412, he reluctantly retired from Prague to save the city from the interdict and, in desperation at maltreatment by Christ's earthly vicar, appealed his case directly to Jesus Christ himself, "who is neither influenced by gifts nor deceived by false witnesses."

All attempts at reconciliation between Hus and his accusers failed. The orthodox party on the faculty of the University insisted that the pope is the head of the church while the College of Cardinals is its body. Theirs is the right to define true doctrine for all Christians. Hus and his supporters, in opposition, insisted with equal vehemence that the church consists of all who worship Christ. Every sincere bishop and priest is a successor of the apostles. Christ alone, not the pope, is head of the church. Popes are not infallible; they have erred again and again. Many have repudiated their own bulls and corrected former opinions. When popes and cardinals live ungodly lives, they are not worthy of support and obedience. Hus formally adopted Wycliffe's views on the church and its government and openly announced those views as his own in a tract on the church. He called upon the state to correct clerical abuses and enforce morality and decency upon priests and laymen alike. Reformation must be effected even in opposition to church and pope. So sincere was Hus, and so convinced was he of his orthodoxy and the rightness of his cause, that he consented to a hearing before the pope, cardinals, and theologians of the church at the Council of Constance, which was about to convene. "If I shall be convicted of heresy," he exclaimed, "I do not refuse to suffer the penalties of a heretic." The Emperor Sigismund, however, promised his safe conduct to and from the council.

Yet in those days of inquisition and heresy-hunting safe conduct, even from an emperor, meant little. "Faith is not to be kept with him," affirmed Pope Innocent III "who keeps not faith with God." The cardinals took charge of Hus, imprisoned and maltreated him before he even had a hearing. The method of the inquisition was to act as if the accused were guilty of heresy until he proved himself innocent. At least six months elapsed before Hus was allowed to appear before the council, months in which an already noble soul was refined into the pure metal of saintliness through the unrelenting fires of persecution it was made to undergo. **The Council of Constance sentenced John Hus to be burned as a heretic at the stake** and caused its sentence to be executed by the secular authority immediately. Hus heard his sentence in the cathedral. A paper crown with pictures of demons tearing his soul to threads was placed on his head. His books were piled up to be burned. He was escorted from the cathedral by an armed guard of one thousand men to a meadow nearby. There he was burned to ashes, his remains being thrown into the Rhine. It is said that at the last Hus, with countenance radiant like an angel's, invoked the mercy of Christ until his voice died away with his body in the encircling flames.[37]

His movement did not die. As soon as the announcement of his martyrdom reached Bohemia, 452 noblemen immediately denounced his disgraceful treatment and shameful death at the hands of the faithless council. He became the religious symbol of incipient Bohemian nationalism. When King Wenzel died (August, 1419), the people refused to accept his brother the Emperor Sigismund as their king. Fifteen bloody years of civil war ensued. In this conflict two distinct nationalistic parties emerged. The moderates, called **Calixtines,** though they wanted to preserve Catholic unity, insisted on four articles to be observed in Bohemia: (1) free preaching of the Word of God; (2) communion in both kinds for laity as well as clergy; (3) reform of morals; (4) deprivation of power and wealth of the clergy. The extremists, called the **Taborites,** desired definitely to break away from what they took to be the false church. They insisted that the Bible alone is the sole norm of Christian belief and practice; that transubstantiation is erroneous; penance and extreme unction should be abandoned; and that purgatory, prayers to saints and for the dead, veneration of images and relics are all superstitions. Yet both parties acted as one socially and militarily for the duration of the war, successfully prosecuted first by Zizka and then by Procopius. Compromise was effected and peace attained only with the death of Procopius in May, 1434. The beliefs of Hus survived

---

[37] *Documenta Magistri Johannis Hus vitam, doctrinam, causam in Constantiensi Concilio actam illustrantia* (ed. F. Palacky, Prague, 1869).

and formed a segment of the new Protestantism in the *Unitas Fratrum* (Moravian Brethren).

John Wycliffe and John Hus shone forth as bright lights of moral and doctrinal reform of church and society in a time too dark to be illuminated by their glow. They have therefore been properly styled "morning stars of the Reformation."

VI. Foreign Missions and the Sacraments

Despite schism, clerical worldliness in high positions, philosophical skepticism, and the intrusion of nationalistic interests into ecclesiastical affairs, the Church Catholic during this period was not without its moments of glory, and some of the accomplishments wrought within the established order were as noteworthy as those of any other time.

Not least among such accomplishments was the missionary enterprise. There was no break here, either in enthusiasm or success, with the thirteenth century, for what was started then came to real fruition later. Raymond Lull (1235-1315) for example, though the major portion of his life was lived during that earlier century, really belongs historically to the fourteenth, when his counsel was heeded and his recommendations adopted. He was far-sighted enough to master Arabic and to insist that special missionaries be trained in oriental languages and sent out to win oriental peoples to the Christian faith. Until the turn of the century he had been looked upon as a madman, and at the request of his own wife his property had been turned over to an administrator to manage. Yet at the Council of Vienne in 1311 he personally witnessed the formal, though unfortunately only nominal, adoption of his proposals. Later, however, under the able Pope John XXII, the great universities of Paris, Oxford, Salamanca, and Bologna, as we have indicated, added Hebrew, Arabic, and Chaldean to their curriculum. Lull himself, though past eighty years of age, crossed back into North Africa where he had tried unsuccessfully to do the work of an evangelist before, and launched a gospel crusade against Islam. As a result, he was stoned outside the walls of Bougie and so sealed his untiring, unappreciated efforts with the martyr's crown. This was the beginning of the opening of Africa to Christianity.

Lull and his supporters however were not the chief missioners of this age. The Dominicans and Franciscans kept the lead in all missionary endeavors even among the Moslems. The *Societas fratrum peregrinantium propter Christum* of the one and the *Societas peregrinantium* of the other were agencies designed specifically for the winning of infidels. All across the Near East from Morocco and Tunis to the Tigris-Euphrates valleys, the terrain was dotted with mendicant outposts. Likewise, the asylums of the Trinitarians and the Mercedarians radiated the passion of evangelism for the unsaved as well as the sacrificial zeal to ransom Christian captives. In Libya Conrad of Ascoli won 6,400 persons to the Christian faith.

The strategy of the two great mendicant orders was to encircle Islam with a vigorous and aggressive Christianity. Consequently their missioners addressed themselves to the task of winning the Cumans (Turkish-speaking people) on the steppes between the Dnieper River and Ural Mountains. Greeks and Latins alike labored among them; and though not all were won, in the fifteenth century the inhabitants of the western portion of this territory were about evenly divided between the Western and Eastern churches. The Dominicans and Franciscans likewise joined with Greek missionaries and some Nestorians in trying to convert the Mongols. This led to the expansion of Christianity into China. The first Roman Catholic missionary to reach this eastern outpost was the Franciscan, John of Montecorvino, who attracted others to follow in his footsteps so that by the time of his death in 1329, the Christian enterprise in the Far East was a going concern. Still other Franciscans, joined now by the Dominicans, made India their major mission field. The Mongols who took Persia were, partially at least, taken themselves by Christianity, first in its native Nestorian form, and later, through the Dominicans and Franciscans, in its Latin form. These conversions unfortunately were not too extensive. A catholicus of Nestorianism was not elected for a period of ten years (1369-1378), while the see of the Jacobite Maphrianus was unfilled for twenty-five years (1379-1404).

On the continent of Europe the mendicant orders entered the Jewish quarters and compelled the Jews to listen to their sermons. By the close of the fourteenth century, for example, Jews by the scores accepted baptism to escape persecution. Some such converts actually rose to high position in the church. In similar fashion the recalcitrant Lithuanians were won by the swords of the Teutonic knights, while in Spain Christianity as a political and social force was revitalized in the successful campaigns against the Moors.[38]

Another accomplishment of the Bodies Catholic during this period, though it proved transient and illusory, was the effecting of union at the **Council of Florence**. This is seen more especially in its theological understanding and interpretation. After the work of that council not only Greek Catholicism, but also the major Eastern schismatic churches were able to accept the standards of Rome. This work, as we have seen already, was the joint accomplishment of the Latins and the Greeks. The major issue, the addition of the filioque to the creed by the West, was made acceptable to the Greeks when the Latins confessed it was not the addition of a new element but merely the explanation of what all Christians believed, namely, that "everything is in

[38] Latourette, op. cit., II, 206-222; 311-316; 324-342. R. Lull, Opera (ed. I. Salzinger, Mainz, 1721-1748), 8 Vols.

common between the Father and the Son, except that the Son is not the Father." Since the Holy Ghost is believed by the West to proceed from the Father and the Son as by a single act from a single principle, the East conceded there was nothing between them.[39] The Latins confessed that transubstantiation could take place with leavened as well as unleavened bread, so this issue was reduced from a difference in doctrine to a mere variation in liturgical practice. Both parties agreed that purgatory is a state where souls which have not completely satisfied for their sins by sufficient works of penance are purified for heaven.

The chief doctrine to emerge as dogma was the doctrine of the sacraments. Only after this was defined by Pope Eugenius IV, November 22, 1439, in his bull *Exultate Deo* containing the *Decretum pro Armenis* were the Jacobites, Syrians, Chaldeans, and Maronites able to join the union. Here again the declarative act was that of the Latin mind, yet at this time it seemed from the response of the leaders to express the belief of all Christendom. **The formulation of the dogma of the sacraments** was the outstanding theological accomplishment of the medieval church. Though all the ideas had been taught earlier, and Pope Eugenius IV in preparing his bull but picked the brains of Abelard, Peter the Lombard, the Victorines, and the great schoolmen of the thirteenth century, still what had been only doctrines—that is, mere theological opinions of varying and sundry influence throughout different parts of the church—were translated in 1439 into dogma, dogma being the required belief of all Roman Catholic Christians. Eugenius IV acted in compliance with the role the Council of Florence had conferred upon him and to which Greeks as well as Latins at least temporarily agreed when they affirmed "the Roman pontiff is the successor of blessed Peter, Vicar of Christ, Father and Doctor of all Christians." [40]

The number of the sacraments was fixed by the papal bull and the Council of Florence at seven. These sacraments are the effects of the work of Christ, continuing in history his passion and applying its benefits to the individual. They are objective acts of divine grace—that is, they confer in and of themselves God's benefits upon those who receive them regardless of the character of either the clerical ministrant or the lay recipient. A thief or murderer who takes the Eucharist eats the body of Christ as surely as the saint who kneels beside him, and the cleansing power of the waters of baptism is as potent from the defiled hands of an unworthy priest as from those of the consecrated shepherd who is willing to lay down his life for the sheep of his parish. The only human stipulation which in any way affects the celebration of these divine rites is the intention of the participants that they be what the church

[39] Mansi, XXXI, 551-556.
[40] *Monumenta Conciliorum*, III, 336.

says they are. For example, the enactment of marriage in a play would not reproduce the sacrament of marriage.

(1) Baptism washes the recipient clean of original sin, confers upon him forgiveness of guilt and its penalty, and gives him the capacity to do good works—in short, it infuses into his nature its spiritual character. Its material is water. Its form is the words of institution: "I baptize thee in the name of the Father, and of the Son, and of the Holy Ghost." Ordinarily it is administered by a priest, but in times of emergency a layman, even an unbeliever, can administer it, and it is effective. The recipient must have faith—that is, he must want it and believe it is effective. In the case of an infant, the intention of the sponsors to rear the child in the Christian religion takes the place of the child's own faith.

(2) Confirmation enables the recipient to fulfill his public duty as a Christian; it confers upon him the status of Christian manhood and spiritual maturity; it infuses into his nature the power of the Holy Spirit. Its material is oil. Its form is the words: "I sign thee with the sign of the cross, and confirm thee in the chrism of salvation in the name of the Father, and of the Son, and of the Holy Ghost." In the Latin church, the bishop performs this sacrament by placing his right hand on the head of the recipient and making the sign of the cross with his thumb on the forehead, having moistened his thumb with oil. In the Greek church, the sacrament is performed by the priest at the same time as baptism.

(3) The Eucharist, performed by the priest, confers upon the recipient replenishing grace—that is, strength for his daily spiritual needs. It takes the effect of the passion of Christ for the whole world and applies it to the individual. In other words, it reproduces the benefits of Christ's passion and at the same time makes them efficacious in the personal life of the communicant. It is therefore both a sacrifice and a meal. The mass is a perpetual immolation of Christ for our sins and is effective even for souls in purgatory. As we eat the meal, we receive the actual body and blood of the Savior into our own bodies. The matter is bread and wine. The form is the words of institution said by the priest above the elements: "This is my body" (said over the bread) and "This is the chalice of my blood of the new and eternal testament—mystery of faith—which shall be shed for you and for many unto the remission of sins." The transformation of the elements into the actual body and blood of Jesus takes place immediately on the pronouncement of these words of institution by the priest, the bread becomes the body and the wine blood, yet "in such a way that Christ is contained entire under the form of the bread, and entire under the form of the wine, and under any part whatever of the consecrated wafer and consecrated wine. . . ." A layman eats only the bread, yet he receives the whole of Christ thereby. This sacrament is a remedy for venial sins.

(4) The sacrament of penance dispels the ill effects of mortal sins. The material of this sacrament is the act of penitence—attrition which brings the sinner to confession. He tells his priest all the sins he can recollect which he has committed. The form is the absolution the priest pronounces after confession. It produces genuine contrition which merits God's forgiveness and pardon from eternal punishment. Yet temporal punishment can be averted only through works of satisfaction. The priest imposes upon the sinner such works, for the church itself has direct control over temporal satisfaction. Since Christ and the saints accumulated far more merit than they needed for themselves and entrusted the control of the use of this merit to the church, the church can through indulgences dole it out to any who need it. Hence indulgences can reduce the works of satisfaction for the living and shorten the stay of the dead in purgatory.

(5) Extreme unction blots out the dregs of sin remaining after the use of the other sacraments. It removes venial sins and thereby heals the soul. It does not necessarily alleviate the need to do works of satisfaction for mortal sins since the measure of grace bestowed depends on the disposition of the recipient. Its material is the oil of the olive blessed by the bishop. Its form is the statement: "By this holy anointing and by his most tender mercy may the Lord forgive thee whatever thou hast done amiss by thy sight, hearing, smell, speech, taste, touch, and walk." The eyes, the ears, the nose, the mouth, the hands, the feet, and the loins are anointed, the anointing being done by the priest with his thumb making the sign of the cross. In the Greek church several priests if possible take part in the ceremony. This is done at the hour of death.

(6) Ordination is the sacrament which empowers the recipient to perform properly the duties of the priestly order. There are two ranks in this one order: simple priests and bishops. Below the priesthood are the inferior ministerial orders. Ordination, however, applies only to the priesthood and confers on the recipient the grace necessary to administer the sacraments. Its material is the vessel used in conferring the order, for example, the cup with wine and the plate with bread. The form is the authorization said by the bishop: "Receive thou authority for the offering of sacrifice in the Church for the living and the dead in the name of the Father, and of the Son, and of the Holy Spirit." Celibacy is mandatory at and subsequent to ordination in the Latin church; it is not in the Eastern churches. However, Greek priests must get married, if at all, before ordination.

(7) The sacrament of marriage lifts the sexual act above fornication and thereby excuses those who participate in it of sin. The matter of the sacrament seems to be the conjugal act itself, since marriage is null if either party is unable to render to the other the physical benefits of union. The form is

the words of consent where each pledges his troth to the other. The blessings of marriage are children and fidelity. It is for the purpose of propagation. Since it typifies for the two persons who enter into its relationship the union between Christ and the church, it is indissoluble.[41]

Such, then, is the sacramental structure of Catholicism which, like the university, was the creation of the Middle Ages and their bequest to subsequent times.

The Council of Florence dissolved in 1445; Pope Eugenius IV, its guiding spirit, died two years later in 1447; the Eastern empire collapsed with the fall of Constantinople in 1453. The Renaissance was now already a reality in the West. The Middle Ages passed away as they had begun—imperceptibly—the new order having been established scarcely before men realized the old order had gone.

[41] Mansi, XXXI, 1055 ff.

List of Sources in English Translation

These suggestions for further reading are arranged according to the chapters of the book and the major divisions within the chapters.

CHAPTER ONE

I

Gregory of Tours. *History of the Franks.* Tr. O. M. Dalton. Oxford: Clarendon Press, 1927. 2 vols. Books II-X. Vol. II, 31-478.

Jordanes. *The Origin and Deeds of the Goths.* Ed. C. C. Mierow. Princeton: Princeton University Press, 1915.

Procopius. *History of the Wars.* Tr. H. B. Dewing. *The Loeb Classical Library.* Cambridge: Harvard University Press, 1916 ff., 5 vols.

The Visigothic Code. Tr. S. P. Scott. Boston: Boston Book Co., 1909.

II

Boethius. *The Theological Tractates.* Tr. H. F. Stewart, E. K. Rand. *The Consolation of Philosophy.* Tr. "I. T." and revised by H. F. Stewart. *The Loeb Classical Library.* New York: G. P. Putnam's Sons, 1919.

Caesarius of Arles. *Sermons.* Tr. Mary M. Mueller. New York: Fathers of the Church, Inc., 1956. Sermons 3, 10, 25, 40, 64, 70.

Cassiodorus, Flavius Aurelius. *An Introduction to Divine and Human Readings.* Tr. L. W. Jones. New York: Columbia University Press, 1946. Pp. 67-209.

————. *Letters.* Tr. Thomas Hodgkin. London: H. Frowde, 1886. I, 1, 24; II, 8, 14; III, 1; V, 37; XI, 2, 40; XII, 14, 20.

The Synod of Orange, Canons 1-12 and 25. *Documents of the Christian Church.* Selected and edited by H. Bettenson. New York and London: Oxford University Press, 1947. Pp. 83-85.

III

Adamnan. *Life of Saint Columba.* Tr. William Reeves. *The Historians of Scotland.* Edinburgh: Edmonston and Douglas, 1874. Vol. VI.

Gregory the Great. *Dialogues.* Tr. O. J. Zimmerman. New York: Fathers of the Church, Inc., 1959. Dialogue II (pp. 55-110).

Jonas of Bobbio. *The Life of Saint Columban.* Tr. D. C. Munro. Philadelphia: University of Pennsylvania Press, 1902.

The Rule of Saint Benedict. Tr. Cardinal Gasquet. London: Chatto and Windus, 1936. Also, *Western Asceticism.* Ed. O. Chadwick. *Library of Christian Classics.* Philadelphia: Westminster Press, 1958. Vol. XII. Pp. 290-337. *Documents of the Christian Church.* Ed. Bettenson. Pp. 164-81.

IV

Evagrius. *Ecclesiastical History.* London: Bohn, 1854. Book III.

_____. "The Henoticon of Zeno." *Documents of the Christian Church.* Pp. 125-128.

V

Evagrius. *Ecclesiastical History.* Book IV.

Procopius. *Anecdota or Secret History.* Tr. H. B. Dewing. *Loeb Classical Library.* Cambridge: Harvard University Press, 1935.

_____. *Buildings.* Tr. H. B. Dewing in collaboration with G. Downey. *Loeb Classical Library.* Cambridge: Harvard University Press, 1940. Book I (pp. 3-97).

The Institutes of Justinian. Tr. J. B. Moyle. Oxford: Clarendon Press, 1937. Also, Tr. C. H. Munro. Cambridge: Cambridge University Press, 1909. 2 vols. Book I.

The Fifth Ecumenical Council, or the Second Council of Constantinople. *The Seven Ecumenical Councils of the Undivided Church.* Ed. H. R. Percival. *The Nicene and Post Nicene Fathers.* Second Series. New York: Charles Scribner's Sons, 1900. Vol. XIV, 299-323. (Reprinted, W. B. Eerdmans, Grand Rapids, Michigan.)

VI

Agapetus, Counsel to Justinian I. *Social and Political Thought in Byzantium from Justinian I to the Last Palaeologus.* Tr. E. Barker. Oxford: Clarendon Press, 1957. Pp. 54-62.

A Novella of Justinian I on the Empire and the Priesthood. *Social and Political Thought in Byzantium.* Pp. 75-76.

Salvian. *Writings.* Tr. J. F. O'Sullivan. *The Fathers of the Church.* New York: Cima Publishing Co., Inc., 1947.

CHAPTER TWO
I

Gregory the Great, Selected Epistles. Tr. J. Barmby. *The Nicene and Post Nicene Fathers.* Second Series. New York: Christian Literature Co., 1895.

Vol. XII, pp. 73-243. Vol. XIII, pp. 1-111.

"The Oldest Life of Pope St. Gregory the Great." *Saints' Lives and Chronicles in Early England*. Tr. and ed. C. W. Jones. Ithaca: Cornell University Press, 1947. Pp. 99-119.

II

Bede. *The Ecclesiastical History of the English Nation*. The Everyman Library. New York: E. P. Dutton and Co., 1930. Book I, chapters 22-34; Book II, chapters 2-20; Books III and IV; Book V, chapters 1-8, 23.

III

Alcuin of York. *The Life of Willibrord*. Tr. A. Grieve. London, 1923.

Bede. *The Ecclesiastical History of the English Nation*. Book V, chapters 9-11, 19.

Boniface. *Letters*. Tr. E. Emerton. New York: Columbia University Press, 1940.

Willibrord. *The Life of Saint Boniface*. Tr. G. W. Robinson. Cambridge: Harvard University Press, 1916.

IV

Bede. *The Ecclesiastical History of the English Nation*. Book V, chapters 12-14.

Gregory the Great. *Dialogues*, III and IV.

————. *Pastoral Care*. Tr. H. Davis. *Ancient Christian Writers*. Westminster: Newman Press, 1950. Vol. XI. Also, *Book of the Pastoral Rule*. Tr. J. Barmby. *The Nicene and Post Nicene Fathers*. Second Series. Vol. XII, 1-72.

————. Selections from the Commentary on Job. *Early Medieval Theology*. Tr. and ed. G. E. McCracken in collaboration with A. Cabaniss. *The Library of Christian Classics*. Philadelphia: Westminster Press, 1957. Vol. IX. Pp. 179-191.

V

Letter of Pope Gregory III to Karl Martel. *A Source Book for Medieval History*. Ed. O. J. Thatcher, E. H. McNeal. New York: Charles Scribner's Sons, 1905. Pp. 101-102.

Papal Authorization for the Coronation of Pippin. *Readings in European History*. Ed. J. H. Robinson. Boston: Ginn and Co., 1906. Pp. 62-63.

The Coronation of Pippin. *A Source Book for Medieval History*. Pp. 37-38. Also, *Readings in European History*. P. 63.

"The Donation of Pippin," *A Source Book for Medieval History*. Pp. 104-105.

The Promise of Pippin to Pope Stephen II. *A Source Book for Medieval History*. Pp. 102-104.

CHAPTER THREE

I

Evagrius. *Ecclesiastical History*. Books V, VI.

John of Ephesus. *Ecclesiastical History*. Tr. R. P. Smith. Oxford: Oxford University Press, 1860. Part III.

————, *Lives of the Eastern Saints*. Ed. and tr. E. W. Brooks. Paris: 1923-1926.

The Liturgies of the Syrian and Coptic Jacobites and the Armenians. *Liturgies Eastern and Western*. Ed. F. E. Brightman. Oxford: Clarendon Press, 1895. Vol. I, pp. 69-110, 144-188, 412-457. Also, *Eastern Catholic Worship*. Ed. D. Attwater. New York: Devin-Adair Co., 1945. Pp. 45-93, 114-138.

II

Narsai. *Liturgical Homilies*. Tr. R. H. Connolly. Cambridge: Cambridge University Press, 1909.

The Liturgy of the Nestorians. *Liturgies Eastern and Western*. Ed. F. E. Brightman. Vol. I, 247-305.

The Statutes of Narsai and Mar Hannona. Tr. F. K. E. Albert, "The School of Nisbis; Its History and Statutes." *Catholic University Bulletin*, Vol. XII (1906), 134-151.

III

The Sixth Ecumenical Council: Third Council of Constantinople, A.D. 680-681. *The Nicene and Post Nicene Fathers*. Second Series. Vol. XIV, 325-354.

IV

The Koran. Tr. J. M. Rodwell. *Everyman's Library*. London, 1909.

V

The Canons of the Council in Trullo: Quinisext Council, A.D. 692. *The Nicene and Post Nicene Fathers*. Second Series. Vol. XIV, 355-408.

The Liturgy of the Eastern Orthodox Church. Ed. H. H. Maughan. London: Faith Press. Milwaukee: The Young Churchman Co., 1916. Also, "The Byzantine Liturgy," *Eastern Catholic Worship*, pp. 19-44. *The Divine Liturgies of Our Holy Fathers John Chrysostom and Basil the Great*. New York: E. P. Dutton and Co., 1873.

CHAPTER FOUR

I

Coronation of Charles the Great. *Parallel Source Problems in Medieval History.* Ed. F. C. Duncalf and A. C. Krey. New York: Harper and Brothers, 1912. Pp. 3-26.

Documents Concerning Charlemagne's Relationships with Rome and the Papacy. *A Source Book for Medieval History.* Ed. Thatcher and McNeal. Pp. 105-109.

Einhardt and the Monk of St. Gaul. *Early Lives of Charlemagne.* Tr. and ed. A. J. Grant. London: Chatto and Windus, 1926.

II

Alcuin of York. Selections from the Commentary on the Epistle of Titus. *Early Medieval Theology.* Tr. and ed. G. E. McCracken in collaboration with A. Cabaniss. *Library of Christian Classics.* Vol. IX. Pp. 192-210.

Documents on Education and Government. *Readings in European History.* Ed. Robinson. Pp. 71-77.

Prologue to the Rule of St. Chrodegang. *A Source Book for Medieval History.* Pp. 491-492.

Selections from the Laws of Charles the Great. Ed. D. C. Munro. *Translations and Reprints from the Original Sources of European History.* Philadelphia: University of Pennsylvania, 1900. Vol. VI, no. 5.

The Rhetoric of Alcuin and Charlemagne. Tr. W. S. Howell. Princeton: Princeton University Press, 1941.

III

Rimbert. *Anskar, the Apostle of the North, 801-864.* Tr. C. H. Robinson. London: Society for the Propagation of the Gospel in Foreign Parts, 1921.

IV

"The Forged Donation of Constantine." *Select Historical Documents of the Middle Ages.* Tr. and ed. E. F. Henderson. *Bohn's Antiquarian Library.* London: George Bell and Sons, 1896. Pp. 319-329.

The Letter of Nicholas I to the Emperor Michael on the Apostolic See. *Documents of the Christian Church.* Ed. Bettenson. Pp. 132-135.

V

John Scotus Eriugena. *On the Division of Nature. Selections from Medieval Philosophers.* Ed. and tr. R. McKeon. New York: Charles Scribner's Sons, 1920. Vol. I, 106-141.

Paschasius Radbertus. *The Lord's Body and Blood* and Ratramnus, *Christ's Body and Blood. Early Medieval Theology.* Pp. 90-147.

Rabanus Maurus. Five Sermons. *Early Medieval Theology.* Pp. 300-313.

VI

Asser. *Life of King Alfred.* Tr. L. C. Jane. London: Chatto and Windus, 1926.

CHAPTER FIVE

I

John of Damascus. *On Holy Images.* Tr. Mary H. Allies. Philadelphia: J. M. McVey and London: T. Baker, 1898.

The Seventh Ecumenical Council: the Second Council of Nicene. A.D. 787. Ed. H. R. Percival. *The Nicene and Post Nicene Fathers.* Second Series. Vol. XIV. Pp. 523-587.

II

John of Damascus. *An Exposition of the Orthodox Faith.* Tr. S. D. F. Salmond. *The Nicene and Post Nicene Fathers.* Second Series. Vol. X. Pp. 1-101.

———. Writings: *The Fount of Knowledge.* Tr. F. H. Chase, Jr. New York: Fathers of the Church, Inc., 1958. Includes *An Exposition of the Orthodox Faith.*

III

The Key to Truth. Ed. and tr. F. C. Conybeare. Oxford: Clarendon Press, 1898.

Theodore of Studion. On Church and State. *Social and Political Thought in Byzantium.* Pp. 87-88.

IV

Lives of the Serbian Saints. Tr. V. Yanich and C. P. Hankey. London: Society for Promoting Christian Knowledge, 1921.

V

Photius. *Homilies.* Tr. Cyril Mango. London: Oxford University Press, 1958.

———. *Library* (collection). Tr. J. H. Freese. New York: McMillan, 1920.

———. Selections from a Letter to Michael of Bulgaria. *Social and Political Thought in Byzantium.* Pp. 109-116.

Selections from Letters of Nicholas Mysticus. *Social and Political Thought in Byzantium.* Pp. 116-117.

CHAPTER SIX

I

Conditions in the Ninth Century. *Annales Xantenses,* ad an. 844 sqq. *Readings in European History.* Ed. J. H. Robinson. Pp. 82-87.

Documents Relating to Feudalism. *Readings in European History.* Pp. 88-93.

The Charter Establishing Cluny Abbey. *Historical Documents of the Middle Ages.* Ed. E. F. Henderson. Pp. 329-333. *Monks, Friars, and Nuns. Life in the Middle Ages.* Tr. and ed. G. G. Coulton. New York: Macmillan, 1935. Pp. 47-50.

The Oath of Otto I to Pope John XII. *A Source Book for Medieval History.* Ed. Thatcher and McNeal. Pp. 115-116.

II

Documents Illustrating the Control of the Papacy by the German Empire. *A Source Book for Medieval History.* Ed. Thatcher and McNeal. Pp. 115-119, 121-124.

Election of Otto I. *Readings in European History.* Ed. J. H. Robinson. Pp. 124-125.

Germany in the Early Tenth Century. *Readings in European History.* Pp. 120-123.

Letter of Pope Sylvester II to King Stephen of Hungary. *A Source Book for Medieval History.* Pp. 119-121.

The Peace of God and the Truce of God. *A Source Book for Medieval History.* Pp. 412-418.

Trial by Ordeal. *A Source Book for Medieval History.* Pp. 400-410.

III

Legal and Ecclesiastical Documents. *Social and Political Thought in Byzantium.* Pp. 96-104.

Philopatris, Dialogue on Nicephorus and the Monks. *Social and Political Thought in Byzantium.* Pp. 117-120.

Psellus, Michael or Constantine. *The Chronographia.* Tr. E. R. A. Sewter. New Haven: Yale University Press, 1953. Books I-V. Pp. 1-112.

IV

"The Chronicle of Nestor." *The Don Carlos Theme; The Russian Primary Chronicle.* S. H. Cross. *Harvard Studies and Notes in Philosophy and Literature,* Cambridge: Harvard University Press, 1930. Vol. XII. Pp. 77-320. Appendix I: "Testament of Vladimir."

V

Extract from the Letter of the Roman Church to Michael Cerularius. *Documents of the Christian Church.* Ed. Bettenson. Pp. 135-136.

Psellus. *The Chronographia.* Book VI. Pp. 113-208.

VI

Decree of 1059 on Papal Elections: Papal and Imperial Versions. *Historical Documents of the Middle Ages.* Ed. E. F. Henderson. Pp. 361-365. Also, *A Source Book for Medieval History.* Ed. Thatcher and McNeal. Pp. 126-131.

Documents on the Peace of the Land. *A Source Book for Medieval History.* Pp. 418-431.

Oath of Robert Guiscard to Pope Nicholas II. *A Source Book for Medieval History.* Pp. 124-126.

Psellus. *The Chronographia.* Book VI. Pp. 209-290.

Selected Writings of Niculitzas, Psellus, and Michael of Ephesus. *Social and Political Thought in Byzantium.* Pp. 120-145.

CHAPTER SEVEN

I

A Selection of the Letters of Hildebrand, Pope Gregory VII. Tr. G. Finch. London: G. Norman, 1853.

"Church and State," *Documents of the Christian Church.* Ed. Bettenson. Pp. 142-155.

Documents on the "Struggle between the Empire and the Papacy" (Henry IV and Gregory VII). *A Source Book for Medieval History.* Ed. Thatcher and McNeal. Pp. 134-160.

"Canossa: From Oppenheim to Foresheim." *Parallel Source Problems in Medieval History.* Pp. 29-91.

"Documents Relating to the War of the Investitures" (Henry IV and Gregory VII). *Historical Documents of the Middle Ages.* Ed. Henderson. Pp. 365-405.

The Correspondence of Pope Gregory VII. Ed. E. Emerton. *Records of Civilization,* 14. New York: Columbia University Press, 1932.

II

Fulcher of Chartres. *Chronicle of the First Crusade.* Tr. M. E. McGinty. *Translations and Reprints from the Original Sources of European History.* Third Series, I. Philadelphia: University of Pennsylvania Press, 1941.

Remensis, Rodbertus. *The Historie of the First Expedition to Jerusalem.* Tr. and abbreviated S. Purchas. Glasgow: Hakluyt Society, 1905.

Selections from the Sources of the History of the First Crusade. *A Source Book for Medieval History.* Ed. Thatcher and McNeal. Pp. 512-526. *Readings in European History.* Ed. Robinson. Pp. 146-157.

The First Crusade; the Accounts of Eye-witnesses and Participants. Ed. A. C. Krey. Princeton: Princeton University Press, 1921.

Urban and the Crusades. Ed. D. C. Munro. *Translations and Reprints from the Original Sources of European History*, I, no. 2. Philadelphia: University of Pennsylvania, 1895.

III

Comnena, Anna. *The Alexiad.* Tr. E. A. S. Dawes. London: K. Paul, Trench, Truber and Co., Ltd., 1928.

Theophylact. From *Paideia Basilike. Social and Political Thought in Byzantium.* Pp. 141-149.

IV

Documents on the "Struggle between the Empire and the Papacy" (Urban II —Calixtus II). *A Source Book for Medieval History.* Ed. Thatcher and McNeal. Pp. 160-167.

Negotiations between Paschal II and Henry V and the "Concordat of Worms." *Historical Documents of the Middle Ages.* Ed. Henderson. Pp. 405-409.

"Privilegium of Pope Calixtus II" and the Edict of the Emperor Henry V. *Readings in European History.* Ed. Robinson. Pp. 135-136. Also, *Documents of the Christian Church.* Ed. Bettenson. Pp. 156-157.

V

Ivo of Chartres. *Decretum, The Prologue* (Excerpt). *A Scholastic Miscellany.* Ed. and tr. E. R. Fairweather. *The Library of Christian Classics.* Philadelphia: Westminster Press, 1956. Vol. X, pp. 238-242.

Monks, Friars, and Nuns. Life in the Middle Ages. Ed. and tr. G. G. Coulton. New York: Macmillan, 1935. Vol. IV, selections 9, 13, 14, 18, 19, 21-72.

VI

Abailard, P. *Ethics.* Tr. J. R. McCallum. Oxford: Blackwell, 1935.

Anselm. *Proslogium, Monologium, Cur Deus Homo.* Tr. S. N. Dean. *Philosophical Classics.* Religion of Science Library, 54. Chicago: Open Court Publishing Co., 1926.

Selections from the Philosophical Writings of Anselm and Abailard. *Selections from Medieval Philosophers.* Ed. and tr. R. McKeon. New York: Charles Scribner's Sons, 1929. Vol. I, pp. 142-184; 202-258.

Selections from the Theological Writings of Anselm, Eadmer, Anselm of Laon, and Peter Abailard. *A Scholastic Miscellany.* Pp. 69-215; 261-299.

CHAPTER EIGHT

I

Letter of Conrad III to John Comnenus, 1142. *A Source Book for Medieval History.* Ed. Thatcher and McNeal. Pp. 173-174.

Papal Announcement of the Second Crusade. *A Source Book for Medieval History*. Ed. Thatcher and McNeal. Pp. 526-529. Also, *Historical Documents of the Middle Ages*. Pp. 333-336.

Papal Privileges to the Knights of Saint John. *A Source Book for Medieval History*. Pp. 494-496.

II

Bernard of Clairvaux. *Works* (particularly Letters). Ed. John Mabillon. Tr. S. J. Eales. *Catholic Standard Library*. London: Burns and Oates, n. d. 4 vols.

Bernard of Clairvaux. *Life of St. Malachy of Armagh*. Tr. H. J. Lawlor. *Translations of Christian Literature*. Series V, *Lives of Celtic Saints*. New York: Macmillan, 1920.

Imperial and Papal Documents. *A Source Book of Medieval History*. Thatcher and McNeal. Pp. 166-173.

III

Documents Concerning Frederick Barbarossa and the Papacy. *A Source Book of Medieval History*. Ed. Thatcher and McNeal. Pp. 176-207. Also, *Historical Documents of the Middle Ages*. Ed. Henderson. Pp. 410-430.

Laws and Charters of Frederick Barbarossa. *A Source Book of Medieval History*. Pp. 385-387; 422-427. Also, *Historical Documents of the Middle Ages*. Pp. 211-218.

Life and Letters of Thomas à Becket. Ed. J. A. Giles. London: Whitaker and Co., 1846. 2 vols.

St. Thomas of Canterbury; an Account of His Life and Fame from Contemporary Biographers and Other Chronicles. Ed. W. H. Hutton. London: D. Nutt, 1889. Latest revision, Cambridge, 1926.

St. Thomas of Canterbury; His Death and Miracles. Ed. E. A. Abbott. London: Adam and Charles Black, 1898. 2 vols.

IV

Guidonis, Bernardus. *Facts and Documents Illustrative of the History, Doctrine, and Rites of the Ancient Albigenses and Waldenses*. Ed. S. R. Maitland, London, 1832.

Religion, Folklore, and Superstition. *Life in the Middle Ages*. Ed. G. G. Coulton. Vol. I, selections 12, 14, 16, 49, and 65.

V

Ambroise. *The Crusade of Richard Lion-heart*. Tr. M. J. Hubert. *Records of Civilization*, 34. New York: Columbia University Press, 1941. Also, tr. E. N. Stone. *Publications in the Social Sciences*, 10. Seattle: University of Washington, 1939.

Geoffrey de Vinsauf. "Itinerary of Richard I and Others to the Holy Land," *Chronicles of the Crusades.* London: H. G. Bohn, 1848. Pp. 65-339.

Richard of Devizes. *The Chronicle of the Deeds of Richard I.* London: H. G. Bohn, 1848. Many reprints.

VI

Selections from the Writings of Gratian; John of Salisbury; Hugh, Richard, and Adam of St. Victor; Peter Lombard; and Stephen Langton. *A Scholastic Miscellany.* Ed. Fairweather. Pp. 243-260; 300-360. Also, Peter Lombard's *Sentences,* Book IV. *Selections from Medieval Philosophers.* Ed. McKeon. I, pp. 189-201.

Selected Treatises of Bernard of Clairvaux. *Late Medieval Mysticism.* Ed. R. C. Petry. *The Library of Christian Classics.* Philadelphia: Westminster Press, 1957. Vol. XIII, pp. 47-78.

CHAPTER NINE

I

Albigensian and Waldensian Movements. *Readings in European History.* Ed. Robinson. Pp. 170-173.

Concession of England to the Pope. *Historical Documents of the Middle Ages.* Ed. Henderson. Pp. 430-432.

Decree of Fourth Lateran Council on Heresy. *Documents of the Christian Church.* Ed. Bettenson. Pp. 188-189.

Documents Relating to Simony and Monasticism. *A Source Book of Medieval History.* Ed. Thatcher and McNeal. Pp. 496-497.

Documents Relating to the Temporal Power of the Church under Innocent III. *A Source Book for Medieval History.* Pp. 208-233.

Feudal Documents. *A Source Book for Medieval History.* Pp. 369-373.

Papal Orders Forbidding the Venetians to Trade with the Moslems. *A Source Book for Medieval History.* Pp. 535-537.

Papal Summons to the Fourth Crusade. *Historical Documents of the Middle Ages.* Pp. 337-344. Also, *Source Book for Medieval History.* Pp. 537-544.

II

John of Saxony. *A New Life of Saint Dominic.* Ed. Louis Getino. Tr. E. C. McEniry. Columbus, Ohio: Aquinas College, 1926.

The Little Flowers and the Life of Saint Francis with the Mirror of Perfection. Thomas Okey. *Everyman's Library.* New York: E. P. Dutton and Co., 1910.

"The Rule of Saint Francis." *Documents of the Christian Church.* Ed. Bettenson. Pp. 181-187. Also, *Historical Documents of the Middle Ages.* Ed.

Henderson. Pp. 344-349. *A Source Book for Medieval History*. Ed. Thatcher and McNeal. Pp. 498-504.
"The Testament of Saint Francis." *A Source Book for Medieval History*. Pp. 498-507.
Thomas of Celano. *The Lives of Saint Francis of Assisi*. Tr. A. G. Ferris Howell. London: Methuen and Co., 1908.

III

Jean de Joinville. *Saint Louis, King of France*. Tr. J. Hutton. New York: E. P. Dutton and Co., 1906.
Philippe of Novara. *The Wars of Frederick II against the Ibelins in Syria and Cyprus*. Tr. J. L. LaMonte and M. J. Hubert. *Records of Civilization*, 25. New York: Columbia University Press, 1936.

IV

Georgius Acropolites. *Funeral Oration on John Vatatzes*. *Social and Political Thought in Byzantium*. Pp. 159-161.
Nicephorus Blemmydes. *The Andrias Basilikos*. *Social and Political Thought in Byzantium*. Pp. 151-159.
Robert de Clari. *The Conquest of Constantinople*. Tr. E. H. McNeal. *Records of Civilization*, 23. New York: Columbia University Press, 1936. Also, tr. E. N. Stone. *University of Washington Publications in Social Sciences*, 10. Seattle: U. of Washington, 1939.
The Fourth Crusade. Ed. D. C. Munro. *Translations and Reprints from the Original Sources of European History*, 3, no. 1. Philadelphia: University of Pennsylvania, 1897.
Thomas Magister. *Peri Basileias* and *Peri Politeias*. *Social and Political Thought in Byzantium*. Pp. 161-173.
Villehardouin, Geoffri de. *The Chronicle of the Conquest of Constantinople*. Tr. T. Smith. London: W. Pickering, 1829.

V

"Advice of Saint Louis to His Son." *Medieval Civilization*. Ed. and tr. D. C. Munro and G. C. Sellery. New York: 1907. Pp. 366-375.
Bulls: "Clericis Laicos" and "Unam Sanctum." *Historical Documents of the Middle Ages*. Ed. Henderson. Pp. 432-437. Also, *Documents of the Christian Church*. Ed. Bettenson. Pp. 159-163. *A Source Book for Medieval History*. Ed. Thatcher and McNeal. Pp. 311-313; 314-317.
Documents on the Struggle between the Papacy and the Emperor Frederick II. *A Source Book of Medieval History*. Pp. 232-259.

Institution of the Jubilee of 1300. *Historical Documents of the Middle Ages.* Pp. 349-350. Also, *A Source Book for Medieval History.* Pp. 313-314.
Legislation on Heresy. *A Source Book for Medieval History.* Pp. 309-310.

CHAPTER TEN

I

Albert the Great. "On the Intellect and the Intelligible." *Selections from Medieval Philosophers.* Ed. and tr. R. McKeon. Vol. I., pp. 326-375.
Bonaventura. "On the Knowledge of God by Distant Likenesses." *Selections from Medieval Philosophers.* Vol. II, pp. 118-148.
John Duns Scotus. "Distinctions." *Selections from Medieval Philosophers.* Vol. II, pp. 313-350.
Thomas Aquinas. "The Disputed Questions on Truth." *Selections from Medieval Philosophers.* Vol. II, 159-234.

II

Robert Grosseteste. "On Truth." *Selections from Medieval Philosophers.* Vol. I, pp. 263-287.
Roger Bacon. "The Causes of Error." *Selections from Medieval Philosophers.* Vol. II, pp. 7-117.

III

Bonaventura. *Breviloquium.* Tr. E. E. Nemmers. St. Louis: B. Herder, 1947.
Thomas Aquinas. *The Summa Theologica.* Tr. Fathers of the English Dominican Province. New York: Benziger Brothers, Inc., 1947. 3 vols.

IV

Dante Alighieri. *The Divine Comedy.* Tr. M. B. Anderson. New York: World Book Co., 1921. Many translations.
Everyman and Eight Miracle Plays. Everyman's Library. New York: E. P. Dutton and Co., 1909.
Lays of the Minnesingers. Ed. E. Taylor. London: Longman, Hurst, Rees, Orme, Brown, and Green, 1825.
Map, Walter. *De Nugis Curialium.* Tr. M. R. James. Ed. E. S. Hartland, London, 1923.
Medieval Hymns and Sequences. Tr. J. M. Neale. London: J. Masters, 1867.
Polo, Marco. *Travels.* Tr. H. Yule. *Universal Library.* New York: Grosset and Dunlap, 1931.
The History of Reynard the Fox. Tr. S. Naylor. London: Longmans, 1845.
The Lay of the Cid. Tr. S. Rose and L. Bacon. Berkeley: University of California Press, 1919.

The Nibelungenlied. Tr. D. B. Shumway. Boston: Houghton Mifflin Co., 1909.

Trobador Poets; Selections from the Poems of Eight Trobadors. Tr. B. Smythe. New Medieval Library. New York: Duffield and Co., 1911.

V

Documents concerning Cities and Trade and the Hanseatic League. *A Source Book for Medieval History.* Ed. Thatcher and McNeal. Pp. 604-612.

Social Documents. *A Source Book for Medieval History.* Pp. 391-399; 548-550; 583-584; 587-602. Also, *Historical Documents of the Middle Ages.* Ed. Henderson. Pp. 135-168.

VI

Readings in the History of Education; Medieval Universities. Ed. A. O. Norton. Cambridge: Harvard University, 1909.

The Medieval Student. Ed. D. C. Munro. *Translations and Reprints from the Original Sources.* Philadelphia: University of Pennsylvania, 1897.

University Records and Life in the Middle Ages. Ed. L. Thorndike. *Records of Civilization.* New York: Columbia University Press, 1944.

CHAPTER ELEVEN

I

Antonius, the Patriarch of Constantinople. "Letter to Vasil I Grand Prince of Russia." *Social and Political Thought in Byzantium.* Tr. and Ed. E. Barker. Oxford: Clarendon Press, 1957. Pp. 194-196.

Gemistus Plethon. Addresses and Treatise On Laws. *Social and Political Thought in Byzantium.* Pp. 196-219.

Nicolas Cabasilas and Nicephoras Gregoras. On the Zealots of Thessalonica. *Social and Political Thought in Byzantium.* Pp. 184-193.

Theodorus Metochites. *Miscellanea. Social and Political Thought in Byzantium.* Pp. 173-183.

II

"Defensor Pacis" (conclusion). *A Source Book for Medieval History.* Ed. Thatcher and McNeal. Pp. 317-324.

Condemnation of Marsilius of Padua by Pope John XXII. *A Source Book for Medieval History.* Pp. 324-325.

Marsilius of Padua. *The Defensor Pacis.* Ed. C. W. Previte-Orton. Cambridge: University Press, 1928.

Papal Court at Avignon as Petrarch Described It. *The Pre-Reformation Period.* Tr. and ed. J. H. Robinson. *Translations and Reprints from the*

Original Sources of European History. Philadelphia: University of Pennsylvania, 1897. Vol. III, no. 1, pp. 27-28.

Rienzi's Correspondence with Pope Clement VI. Parallel Source Problems in Medieval History. Ed. F. Dunclaf and A. C. Krey. New York: Harper and Brothers, 1912. Pp. 189-237.

Vices of the Church as Seen by Dietrich Vrie and Nicholas Clemanges. The Pre-Reformation Period. Pp. 28-30.

III

Cardinals' Manifesto Causing the Schism and Other Documents Relating Thereto. A Source Book for Medieval History. Ed. Thatcher and McNeal. Pp. 325-328. Readings in European History. Ed. Robinson. Pp. 212-216.

Decrees of the Council of Constance. A Source Book for Medieval History. Pp. 328-332. Documents of the Christian Church. Pp. 192-193. Readings in European History. Pp. 216-218.

IV

Conciliarists' Documents of Henry of Langenstein, John Gerson, Detrich of Neim, and John Major. Advocates of Reform. Ed. Matthew Spinka. The Library of Christian Classics. Philadelphia: Westminster Press, 1953. Pp. 106-184.

Selections from the Writings of Meister Eckhardt, Richard Rolle, Henry Suso, Catherine of Siena, Jan von Ruysbroeck, author of the Theologia Germanica and Nicholas of Cusa. Late Medieval Mysticism. Ed. R. C. Petry. The Library of Christian Classics. Philadelphia: Westminster Press, 1957. Vol. XIII. Pp. 170-391.

William of Ockham. The Seven Quodlibeta (Selection). Selections from Medieval Philosophers. Ed. and tr. R. McKeon. Vol. II, pp. 360-421.

V

Hus, John. Letters. Ed. H. B. Workman and R. M. Pope. London: Hodder and Stoughton, 1904.

————. The Church. Tr. D. S. Schaff. New York: Charles Scribner's Sons, 1915.

————. Treatise on Simony. Advocates of Reform. Pp. 196-278.

Wyclif, John, Pastoral Office and Eucharist. Advocates of Reform. Pp. 32-88.

————. Tracts and Treatises. Tr. and ed. R. Vaughan. London: Blackburn and Pardon, 1845.

————. Writings. London: Religious Tract Society, 1831.

VI

Bull Exultate Deo of Eugene IV (selection). Readings in European History. Ed. Rolinson. Pp. 159-163.

Lull, Ramon. The Blanguerna. The Late Medieval Mystics. Pp. 149-169.

List of Emperors, Popes, and Patriarchs

POPES

Lando 913-14
John X 914-28
Leo VI 928
Stephen VII (VIII) 928-31
John XI 931-36
Leo VII 936-39
Stephen VIII (IX) 939-42
Marinus II (Martin III) 942-46
Agapetus II 946-55
John XII 955-64
Leo VIII 963-65
Benedict V 964
John XIII 965-72
Benedict VI 973-74
    (Boniface VII, 974)
Benedict VII 974-83
John XIV 983-84
Boniface VII 984-85
John XV 985-96
Gregory V 996-99
    (John XVI, 997-98)
Silvester II 999-1003
John XVII 1003
John XVIII 1003-09
Sergius IV 1009-12
Benedict VIII 1012-24
John XIX 1024-32
Benedict IX (a) 1032-45
    (Silvester III, 1045)
Gregory VI 1045-46
Clement II 1046-47
    (Benedict IX [b], 1047-48)
Damasus II 1048
Leo IX 1049-54
Victor II 1055-57
Stephen IX (X) 1057-58
    (Benedict X, 1058-59)
Nicholas II 1059-61
Alexander II 1061-73
    (Honorius II, 1061-64)

Gregory VII ....22 Apr., 1073-25 May, 1085
(Clement III, 1084-1100)
Victor III ....9 May, 1087-16 Sept., 1087
Urban II ....12 March, 1088-29 July, 1099
Paschal II ....13 Aug., 1099-21 Jan., 1118
(Sylvester IV, 1105-11)
Gelasius II ....24 Jan., 1118-28 Jan., 1119
(Gregory VIII, 1118-21)
Calixtus II ....2 Feb., 1119-13 Dec. 1124
Honorius II ....15 Dec., 1124-13 Feb., 1130
(Celestine II, 1124)
Innocent II ....14 Feb., 1130-24 Sept., 1143
(Anacletus II, 1130-38)
(Victor IV, 1138)
Celestine II ....26 Sept., 1143-8 March, 1144
Lucius II ......12 March, 1114 (cons.)-15 Feb., 1145
Eugenius III ....15 Feb., 1145-8 July, 1153
Anastasius IV ......12 July, 1153 (cons.)-3 Dec., 1154
Adrian IV ....4 Dec., 1154-1 Sept., 1159
Alexander III ....7 Sept., 1159-30 Aug., 1181
(Victor IV, 1159-64)
(Paschal III, 1164-68)
(Calixtus III, 1168-78)
(Innocent III, 1179-80)
Lucius III ....1 Sept., 1181-25 Nov., 1185
Urban III ....25 Nov., 1185-20 Oct., 1187
Gregory VIII ....21 Oct.,-17 Dec., 1187
Clement III ....19 Dec., 1187-March, 1191
Celestine III ....30 March, 1191-8 Jan., 1198
Innocent III ....8 Jan., 1198-16 July, 1216
Honorius III ....18 July, 1216-18 March, 1227
Gregory IX ....19 March, 1227-22 Aug., 1241
Celestine IV ....25 Oct.-10 Nov., 1241
Innocent IV ....25 June, 1243-7 Dec., 1254
Alexander IV ....12 Dec., 1254-25 May, 1261
Urban IV ....29 Aug., 1261-2 Oct., 1264
Clement IV ....5 Feb., 1265-29 Nov., 1268
Gregory X ....1 Sept., 1271-10 Jan., 1276
Innocent V ....21 Jan.-22 June, 1276
Adrian V ....11 July-18 Aug., 1276
John XXI ....8 Sept., 1276-20 May, 1277

Nicholas III ....25 Nov., 1277-22 Aug., 1280
Martin IV ....25 Feb., 1281-28 March, 1285
Honorius IV ....2 Apr., 1285-3 Apr., 1287
Nicholas IV ....22 Feb., 1288-4 Apr., 1292
Celestine V ....5 July-13 Dec., 1294
Boniface VIII ....24 Dec., 1294-11 Oct., 1303
Benedict XI ....22 Oct., 1303-7 July, 1304
Clement V ....5 June, 1305-20 Apr., 1314
John XXII ....7 Aug., 1316-4 Dec., 1334
    (Nicholas V, 1328-30)
Benedict XII ....20 Dec., 1334-25 Apr., 1342
Clement VI ....7 May, 1342-6 Dec., 1352
Innocent VI ....18 Dec., 1352-12 Sept., 1362
Urban V ....6 Nov., 1362 (cons.)-19 Dec., 1370
Gregory XI ....30 Dec., 1370-27 March, 1378
Urban VI ....8 Apr., 1378-15 Oct., 1389
    (Clement VII, 1378-94, Schismatic pope at Avignon)
Boniface IX ....2 Nov., 1389-1 Oct., 1404
    (Benedict XIII, 1394-1422, Schismatic pope at
    Avignon)
Innocent VII ....17 Oct., 1404-6 Nov., 1406
Gregory XII ....30 Nov., 1406-4 July, 1415
    (Alexander V, 26 June, 1409-3 May, 1410—
    Elected by Council of Pisa)
    (John XXIII, 17 May, 1410-29 May, 1415—
    Successor of Alexander V; deposed by
    Council of Constance)
Martin V ....11 Nov., 1417-20 Feb., 1431
    (Clement VIII, 1424-29)
    (Benedict XIV, 1424)
Eugenius IV ....3 March, 1431-23 Feb., 1447
    (Felix V, 1439-49)
Nicholas V ....6 March, 1447-24 March, 1455

Holy Roman Emperors

Charlemagne .... 800-814 Frankish King, 768
Louis the Pious 814-840
Lothaire 840-855
Louis II, in Italy 855-875
Charles II, the Bald, West
    Frankish 875-877
Charles III, the Fat, East
    Frankish 881-887
Interregnum 888-891
Guido, in Italy 891-894
Lambert, in Italy 894-898
Arnulf, East Frankish 896-899
Louis, the Child (Made no
    claim to imperial title).... 899-911
Louis III, king of Provence,
    in Italy .... 901 (Year of Accession)
Conrad I (made no claim to
    imperial title) 911-918
Berenger, in Italy .... 915 (Year of Accession)
Henry I of Saxony (Made
    no claim to imperial title).. 919-936
Otto I, crowned king at
    Aachen 936
    and emperor at Rome 962-973
Otto II 973-983
Otto III 983-1002
Henry II 1002-1024
Conrad II of House of
    Franconia 1024-1039
Henry III 1039-1056
Henry IV 1056-1106
Rudolph of Swabia, rival.... 1077-1081
Hermann of Luxemburg,
    rival 1081-1093
Conrad of Franconia, rival... 1093-1101
Henry V 1106-1125
Lothaire II, of Saxony 1125-1137
Conrad III, of House of
    Hohenstauffen (Not for-
    mally crowned emperor) ..1138-1152

Frederick I Barbarossa 1152-1190
Henry VI 1190-1197
*Philip of Swabia and Otto
IV (Uncrowned rivals)* ...1197-1208
Otto IV, House of Brunswick.1208-1212
Frederick II 1212-1250
Henry Raspe, rival 1246-1247
William of Holland, rival 1247-1256
Conrad IV (not formally
crowned emperor) 1250-1254
Interregnum 1254-1257
Richard of Cornwall, rival...1257-1273
Alfonso X of Castile, rival...1257-1272
Rudolph I of Habsburg
(Never formally crowned
emperor) 1273-1292
Adolph of Nassau (Never
formally crowned emperor).1292-1298
Albert I of Habsburg (Never
formally crowned emperor).1298-1308
Henry VII of Luxemburg ...1308-1314
Ludwig IV of Bavaria 1314-1347
Frederick of Austria, rival ...1314-1322
Charles IV of Luxemburg ...1347-1378
*Günther of Schwartzburg,
rival* 1347-1349
Wenzel of Luxemburg (Never
formally crowned emperor).1378-1400
Rupert of the Palatinate
(Never formally crowned
emperor) 1400-1410
Sigismund of Luxemburg ...1410-1437
Jobst of Moravia, rival 1410-1411
Albert II of Habsburg
(Never formally crowned
emperor) 1438-1439
Frederick III 1440-1493

Byzantine Emperors

Romanus II 959-963
Nicephorus II Phocas 963-969
John I Tzimisces 969-976
Basil II Bulgaroctonus 976-1025
Constantine VIII 1025-1028
Romanus III Argyrus 1028-1034
Michael IV the Paphlagonian 1034-1041
Michael V Calaphates 1041-1042
Theodora and Zoë 1042
Constantine IX Monomachus 1042-1055
Theodora 1055-1056
Michael VI Stratioticus 1056-1057
Isaac I Comnenus 1057-1059
Constantine X Ducas 1059-1067
Romanus IV Diogenes 1068-1071
Michael VII Ducas Parapinakes 1071-1078
Nicephorus III Botaniates 1078-1081
Alexius I Comnenus 1081-1118
John II 1118-1143
Manuel I 1143-1180
Alexius II 1180-1183
Andronicus I 1183-1185
Isaac II Angelus 1185-1195
Alexius III 1195-1203
Isaac (for the second time) and Alexius IV ..1203-1204
Alexius V Ducas Mourtzouphlos 1204
Theodore I Lascaris 1206-1222
John III Ducas Vatatzes 1222-1254
Theodore II Lascaris 1254-1258
John IV 1258-1261
Michael VIII Palaeologus 1261-1282
Andronicus II 1282-1328
Michael IX 1295-1320
Andronicus III 1328-1341
John V 1341-1391
John VI Cantacuzene 1347-1354
Andronicus IV 1376-1379
John VII 1390
Manuel II 1391-1425
John VIII 1425-1448
Constantine XI Dragases 1448-1453

Patriarchs of Constantinople

Ignatius ....846-858 (a)
Photius ....858-867 (a)
Ignatius ....867-878 (b)
Photius ....878-886 (b)
Stephen I 886-893
Antony II 893-895
Nicholas I ....Mysticus, 895-906 (a)
Euthymius I 906-911
Nicholas I ....911-925 (b)
Stephen II 925-928
Tryphon 928-931
Theophylactus 933-956
Polyeuctus 956-970
Basil I 970-974
Antony III 974-980
Nicholas II 984-995
Sisinius II 995-998
Sergius II 999-1019
Eustathius 1019-1025
Alexius 1025-1043
Michael I ....Cerularius, 1043-1058
Constantine III ....Leuchudes, 1059-1063
John VIII ....Xiphilinus, 1064-1075
Cosmas I ....Hierosolymites, 1075-1081
Eustratius ....Garidus, 1081-1084
Nicholas III 1084-1111
John IX ....Agapetus, 1111-1134
Leo ....Styppes, 1134-1143
Michael II ....Kurkuas (Oxeites), 1143-1146
Cosmas II ....Atticus, 1146-1147
Nicholas IV ....Muzalon, 1147-1151
Theodotus II 1151-1153
Neophytus I 1153
Constantine IV ....Chliarenus, 1154-1156
Lucas ....Chrysoberges, 1156-1169
Michael III 1169-1177
Chariton ....Eugeniotes, 1177-1178
Theodosius I 1178-1183
Basil II ....Camaterus, 1183-1187
Nicetas II ....Muntanes, 1187-1190
Leontius ....Theotocites, 1190-1191
Dositheus 1191-1192

George II ....Xiphilinus, 1192-1199
John X ....Camaterus, 1199-1206
Michael IV (Autorianus) 1206-1212
Theodore II (Irenicus: Copas) 1212-1215
Maximus II 1215
Manuel I 1215-1222
Germanus II 1222-1240
Methodius 1240
Manuel II 1244-1255
Arsenius ....1255-1260 (a)
Nicephorus II 1260-1261
Arsenius ....1261-1267 (b)
Germanus III 1267
Joseph I ....1268-1275 (a)
John XI (Beccus) 1275-1282
Joseph I ....1282-1283 (b)
Gregory II 1283-1289
Athanasius I 1289-1293
John XII 1294-1303
Athanasius I 1303-1311
Nephon I 1311-1315
John XIII 1316-1320
Gerasimus I 1320-1321
Jesias 1323-1334
John XIV 1334-1347
Isidore I 1347-1349
Callistus I ....1350-1354 (a)
Philotheus ....1354-1355 (a)
Callistus I ....1355-1363 (b)
Philotheus ....1364-1376 (b)
Macarius ....1376-1379 (a)
Nilus 1380-1388
Antonius IV ....1389-1390 (a)
Macarius ....1390-1391 (b)
Antonius IV ....1391-1397 (b)
Matthias 1397-1410
Euthymius II 1410-1416
Joseph II 1416-1439
Metrophanes II 1440-1443
Gregory III 1443-1450
Athanasius II 1450
Gennadius II 1453-1459

Index

2 70, 2
C 226
C. 2

67725

352